2011

FASHION
THE FAIRCHILD DIRECTORY OF
SCHOOLS

fb

2011

FASHION
THE FAIRCHILD DIRECTORY OF
SCHOOLS

Vice President & General Manager, Fairchild Education & Conference Division: **Elizabeth Tighe**
Executive Editor: **Olga T. Kontzias**
Senior Associate Acquiring Editor: **Jaclyn Bergeron**
Assistant Acquisitions Editor: **Amanda Breccia**
Editorial Development Director: **Jennifer Crane**
Creative Director: **Carolyn Eckert**
Production Director: **Ginger Hillman**
Production Editor: **Jessica Rozler**
Assistant Art Director: **Sarah Silberg**
Editorial Assistant: **Lauren Vlassenko**
Editorial Research: **Suzette Lam**
Cover and Text Design: **Carolyn Eckert**
Page Composition: **Mike Suh, Vanessa Han**
Art and Layout Assistants: **Andrea Lau, Carly Grafstein**

Library of Congress Catalog Card Number:
2010 941 932

ISBN: 978-1-60901-182-6

GST R 133004424

TP09

PHOTO CREDITS
Front Cover: Courtesy of Veer/Image Source Photography; *Back Cover* (top to bottom): Courtesy of Veer/
Moodboard Photography; © Image Source/Corbis; Courtesy of Veer/Blend Images Photography; *Title
Page:* ©PhotoAlto/Alamy; *Page 7:* © Yordanka Poleganova/iStockphoto; *Page 8:* Courtesy of WWD/
Delphine Achard; *Page 9:* Courtesy of WWD/John Aquino; *Page 10 (spread):* Courtesy of WWD/Delphine
Achard; *Page 10:* Courtesy of WWD/Steve Eichner; *Page 11:* Courtesy of WWD/Steve Eichner; *Page 12:*
Courtesy of WWD/Thomas Iannaccone; Courtesy of WWD; Courtesy of WWD/Steve Eichner; *Page 13:*
© Jim Jurica/iStockphoto; Courtesy of WWD/John Aquino; Courtesy of WWD/Donato Sardella; *Page
14:* Courtesy of Stores; Courtesy of Footwear News/Fairchild Archive; Courtesy of California Apparel
News; *Page 15:* Courtesy of WWD; *Page 16:* Courtesy of WWD/Kyle Ericksen; *Page 18:* Courtesy of WWD/
Giovanni Giannoni; *Page 21:* © Diana Hirsch/iStockphoto; *Page 22:* Courtesy of WWD/Kyle Ericksen;
Page 23: Courtesy of WWD/Steve Eichner; *Page 24–25:* © Yordanka Poleganova/iStockphoto; *Page 26:*
Courtesy of WWD/Dominique Maitre; *Page 30:* Courtesy of WWD/Dominique Maitre; *Page 59:* Courtesy of
WWD/Giovanni Giannoni; *Page 60:* Courtesy of WWD/Tim Jenkins; *Page 358:* Courtesy of WWD

CONTENTS

INTRODUCTION:
About This Directory

Do you want to go to fashion school, but are unsure of where to apply?
The Fairchild Directory of Fashion Schools was created especially for you.

While most college guides offer information about the overall size, setting, and cost of a school, very few provide additional details about specific majors or departments. And among the more specialized directories available, not one focuses exclusively on the study of Fashion—until now.

The Fairchild Directory of Fashion Schools comprises information about more than 350 schools in the United States and Canada that offer undergraduate and graduate programs in Fashion Design, Fashion Merchandising, and related areas. Each listing includes the school's name and location, the Fashion majors and degrees available, and the school's Web site address. A school's Web site is a great place to learn more about its Fashion program, read about the courses and facilities available to students, and even view examples of student work. We encourage readers to visit the Web sites of schools they find interesting to learn more about what each program has to offer.

Since location plays such an important role in the college selection process, the school listings are arranged alphabetically by state. Additional indexes allow readers to select schools by degree level, major specialization, or alphabetically by name.

Following the state-by-state listing of schools, extended profiles of more than 150 programs provide a detailed picture of what a Fashion student at each school is likely to experience. In addition to general school data on enrollment, tuition, and campus setting, each extended profile features in-depth information about the following:

- Degrees, admission requirements, and graduation rates
- Student demographics including male/female, full-time/part-time, and international/minority
- Faculty demographics including full-time/part-time, certification, and affiliations with professional and/or academic associations
- Scholarships and financial aid
- Program description and philosophy
- Facilities
- Availability of online/distance learning
- Courses of instruction
- Internship requirements and typical placement
- Study abroad opportunities
- Job placement rates
- Notable alumni
- Student activities and organizations
- Faculty specializations and research

The information contained in the extended profiles was collected from questionnaires that Fairchild Books sent to schools offering majors, concentrations, or areas of emphasis in Fashion Design, Fashion Merchandising, or related areas. Schools that returned completed questionnaires received extended profiles in the directory; inclusion of an extended profile in no way indicates endorsement of the school by Fairchild Books.

With the exception of standard editorial revision for length and style, the content of the extended profiles remains exactly as it was submitted by the school officials (usually program directors, department heads, or media personnel) at the institutions themselves. Portions of the questionnaires that were left blank are indicated as "not reported" within the extended profile. All of the data submitted by the schools reflects conditions as of Spring 2010 and Fairchild Books has every reason to believe that the information contained within the extended profiles is accurate. Readers should check with a specific college or university to verify information that may have changed since the publication of this directory, particularly tuition, enrollment statistics, and graduation rates.

As a leading publisher of textbooks for Fashion, Fairchild Books has a unique understanding of Fashion education and the needs of Fashion students. The next few pages of this directory contain readings that will orient prospective students to the Fashion industry and help them navigate their Fashion education. From the importance of the portfolio and choosing the right internship to advice for aspiring designers, these readings provide invaluable insight that will set any Fashion student on the path to success.

It was our goal in creating this directory to provide prospective Fashion students with one complete resource that will help them identify schools they may wish to apply to. We hope this directory serves as a good first step towards finding the Fashion program that is right for you.

About Fairchild Books

Fairchild Books has been the premier publisher of textbooks and educational resources for fashion and textiles since the 1940s. Our titles help educate students and professionals in a broad range of fashion fields: from design, production, and manufacturing to retailing, marketing, and visual merchandising. Our award-winning list also covers costume history; color theory; the social and psychological aspects of dress; and cutting-edge industry software. As part of the Fairchild Fashion Group—publishers of *Women's Wear Daily*—Fairchild Books has a unique, insider access to all aspects of the fashion and design worlds. Learn more about Fairchild Books at www.fairchildbooks.com.

As a leading publisher of textbooks for Fashion, Fairchild Books has a unique understanding of Fashion education and the needs of Fashion students.

SO, YOU WANT TO BE IN FASHION:
A Brief Orientation to a Dynamic Industry

FASHION—the very word conjures up excitement and interest in all of us. Fashion is the ultimate F word! It is faddish, familiar, fantasy, form, fatal, feasible, festive, finite, fit, fresh, and fun. Fashion is the most dynamic of American businesses. It thrives on change, and change is the engine that fuels it.

People long for excitement and variety in their lives and look to the fashion business to show them "what's new." Ever since Adam and Eve wore fig leaves, fashion has had the power to fascinate and excite. This power has been used by the trendsetters of history. Today, past eras conjure up images not only of the philosophy and social mores of the times, but also, in large part, the fashions of the times. Designers, manufacturers, and retailers have enjoyed impressive growth. Press coverage has crossed over from the purely "passion for fashion" to become "hard news" in the *Wall Street Journal*, the *New York Times*, *Newsweek*, global television, and the Internet.

The fashion business is both an art and a science and at the same time both personal and incredibly public. Fashion can be viewed as an art because so much creativity is required to make its products. Unlike most other business where conformity is the norm, fashion nurtures innovation and creativity. Fashion has always been considered a science as well. Modern fashion manufacturing was born during the industrial revolution and has matured in the age of technology. Technology has revolutionized the way fashion is made.

Fashion, always a highly personal business, is in the process of becoming even more so. Mass customization has taken root in the fashion industry. New fashion ideas now come from the world around us; the streets, innovative teenagers, film, a celebrity with his or her unique look. Shifts in the economy, sociological influences, and demographic changes all contribute to change in fashion and therefore affect the fashion business.

THE MATERIALS OF FASHION

All good stories have a terrific beginning. So it is with fashion—all good fashions have good beginnings. They are the fibers, fabrics, leather, and fur industries known in fashion as the primary markets.

The earliest part of the planning function—in both color and texture—takes place on the primary level. It is also the level of the fashion business that works the farthest in advance of the ultimate selling period for the finished goods.

More fashion apparel and accessories are made of textiles than any other kind of material. Fashion textiles are the product of a network of primary industries, such as the cotton industry, the wool industry, the various industries producing manufactured fibers, and the fabric industry.

Changes in the textile industries have been rapid and important, particularly in recent years. Not only have there been radical new methods of producing and blending fibers, but also advances have been made in the methods of making and finishing fabrics. All of these new and fast-moving advances have contributed to the "green scene" and the sustainability of the products.

The fur and leather industries are also changing at a rapid pace, and giving designers a wider range of products to work with. These changes may be the indicators of the

exciting course that fashion in leather and fur may take to satisfy the fashion needs of the future.

THE PRODUCERS OF APPAREL

Fashion has many faces—different faces for different places, different looks for different years. Fashion is also products, and products have a past. The history of a product includes all the designers and manufacturers who have watched their customers and are always trying to give them what they want.

Fashion fascinates, it holds our interest, and it even appears in our dreams. This is quite an extraordinary challenge for the producers of fashion.

In the past few decades, the fashion apparel manufacturing business has changed from an industry composed of many small companies into a much larger one dominated by a growing group of giants. This has changed the way apparel is designed, manufactured, and merchandised. Large companies can afford to invest in the newest technology. Technology, in turn, has helped make high style and quality accessible to everyone.

THE PRODUCERS OF ACCESSORIES, FRAGRANCE, AND COSMETICS

No matter how chic, exquisite, or hip your apparel may look, it is the finishing touches that make your outfit

something special, something that says . . . YOU! For years, intimate apparel, accessories, and cosmetics and fragrances were simply something that you thought of as "maybe yes, maybe no." They were not the most important part of your fashion look. Things have really changed.

Today, producers of accessories, innerwear, cosmetics and fragrances, and home fashions must stay on the cutting edge of fashion trends that affect apparel, because the customer expects them to support and refine each new fashion trend. These producers have evolved from their original role of coordinating with apparel, becoming fashion innovators and trendsetters on their own. What we wear underneath is as important to fashion as what we wear outside. How we choose our accessories, cosmetics, and fragrance, and the items we surround ourselves with at home, all add up to our own personal fashion feel and look.

THE MARKETS FOR FASHION

The explosion of fashion markets and marts across America has been repeated not only in European markets but also in Canada, South America, and several Asian countries, including Japan and China. With the emergence of so many international markets, fashion has truly become global!

The most important market center for fashion in the

> **Fashion fascinates, it holds our interest, and it even appears in our dreams. This is quite an extraordinary challenge for the producers of fashion.**

United States is New York City. For many years it was the only center, but today Los Angeles, Miami, Dallas, Chicago, and Atlanta have captured large shares of the fashion business. Paris, which has reigned as the fashion capital of Europe for many years, now has competition from Italy, England, Belgium, Germany, and Spain. Global sourcing—the buying of foreign goods—is perhaps the most significant development in the fashion industry in many decades.

American manufacturers and retailers now routinely do direct importing and product development around the world. In addition to fashion fairs they hold in their own countries, foreign sellers and producers schedule fashion fairs in the United States to showcase and sell their goods. Popular kinds of buying that are the most successful are specification buying, private label, and product development.

SUPPORTING SERVICES

Just as customers coordinate their fashion looks, including all the fashion products seen or not seen, the fashion industry also coordinates all auxiliary services, seen or not seen, to the successful selling of the latest fashion products to the customer. The auxiliary services that support and enhance all the other levels of the fashion industries have an interconnecting role in the big fashion picture.

Try to imagine a new fashion season without fashion shows, magazines, fashion stylists, trade shows, visual merchandisers, TV, advertising agencies, public relations agencies, and the myriad of other services that support and grow this phenomenon known as the fashion business. What would the fashion world be without these services?

Understanding the roles these individual and specific services play in completing the whole is important to an understanding of how and why the fashion business goes from design to consumer. The services of magazines, newspapers, broadcast and TV media, fashion consultants, visual merchandisers, trade associations, and product development offices may be auxiliary, but—just like the Oscar awarded to supporting roles—they deserve a place of honor in the fashion business.

Excerpted from **The Dynamics of Fashion,** *Third Edition by Elaine Stone. Fairchild Books © 2008*

Fashion Careers

Careers in today's fashion industry are as diverse as the designs walking down the runway. Take a look at some of the many opportunities available to the fashion professional. Where would you like your career to lead?

buyer Typically responsible for all of the product purchases and inventories for a company or particular department of a company, within a certain budget.

collections manager Supervises museum personnel working in a specific area within a museum classification, such as historical textiles, 18th-century millinery, or Egyptian jewelry.

colorist Chooses the color palette or color combinations that will be used in creating product lines.

designer The creator of a product line; he or she is a trend forecaster in his or her own right by determining what the customer will be ready for next.

distribution manager Responsible for planning and managing the flow of goods received from the vendors, as ordered by the buyers, to the retail locations.

esthetician A licensed professional who provides services such as facials, makeup application, and hair removal to aid in improving someone's physical appearance.

fashion director Determines the trends, colors, themes, and textures for piece goods or fabrics that the apparel firm or retailer will feature for a specific season.

fashion editor Supervises the process of creating and presenting content for fashion-specific magazines, websites, newspaper sections, or television shows.

fashion photographer Works with models and art directors in apparel, accessories, or home products and is often commissioned by the art directors of catalogs and magazines.

fashion show/event planner Responsible for developing and implementing a variety of promotional activities for a designer, manufacturer, or retailer, such as a fashion show, party, or conference. Works with budgets, media, and customers in producing cost-effective and high-profile events.

fashion stylist Responsible for bringing to life a photographer's or director's vision for a fashion photography shoot, magazine layout, music video, television or film commercial, or print advertisement.

findings buyer Responsible for purchasing zippers, threads, linings, and such for a manufacturer.

illustrator Works freelance or within the advertising divisions of major retailers, designers, or manufacturers to sketch garments for print advertisements.

merchandiser Collaborates with the director of product development to decide what to produce and organizes and manages the entire product development process; this person is responsible for the development of a balanced, marketable, profitable, and timely line.

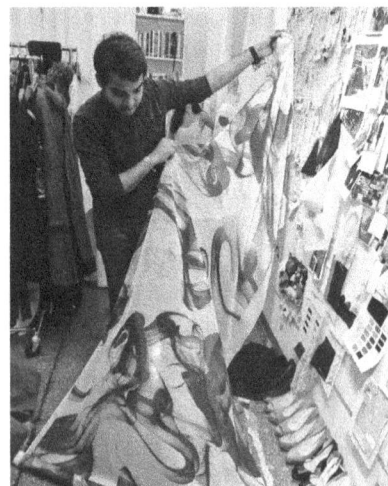

modeling/talent agency director Ultimately responsible for locating and contracting new models, training them, and, later, securing modeling jobs for them.

pattern maker Translates the design concept into a flat pattern to create an actual garment.

personal shopper Assists an individual in selecting an entire season's wardrobe or an outfit for a specific occasion, based on the needs of the customer, including his or her budget, activities, and personal style; a personal shopper may be employed by an individual, boutique, upscale department store, or specialty store.

photographer Freelance or employed by large retailers in the promotion division to photograph the visual components of promotions.

photographic model Hired to be photographed in the studio or on location. While a select few top models work in high-fashion magazines, a large number of opportunities exist through mail order catalogs, newspaper advertisements, and television.

piece goods buyer Purchases the textiles used in the production of final products.

production planner Estimates the amount and types of products a company will manufacture, either based on previous seasonal sales or on orders being received from the sales representatives on the road and in the showroom.

public relations account executive Works with media contacts such as fashion publications like Vogue, Elle, W, and InStyle to promote the line in magazine editorials and feature stories.

quality control manager Also known as the quality control engineer, this person develops specifications for the products that will be manufactured and is responsible for the final inspection for garments from the manufacturer, checking fabric, fit, construction for quality and adherence to product specification guidelines

retail account executive This person sells a product line to retail accounts and oversees the sales performance of the line in large retail accounts.

retail store manager Oversees all aspects of a retail store's operation, from advertising and special events to the customers and employees, often consisting of assistant managers, department managers, sales associates, and staff.

sourcing manager Director of the activities related to locating goods and producers of goods.

textile designer Creates original patterns, prints, and textures for the fabrics used in many types of industry, from fashion to interiors.

textile engineer Works with designers to determine how a design can be applied to a fabric in terms of more practical variables, such as durability, washability, and colorfastness.

trend forecaster Continually monitors the consumer and the industry through traveling, reading, networking, and, most important, observing; this person creates formal reports that summarize important fashion trends with seasonal themes. The trend forecaster in the product development division of a retailer identifies the fashion trends and then interprets them for the retailer's particular customer or market.

visual merchandiser Responsible for the window installations, displays, signage, fixtures, mannequins, and decorations that give a retail operation esthetic appeal and a distinct image.

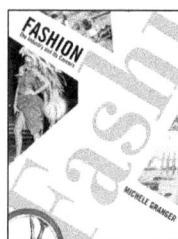

Excerpted from **Fashion: The Industry and Its Careers** *by Michele Granger. Fairchild Books © 2007*

BEYOND CONSUMER MAGAZINES:
Trade Publications
You Should Be Reading

One of the best sources of information about the fashion industry is the trade publication. Published on a daily, weekly, or monthly basis, trade publications provide up-to-the-minute details on what is current in the industry and what can be expected. For a nominal cost, designers, manufacturers, retailers, and anyone with an interest in fashion can quickly learn about the industry. Some periodicals are directed toward a specific market segment; others provide a general market overview.

The principal player in fashion-oriented trade publications is Fairchild Fashion Group. Based in New York City, it publishes such influential newspapers as *Women's Wear Daily (WWD)*, which covers both the domestic and international scene on women's, men's, and children's clothing, accessories, and textiles. *Footwear News (FN)* is another Fairchild publication for the footwear fashion and retail industries. Other U.S.-produced trade periodicals include *Fashion International, Fashion Showcase Retailer,* and the *California Apparel News*.

An excellent monthly publication for retailers is *Stores* magazine, which features every aspect of retail management and merchandising from industry trends to current interests. It is published by the National Retail Federation.

VM&SD (Visual Merchandising and Store Design) is a monthly publication of particular importance to people responsible for visual merchandising and display programs. It features articles on display innovation, prop acquisition, new materials, and lighting and general store design.

Trade publications from abroad help decision makers in the United States keep abreast of what is happening all over the world. Excellent sources of information about the international fashion scene include *Style* from Canada; *Gap* from France; *Textile Forecast, Fashion Forecast, Fashion Update, Fashionews, Fashion Record, Fashion Weekly,* and *Fashion Extras* from Great Britain; *Femme Elegant* from Spain; *Mode* from Australia; and *Italian Design Fashion* and *Sposabella* from Italy.

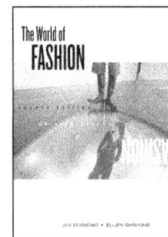

Adapted From **The World of Fashion**, *Fourth Edition by Jay and Ellen Diamond. Fairchild Books © 2008*

WWD

men's Wear Daily • Wednesday, October 13, 2010 • $3.00

Back in Blue

the past three seasons, Phoebe Philo has
eated a stylish new identity for Celine.
e key to it: precision-cut sportswear,
ten with workwear references. Here, her
rsion of the denim looks that have been
important trend this season: a cotton
atneck top and pants with an industrial
per. For more, see pages 6 and 7.

Penney's Preps
Taps Goldman In Ackman Battle

By Evan Clark and David Moin

J.C. PENNEY CO. INC. HAS TAKEN A page from the Target Corp. playbook and hired Goldman Sachs to help play defense against activist investor William Ackman, sources said.

Ackman plans to "engage in discussions" with Penney's management and other stakeholders concerning the firm's "business, assets, capitalization, financial condition, operations, governance, management, strategy and future plans." Little is known of Ackman's plans beyond that catchall laundry list, which was included in one of last week's regulatory filings from Pershing Square Capital Management, where he is chief executive officer.

Last week Ackman unveiled a 16.5 percent stake in Penney's, and said he was working in tandem with Vornado Realty Trust, which holds another 9.9 percent of the retailer's shares.

"It's the most economically sensitive stock we've invested in," said Ackman, touching on the topic at the Value Investing Congress in New York Tuesday. "Most of the retail sector doubled and tripled from the bottom, but Penney was a laggard," Ackman said, according to Barron's coverage of the conference./8

TODAY

Coach Expands Into the U.K./3
Accessories: The U.S. brand plans to open up to 15 stores in Britain over the next three years as it moves aggressively into Europe. ▲

India's Fast-Fashion Influx/8
Retail: Forever 21 is the latest fast-fashion chain to tap into India's booming market.

Versace Ups Sales Forecast/2
Financial: After trimming staff and rejigging collections, the brand is back on the growth path under new chief executive officer Gian Giacomo Ferraris.

Gian Giacomo Ferraris

Avon Shares Climb On Rumor/2
Beauty: The beauty group's shares jump after reports of a possible bid from L'Oréal.

INTERPRETING THE INITIALS:
A Breakdown of Professional & Academic Associations

American Apparel and Footwear Association (AAFA)—The national trade association representing apparel, footwear and other sewn products companies, and their suppliers, which compete in the global market. http://apparelandfootwear.org

American Collegiate Retailing Association (ACRA)—Educational association affiliated with the NRF that supports retail education at 4-year colleges and graduate schools. www.acraretail.org

American Marketing Association (AMA)—The professional association for individuals and organizations who are leading the practice, teaching, and development of marketing worldwide. www.marketingpower.com

Association for Consumer Research (ACR)—Educational association that supports the advancement of consumer research and facilitates the exchange of scholarly information among members of academia, industry, and government worldwide. www.acrwebsite.org

California Fashion Association—A non-profit organization established to provide information for business expansion and growth to the apparel and textile industry of California. www.calfashion.org

Canadian Apparel Federation (CAF)—Professional association for Canada's apparel industry. www.apparel.ca

Costume Society of America (CSA)—An academic organization that advances the global understanding of all aspects of dress and appearance and works to stimulate scholarship and encourage the study of costume. www.costumesocietyamerica.com

Council of Fashion Designers of America (CFDA)—A not-for-profit trade association that leads industry-wide initiatives to support professional development through awards, scholarships, and other programs. www.cfda.com

DECA—A non-profit student organization that sponsors programs and activities for high school and college level students interested in the areas of marketing, finance, hospitality and management. www.deca.org

Fashion Group International, Inc. (FGI)—A global, non-profit, professional organization that works to advance professionalism in fashion and its related lifestyle industries. http://fgi.org

International Apparel Federation (IAF)—Politically-neutral global association, open to entrepreneurs, executives, and educational institutions from the apparel chain worldwide. www.iafnet.com

International Association of Clothing Designers and Executives (IACDE)—Global professional organization for pattern designers, technical designers, manufacturing executives and suppliers of the clothing industry. http://iacde.com

International Council of Shopping Centers (ICSC)—The global trade association of the shopping center industry, including owners, developers, managers, marketing specialists, investors, lenders, retailers and other professionals as well as academics and public officials. www.icsc.org

International Textile and Apparel Association (ITAA)—A professional and educational association composed of scholars, educators, and students in the textile, apparel, and merchandising disciplines in higher education. www.itaaonline.org

Men's Apparel Guild in California (MAGIC International)—The preeminent trade event in the international fashion industry, hosting global buyers and sellers of men's, women's and children's apparel, footwear, accessories and sourcing resources. http://show.magiconline.com

National Retail Federation (NRF)—The world's largest retail trade association, it's mission is to advance and protect the interests of the retail industry and to help retailers achieve excellence in all areas of their business. http://nrf.com

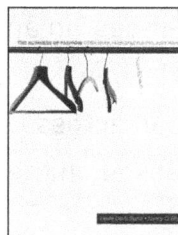

Adapted from **The Business of Fashion**, *Third Edition, by Leslie Davis Burns and Nancy O. Bryant. Fairchild Books © 2007*

17

SAY IT WITH STYLE:
A Fashionista's Guide to Correct Pronunciation

One of the easiest ways a budding fashionista can burn valuable networking bridges is to mispronounce key words of the business. There can be nothing worse than dropping a bomb like "Her-mees" in an interview when one means to reference master silk-and-leather designer Hermès (air-mez). Stumbling through those French and Italian words so amply spread across fashion jargon can jeopardize a career. Imagine if Scarlett Johansson, when asked on the red carpet whom she happened to be wearing, were to reply, "Give-in-chee."

Terms

Aesthetic (ehs-*theh*-tik)
Appliqué (ap-plee-*kay*)
Atelier (at-tell-ee-*ay*)
Avant-garde (av-ahn-*gahrd*)
Bandeau (band-*oh*)
Basque (bask)
Boutique (boo-*teek*)
Bourgeois (boor-*zhwah*)
Bustier (boo-stee-*ay*)
Charmeuse (shar-*mewz*)
Chartreuse (shar-*trewz*)
Chemise (shem-*eez*)
Chic (sheek)
Couturier (coh-too-ree-*air*)
Gaucho (*gow*-cho)
Faux Pas (foh *paw*)
Fuchsia (*few*-shuh)
Femme (fem)
Haute Couture (oat ko-*tour*)
Kimono (kee-*moh-no*)
Madras (*mad*-dress)
Mannequin (*man*-uh-kin)
Moda (*mo*-dah)
Outré (*oh*-tray)
Palette (*pal*-et)
Passé (pass-*ay*)
Pique (as in "to pique interest") (peek)
Piqué (as in cotton weave) (pee-kay)
Prêt-à-Porter (pret-ah-pohr-*tay*)
Silhouette (sill-ew-*et*)
Vermilion (ver-*mill*-yuhn)
Voile (vwall)

Designers

Anna Sui (anna swee)
Balenciaga (bal-lawn-see-*ah*-gah)
Christian Dior (chris-tee-ahn dee-*or*)
Dolce & Gabbana (dohl-chay and gahb-*bah*-nah)
Donna Karan (donna ke-*rahn*)
Dries Van Noten (drees van note-*ahn*)
Fendi (*fen*-dee)
Givenchy (zhee-*von*-she)
Hermès (air-*mez*)
Jean Paul Gaultier (zhahn paul gol-tee-*yeh*)
Lacroix (lah-*cwa*)
Louis Vuitton (loo-*ee vwee*-ton)
Ralph Lauren (*lor*-uhn)
Versace (ver-*sah*-chay)
Yohji Yamamoto (*yo*-jee yah-mah-*mo*-to)
Yves Saint Laurent (eve sanh-la-*rahn*)

The press would be all over it. The ramifications would be horrific for celebrity credibility as well as for product marketing.

To avoid problems, it is wise to invest in a fashion dictionary, complete with pronunciation keys and examples of usage. One great reference is *The Fairchild Dictionary of Fashion*, by Charlotte Mankey Calasibetta and Phyllis G. Tortora. *Merriam-Webster* online also has a pronunciation feature, but not every designer is listed.

The following is a brief list of some must-know words and names. The italicized syllable is generally recognized as stressed. Japanese words ideally do not have accented syllables (i.e., intonation and inflection are more important than stress).

Excerpted from **Uncovering Fashion** *by Marian Francis Wolbers.* *Fairchild Books © 2009*

EXPERIENCE IS THE BEST TEACHER:
The Fashion Internship

An internship is a supervised on-the-job experience that combines work, an analysis of the organization, employer and academic sponsor feedback, and, frequently, special assignments. An internship provides students with an excellent opportunity to apply their education to the work environment; it also allows the employer to assess and train future employees while gaining new perspectives. An internship may be paid or unpaid, and enrolled in for college credit or no credit, depending on the requirements of the academic institution, the students, and the internship organization.

An internship can truly be a win-win situation for all three partners. The student can benefit from hands-on experience, the opportunity to apply academic theory to the real world, and, possibly, procure the additional benefit of post-graduation employment. The internship supervisor can gain a new and enthusiastic perspective from the student as well as a candidate for future employment. The academic internship sponsor is exposed to various fashion industry businesses and given the chance to assess not only student performance on the job but also the relationship between academic course content and current and future industry needs and trends.

There are two categories of internships: formal and informal. A formal internship program is most often offered by a large company. For example, a group of student interns may go through preplanned classes and activities in a formal internship program. In an informal internship, the internship supervisor and student develop an individual program that will meet the employer's needs, the student's goals, and the academic institution's internship requirements. In an informal internship, developing a specific work plan that meets the needs of the intern, the employer, and the academic sponsor is extremely important.

WHY AN INTERNSHIP?

An internship is one of the best ways to get your foot in the door of a fashion business. Interning is a route to meeting and working with successful industry professionals who will model success and may later help you land a position after graduation; it is a path to learning firsthand about the multitude of career options in the industry. This path may not be available to others—those not pursuing a college degree or not enrolled in an academic program that provides the necessary prerequisite training and support. An internship is the part of your education that introduces you to the professional world. Why complete an internship? The following are a few of the many reasons for working diligently to secure and successfully complete the best internship for you.

- **Gain essential on-the-job experience in the industry.** The classroom is the fundamental part of your education and will afford you opportunities to learn about theory, best practices, and techniques; however, one of the most difficult lessons to teach in a classroom is how to work within the industry, with clients, coworkers, teams, and supervisors. An internship provides real-world work experience, such as meeting an immediate and unexpected deadline, pleasing a difficult customer, working with a challenging supervisor, or motivating an uncertain employee.

- **Build an industry network.** Because you will be interning in a showroom, buying office, design studio, retail store, costume collection, or any one of the multitude of places of business in the industry, nearly every person you meet will be someone to add to your career network. Many students say, "It's who you know . . . and I don't know

Interning is a route to meeting and working with successful industry professionals who will model success and may later help you land a position after graduation; it is a path to learning firsthand about the multitude of career options in the industry.

anybody when it comes to finding a job." You know your faculty, alumni, and peers. During the internship, you can expand this network by taking the time to get to know professionals you meet on the job and recording their contact information.

- **Expand your portfolio.** Nothing enhances a portfolio like actual professional work. Your college projects and writing assignments are significant to employers; they show the diversity of your skills and provide outside assessment. Work completed on the job, such as newsletters, memos, trend boards, and other projects, help establish you as a professional.

- **Learn what is out there.** While working as an intern, you will be exposed to many professionals in positions and careers tracks that you may not have studied in college or read about in your research. A former student who interned with a fiber trade organization, Cotton Incorporated, learned that there was an employee who organized sample garments and accessories, catalogued fabric samples, and assisted with the development of trend boards. It was the ideal position for this ultra-organized, color-coded, and fashion-forward young woman. She completed the internship with flying colors and applied for this job when a new graduate. The company knew she was a talented and tireless employee; she got the job.

- **Land a job.** Can you imagine that your job search may be over before it is ever started? Can you envision having

a position in the industry before you graduate from college? Many employers prefer to offer an entry-level position to one of their successful, hardworking interns, rather than pay to advertise the position, spend valuable time interviewing candidates, and take a risk in hiring someone with whom they have no experience. Companies offer internships for two main reasons. First, interns provide extra help in the workplace, often offering a fresh look at how business is conducted. Second, an internship provides a company with a test drive of a potential employee. If you are interning for a firm that does not have a job opening now, it may have one tomorrow. In addition, if your internship company does not have a position, the executives may know of another person or business that is hiring. It all comes back to building both a network and a top professional reputation.

COMMON INTERNSHIP QUESTIONS AND ANSWERS

When should I start to plan for my internship?
Begin to plan at least two semesters prior to when you expect to complete the internship. For example, start planning during a current fall semester at the very latest for a prospective internship for the following summer.

What should I do first?
Before contacting prospective employers, it is important to clarify personal goals and expectations for the internship experience. What do you want to do in the internship? Assist in production planning? Learn how to buy? Help plan and coordinate fashion promotion activities? Assist a

While working as an intern, you will be exposed to many professionals in positions and career tracks that you may not have studied in college or read about in your research.

designer? Work in finance or in control? Learn about visual merchandising or, perhaps, the functions of personnel?

Assist in merchandising? Construct patterns? Work in product development?

Now I'm ready to contact employers, right?
Not quite. The next step involves investigation: researching employers and employment opportunities. The Internet is an excellent source of information. Additional resources are presented in this chapter. If you are interested in returning home, or perhaps working in your college town during the school year or summer, you may find it advisable to identify the specific employers you are interested in and to apply directly to those organizations. Knowing something about the company before you begin will help you know how better to present yourself and possibly prevent an embarrassing moment or comment. In addition, the company representative may be impressed by your wealth of knowledge.

So, what next?
Now you are faced with important choices. Do you want to apply for an existing internship program, or should you create your own? For example, Liz Claiborne, Inc., and Saks Fifth Avenue offer structured, or formal, internship programs. Can you complete the internship during the summer or during a semester of the traditional academic year? Can you work full-time or part-time? Applying for internship programs requires careful, long-range planning, perhaps including arranging for a lighter academic load during the appointed internship semester. An internship is a real job that requires time and effort.

After I have decided between creating my own internship and applying for an existing one, how do I present myself?

It is necessary to develop an appropriate résumé and letter of application describing yourself, your experiences, the position sought, and what you bring to this position.

To how many companies should I apply for an internship?
Although there is no right answer, as it depends entirely upon your personal goals and objectives, one should consider a minimum of five to ten applications. If possible, do not limit yourself to one location.

Will I get paid for my internship?
Yes and no. Some companies pay interns the minimum hourly wage; others pay a stipend. Some organizations may not pay at all for the internship experience. It is up to you and your academic institution to decide whether or not you can accept an unpaid internship.

What if I receive more than one offer?
Lucky you! Choosing among offers is never easy. If, however, you have clarified your goals and objectives in applying for the internship early in your search, you will be in a better position to evaluate offers as they are presented.

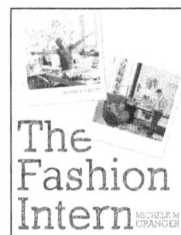

The Fashion Intern

Excerpted from **The Fashion Intern,** *Second Edition by Michele Granger. Fairchild Books © 2010*

THE FASHION PORTFOLIO:
Your Statement of Style

In today's competitive fashion industry, your portfolio is your ultimate sales tool.
It must express the unique qualities that set you apart from others, and should
include samples that reflect your best efforts and indicate your range of skills and
expertise. In short, your portfolio promotes your most important product—you.

Potential employers are articulate, creative, visually sensitive
individuals who work under pressure and tight schedules.
Not surprisingly, they seek to hire equally capable designers.
A strong portfolio, coupled with an impressive résumé, is

your key into the creative business of fashion.

Your portfolio is also an effective interviewing tool.
Although you can claim certain skills, your portfolio
provides the visual evidence, showcasing your creativity,

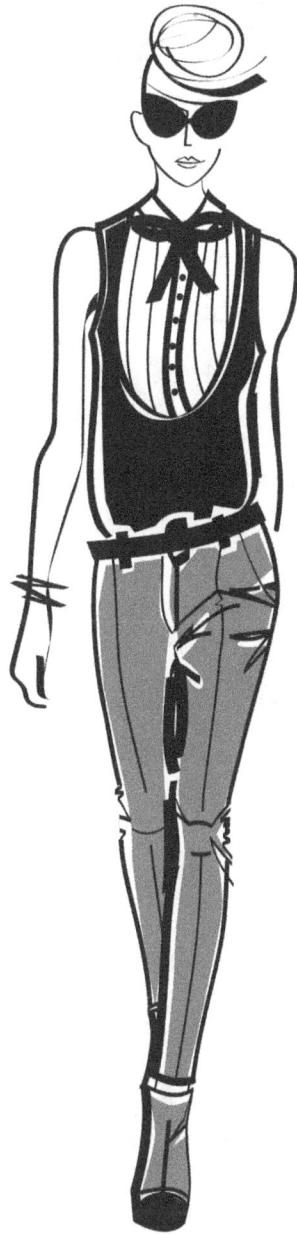

organizational and technical skills (knowledge of sewing, draping, and pattern making), drawing ability, and awareness of fashion trends.

Fashion designers assemble several portfolios over the course of their student careers: one for entry into design school, an internship portfolio, and an exit portfolio representing the culmination of their studies, abilities, and fashion awareness. In addition, you'll need a portfolio for admission to a graduate program and, as a professional reentering the job market, an up-dated book including recent samples, press clippings, and published work.

The creative fashion portfolio should constantly evolve and never stagnate. You should also make sure to target

each company individually by including designs that have their "look," thus promising growth potential and enthusiasm for what they do.

Excerpted from **Portfolio Presentation for Fashion Designers**, *Third Edition by Linda Tain. Fairchild Books © 2010*

NEVER TOO EARLY TO PLAN:
Advice for Aspiring Designers

Those who believe that designers spend all day sketching in their studios should reconsider their choice of career. It takes a mountain of concerns and then some for designers to convey their message. Be media-savvy, aware of global issues, and clever enough to bottle these qualities into a brand identity that speaks to the consumer. Oh, and don't forget to bring along design talent! That's the advice those in the know offer to anyone who aspires to the glamorous title of fashion designers.

In the past, designers spent their days—and their nights—sketching, sewing, and draping, but the role has shifted as fashion has evolved into a billion-dollar global business over the past two decades. As a result, designers have to represent their labels 24/7. Ideally, they should become their brand. And, while they are at it, they shouldn't neglect world events!

Designers must also predict what their customers will want months before they know themselves. In fact, the laundry list of what designers have to do today appears endless.

Now there is the growing competition from celebrity designers who enter the fashion fray with well-established names and a solid following of fans around the world. Young designers can find other avenues to help them gain recognition. Fashion festivals and scholarships certainly help. Globally, fashion philanthropists are doing more than doling out cash. Nathalie Dufour, who runs France's Andam prize, says, "The idea is to help designers who are starting out to understand what type of business strategy could help them to develop."

The steps to becoming a fashion designer mirror what the Council of Fashion Designers of America (CFDA) is doing with its CFDA/Vogue Fashion Fund. The CFDA selects three designers each season for financing of up to $200,000, as well as mentoring from a senior executive from within the industry. In the United States generally, though, young designers tend to get funding more by doing consultancy work for large companies and assisting on teams of leading designers than by participation in festivals or through scholarships.

France's Chambre Syndicale also is involved in supporting young designers. The biggest hurdle a young designer often faces his naïveté in the ways of the world and the fast-changing nature of today's fashion business. It is not enough to design! Young designers must have a product that is produced in an innovative way.

Today, young designers have a new set of eyes analyzing their designs: private equity firms and investment bankers. These investors are interested in young designers who have already grown to the $2 million mark and have the potential to grow further. Among recent designers have been Anna Sui, Catherine Malandrino, Hussein Chalayan, and Phoebe Philo.

And let's not forget Jason Wu, who interned with Narciso Rodriguez; or Derek Lam, who as a young designer worked as an assistant to Geoffrey Beene and for Michael Kors; or Peter Som, who was recognized in 1997 by the CFDA as a rising young talent in the scholarship competition and honed his skills in the design rooms of Bill Blass, Michael Kors, and Calvin Klein.

You have to hone your skills and spend time working with and learning from the star designers. As a young designer, your path to star success is Go! Go! Go!—but go slow!

Excerpted from **The Dynamics of Fashion**, *Third Edition by Elaine Stone. Fairchild Books © 2008*

Build Your Fashion Library with Fairchild Books

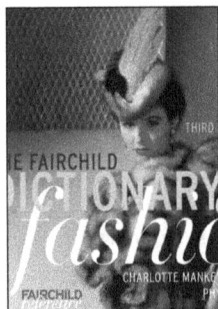

The Fairchild Dictionary of Fashion

Third Edition

Charlotte Mankey Calasibetta and Phyllis Tortora

Who's Who in Fashion

Fifth Edition

Holly Price Alford and Anne Stegemeyer

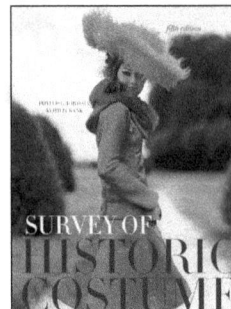

Survey of Historic Costume

Fourth Edition

Phyllis Tortora

Fabric Science

Ninth Edition

Allen C. Cohen, Ingrid Johnson, Joseph J. Pizzuto

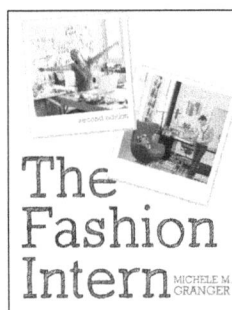

The Fashion Intern,

Second Edition

Michele Granger

Portfolio Presentation for Fashion Designers

Third Edition

Linda Tain

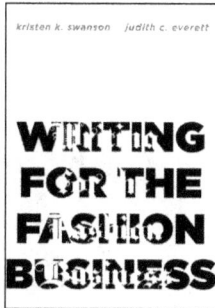

Writing for the Fashion Business

Kristen Swanson and
Judith Everett

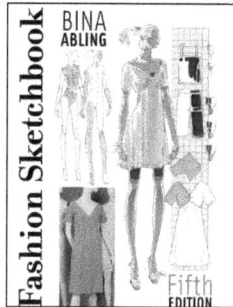

The Fashion Sketchbook

Fifth Edition

Bina Abling

Draping Basics

Sally DiMarco

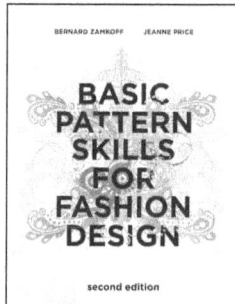

Basic Pattern Skills for Fashion Design,

Second Edition

Bernard Zamkoff and
Jeanne Price

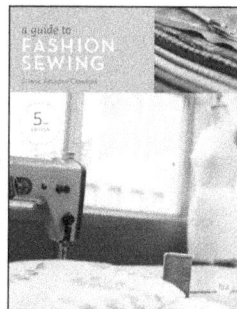

A Guide to Fashion Sewing

Fifth Edition

Connie Amaden-Crawford

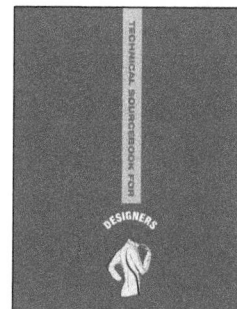

Technical Designer's Sourcebook

Jaeil Lee and
Camille Steen

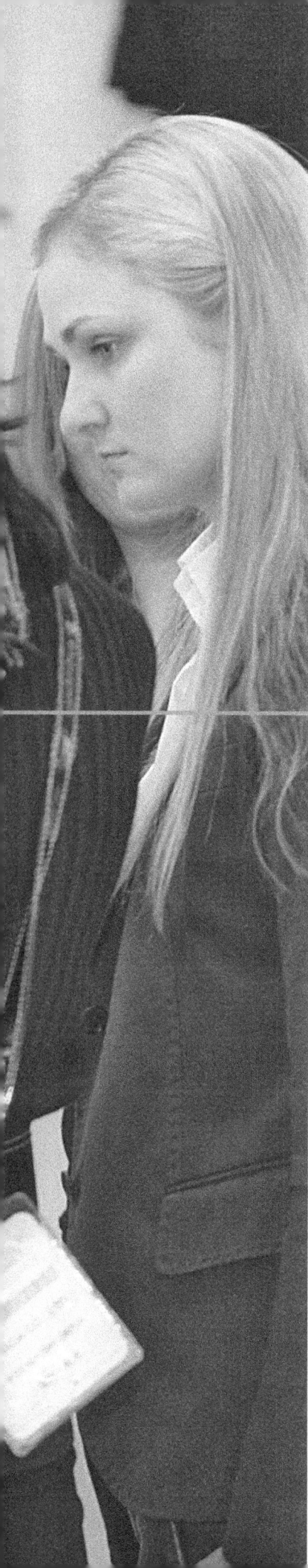

State-by-State Listing of Schools

ALABAMA

Alabama A & M University
Normal, AL
School of Agricultural & Environmental Sciences
Department of Family & Consumer Sciences
Apparel, Merchandising & Design (B.S.)
www.aamu.edu/saes/FCS/amd_intro.aspx

Auburn University
Auburn University, AL
Department of Consumer Affairs
Apparel Merchandising (B.S.)
Product Design & Product Management (B.S.)
Consumer Affairs: Apparel (M.S.)
Integrated Textile & Apparel Science (PhD)
www.humsci.auburn.edu/cahs
- **EXTENDED PROFILE ON PAGE 62**

Trenholm State Technical College
Montgomery, AL
Department of Apparel & Designs
Apparel & Designs Special Training (certificate)
www.trenholmstate.edu
- **EXTENDED PROFILE ON PAGE 64**

University of Alabama
Tuscaloosa, AL
Department of Clothing, Textiles & Interior Design
Apparel & Textiles: Apparel Design (B.S.)
Apparel & Textiles: Fashion Retailing (B.S.)
www.ches.ua.edu
- **EXTENDED PROFILE ON PAGE 66**

ARIZONA

Art Institute of Phoenix, The
Phoenix, AZ
Fashion Marketing (B.A.)
www.artinstitutes.edu/phoenix

Art Institute of Tucson, The
Tucson, AZ
Fashion Marketing (B.A.)
www.artinstitutes.edu/tucson
- **EXTENDED PROFILE ON PAGE 70**

Collins College
Phoenix, AZ
Department of Fashion Design & Merchandising
Fashion Design & Merchandising (B.F.A.)
www.collinscollege.edu
- **EXTENDED PROFILE ON PAGE 72**

Gateway Community College
Phoenix, AZ
Retail Management (A.A.S., certificate)
www.gatewaycc.edu/Programs/RetailManagement

Mesa Community College
Mesa, AZ
Fashion Merchandising & Design Department
Fashion Merchandising; Fashion Design;
    Retailing (A.A.S.)
www.mc.maricopa.edu/fashion
- **EXTENDED PROFILE ON PAGE 74**

Northern Arizona University
Flagstaff, AZ
School of Communication
Merchandising (B.S.)
www.nau.edu/sbs/communication
- **EXTENDED PROFILE ON PAGE 76**

Phoenix College
Phoenix, AZ
Applied Technology, Family & Consumer Sciences
Fashion Design (A.A.S.)
www.pc.maricopa.edu

Pima Community College
Tucson, AZ
Business Careers
Fashion Merchandising (A.A.S.)
www.pima.edu/program/business/apparel-
merchandising-aas.shtml

University of Arizona
Tucson, AZ
College of Agriculture & Life Sciences
John & Doris School of Family & Consumer Sciences
Retailing & Consumer Sciences (B.S., M.S., PhD)
http://ag.arizona.edu/fcs/rcsc

ARKANSAS

Harding University
Searcy, AR
Family & Consumer Sciences Department
Fashion Merchandising (B.S.)
Interiors Merchandising (B.S.)
www.harding.edu/fcs
- **EXTENDED PROFILE ON PAGE 68**

Henderson State University
Arkadelphia, AR
Teacher's College
Department of Family & Consumer Sciences
Fashion Merchandising (B.S.)
www.hsu.edu/content.aspx?id=505

University of Arkansas
Fayetteville, AR
School of Human Environmental Sciences
Apparel Studies (B.S., M.A.)
http://hesc.uark.edu/2618.htm

University of Arkansas
Pinebluff, AR
School of Agriculture, Fisheries & Human Sciences
Department of Human Sciences
Merchandising, Textiles & Design (B.S.)
www.uapb.edu

CALIFORNIA

Academy of Art University
San Francisco, CA
School of Fashion
Fashion Design (A.A., B.F.A., M.F.A.)
Knitwear (A.A., B.F.A., M.F.A.)
Menswear (A.A.)
Merchandising (A.A., B.F.A., M.F.A.)
Textiles Design (A.A., B.F.A., M.F.A)
Visual Merchandising (A.A., B.F.A)
www.academyart.edu/fashion-school
• **EXTENDED PROFILE ON PAGE 78**

Academy of Couture Art
West Hollywood, CA
Fashion Design & Pattern Design (A.A., B.A., B.S.)
www.academyofcoutureart.com/

Allan Hancock College
Santa Maria, CA
Fashion Studies (A.S., certificate)
www.hancockcollege.edu/Default.asp?Page=1360

American River College
Sacramento, CA
Fine & Applied Arts
Fashion Design (A.A.)
Fashion Merchandising (A.A.)
www.arc.losrios.edu/Programs_of_Study/FAA/Fashion.htm

Antelope Valley College
Lancaster, CA
Technical Education
Clothing & Textiles (A.A., certificate)
www.avc.edu/information/catalog/common/documents/clothing.pdf

Art Institute of California (The)—Hollywood
North Hollywood, CA
Fashion Design (A.S.)
Fashion Marketing (A.S.)
Fashion Design (B.F.A.)
Fashion Marketing & Management (B.S.)
www.artinstitutes.edu/hollywood

Art Institute of California (The)–Inland Empire
San Bernardino, CA
Fashion & Retail Management (B.S.)
Fashion Design (B.F.A.)
www.artinstitutes.edu/inland-empire
• **EXTENDED PROFILE ON PAGE 80**

Art Institute of California (The)—Orange County
Santa Ana, CA
Fashion Design (B.F.A.)
Fashion Marketing & Management (B.S.)
www.artinstitutes.edu/orange-county

Art Institute of California (The)—San Diego
San Diego, CA
Fashion Design (B.F.A.)
Fashion Marketing & Management (B.S.)
www.artinstitutes.edu/san-diego

Art Institute of California (The)–San Francisco
San Francisco, CA
Fashion Design (A.A.S., B.F.A.)
Fashion Marketing (A.A.S.)
Fashion Marketing & Management (B.A.)
www.artinstitutes.edu/san-francisco
• **EXTENDED PROFILE ON PAGE 82**

Art Institute of California (The)–Sunnyvale
Sunnyvale, CA
Fashion Marking & Management (B.S.)
www.artsinstitues.edu/sunnyvale
• **EXTENDED PROFILE ON PAGE 84**

Butte College
Oroville, CA
Art/Digital Art & Design Department
Fashion Merchandising (A.S., certificate)
Fashion Design (certificate)
www.butte.edu/

California College of the Arts
San Francisco, CA
Fashion Design Program
Fashion Design (B.F.A.)
www.cca.edu/academics/fashion-design
- **EXTENDED PROFILE ON PAGE 86**

California State Polytechnic University, Pomona
Pomona, CA
College of Agriculture
Apparel Merchandising & Management:
    Apparel Production (B.S.)
Apparel Merchandising & Management:
    Fashion Retailing (B.S.)
www.csupomona.edu/~amm/

California State University, Fresno
Fresno, CA
Department of Child, Family & Consumer Sciences
Family & Consumer Sciences: Fashion Merchandising
    (B.A.)
http://cast.csufresno.edu
- **EXTENDED PROFILE ON PAGE 88**

California State University, Long Beach
Long Beach, CA
Department of Family & Consumer Sciences
Family & Consumer Sciences: Merchandising & Design
    (B.A., M.A.)
Family & Consumer Sciences: Textiles & Clothing
    (B.A., M.A.)
http://csulb.edu/fcs
- **EXTENDED PROFILE ON PAGE 90**

California State University, Los Angeles
Los Angeles, CA
College of Arts & Letters
Art Department
Fashion & Textiles: Fashion Design (B.A., M.A.,
    certificate)
Fashion & Textiles: Fashion Merchandising (B.A., M.A.,
    certificate)
Fashion & Textiles: Textiles (B.A., M.A., certificate)
www.calstatela.edu/academic/art/fashion.php

California State University, Northridge
Northridge, CA
Department of Family & Consumer Sciences
Apparel Design & Merchandising (B.S., M.S.)
www.csun.edu/hhd/fcs/fcsadm.html

California State University, Sacramento
Sacramento, CA
Department of Family & Consumer Sciences
Family & Consumer Sciences: Apparel Marketing &
    Design (B.A.)
www.asn.csus.edu/facs/APMD/apparel.htm
- **EXTENDED PROFILE ON PAGE 92**

Cañada College
Redwood City, CA
Fashion Design Merchandising (A.S., certificate)
http://canadacollege.net/fashion/

City College of San Francisco
San Francisco, CA
Fashion Department
Fashion Merchandising (certificate)
Fashion Design (certificate)
www.ccsf.edu/fashion
- **EXTENDED PROFILE ON PAGE 94**

College of Alameda
Alameda, CA
Apparel Design & Merchandising Program
Apparel Design & Merchandising (A.A., certificate)
http://adamcoa.com
- **EXTENDED PROFILE ON PAGE 96**

College of the Sequoias
Visalia, CA
Consumer/Family Studies Division
Fashion Design (certificate)
Fashion Merchandising (certificate)
www.cos.edu/

Cuesta College
San Luis Obispo, CA
Department of Fashion Design & Merchandising
Fashion Design (A.A., certificate)
Fashion: Merchandising (A.A.)
Fashion Merchandising (certificate)
www.cuesta.edu
- **EXTENDED PROFILE ON PAGE 98**

El Camino College
Torrance, CA
Fashion & Related Technologies
Fashion Design & Production (A.S., certificate)
Fashion Merchandising (A.S.)
Computer Patternmaking Technician (certificate)
Costume Technician (certificate)
www.elcamino.edu/academics/indtech/fashion/
- **EXTENDED PROFILE ON PAGE 100**

Evergreen Valley College
San Jose, CA
Business & Workforce Development Division
Retail Management (A.S., certificate)
www.evc.edu/bat/

Fashion Careers College
San Diego, CA
Fashion Design & Technology (Specialized Associate
    Degree, certificate)
Fashion Business & Technology (Specialized Associate
    Degree, certificate)
www.fashioncareercollege.com
• **EXTENDED PROFILE ON PAGE 102**

Fashion Institute of Design & Merchandising
Los Angeles, CA
Apparel Industry Management (A.A.)
Fashion Design (A.A.)
Fashion Knitwear Design (A.A.)
Merchandise Marketing (A.A.)
Merchandise Product Development (A.A.)
Advanced Fashion Design (A.A.)
International Manufacturing & Product
    Development (A.A.)
www.fidm.edu
• **EXTENDED PROFILE ON PAGE 104**

Fresno City College
Fresno, CA
Social Sciences Division
Home Economics & Fashion Merchandising (A.A.,
    certificate)
www.fresnocitycollege.edu/index.aspx?page=809

Fullerton College
Fullerton, CA
Division of Technology & Engineering
Fashion Design (A.A., certificate)
Fashion Merchandising (A.A., certificate)
Fashion Journalism (A.A.)
http://techneng.fullcoll.edu/degree.htm

International Academy of Art & Design— Sacramento
Sacramento, CA
Fashion Design & Merchandising (B.F.A., A.A.S.)
www.iadtsacramento.com/fashion-ba.asp

Los Angeles Trade-Tech
Fashion Design (A.A., certificate)
Fashion Merchandising (A.S., certificate)
http://college.lattc.edu/fashion/

Monterey Peninsula College
Monterey, CA
Department of Fashion
Fashion Design (A.S.)
Fashion Merchandising (A.S.)
Fashion Production (A.S.)
Fashion Costuming (A.S.)
www.mpc.edu
• **EXTENDED PROFILE ON PAGE 106**

Mount San Antonio College
Walnut, CA
Business Division
Consumer Sciences & Design Technology Department
Fashion Design & Merchandising (A.S.)
www.mtsac.edu/instruction/business

Orange Coast College
Costa Mesa, CA
Fashion Department
Apparel Construction (A.A., A.S., certificate)
Fashion Design (A.A., A.S., certificate)
Fashion Merchandising (A.A., A.S., certificate)
Production/Product Development (A.A., A.S., certificate)
www.orangecoastcollege.edu/academics/course_cat/
cert.htm

Otis College of Art & Design
Los Angeles, CA
Department of Fashion
Fashion Design (B.F.A.)
www.otis.edu
• **EXTENDED PROFILE ON PAGE 108**

Palomar College
San Marcos, CA
Design & Consumer Education Department
Fashion: Buying & Management (A.A., certificate)
Fashion Design/Technical (A.A.)
Fashion Merchandising (A.A.)
www.palomar.edu/fashion/

Pasadena City College
Pasadena, CA
Business & Computer Technology Division
Fashion Design (certificate)
www.pasadena.edu/divisions/business-computertech/

Point Loma Nazarene University
San Diego, CA
Family & Consumer Sciences Department
Fashion Merchandising (B.S.)
www.pointloma.edu/experience/academics/areas-study/
fashion-merchandising

Sacramento City College

Sacramento, CA
Behavioral & Social Sciences Division
Family & Consumer Science Department
Fashion Design & Production (A.A., certificate)
Custom Apparel Construction & Alterations (A.A.,
    certificate)
http://web.scc.losrios.edu/fashn/

Saddleback College

Mission, CA
Fashion Department
Fashion Design (A.A., A.S., certificate)
Advanced Fashion Design & Apparel Manufacturing
    (A.A., A.S., certificate)
Fashion Merchandising (A.A., A.S., certificate)
www.saddleback.edu/atas/Fashion
• **EXTENDED PROFILE ON PAGE 110**

San Diego Mesa College

San Diego, CA
School of Health Science & Public Service
Fashion Design (A.S., certificate)
Fashion Merchandising (A.S., certificate)
Computer Fashion Technology (A.S., certificate)
www.sdmesa.edu/academic-programs/index.
cfm?DeptID=26

San Francisco State University

San Francisco, CA
Consumer & Family Studies/Dietetics
Apparel Design & Merchandising (B.S.)
http://cfsd.sfsu.edu

San Joaquin Delta College

Stockton, CA
Department of Fashion
Fashion Merchandising (A.A.)
Apparel Design (A.A.)
www.deltacollege.edu/div/finearts/fashion/fashion.html
• **EXTENDED PROFILE ON PAGE 112**

Santa Ana College

Santa Ana, CA
Family & Consumer Studies Department
Fashion Design (A.A., A.S., certificate)
Fashion Merchandising (A.A., A.S., certificate)
www.sac.edu/faculty_staff/academic_progs/
departments/family/

Santa Monica College

Santa Monica, CA
Fashion Design (A.A., certificate)
Fashion Merchandising (A.A., certificate)
www.smc.edu

Santa Rosa Junior College

Santa Rosa, CA
Consumer & Family Studies Department
Fashion Studies: Design (A.A.)
Fashion Studies: Merchandising (A.A.)
www.santarosa.edu/instruction/instructional_
departments/consumer-and-family-studies

Sierra College

Rocklin, CA
Liberal Arts Division
Fashion Design & Merchandising Department
Apparel Design & Production (A.A., A.S., certificate)
Fashion Merchandising (A.A., A.S., certificate)
www.sierracollege.edu/programs/divisions/LiberalArts/
fashion/index.html

University of California, Davis

Davis, CA
Division of Clothing & Textiles
Textiles & Clothing: Textile Science (B.S.)
Textiles & Clothing: Marketing/Economics (B.S.)
Fiber & Polymer Science (B.S.)
Textiles (M.S.)
Cultural Studies (M.A., PhD)
http://textiles.ucdavis.edu

Ventura College

Ventura, CA
Fashion Design (A.S., certificate)
Fashion Merchandising (A.S., certificate)
www.venturacollege.edu/departments/academic

West Valley College

Saratoga, CA
Department of Fashion Design & Apparel Technologies
Apparel Design (A.S., certificate)
Apparel Production (A.S., certificate)
www.westvalley.edu/fd
• **EXTENDED PROFILE ON PAGE 114**

Woodbury University

Burbank, CA
Department of Fashion Design
Fashion Design (B.F.A.)
http://mcd.woodbury.edu/fashiondesign
• **EXTENDED PROFILE ON PAGE 116**

COLORADO

Art Institute of Colorado, The
Denver, CO
Fashion Design (B.A.)
Fashion Retail Management (B.A.)
www.artinstitutes.edu/denver
- **EXTENDED PROFILE ON PAGE 120**

Colorado State University
Fort Collins, CO
Department of Design & Merchandising
Design & Merchandising: Apparel Design & Production
   (B.S.)
Design & Merchandising: Merchandising (B.S.)
Design & Merchandising: Apparel & Merchandising
   (B.S., M.S.)
www.dm.cahs.colostate.edu
- **EXTENDED PROFILE ON PAGE 122**

Johnson & Wales University
Denver, CO
College of Business
Fashion Merchandising & Retail Marketing (B.S.)
www.jwu.edu

Westwood College
Denver, CO
School of Business
Fashion Merchandising (B.S.)
www.westwoodcollegecolorado.com/fashion-
merchandising-college.aspx

CONNECTICUT

Sanford-Brown
Farmington, CT
Fashion Design & Merchandising (A.A.S.)
www.sanfordbrown.edu

University of Bridgeport
Bridgeport, CT
Department of Fashion Merchandising & Retailing
Fashion Merchandising & Retailing (A.A., B.S.)
www.bridgeport.edu
- **EXTENDED PROFILE ON PAGE 124**

DELAWARE

Delaware State University
Dover, DE
Department of Human Ecology
Textile & Apparel Studies (B.S.)
www.desu.edu
- **EXTENDED PROFILE ON PAGE 126**

University of Delaware
Newark, DE
Department of Fashion & Apparel Studies
Fashion Merchandising (B.S.)
Apparel Design (B.S.)
Fashion Studies (M.S.)
www.udel.edu/fash
- **EXTENDED PROFILE ON PAGE 128**

FLORIDA

Art Institute of Ft. Lauderdale, The
Ft. Lauderdale, FL
Fashion Design (B.S., A.S.)
Fashion Merchandising (B.S.)
www.artinstitutes.edu/fort-lauderdale

Art Institute of Tampa, The
Tampa, FL
Fashion & Retail Management (B.A.)
www.artinstitutes.edu/tampa

Florida State University
College of Human Sciences
Retail Merchandising & Product Development (B.S.,
Graduate Certificate)
www.chs.fsu.edu/rmpd

International Academy of Design & Technology–Orlando
Orlando, FL
Fashion Design & Merchandising (B.F.A.)
www.iadt.edu
- **EXTENDED PROFILE ON PAGE 130**

International Academy of Design & Technology–Tampa
Tampa, FL
Fashion Design (B.F.A.)
Fashion Merchandising (B.A.)
www.academy.edu
- **EXTENDED PROFILE ON PAGE 132**

Johnson & Wales
North Miami, FL
College of Business
Fashion Merchandising & Retail Marketing (B.S.)
www.jwu.edu

Keiser University
Ft. Lauderdale, FL
Fashion Design & Merchandising (A.S.)
www.keiseruniversity.edu/fashion-design-merch-AS.php

Lynn University
Boca Raton, FL
College of Business & Management
Fashion Management (B.S.)
www.lynn.edu/academics/colleges/business-and-management/programs

Miami University of Art & Design
Miami, FL
Accessory Design (A.A.)
Fashion Design (A.A., B.F.A.,)
Fashion Merchandising (A.A., B.F.A.)
www.artinstitutes.edu/miami/fashion-702.aspx

GEORGIA

Art Institute of Atlanta, The
Atlanta, GA
Fashion & Retail Management (B.A.)
www.artinstitutes.edu/atlanta

Bauder College
Atlanta, GA
Fashion Design (A.A.)
Fashion Merchandising (A.A.)
http://atlanta.bauder.edu/Pages/Areas_Of_Study.aspx#Design

Brenau University
Gainesville, GA
Fashion Design (B.F.A.)
www.brenau.edu
- **EXTENDED PROFILE ON PAGE 134**

Clark Atlanta University
Atlanta, GA
Department of Art
Fashion Design & Merchandising (B.A.)
www.cau.edu/Academics_DegreeProgramsFashion_Art.aspx

Georgia Southern University
Statesboro, GA
College of Health & Human Sciences
Hospitality, Tourism, Family & Consumer Sciences
    Department
Fashion Merchandising & Apparel Design (B.S.)
http://chhs.georgiasouthern.edu/htfcs

Savannah College of Art & Design
Savannah, GA
School of Fashion
Fashion Design (B.F.A., M.A., M.F.A.)
Accessory Design (B.F.A., M.A., M.F.A.)
Fashion Marketing & Management (B.F.A)
Luxury & Fashion Management (M.A., M.F.A.)
Menswear Design (minor)
www.scad.edu/programs/fashion/idex.cfm
- **EXTENDED PROFILE ON PAGE 136**

Southern Polytechnic State University
Marietta, GA
School of Engineering Technology & Management
Fashion Design & Product Development (B.S., certificate)
http://atet.spsu.edu/

University of Georgia
Athens, GA
Department of Textiles, Merchandising, & Interiors
Fashion Merchandising (B.S. in Family & Consumer
    Sciences)
Fashion Merchandising: Global Soft Goods Emphasis
    (B.S. in Family & Consumer Sciences)
Furnishings and Interiors Fashion Merchandising
    (B.S. in Family & Consumer Sciences)
Textiles, Merchandising & Interiors: Textile Science
    (M.S., PhD)
Textiles, Merchandising & Interiors: Historic/Cultural
    Aspects of Dress (M.S.)
Textiles, Merchandising & Interiors: Textile/
Merchandising/International Trade (M.S., PhD)
www.fcs.uga.edu/tmi
- **EXTENDED PROFILE ON PAGE 138**

HAWAII

Honolulu Community College
Honolulu, HI
Fashion Technology (A.A.S.)
http://tech.honolulu.hawaii.edu/ft/

Maui Community College
Kahului, HI
Fashion Technology (A.A.S.)
http://maui.hawaii.edu/programs/programs.php

University of Hawaii

Honolulu, HI
Department of Apparel Product Design & Merchandising
Apparel Product Design & Merchandising (B.S.)
www.hawaii.edu

- **EXTENDED PROFILE ON PAGE 140**

IDAHO

University of Idaho

Moscow, ID
College of Agriculture & Life Sciences
Department of Family & Consumer Sciences
Clothing, Textiles & Design (B.S.)
www.uidaho.edu/cals/fcs/clothingtextilesanddesign

ILLINOIS

Art Institute of Chicago, The

Chicago, IL
Fashion Merchandising (A.A.S.)
Fashion Design (B.F.A.)
Fashion Marketing & Management (B.A.)
www.artinstitutes.edu/chicago/fashion-702.aspx

Bradley University

Peoria, IL
Retail Merchandising (B.A., B.S.)
www.bradley.edu/academic/departments/fcs/programs/
retail/index.dot

College of DuPage

Glen Ellyn, IL
Department of Fashion Merchandising & Design
Fashion Design (A.A.S., Certificate)
Fashion Merchandising (A.A.S., Certificate)
Fashion Entrepreneurship (Certificate)
www.cod.edu/fashion/

- **EXTENDED PROFILE ON PAGE 144**

Columbia College, Chicago

Chicago, IL
Fashion Studies & Fashion Retail Management
Fashion Design (B.F.A.)
Fashion Retail Management (B.A.)
www.colum.edu/Academics

- **EXTENDED PROFILE ON PAGE 146**

Dominican University

River Forest, IL
Department of Apparel Design & Merchandising
Apparel Design: Fashion Development (B.A.)
Apparel Design: Surface Design (B.A.)
Apparel Design: Dress & Textile Studies (B.A.)
Apparel Merchandising (B.A.)
www.dom.edu

- **EXTENDED PROFILE ON PAGE 148**

Eastern Illinois University

Charleston, IL
Lumpkin College of Business & Applied Sciences
School of Family & Consumer Sciences
Family & Consumer Science: Merchandising (B.S.)
www.eiu.edu/famsci/bachelor.php

Harper College

Palatine, IL
Arts, Communication & Media
Fashion Design (A.A.S., certificate)
Fashion Merchandising (A.A.S.)
http://goforward.harpercollege.edu/page.cfm?p=4577

Illinois Institute of Art—Chicago

Chicago, IL
Fashion Merchandising (A.A.S.)
Fashion Design (B.F.A.)
Fashion Marketing & Management (B.A.)
www.artinstitutes.edu/chicago

Illinois Institute of Art—Schaumburg

Schaumburg, IL
Fashion Design (B.F.A.)
Fashion Marketing & Management (B.A.)
www.artinstitutes.edu/schaumburg

Illinois State University

Normal, IL
Department of Family & Consumer Sciences
Family & Consumer Sciences: Apparel Design (B.A., B.S.)
Family & Consumer Sciences: Apparel Merchandising
    (B.A., B.S.)
Family & Consumer Sciences: Apparel Merchandising &
    Design (M.A., M.S.)
http://fcs.illinoisstate.edu

- **EXTENDED PROFILE ON PAGE 150**

International Academy of Design & Technology—Chicago

Chicago, IL
Fashion Design Department
Fashion Design (B.S., A.A.S)
Merchandising Management (B.S., A.A.S)
www.iadtchicago.edu

- **EXTENDED PROFILE ON PAGE 152**

International Academy of Design & Technology—Schaumburg
Schaumburg, IL
Fashion Design Department
Fashion Design (B.S.)
www.iadtschaumburg.com
* **EXTENDED PROFILE ON PAGE 154**

Joliet Junior College
Joliet, IL
Career & Technical Education Division
Retail Business Management (certificate)
www.jjc.edu/academics/divisions/career-technical/
business/Pages/retail-management.aspx

North Illinois University
DeKalb, IL
School of Family, Consumer, & Nutrition Sciences
Textiles, Apparel & Merchandising (B.S.)
Family & Consumer Sciences: Apparel Studies (M.S.)
www.chhs.niu.edu/
* **EXTENDED PROFILE ON PAGE 156**

Olivet Nazarene University
Bourbonnais, IL
Family & Consumer Sciences
Fashion Merchandising (B.S.)
www.olivet.edu/academics/SPS/consumers.aspx

School of the Art Institute of Chicago
Chicago, IL
Fashion Design Department
Fashion Design (B.F.A., certificate)
Fashion, Body & Garment (Master of Design)
www.saic.edu/degrees_resources/departments/
fash/#overview

Southern Illinois University Carbondale
Carbondale, IL
School of Architecture
Fashion Design & Merchandising
Fashion & Merchandising: Fashion Design (B.S.)
Fashion & Merchandising: Fashion Merchandising (B.S.)
http://architecture.siuc.edu/
* **EXTENDED PROFILE ON PAGE 158**

Triton College
River Grove, IL
Division of Career Education
Marketing: Fashion Management (A.A.S.)
www.triton.edu

Western Illinois University
Macomb, IL
Department of Dietetics, Fashion Merchandising &
	Hospitality
Fashion Merchandising (B.S.)
www.wiu.edu/dfmh
* **EXTENDED PROFILE ON PAGE 160**

William Rainey Harper College
Palatine, IL
Fashion Department
Fashion Design (A.A., Certificate)
Fashion Merchandising (A.A., Certificate)
www.harpercollege.edu
* **EXTENDED PROFILE ON PAGE 162**

INDIANA

Art Institute of Indianapolis, The
Indianapolis, IN
Fashion & Retail Management (B.S.)
Fashion Design (B.S.)
www.artinstitutes.edu/indianapolis

Ball State University
Muncie, IN
Department of Family & Consumer Sciences
Family & Consumer Sciences: Fashion Merchandizing
	(B.S., B.A.)
Family & Consumer Sciences: Fashion Design (B.S., B.A.)
Family & Consumer Sciences: Fashion (M.S., M.A.)
www.bs.edu/fcs/
* **EXTENDED PROFILE ON PAGE 164**

Harrison College
Indianapolis, IN
Fashion Merchandising, School of Business
Apparel Merchandising (A.A.S.)
www.harrison.edu
* **EXTENDED PROFILE ON PAGE 166**

Indiana State University
Terre Haute, IN
College of Technology
Textiles, Design & Merchandising (B.A., B.S.)
www.indstate.edu/majors/fashionmerchandising.htm

Indiana University, Bloomington
Bloomington, IN
College of Arts & Sciences
Department of Apparel Merchandising & Interior Design
Apparel Merchandising (B.S., M.S.)
Fashion Design (certificate)
http://design.iub.edu/rdmg/

Purdue University
Lafayette, IN
Consumer Sciences & Retailing
Apparel Design & Technology (B.S.)
www.cfs.purdue.edu/csr
• **EXTENDED PROFILE ON PAGE 168**

Vincennes University
Vincennes, IN
Department of Family & Consumer Sciences
Fashion Merchandising (A.S., A.A.S.)
Interior Design (A.S., A.A.S.)
www.vinu.edu
• **EXTENDED PROFILE ON PAGE 170**

IOWA

Des Moines Area Community College
Ankeny, IA
Fashion Design (A.A.S., certificate)
https://go.dmacc.edu/programs/marketing/pages/
fashion.aspx

Iowa Lakes Community College
Emmetsburg, IA
Sales & Fashion (diploma)
www.iowalakes.edu/programs_study/business/sales_
fashion.htm

Iowa State University
Ames, IA
Apparel, Educational Studies & Hospitality Department
Apparel Merchandising & Design: Merchandising (B.S.)
Apparel Merchandising & Design: Creative Design (B.S.)
Apparel Merchandising & Design: Technical Design (B.S.)
Apparel Merchandising & Design: Product Development
   (B.S.)
Apparel Merchandising & Design: Production & Sourcing
   Management (B.S.)
Textiles & Clothing: Merchandising & Management (M.S.,
PhD)
Textiles & Clothing: Consumer Behavior (M.S., PhD)
Textiles & Clothing: Design-Creative, Technical,
Functional (M.S., PhD)
Textiles & Clothing: Historic Textiles/Costume, Consumer
Textiles & Conservation (M.S., PhD)
www.aeshm.hs.iastate.edu
• **EXTENDED PROFILE ON PAGE 142**

Iowa Western Community College
Council Bluffs, IA
Marketing: Fashion (A.A.S.)
www.iwcc.edu/programs/program.
asp?id=mrktfshnmrktaas

University of Northern Iowa
Cedar Falls, IA
Textiles & Apparel (B.A.)
www.uni.edu/tapp

KANSAS

Art Institute of Kansas City, The
Lenexa, KS
Fashion Marketing (B.A.)
www.artinstitutes.edu/kansas-city

Johnson County Community College
Overland Park, KS
Fashion Merchandising & Design
Fashion Merchandising (A.A.S.)
Fashion Design (A.A.S.)
www.jccc.edu/home/depts/1201
• **EXTENDED PROFILE ON PAGE 172**

Kansas State University
Manhattan, KS
Department of Apparel, Textiles & Interior Design
Apparel & Textiles: Apparel Design & Production (B.S.)
Apparel & Textiles: Apparel Marketing (B.S.)
Apparel & Textiles (M.S.)
Apparel & Textiles: Merchandising GP-IDEA (M.S.)
Human Ecology (PhD)
www.humec.k-state.edu/atid/
• **EXTENDED PROFILE ON PAGE 174**

Pittsburgh State University
Pittsburgh, KS
College of Arts & Sciences
Department of Family & Consumer Sciences
Fashion Merchandising (B.S.)
www.pittstate.edu/academics/program-detail.
dot?id=15624

KENTUCKY

Eastern Kentucky University
Richmond, KY
Department of Family & Consumer Sciences
Apparel Design & Merchandising (B.S.)
www.fcs.eku.edu/appareldesignmerchandising.php

University of Kentucky
Lexington, KY
Department of Merchandising, Apparel & Textiles
Merchandising, Apparel, & Textiles (B.A., M.S.)
www.ca.uky.edu/hes/?p=27
• **EXTENDED PROFILE ON PAGE 176**

Western Kentucky University
Bowling Green, KY
Department of Family & Consumer Sciences
Textiles & Apparel Merchandising (B.S.)
www.wku.edu/Dept/Academic/chhs
• **EXTENDED PROFILE ON PAGE 178**

LOUISIANA

Louisiana State University
Baton Rouge, LA
School of Human Ecology
Division of Textiles, Apparel Design & Merchandising
Apparel Design (B.S., M.S., PhD)
Merchandising (B.S., M.S., PhD)
Textile Science (B.S., M.S., PhD)
www.tam.huec.lsu.edu/

University of Louisiana, Lafayette
Lafayette, LA
School of Architecture & Design
College of the Arts
Apparel Design (B.S.)
Apparel Merchandising (B.S.)
www.ucs.louisiana.edu/~jmr3438/index.html

MARYLAND

Baltimore City Community College
Baltimore, MD
Fashion Design Program
Fashion Design (A.A.A., certificate)
Fashion Retailing (A.A.A.)
www.bccc.edu
• **EXTENDED PROFILE ON PAGE 186**

University of Maryland Eastern Shore
Princess Anne, MD
Department of Human Ecology
Human Ecology: Fashion; Merchandising (B.S.)
http://umes.edu/HE
• **EXTENDED PROFILE ON PAGE 188**

MASSACHUSETTS

Bay State College
Boston, MA
Fashion Design (A.S., A.A.S.)
Fashion Merchandising (A.S., A.A.S., B.S.)
http://baystate.edu

Bristol Community College
Fall River, MA
Fashion Merchandising (certificate)
Business Administration: Retail Management
    (A.S., certificate)
www.bristolcc.edu

Fisher College
Boston, MA
Fashion Design (A.S.)
Fashion Merchandising (A.S.)
www.fisher.edu/academics/associate-degrees.html

Framingham State College
Framingham, MA
Consumer Sciences Department
Fashion Design & Retailing: Apparel Design (B.S.)
Fashion Design & Retailing: Merchandising (B.S.)
Fashion Design: Apparel Design (certificate)
Merchandising (Graduate Certificate)
www.framingham.edu/fashion
• **EXTENDED PROFILE ON PAGE 180**

Lasell College
Newton, MA
Fashion Department
Fashion Design & Production (B.A.)
Fashion Design & Retail Merchandising (B.S.)
Fashion Communication & Promotion (B.S.)
www.lasell.edu
• **EXTENDED PROFILE ON PAGE 182**

Marian Court Community College
Swampscott, MA
Fashion Merchandising (A.S.)
www.mariancourt.edu/academics/fashion-merchandising.html

Massachusetts College of Art & Design
Boston, MA
Fashion Design Department
Fashion Design (B.F.A.)
www.massart.edu/Academic_Programs/Fashion_Design
• **EXTENDED PROFILE ON PAGE 184**

Middlesex Community College
Bedford, MA
Fashion Merchandising (A.S.)
http://catalog.middlesex.mass.edu/preview_program.php
?catoid=4&poid=310&returnto=317

Mount Ida College
Newton, MA
School of Design
Fashion Design (B.S.)
Fashion Merchandising & Marketing (B.S.)
www.mountida.edu/sp.cfm?pageid=320

New England Institute of Art
Brookline, MA
Fashion & Retail Management (B.S.)
www.artinstitutes.edu/boston

Newbury College
Brookline, MA
School of Business & Management
Fashion Merchandising (B.S.)
www.newbury.edu/RelId/606766/ISvars/default/
Introduction.htm

School of Fashion Design
Boston, MA
Fashion Design (certificate, diploma)
www.schooloffashiondesign.org/

MICHIGAN

Art Institute of Michigan, The
Novi, MI
Fashion Merchandising (A.S.)
Fashion Marketing & Management (B.A.)
www.artinstitutes.edu/detroit

Central Michigan University
Pleasant, MI
Department of Human Environmental Studies
Apparel Merchandising & Design: Apparel Design
   (B.A., B.A.A.)
Apparel Merchandising & Design: Merchandising
   (B.A., B.A.A.)
Apparel Product Development & Merchandising
   Technology (M.S.)
www.ehs.cmich.edu/hev
• **EXTENDED PROFILE ON PAGE 190**

Eastern Michigan University
Ypsilanti, MI
College of Technology
Apparel, Textiles & Merchandising
Fashion Design (B.S., M.S.)
Fashion Merchandising (B.S., M.S.)
Textiles (B.S., M.S.)
www.emich.edu/cot/progsites/atm

Finlandia University
Hancock, MI
International School of Art & Design
Fiber and Fashion Design (B.F.A.)
www.finlandia.edu
• **EXTENDED PROFILE ON PAGE 192**

International Academy of Design & Technology—Detroit
Troy, MI
Fashion Design & Merchandising (B.F.A.)
www.iadtdetroit.com

Lansing Community College
Lansing, MI
Environmental, Design & Building Technologies
   Department
Fashion Technology (A.A.S., certificate)
www.lcc.edu/edbt/fashion/

Michigan State University
Lansing, MI
Art & Art History
Apparel & Textile Design (B.A., B.F.A.)
www.art.msu.edu
• **EXTENDED PROFILE ON PAGE 194**

Wayne State University
Detroit, MI
College of Fine, Performing & Communication Arts
Department of Art & Art History
Fashion Design & Merchandising (B.A., B.S., M.A.)
http://art.wayne.edu/fashion.php

Western Michigan University
Kalamazoo, MI
College of Education & Human Development
Family & Consumer Sciences Department
Textile & Apparel Studies: Fashion Design (B.S., M.A.)
Textile & Apparel Studies: Merchandising (B.S., M.A.)
Textile & Apparel Studies: Product Development
   (B.S., M.A.)
www.wmich.edu/consumer/tex/undergrad.htm

MINNESOTA

Alexandria Technical Institute
Alexandria, MN
Business Management & Finance Professionals
Fashion Management (A.A.S.)
www.alextech.edu

Art Institutes International Minnesota, The
Minneapolis, MN
Department of Fashion & Retail Management
Fashion & Retail Management (B.S.)
www.artinstitutes.edu/minneapolis
- **EXTENDED PROFILE ON PAGE 196**

Minneapolis Community and Technical College
Minneapolis, MN
Apparel Technologies
Apparel Design/Technical Design (diploma, certificate)
www.minneapolis.edu
- **EXTENDED PROFILE ON PAGE 198**

St. Catherine University
St. Paul, MN
Department of Family, Consumer, & Nutritional Sciences
Fashion & Apparel: Apparel Design (B.A., B.S.)
Fashion & Apparel: Fashion Merchandising (B.A., B.S.)
www.stkate.edu/academic/
- **EXTENDED PROFILE ON PAGE 200**

University of Minnesota
Saint Paul, MN
Department of Design, Housing & Apparel
Apparel Design (B.S.)
Retail Merchandising (B.S.)
Design Apparel Studies (M.A., M.S., PhD)
www.dha.design.umn.edu
- **EXTENDED PROFILE ON PAGE 202**

MISSISSIPPI

Delta State University
Cleveland, MS
Division of Family & Consumer Sciences
Family & Consumer Sciences: Fashion Merchandising (B.S.)
www.deltastate.edu/pages/444.asp
- **EXTENDED PROFILE ON PAGE 214**

Hinds Community College
Pearl, MS
Business & Marketing Management
Fashion Marketing Technology (A.A.S.)
www.hindscc.edu/Departments/marketing_management_technology/default.aspx

Jones County Junior College
Ellisville, MS
Business & Marketing Management Technology
Fashion Merchandising (A.A.S.)
www.jcjc.edu/programs/businessmarketingmanagement/index.php

Mississippi Gulf Coast Community College
Perkinston, MS
Fashion Marketing Technology (A.A.S.)
www.mgccc.edu/programs_of_study/technical_programs/program.php?id=44

Mississippi State University
Mississippi State, MS
College of Agriculture & Life Sciences
School of Human Sciences
Apparel, Textiles, & Merchandising
Apparel Production & Design (B.S.)
Merchandising (B.S.)
www.msstate.edu/school/humansciences/academic_majors/atm.html

Northeast Mississippi Community College
Booneville, MS
Fashion Merchandising (A.A.)
www.nemcc.edu

University of Southern Mississippi
Hattiesburg, MS
Department of Marketing & Fashion Merchandising
Fashion Merchandising & Apparel Studies (B.S.)
www.usm.edu/undergraduate/fashion-merchandising-and-apparel-studies-bs

MISSOURI

Fontbonne University
St. Louis, MO
Human Environmental Sciences
Fashion Merchandising (B.S.)
www.fontbonne.edu
- **EXTENDED PROFILE ON PAGE 204**

Lindenwood University
St. Charles, MO
School of Fine & Performing Arts
Fashion Design (B.A., B.F.A.)
www.lindenwood.edu/arts/fashion.cfm

Metropolitan Community College— Penn Valley
Kansas City, MO
Apparel & Textiles: Product Development & Design (A.A.S)
Apparel & Textiles: Marketing & Merchandising (A.A.S)
www.mcckc.edu/aptx
- **EXTENDED PROFILE ON PAGE 206**

Missouri State University

Springfield, MO
Department of Fashion & Interior Design
Fashion Design & Product Development (B.S.)
Fashion Merchandising & Management (B.S.)
www.missouristate.edu/fid
• **EXTENDED PROFILE ON PAGE 208**

Southeast Missouri State University

Cape Girardeau, MO
Department of Human Environmental Studies
Human Environmental Studies: Fashion Merchandising
    (B.S., M.A.)
www.semo.edu/study/fashion/index.htm

Stephens College

Columbia, MO
School of Design & Fashion
Fashion Communication (B.F.A.)
Fashion Design & Product Development (B.F.A.)
Fashion Marketing & Management (B.S.)
www.stephens.edu/academics/programs/fashion
• **EXTENDED PROFILE ON PAGE 210**

Stevens Institute of Business & Arts

Saint Louis, MO
Department of Retail Management & Fashion
Merchandising
Retail Management/Fashion Merchandising (B.A., A.A.S.)
www.siba.edu
• **EXTENDED PROFILE ON PAGE 212**

University of Central Missouri

Warrensburg, MO
School of Technology
Fashion: Textiles & Clothing in Business (B.S.)
www.ucmo.edu/majors/print/4yearplan.cfm?ftd=59

University of Missouri, Columbia

Columbia, MO
College of Human Environmental Sciences
Department of Textile & Apparel Management
Apparel Marketing & Merchandising (B.S.)
Apparel Product Development & Management (B.S.)
International Apparel Marketing & Merchandising (B.S.)
International Apparel Product Development &
    Management (B.S.)
Home Furnishing & Merchandising (B.S.)
Textile & Apparel Science (M.S.)
http://tam.missouri.edu/academics.html

Washington University

St. Louis, MO
Sam Fox School of Design & Visual Arts
Art: Fashion Design (B.F.A.)
http://samfoxschool.wustl.edu/node/4154

NEBRASKA

Chadron College

Chadron, NE
Department of Applied Sciences
Family & Consumer Sciences: Design & Merchandising
    (B.A.)
www.csc.edu/appliedsciences/fcs/degrees.
csc#desmerchopt

University of Nebraska, Lincoln

Lincoln, NE
College of Education & Human Sciences
Department of Textiles, Clothing & Design
Textiles & Apparel Design (B.S., M.A., M.S., PhD)
Merchandising (B.S., M.A., M.S., PhD)
Textile Science (B.S., M.A., M.S., PhD)
Textiles, Clothing & Design/Journalism & Mass
    Communications (B.S.)
http://cehsbeta.unl.edu/tcd

Wayne State College

Wayne, NE
School of Business & Technology
Technology & Applied Science Department
Family & Consumer Science: Fashion Merchandising
    (B.A., B.S.)
www.wsc.edu/schools/bst/tasc/academic_programs

NEVADA

Art Institute of Las Vegas, The

Henderson, NV
Fashion & Retail Management (B.S.)
www.artinstitutes.edu/las-vegas

International Academy of Design & Technology–Las Vegas

Henderson, NV
Fashion Merchandising Department
Fashion Design (B.F.A., A.S.)
Fashion Merchandising (B.F.A.)
www.iadtvegas.com
• **EXTENDED PROFILE ON PAGE 228**

University of Nevada, Las Vegas

Las Vegas, NV
Continuing Education
Fashion Design (certificate)
http://edoutreach.unlv.edu/continuingeducation/catalog/
fashion_design.html

NEW JERSEY

Berkeley College
Paramus, NJ
Fashion Marketing & Management (A.A.S., B.B.A., B.S.)
http://berkeleycollege.edu/bachelors/Fashion_
Marketing/index.htm

Brookdale Community College
Lincroft, NJ
Fashion Merchandising (A.A.S.)
www.brookdalecc.edu/pages/528.asp

Burlington County College
Pemberton, NJ
Fashion Design (A.A.S.)
Fashion Product Merchandising (A.S.)
Fashion Studies (A.A.)
Specification Tech for Fashion (certificate)
www.bcc.edu/pages/490.asp

Centenary College
Hackettstown, NJ
Communication & Fine Arts
Fashion Design (B.F.A.)
www.centenarycollege.edu/cms/?id=856

County College of Morris
Randolph, NJ
Design: Fashion Design/Merchandising (A.F.A.)
www.ccm.edu/academics/degrees/design.aspx

Middlesex County College
Edison, NJ
Department of Business Administration & Management
Fashion Merchandising & Retail Management (A.A.S.)
www.middlesexcc.edu/departments/bam/control.cfm/
ID/979/

Montclair State University
Montclair, NJ
Fashion Studies Program, Department of Art & Design
Fashion Studies (B.A.)
www.montclair.edu/arts/deptdesign
• **EXTENDED PROFILE ON PAGE 226**

NEW MEXICO

New Mexico State University
College of Agricultural, Consumer & Environmental
  Sciences
Department of Family & Consumer Sciences
Clothing, Textiles & Fashion Merchandising (B.S.)
http://aces.nmsu.edu/academics/fcs/clothing-textiles--
fashi.html

Santa Fe Community College
Santa Fe, NM
School of Arts & Design
Fashion Design (A.A.A., certificate)
www.sfcc.edu/school_of_arts_and_design/fashion_
design

NEW YORK

Art Institute of New York City, The
New York, NY
Fashion Design (A.A.S.)
Fashion Merchandising & Marketing (A.A.S.)
www.artinstitutes.edu/new-york

Berkeley College
New York, NY
Fashion Marketing & Management (A.A.S., B.B.A., B.S.)
http://berkeleycollege.edu/bachelors/Fashion_
Marketing/INDEX.HTM

Buffalo State (SUNY)
Buffalo, NY
Technology Department
Fashion & Textile Technology: Apparel Design (B.S.)
Fashion & Textile Technology: Fashion Merchandising (B.S.)
Fashion & Textile Technology: Fashion/Textile Design (B.S.)
Fashion & Textile Technology: Product Development (B.S.)
www.buffalostate.edu/technology/x536.xml?bpid=72

Cazenovia College
Cazenovia, NY
Fashion Design (B.F.A.)
Fashion Merchandising (B.P.S.)
www.cazenovia.edu/default.aspx?tabid=484

Cornell University
Ithaca, NY
College of Human Ecology
Fiber Science & Apparel Design
Fiber Science & Apparel Design: Apparel Design
  (B.S., M.A., PhD)
Fiber Science & Apparel Design: Apparel/Textile
  Management (B.S.)
Fiber Science & Apparel Design: Fiber Science
  (B.S., M.S., PhD)
www.human.cornell.edu
• **EXTENDED PROFILE ON PAGE 230**

Fashion Institute of Technology
New York, NY
Department of Accessories Design
Accessories Design (A.A.S.)
Accessories Design & Fabrication (B.F.A)
www.fitnyc.edu/accessoriesdesign
• **EXTENDED PROFILE ON PAGE 232**

Fashion Institute of Technology
New York, NY
Department of Fashion Design
Fashion Design (A.A.S.)
Fashion Design: Children's Wear, Intimate Apparel, Knitwear, Special Occasion, Sportswear (B.F.A.)
www.fitnyc.edu/fashiondesign
• **EXTENDED PROFILE ON PAGE 234**

Fashion Institute of Technology
New York, NY
Department of Fashion Merchandising Management
Fashion Merchandising Management (A.A.S., B.S.)
www.fitnyc.edu/fmm
• **EXTENDED PROFILE ON PAGE 236**

Fashion Institute of Technology
New York, NY
Department of Global Fashion Management
Global Fashion Management (M.P.S.)
www.fitnyc.edu/2865.asp
• **EXTENDED PROFILE ON PAGE 238**

Fashion Institute of Technology
New York, NY
Menswear
Menswear (A.A.S.)
www.fitnyc.edu/menswear
• **EXTENDED PROFILE ON PAGE 240**

Fashion Institute of Technology
New York, NY
Department of Technical Design
Technical Design (A.A.S)
www.fitnyc.edu
• **EXTENDED PROFILE ON PAGE 242**

Genesee Community College
Batavia, NY
Business/Fashion Merchandising Management
Fashion Merchandising Management (A.A.S.)
www.genesee.edu
• **EXTENDED PROFILE ON PAGE 244**

Herkimer County Community College
Herkimer, NY
Business: Fashion Buying & Merchandising
Fashion Buying & Merchandising (A.A.S.)
www.herkimer.edu/academics/
• **EXTENDED PROFILE ON PAGE 246**

Kingsborough Community College
Department of Business
Retail Merchandising (A.A.S.)
Fashion Design (A.A.S.)
www.kingsborough.edu/academicDepartments/BA/
programs.htm#rm

LIM College
New York, NY
Fashion Merchandising
Fashion Merchandising (B.B.A., B.P.S., A.A.S, A.O.S.)
Marketing (B.B.A.)
Visual Merchandising (B.B.A.)
Master's of Business Administration (M.B.A.)
www.limcollege.edu
• **EXTENDED PROFILE ON PAGE 248**

Marist College
Poughkeepsie, NY
The Fashion Program
Fashion Design: Merchandising or Product Development (B.P.S.)
Fashion Merchandising (B.P.S.)
www.marist.edu/commarts/fashion
• **EXTENDED PROFILE ON PAGE 250**

Nassau Community College
Garden City, NY
Marketing/Retailing/Fashion
Apparel Design (A.A.S.)
Fashion Buying & Merchandising (A.A.S.)
Marketing (A.A.S.)
Interior Design/Home Furnishings (A.A.S.)
Retail Business Management (A.A.S.)
www.ncc.edu/Academics/AcademicDepartments/
MarketingRetailingFashion

New York City College of Technology
Brooklyn, NY
Business: Fashion Marketing (A.A.S.)
www.citytech.cuny.edu/academics/deptsites/business/
programs.shtml

Parsons The New School for Design
New York, NY
School of Fashion
Fashion Design (A.A.S., B.F.A.)
Fashion Marketing (A.A.S.)
Fashion Design and Society (M.F.A.)
www.newschool.edu/parsons/fashion-school/

Pratt Institute
Brooklyn, NY
Fashion Design Department
Fashion Design (B.F.A.)
www.pratt.edu
● **EXTENDED PROFILE ON PAGE 252**

Queens College
Flushing, NY
Family, Nutrition & Exercise Sciences
Family & Consumer Science: Textiles & Apparel (B.A.)
www.qc.cuny.edu/ACADEMICS/DEGREES/DMNS/FNES/
Pages/default.aspx

Suffolk Community College
Riverhead, NY
Fashion/Interior Design (A.A.S.)
www.sunysuffolk.edu/Curricula/INDA-AAS.asp

State University of New York at Oneonta
Oneonta, NY
Department of Human Ecology
Apparel & Textiles: Design (B.S.)
Apparel & Textiles: Merchandising Management (B.S.)
Apparel & Textiles: Textile Development & Marketing
    (B.S.)
Apparel & Textiles: Textiles/Surface Design (B.S.)
Apparel & Textiles: Jewelry Design (B.S.)
Apparel & Textiles: Accessory Design (B.S.)
Apparel & Textiles: Merchandising (B.S.)
www.oneonta.edu/academics/huec/Apparel2.asp

Syracuse University
Syracuse, NY
College of Visual & Performing Arts
School of Art & Design
Fashion Design (B.F.A.)
http://vpa.syr.edu/art-design/design/undergraduate/
fashion-design

Villa Maria College
Buffalo, NY
Fashion Design & Merchandising Department
Fashion Design & Merchandising (B.F.A.)
www.villa.edu
● **EXTENDED PROFILE ON PAGE 256**

Westchester Community College
Valhalla, NY
Department of Fashion Merchandising
Fashion Merchandising (A.A.S.)
Fashion Technology & Construction (A.A.S.)
www.sunywcc.edu/fashion
● **EXTENDED PROFILE ON PAGE 254**

Wood Tobé-Coburn School
New York, NY
Fashion Design (A.A.)
Fashion Merchandising, Marketing & Management (A.A.)
www.woodtobecoburn.edu/programs/fashion#67

NORTH CAROLINA

Appalachian State University
Boone, NC
Reich College of Education
Department of Family & Consumer Sciences
Apparel & Textiles (B.S.)
www.fcs.appstate.edu/students/ug_programs/app_
textiles.aspx

Art Institute of Charlotte, The
Charlotte, NC
Fashion Marketing & Management (B.A., A.A.S.)
www.artinstitutes.edu/charlotte

East Carolina University
Greenville, NC
Department of Interior Design & Merchandising
Merchandising (B.S.)
www.ecu.edu/che/idmr
● **EXTENDED PROFILE ON PAGE 216**

Johnson & Wales University
Charlotte, NC
The College of Business
Fashion Merchandising & Retail Marketing (B.S.)
www.jwu.edu/content.aspx?id=17926#fbid=7CVuN2XFaPw

Mars Hill College
Mars Hill, NC
Fashion & Interior Merchandising (B.S.)
www.mhc.edu/academics/majors/fim
● **EXTENDED PROFILE ON PAGE 218**

Meredith College
Raleigh, NC
Department of Human Environmental Sciences
Fashion Design (B.S.)
Fashion Merchandising (B.S.)
www.meredith.edu/hes/fashion/default.htm

North Carolina Agricultural & Technical State University

Greensboro, NC
School of Agriculture & Environmental Science
Department of Family & Consumer Sciences
Family & Consumer Science: Fashion Merchandising & Design (B.S.)
www.ag.ncat.edu/academics/fcs/fashion_merchandising/index.htm

North Carolina State University

Raleigh, NC
College of Textiles
Department of Textile & Apparel Technology & Management,
Fashion & Textile Management: Fashion Development & Product Management (B.S., Graduate Certificate)
Fashion & Textile Management: Brand Management & Marketing (B.S, Graduate Certificate.)
Fashion & Textile Management: Retail & Supply Chain (B.S.)
Textile Technology: Design (B.S.)
Textiles (M.S.)
Textile Technology Management (PhD)
www.tx.ncsu.edu/departments/tatm/
• **EXTENDED PROFILE ON PAGE 220**

University of North Carolina at Greensboro

Greensboro, NC
Department of Consumer, Apparel, & Retail Studies
Consumer, Apparel, & Retail Studies: Apparel Product Design (B.S.)
Consumer, Apparel, & Retail Studies: Retailing & Consumer Studies (B.S.)
Consumer, Apparel, & Retail Studies: Global Apparel & Related Industries Studies (B.S., M.S., PhD)
www.uncg.edu/crs
• **EXTENDED PROFILE ON PAGE 222**

NORTH DAKOTA

North Dakota State University

Fargo, ND
Department of Apparel, Design & Hospitality Management
Apparel & Textiles: Apparel Studies (B.S.)
Apparel & Textiles: Retail Merchandising: Textile Product Merchandising (B.S.)
Apparel & Textiles: Retail Merchandising: Interior Merchandising (B.S.)
Merchandising (M.S.)
www.ndsu.edu/adhm
• **EXTENDED PROFILE ON PAGE 224**

OHIO

Art Institute of Ohio (The)—Cincinnati

Cincinnati, OH
Fashion Merchandising (A.A.S.)
Fashion Marketing & Management (B.A.)
www.artinstitutes.edu/cincinnati

Ashland University

Ashland, OH
Family & Consumer Sciences
Fashion Merchandising (B.S.)
www.ashland.edu/departments/family-consumer-sciences

Bluffton University

Bluffton, OH
Family & Consumer Sciences
Fashion, Interiors, Retail Merchandising & Design (B.A.)
www.bluffton.edu/fcs/apparel

Bowling Green State University

Bowling Green, OH
College of Education & Human Development
School of Family & Consumer Sciences
Apparel Merchandising & Product Development (B.S.)
www.bgsu.edu/colleges/edhd/fcs/ampd/index.html

Columbus College of Art & Design

Columbus, OH
Fashion Design (B.F.A.)
www.ccad.edu/programs-of-study/majors/fashion-design

Davis College

Toledo, OH
Department of Business Administration & Information Technology
Retail Management & Fashion Merchandising (A.A.B.)
www.daviscollege.edu/programs.html

Kent State University

Kent, OH
Shannon Rodgers & Jerry Silverman School of Fashion Design & Merchandising
Fashion Design: Conceptual (B.A.)
Fashion Design: Technical (B.A.)
Fashion Merchandising (B.S.)
www.fashionschool.kent.edu
• **EXTENDED PROFILE ON PAGE 258**

Mount Vernon Nazarene University

Mount Vernon, OH
Family & Consumer Sciences Department
Family & Consumer Sciences: Fashion Merchandising (B.A.)
www.mvnu.edu/academics/eduprofstud/fcs/fcs.asp

Ohio State University

Columbus, OH
College of Education & Human Ecology
Department of Consumer Sciences
Fashion & Retail Studies: Merchandising (B.S., M.S., PhD)
Fashion & Retail Studies: Product Development
    (B.S., M.S., PhD)
http://ehe.osu.edu/cs/programs/undergraduate/frs.cfm

Ohio University

Athens, OH
Patton College of Education & Human Services
Retail Merchandising & Fashion Product Development
    (B.S.)
Apparel, Textiles & Merchandising (M.S.)
www.cehs.ohio.edu/academics/hcse/rm/index.htm

University of Akron

Akron, OH
College of Health Sciences & Human Services
School of Family & Consumer Sciences
Fashion Merchandising (B.A.)
www.uakron.edu/healthcollege

University of Cincinnati

Cincinnati, OH
College of Design, Architecture & Planning
School of Design
Fashion Design (B.S.)
Fashion Design: Product Development (B.S., Master of
    Design)
www.daap.uc.edu/design/

Ursuline College

Pepperpike, OH
School of Professional Studies
Fashion Design (A.A.S.)
Fashion Merchandising (A.A.S.)
www.ursuline.edu/Academics/Graduate_Professional/
Bachelors_Programs/Fashion

Virginia Marti College of Art & Design

Lakewood, OH
Fashion Design (A.A.B)
Fashion Merchandising (A.A.B.)
www.vmcad.edu

Youngstown State University

Bitonte College of Health & Human Services
Department of Human Ecology
Fashion & Interiors (B.S.A.S.)
http://bchhs.ysu.edu/dhe/merch.shtml

OKLAHOMA

East Central University

Ada, OK
Department of Family & Consumer Sciences
Family & Consumer Sciences: Retail Management (B.S.)
www.ecok.edu/colleges/health_sciences/family_
consumer/fcs/index.htm

Oklahoma State University

Stillwater, OK
College of Human Environmental Sciences
Department of Design, Housing & Merchandising
Apparel Design & Production (B.S., M.S., PhD)
http://ches.okstate.edu/dhm/

University of Central Oklahoma

Edmond, OK
Human Environmental Sciences
Fashion Marketing (B.S.)
www.uco.edu
• **EXTENDED PROFILE ON PAGE 260**

OREGON

Art Institute of Portland, The

Portland, OR
Apparel Design (A.A.S., B.F.A.)
Accessory Design (A.A.S., B.F.A.)
Fashion Marketing (A.A.S., B.F.A.)
www.artinstitutes.edu/portland
• **EXTENDED PROFILE ON PAGE 262**

George Fox University

Newberg, OR
Family & Consumer Sciences: Fashion Merchandising/
    Interior Design (B.S.)
www.georgefox.edu/college-admissions/academics

Oregon State University

Corvallis, OR
Department of Design & Human Environment
Apparel Design (B.S., H.B.S.)
Merchandising Management (B.S., H.B.S.)
Design & Human Environment (M.A., M.S., PhD)
www.hhs.oregonstate.edu/dhe
• **EXTENDED PROFILE ON PAGE 264**

PENNSYLVANIA

Albright College
Reading, PA
Fashion Department
Fashion: Merchandising, Costume Design, Design &
    Merchandising (B.A.)
www.albright/edu/fashion
• **EXTENDED PROFILE ON PAGE 266**

Art Institute of Philadelphia, The
Philadelphia, PA
Department of Fashion Design
Fashion Design (A.S., B.S.)
Fashion Marketing (A.S., B.S.)
Visual Merchandising (A.S.)
www.artinstitutes.edu/philadelphia
• **EXTENDED PROFILE ON PAGE 268**

Art Institute of Pittsburgh, The
Pittsburgh, PA
Fashion & Retail Management (B.S.)
Fashion Design (B.S.)
www.artinstitutes.edu/pittsburgh

Art Institute of York Pennsylvania, The
York, PA
Fashion & Retail Management (B.S.)
www.artinstitutes.edu/york/

Bucks County Community College
Newtown, PA
Continuing Education
Fashion Design (certificate)
www.bucks.edu/coned/certfashion.php

Cheyney University of Pennsylvania
Cheyney, PA
School of Education & Professional Studies
Fashion Merchandising & Management (B.S.)
www.cheyney.edu/professional-studies/index.cfm

Drexel University
Philadelphia, PA
Department of Fashion & Design & Merchandising
Fashion Design (B.S., M.S.)
Design & Merchandising (B.S.)
Product Design (B.S.)
www.drexel.edu/westphal
• **EXTENDED PROFILE ON PAGE 270**

Harcum College
Bryn Mawr, PA
Center for Business & Professional Studies
Fashion Design (A.A., A.S.)
Fashion Merchandising (A.A., A.S.)
www.harcum.edu

Immaculata University
Immaculata, PA
Department of Fashion-Family & Consumer Sciences
Fashion Merchandising (B.S.)
www.immaculata.edu/node/25

Indiana University of Pennsylvania
Indiana, PA
Fashion Merchandising Program, Human Development,
& Environmental Studies
Fashion Merchandising (B.S.)
Business Administration Minor: Marking, Small
    Business, Management
www.iup.edu/
• **EXTENDED PROFILE ON PAGE 272**

Kaplan Career Institute
Pittsburgh, PA
Fashion Merchandising (A.S.B.)
http://pittsburgh.kaplancareerinstitute.com

Lehigh Carbon Community College
Schnecksville, PA
School of Computer Science & the Arts
Fashion Design (A.A.)
www.lccc.edu/academics/school-computer-science-and-
arts/fashion-design-aa

Mercyhurst College
Erie, PA
Walker School of Business & Communication
Fashion Merchandising (B.S.)
http://fashion.mercyhurst.edu

Moore College of Art & Design
Philadelphia, PA
Fashion Design (B.F.A.)
Textile Design (B.F.A.)
www.moore.edu/site/bfa_programs/fashion_design/
summary

Philadelphia University
Philadelphia, PA
Department of Fashion Design
Fashion Design (B.S.)
Textile Design (B.S.)
www.philau.edu/fashiondesign/
• **EXTENDED PROFILE ON PAGE 274**

Philadelphia University
Philadelphia, PA
School of Business Administration
Fashion Industry Management (B.S.)
Fashion Design (B.S.)
Fashion Merchandising (B.S., M.B.A.)
www.philau.edu/schools/tmt/Ugrad_Majors/fim/
• **EXTENDED PROFILE ON PAGE 276**

RHODE ISLAND

Johnson & Wales University
Providence, RI
College of Business
Fashion Merchandising & Retail Marketing (B.S.)
www.jwu.edu/content.aspx?id=18126#fbid=7CVuN2XFaPw

Rhode Island School of Design
Providence, RI
Apparel Design (B.F.A.)
Textiles (B.F.A., M.F.A.)
www.risd.edu

University of Rhode Island
Kingston, RI
Department of Textiles, Fashion Merchandising & Design
Textiles, Fashion Merchandising & Design (B.S.. M.S.)
Textile marketing (B.S.)
www.uri.edu/hss/tmd
• **EXTENDED PROFILE ON PAGE 278**

SOUTH CAROLINA

Art Institute of Charleston, The
Charleston, SC
Fashion & Retail Management (B.A.)
www.artinstitutes.edu/charleston

Bob Jones University
Greenville, SC
Apparel, Textiles & Design (B.S.)
www.bju.edu/academics/majors

South Carolina State University
Orangeburg, SC
Department of Family & Consumer Sciences
Family & Consumer Sciences Business: Fashion
    Merchandising (B.S.)
www.scsu.edu/academicdepartments/
departmentoffamilyconsumersciences.aspx

University of South Carolina
Columbia, SC
College of Hospitality, Retail & Sport Management
Department of Retailing
Retailing: Fashion Merchandising (B.S.)
Retailing: Retail Management (B.S.)
Master of Retailing (M.R.)
www.hrsm.sc.edu/retail/
• **EXTENDED PROFILE ON PAGE 280**

SOUTH DAKOTA

South Dakota State University
Brookings, SD
College of Education & Human Sciences
Department of Consumer Sciences
Apparel Merchandising (B.S.)
Merchandising (M.S.)
www.sdstate.edu/cs/programs/apparel-merchandising.cfm

TENNESSEE

Art Institute of Tennessee (The)—Nashville
Nashville, TN
Fashion & Retail Management (B.A.)
www.artinstitutes.edu/nashville

Carson Newman College
Jefferson City, TN
School of Family & Consumer Sciences
Retailing (B.S.)
www.cn.edu/fcs/default.htm

East Tennessee State University
Johnson City, TN
Department of Management & Marketing
Management & Marketing: Merchandising (B.B.A)
http://business.etsu.edu/mgmtmkt/academics
• **EXTENDED PROFILE ON PAGE 282**

International Academy of Design &
Technology–Nashville
Nashville, TN
Fashion Design & Merchandising (A.A.S., B.A.S.)
www.iadtnashville.com
• **EXTENDED PROFILE ON PAGE 284**

Lambuth University
Jackson, TN
School of Arts & Communications
Family & Consumer Sciences: Fashion Merchandising
    (B.A., B.S.)
www.lambuth.edu/courses-a-programs/majors/345-
family-a-consumer-sciences

Lipscomb University
Nashville, TN
College of Arts & Sciences
Department of Family & Consumer Sciences
Family & Consumer Sciences: Fashion Merchandising
(B.S.)
Family & Consumer Sciences: Textiles & Apparel (B.S.)
http://fcs.lipscomb.edu/

Middle Tennessee State University
Murfreeboro, TN
Department of Human Sciences
Textiles, Merchandising & Design: Apparel Design (B.S.)
Textiles, Merchandising & Design: Fashion Merchandising
(B.S.)
www.mtsu.edu/humansciences/
• **EXTENDED PROFILE ON PAGE 286**

O'More College of Design
Franklin, TN
Fashion Design (B.F.A.)
www.omorecollege.edu/content/fashionoverview.html

Tennessee State University
Nashville, TN
Department of Family & Consumer Sciences
Family & Consumer Sciences: Fashion Merchandising
(B.S.)
Family & Consumer Sciences: Design (B.S.)
http://agfacs.tnstate.edu
• **EXTENDED PROFILE ON PAGE 288**

Tennessee Technological University
Cookeville, TN
School of Human Ecology
Human Ecology: Merchandising & Design (B.S.)
Human Ecology: Housing & Design (B.S.)
www.tntech.edu/hec
• **EXTENDED PROFILE ON PAGE 290**

University of Tennessee, Knoxville
Knoxville, TN
College of Education, Health & Human Sciences
Department of Retail, Hospitality & Tourism Management
Retail & Consumer Sciences (B.S.)
http://csm.utk.edu/ug/rcs.html

University of Tennessee, Martin
Martin, TN
College of Agriculture & Applied Sciences
Department of Family & Consumer Sciences
Family & Consumer Sciences: Fashion Merchandising
(B.S.)
www.utm.edu/departments/caas/fcs/fashion.php

TEXAS

Art Institute of Austin, The
Austin, TX
Fashion Retail & Management (B.S.)
www.artinstitutes.edu/Austin

Art Institute of Dallas, The
Dallas, TX
Fashion Design (A.A.A., B.F.A.)
www.artinstitutes.edu/dallas
• **EXTENDED PROFILE ON PAGE 292**

Art Institute of Houston, The
Houston, TX
Fashion Retail & Management (B.S.)
Fashion Design (B.F.A.)
www.artinstitutes.edu/houston

Austin Community College
Austin, TX
Marketing & Fashion Marketing (A.A.S., certificate)
www.austincc.edu/info/marketing

Baylor University
Waco, TX
Family & Consumer Sciences: Fashion Division
Fashion Design (B.A., B.S.)
Fashion Merchandising (B.A., B.S.)
www.baylor.edu/fcs
• **EXTENDED PROFILE ON PAGE 294**

El Centro College
Dallas, TX
Fashion Design (A.A.S.)
Fashion Marketing (A.A.S.)
www.elcentrocollege.edu

El Paso Community College
El Paso, TX
Department of Fashion Technology
Fashion Technology: Fashion Merchandising (A.A.S.)
Fashion Technology: Fashion Design (A.A.S.)
Fashion Technology: Fashion Illustration (A.A.S.)
Fashion Technology: Industrial Patternmaking
(Certificate of Completion)
www.epcc.edu
• **EXTENDED PROFILE ON PAGE 296**

Houston Community College, Central College
Houston, TX
Lifestyle Arts & Design Careers Division
Fashion Design: Science Theatrical, Costume Design
(A.A.)
Fashion Merchandising (A.A.)
http://central.hccs.edu/lifestylearts
● EXTENDED PROFILE ON PAGE 298

International Academy of Design & Technology–San Antonio
San Antonio, TX
Fashion Design & Merchandising
Fashion Design & Merchandising (A.A.S., B.F.A.)
www.iadtsanantoio.com
● EXTENDED PROFILE ON PAGE 300

Lamar University
Beaumont, TX
Family & Consumer Sciences Department
Fashion Retailing & Merchandising (B.S.)
http://dept.lamar.edu/fcs/fash_merch/prog_descr.htm

Northwood University
Cedar Hill, TX
Management: Fashion Marketing (B.B.A.)
Marketing: Fashion Marketing (B.B.A.)
www.northwood.edu/tx/academics/fashion-marketing

Sam Houston State University
Huntsville, TX
Department of Family & Consumer Sciences
Fashion Merchandising (B.A., B.S.)
www.shsu.edu/~hec_www
● EXTENDED PROFILE ON PAGE 302

Stephen F. Austin State University
Nacogdoches, TX
School of Human Sciences
Fashion Merchandising (B.S., M.S.)
www.sfasu.edu/go/human-sciences
● EXTENDED PROFILE ON PAGE 304

Tarrant County College
Fort Worth, TX
Business Administration: Fashion Merchandising (A.A.S.,
certificate)
www.tccd.edu/Courses_and_Programs/Program_
Offerings/Fashion_Merchandising.html

Texas Christian University
Forth Worth, TX
Department of Design, Merchandising & Textiles
Fashion Merchandising (B.S.)
www.demt.tcu.edu
● EXTENDED PROFILE ON PAGE 306

Texas State University
San Marcos, TX
College of Applied Arts
Department of Family & Consumer Sciences
Fashion Merchandising (B.S., minor in Business)
www.txstate.edu/fcs
● EXTENDED PROFILE ON PAGE 308

Texas Tech University
Lubbock, TX
College of Human Science
Department of Design
Apparel Design & Manufacturing (B.S.)
www.depts.ttu.edu/hs/dod/adm/index.php
● EXTENDED PROFILE ON PAGE 310

Texas Women's University
Denton, TX
Fashion Design (B.A.)
Fashion Merchandising (B.A., B.S.)
www.twu.edu/fashion/programs.asp

University of Houston
Houston, TX
Department of Human Development & Consumer
Sciences
Consumer Science & Merchandising (B.S., certificate)
www.tech.uh.edu/Programs/Consumer_Merchandising
● EXTENDED PROFILE ON PAGE 312

University of the Incarnate Word
San Antonio, TX
School of Interactive Media & Design
Fashion Management: Design (A.A., B.A.)
Fashion Management: Merchandising (A.A., B.A.)
www.uiw.edu/fashion/index.htm

University of North Texas
Denton, TX
College of Visual Arts & Design
Fashion Design (B.F.A., M.F.A.)
http://art.unt.edu/fashion-design.html

University of North Texas
Denton, TX
School of Merchandising & Hospitality Management
Merchandising (B.S., M.S.)
Home Furnishings Merchandising (B.S.)
E-Merchandising (B.S.)
Merchandising/Business (M.B.A)
www.smhm.unt.edu
● EXTENDED PROFILE ON PAGE 314

University of Texas, Austin
College of Natural Sciences
School of Human Ecology
Textiles & Apparel: Apparel Design (B.S.)
Textiles & Apparel: Apparel Conservation (B.S.)
Textiles & Apparel: Retail Merchandising (B.S.)
Textile & Apparel Technology (M.S.)
www.he.utexas.edu/txa/index.php

Wade College
Dallas, TX
Fashion Merchandising & Design (A.A.)
www.wadecollege.edu/content/index.php?page=fashion-design

UTAH

Salt Lake Community College
Salt Lake City, UT
The Fashion Institute
Fashion Design (certificate)
www.slcc.edu/fashion/

Weber State University
Ogden, UT
Sales & Merchandising (A.A.S.)
www.weber.edu/coast/programs/salesmerchandising.html

VIRGINIA

Art Institute of Virginia Beach, The
Virginia Beach, VA
Department of Fashion & Retail Management
Fashion Retail Management (B.A.)
www.artinstitutes.edu/virginia-beach
• **EXTENDED PROFILE ON PAGE 316**

Art Institute of Washington, The
Arlington, VA
Fashion & Retail Management (B.A.)
www.artinstitutes.edu/arlington

Liberty University
Lynchburg, VA
College of Arts & Sciences
Department of Family & Consumer Sciences
Fashion Merchandising & Interiors (B.S.)
www.liberty.edu/academics/arts-sciences/facs

Marymount University
Arlington, VA
Fashion Design & Merchandising
Fashion Design (B.A.)
Fashion Merchandising (B.A.)
www.marymount.edu/academics
• **EXTENDED PROFILE ON PAGE 318**

Old Dominion University
Norfolk, VA
Darden College of Education
Department of STEM Education & Professional Studies
Occupational & Technical Studies: Fashion (B.S.)
http://education.odu.edu/ots/academics/undergrad/fashion.shtml

Radford University
Radford, VA
College of Visual & Performing Arts
Department of Interior Design & Fashion
Design: Fashion Design (B.F.A.)
Design: Merchandising for Design (B.S.)
Design: Design Management (B.S.)
Design: Design Culture (B.S.)
http://id-f.asp.radford.edu

Virginia Commonwealth University
Richmond, VA
Department of Fashion Design & Merchandising
Fashion Design (B.A.)
Fashion Merchandising (B.A.)
www.vcu.edu/arts/fashion/dept/
• **EXTENDED PROFILE ON PAGE 320**

Virginia Polytechnic Institute & State University
Blacksburg, VA
Department of Apparel, Housing & Resource Management
Apparel Product Development & Merchandising Management (B.S.)
www.ahrm.vt.edu
• **EXTENDED PROFILE ON PAGE 322**

WASHINGTON

Art Institute of Seattle, The
Fashion Design (A.A.A., B.F.A.)
Fashion Marketing (A.A.A., B.S.)
www.artinstitutes.edu/seattle

Bates Technical College
Tacoma, WA
Fashion Construction & Design (certificate)
www.bates.ctc.edu/Fashion

Central Washington University
Ellensburg, WA
Family & Consumer Sciences
Fashion Merchandising (B.S., minor)
www.cwu.edu/~fandcs/fcsa
- **EXTENDED PROFILE ON PAGE 324**

Edmonds Community College
Lynnwood, WA
Business Management: Fashion/Retail Merchandising
   (certificate)
http://mgmt.edcc.edu/

Highline Community College
Des Moines, WA
Retail Management (A.A.S., certificate)
http://business.highline.edu/

International Academy of Design & Technology—Seattle
Seattle, WA
Fashion Design (B.F.A., A.A.S)
Fashion Merchandising (B.F.A., A.A.S.)
www.iadtseattle.com/programs/fashion-design.asp

Seattle Pacific University
Family & Consumer Sciences Department
Clothing & Textiles: Apparel Design (B.A.)
Clothing & Textiles: Fashion Merchandising (B.A.)
www.spu.edu/depts/fcs/textiles/index.html

Shoreline Community College
Shoreline, WA
Business Administration
Fashion Merchandising (A.A.A.S., certificate)
Retail Management (A.A.A.S., certificate)
www.shoreline.edu/genbusad.aspx

Washington State University
Pullman, WA
Department of Apparel, Merchandising, Design, &
   Textiles
Apparel, Merchandising, & Textiles: Apparel Design
   (B.A., M.A.)
Apparel, Merchandising, & Textiles: Merchandising
   (B.A., M.A.)
http://amdt.wsu.edu
- **EXTENDED PROFILE ON PAGE 326**

WASHINGTON, DC

Howard University
Washington, DC
Art Department
Fashion Merchandising (B.A.)
www.coas.howard.edu/art/Undergraduate/under_
Fashion.html

WEST VIRGINIA

Marshall University
Huntington, WV
College of Education & Human Services
Family & Consumer Sciences: Apparel Design &
   Merchandising (B.A.)
www.marshall.edu/fcs/degrees/

Pierpont Community & Technical College
Fairmont, WV
School of Human Services
Fashion Design (A.A.S.)
www.pierpont.edu/schoolofhumanservices/
- **EXTENDED PROFILE ON PAGE 336**

West Virginia University
Morgantown, WV
Division of Design & Merchandising
Fashion Design & Merchandising: Fashion Design (B.S.)
Fashion Design & Merchandising: Merchandising (B.S.)
www.design.wvu.edu
- **EXTENDED PROFILE ON PAGE 338**

WISCONSIN

Madison College
Madison, WI
Fashion Marketing
Fashion Marketing (A.A.S.)
http://matcmadison.edu/program-info/fashion-marketing
- **EXTENDED PROFILE ON PAGE 328**

Milwaukee Area Technical College
Oak Creek, WI
Department of Marketing
Fashion Marketing: Fashion (A.A.S.)
Fashion Marketing: Retail Management (A.A.S.)
http://oncampus.matc.edu/luchta/fashionretail/
- **EXTENDED PROFILE ON PAGE 330**

Mount Mary College

Milwaukee, WI
Fashion Department
Apparel Product Development: Creative Design (B.A.)
Apparel Product Development: Technical Design (B.A.)
Merchandise Management (B.A.)
www.mtmary.edu/dept_fashion.htm
- **EXTENDED PROFILE ON PAGE 332**

University of Wisconsin-Madison

Madison, WI
School of Human Ecology
Design Studies Department
Textile & Apparel Design (B.S.)
Design Studies: Textiles (M.S., PhD)
www.sohe.wisc.edu/etd

University of Wisconsin-Stout

Menomonie, WI
Department of Apparel Design & Development
Apparel Design & Development (B.S.)
www.uwstout.edu/programs/bsadd/index.cfm
- **EXTENDED PROFILE ON PAGE 334**

CANADA

Algonquin College of Applied Arts and Technology

Ottawa, ON
School of Part-time Studies
Fashion Design (certificate)
www.algonquincollege.com
- **EXTENDED PROFILE ON PAGE 340**

Blanche Macdonald Centre for Applied Design

Vancouver, BC
Department Fashion Merchandising/Fashion Design
Fashion Merchandising (diploma)
Fashion Design (diploma)
www.blanchemacdonald.com
- **EXTENDED PROFILE ON PAGE 342**

Center for Arts & Technology

Kelowna, BC
Fashion Design & Merchandising (diploma)
www.digitalartschool.com/programs/fashion_design

George Brown College

Toronto, ON
School of Fashion Studies
Fashion Management (diploma)
Fashion Business Industry (diploma)
Fashion Techniques & Design (diploma)
International Fashion Development & Management
    (advanced diploma)
www.georgebrown.ca/fashionstudies/
- **EXTENDED PROFILE ON PAGE 344**

Humber College

Toronto, ON
Fashion Institute
Fashion Arts (diploma)
Cosmetic Management (diploma)
Esthetician Spa Management (diploma)
www.humber.ca
- **EXTENDED PROFILE ON PAGE 346**

John Casablancas Institute

Vancouver, BC
Fashion Business & Creative Arts (diploma)
www.jcinstitute.com/#/fashion

Kwantlen Polytechnic University

Richmond, BC
Fashion & Technology (B.D)
Fashion Marketing (diploma)
www.kwantlen.ca/fashion
- **EXTENDED PROFILE ON PAGE 348**

LaSalle College

Montreal, QC
Fashion Design (diploma)
Fashion Marketing (diploma)
www.collegelasalle.com/schools/fashion.aspx

Marvel College

Edmonton, AB
Fashion Design & Apparel Production (diploma)
www.mccollege.ca/fashion.shtml

Mohawk College

Hamilton, ON
School of Continuing Education
Fashion Design (certificate)
www.mohawkcollege.ca/discover/ce/carts/fashion.html

Olds College Calgary Campus

Olds, Alberta
Department of Apparel Technology
Apparel Technology (Diploma)
www.oldscollege.ca
- **EXTENDED PROFILE ON PAGE 350**

CANADA

Olds College Calgary Campus
Olds, Alberta
School of Business
Fashion Marketing Technology (Diploma)
www.oldscollege.ca
• **EXTENDED PROFILE ON PAGE 352**

Pacific Design Academy
Victoria, BC
Fashion Design (diploma)
www.pacificdesignacademy.com/program.htm

RCC Institute of Technology
Concord, ON
Academy of Design
Fashion Design (diploma)
Fashion Merchandising (diploma)
www.aodt.ca/programs.asp

Richard Robinson Fashion Design Academy
Fashion Design (diploma)
Ottawa, ON
www.richardrobinson.com/english.html

Ryerson University
Toronto, ON
School of Fashion
Fashion Design (B.D.)
Fashion Communication (B.D.)
Fashion (M.A.)
www.ryerson.ca/fashion
• **EXTENDED PROFILE ON PAGE 354**

Seminaire de Sherbrooke
Sherbrooke, QC
Fashion Marketing (diploma)
www.seminaire-sherbrooke.qc.ca

Seneca College
Toronto, ON
Department of Fashion Arts
Fashion Arts (diploma)
www.senecac.on.ca/fashion/faa

University of Alberta
Edmonton, AB
Department of Human Ecology
Clothing, Textiles & Material Culture (B.S.)
www.ualberta.ca
• **EXTENDED PROFILE ON PAGE 356**

University of the Fraser Valley
Abbotsford, BC
Fashion Design (diploma)
www.ufv.ca/Fashion/Fashion_Design_Program_Overview.
htm#

University of Manitoba
Winnipeg, MB
Faculty of Human Ecology
Textile Science (B.S., M.S.)
http://umanitoba.ca/faculties/human_ecology/
departments/ts/index.html

Vancouver College of Art & Design
Vancouver, BC
Fashion Design (diploma)
Marketing & Merchandising for Fashion (diploma)
www.vcad.ca/Programs

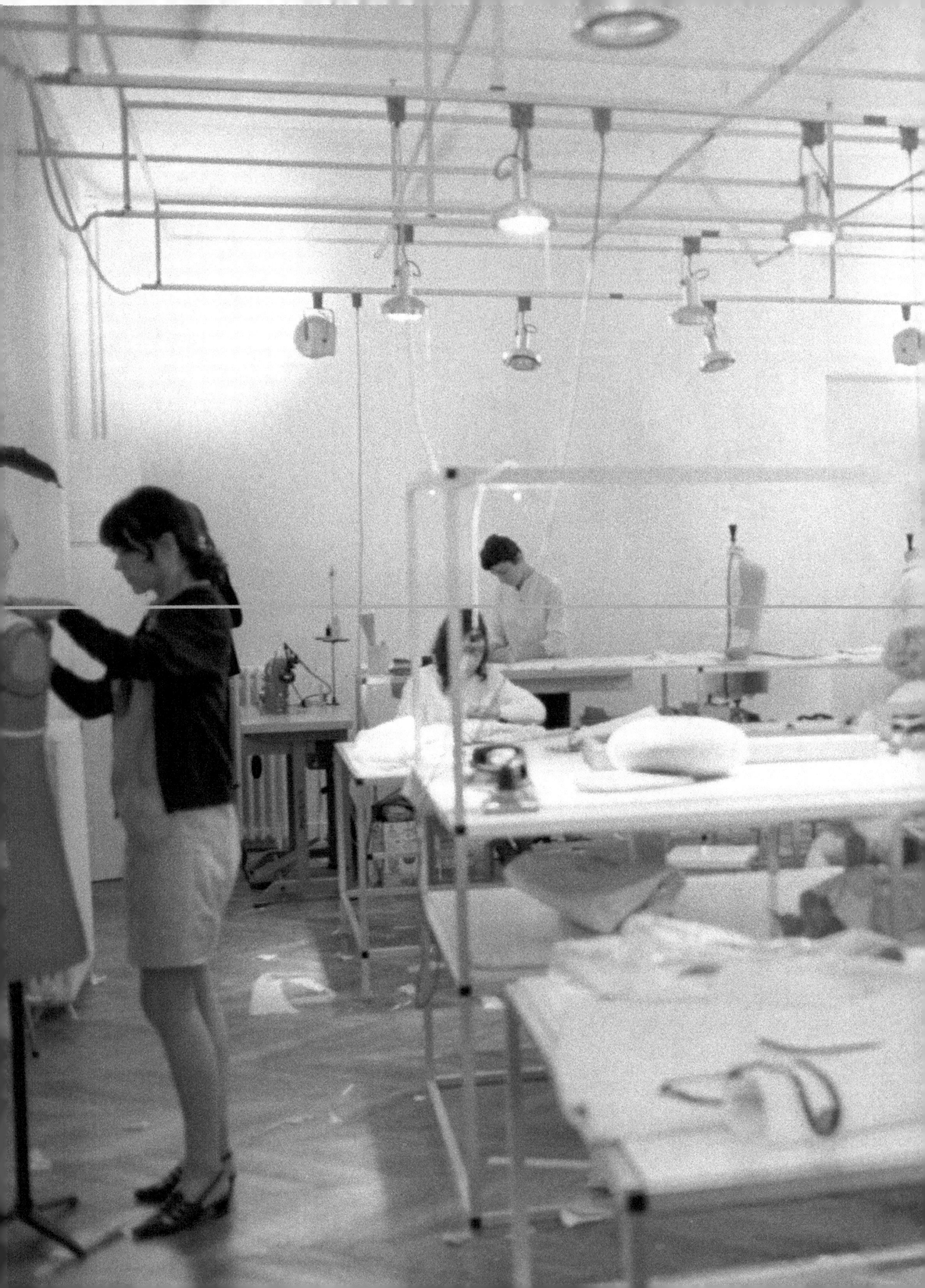

Extended Profiles

Auburn University

Department of Consumer Affairs

308 Spidle Hall, Auburn University, AL 36849 | 334-844-3789 | www.humsci.auburn.edu/cahs/index.php

UNIVERSITY PROFILE
Public
Suburban
Residential
Semester Schedule
Co-ed

STUDENT DEMOGRAPHICS
STUDENT DEMOGRAPHICS
Undergraduate: 20,913
Graduate: 3,689

Male: 51%
Female: 49%

Full-time: Not reported
Part-time: Not reported

EXPENSES
Tuition: $7,900 (in-state)
$21,916 (out-of-state)

Room & Board: $9,630

ADMISSIONS
Quad Center
Auburn University, AL 36849
334-844-6425

DEGREE INFORMATION

Major / Degree / Concentration	Enrollment	Requirements for entry	Graduation rate
Apparel Merchandising, Design & Production Management Bachelor of Science Apparel Merchandising Option	200	2.5 gpa for off-campus transfer; 2.0 for on-campus transfer	Not reported
Apparel Merchansising, Design & Production Management Bachelor of Science Product Design & Production Management Option	90	2.5 gpa for off-campus transfer; 2.0 for on-campus transfer	Not reported
Consumer Affairs-Apparel Master of Science	12	3.0 gpa; 900 GRE	Not reported
Integrated Textile and Apparel Science Doctor of Philosophy	13	3.0 gpa; 1,000 GRE	Not reported

TOTAL PROGRAM ENROLLMENT
Undergraduate: 290
Graduate: 25

Male: 2.3%
Female: 97.7%

Full-time: Not reported
Part-time: Not reported
Online: 0%

International: Not reported
Minority: Not reported

Job Placement Rate: Not reported

SCHOLARSHIPS / FINANCIAL AID
Most scholarships are for students demonstrating need and/or academic achievement and promise. AAFA scholarships for design/production; University scholarships for students with ACT of 30 or higher.

TOTAL FACULTY: 9
Full-time: 100%
Part-time: 0%

FASHION ADMINISTRATION
Dr. Carol L. Warfield, Head Department of Consumer Affairs

PROFESSIONAL / ACADEMIC AFFILIATIONS
American Apparel and Footwear Association
American Collegiate Retailing Association

PROGRAM DESCRIPTION AND PHILOSOPHY

Auburn's Apparel, Merchandising, Design, and Product Management curriculum is an integrated study of the apparel supply chain. It provides an understanding of the consumer-driven textile/apparel/ retail complex from textile fiber to design and production to sourcing and merchandising. Two options: Merchandising or Design/Production Management each have capstone courses which build upon all of the academic coursework in the major. A 10-week supervised professional internship is a graduation requirement. Students intern all over the U.S. and overseas. The Internship is our best placement asset.

FACILITIES

Two state-of-the-art computer labs house digitizing, patternmaking, marking and grading and plotting (GERBER/Lectra) software and Photoshop and Illustrator for apparel product development. The sewn products lab is equipped with industrial as well as custom construction equipment. An archive of historic designs is available.

ONLINE / DISTANCE LEARNING

Not available

COURSES OF INSTRUCTION

Merchandising Option:
- Global Consumer Culture
- Textile Industrial Complex
- Merchandising Planning and Control, Visual Merchandising
- Consumer Decision Making/Apparel and Fashion
- Global Sourcing
- Fashion Analysis and Forecasting
- Apparel Merchandising and Retail Management
- History of Costume
- Textiles
- Marketing
- Management
- Accounting
- Microeconomics
- Chemistry
- History
- Statistics
- Internship

Design Option:
- Global Consumer Culture
- Textile Industrial Complex
- Apparel Production Management
- Aesthetics for Apparel Design
- Technical Design
- Creative Design
- Portfolio
- Merchandise Planning and Control
- Textiles
- Chemistry
- Microeconomics
- Apparel Engineering
- Fashion Analysis and Forecasting
- Global Sourcing
- History of Costume
- Apparel Line Development
- Internship

INTERNSHIPS

Required of majors at the Senior level. Interns are typically placed at apparel design and product development firms, retail sites, and fashion-related publications around the U.S. and abroad, e.g., Macy's, Kay Unger, Under Armour, Tuleh, Betsey Johnson, Anthropologie, J. Crew, Belk's, Armani Exchange, Zac Posen, Michael Kors, BCBG Max Azria, Bergdorf Goodman, Nordstrom, Shoshanna, America's Mart, Billy Reid, Kohl's, Target, Erica Angeline, Caruana Group, Alabama Shakespeare Festival.

STUDY ABROAD

A12-week immersion program, Joseph S. Bruno Auburn Abroad in Italy program, is available to all students in the College. Students earn 16 semester hours of credit and an International Minor. Other study abroad opportunities are available as well.

NOTABLE ALUMNI

Dawn Robertson, President, Sean John

STUDENT ACTIVITIES AND ORGANIZATIONS

Not reported

FACULTY SPECIALIZATIONS AND RESEARCH

Merchandising, branding, fast fashion, 3D whole -body scanning, body size and shape analysis for women, men, & teens/tweens; body image, online retailing, consumer decision making, historic costume and textiles, ethnic retailing, apparel fit and preferences for teens and tweens, especially for the overweight and obese, global retailing

Trenholm State Technical College

Department of Apparel & Designs

3920 Troy Highway, Montgomery, AL 36116　|　334-420-4352　|　www.trenholmstate.edu

UNIVERSITY PROFILE
Public
Urban
Commuter
Semester Schedule
Co-ed

STUDENT DEMOGRAPHICS
Undergraduate: 1,733
Graduate: NA

Male: 50.3%
Female: 49.7%

Full-time: 62.2%
Part-time: 38.8%

EXPENSES
Tuition: $1,560
Room & Board: n/a

ADMISSIONS
1225 Air Base Blvd.
Montgomery, AL 36108
334-420-4300
tmcbryde@trenholmstate.edu

DEGREE INFORMATION

Major / Degree / Concentration	Enrollment	Requirements for entry	Graduation rate
Apparel & Designs Special Training Certificate 1	Not reported	2.0 gpa	Not reported
Apparel & Designs Special Training Certificate 2	Not reported	2.0 gpa	Not reported
Apparel & Designs Special Training Certificate 3	Not reported	2.0 gpa	Not reported

TOTAL PROGRAM ENROLLMENT
Undergraduate: 16
Graduate: n/a

Male: 25%
Female: 75%

Full-time: 37.5%
Part-time: 62.5%
Online: n/a

International: 0%
Minority: 93.8%

Job Placement Rate: 60%

SCHOLARSHIPS / FINANCIAL AID
Federal Pell Grant, FSEOG, Federal Work Study, Federal Academic Competiveness Grant, Trenholm Foundation Scholarships, Institutional Scholarships

TOTAL FACULTY: 1
Full-time: 100%
Part-time: Not reported

FASHION DESIGN ADMINISTRATION
Margaret Law, Program Coordinator/ Instructor
Jean Stockman, Service Occupations Division Head
Wilford Holt, Assistant Dean, Technical Education

PROFESSIONAL / ACADEMIC AFFILIATIONS
International Textile and Apparel Association

PROGRAM DESCRIPTION AND PHILOSOPHY

The Apparel and Designs Program is designed to provide individuals with the knowledge and proficiencies to provide safe and productive service and/or products in the apparel field. Individuals will be able to tailor and alter/remodel apparel, analyze body figure types, demonstrate knowledge of textiles, create custom apparel, and produce interior furnishings.

FACILITIES

Computer Labs, Archives, Classroom, Construction Lab

ONLINE / DISTANCE LEARNING

Not available

COURSES OF INSTRUCTION

- Introduction to Apparel Trades
- Apparel Industry Tools/Machine
- Concepts Apparel Construction
- Basic Apparel Construction Lab
- Introduction to Textiles
- Textile Analysis & Testing

INTERNSHIPS

Not required. Interns are typically placed at Fabric stores, tailoring/dress-making shops, department stores, furniture stores, accessories stores, custom home furnishing stores, and self-employed.

STUDY ABROAD

Not available

NOTABLE ALUMNI

Not reported

STUDENT ACTIVITIES AND ORGANIZATIONS

SGA, Student Ambassadors, Skills USA, Photography Club

FACULTY SPECIALIZATIONS AND RESEARCH

Apparel designs and interior decorating

COMMUNITY COLLEGE TRANSFERS

Certain courses are transferable: Textiles, Pattern Adjusting and Fitting, Basic Apparel Construction, Accessories and Related Merchandise

University of Alabama

Department of Clothing, Textiles and Interior Design

Box 870158, Tuscaloosa, AL 35487 | 205-348-6176 | www.ches.ua.edu

UNIVERSITY PROFILE
Public
Urban
Residential
Semester Schedule
Co-ed

STUDENT DEMOGRAPHICS
Undergraduate: 23,702
Graduate: 5,105

Male: 47.6%
Female: 52.4%

Full-time: 91.7%
Part-time: 8.3%

EXPENSES
Tuition: www.cost.ua.edu
Room & Board: www.cost.
ua.edu

ADMISSIONS
Box 870132
Tuscaloosa, AL 35487-0132
205-348-88197
www.ua.edu

DEGREE INFORMATION

Major / Degree / Concentration	Enrollment	Requirements for entry	Graduation rate
Apparel and Textiles Bachelor of Science Apparel Design	110	2.0 gpa Senior Portfolio Review	95%
Apparel and Textiles Bachelor of Science Fashion Retailing	210	Internship dependent upon 2.5 gpa on block of specified classes	90%

TOTAL PROGRAM ENROLLMENT
Undergraduate: 362
Graduate: 1

Male: 1.8%
Female: 97.2%

Full-time: 97%
Part-time: 3%
Online: 0%

International: Not reported
Minority: 7.1%

Job Placement Rate: 90%

SCHOLARSHIPS / FINANCIAL AID
Many scholarships and Financial aid awards are given through the College of Human Environmental Sciences Dean's Office in addition to University-wide awards. Students fill out one application form and they are then reviewed for all scholarships and aid for which they qualify.

Students receiving Scholarships or Financial Aid: 48%

TOTAL FACULTY: 8
Full-time: 7
Part-time: 1

FASHION DESIGN ADMINISTRATION
Dr. Milla Boshung, Dean of College of Human Environmental Sciences
Dr. Shirley Foster, Interim Department Chair for Clothing Textiles and Interior Design
Mrs. Paula Robinson, Program Contact for Apparel Design

PROFESSIONAL / ACADEMIC AFFILIATIONS
International Textile and Apparel Association
Marketing Science Institute
Society for American Archaeology

PROGRAM DESCRIPTION AND PHILOSOPHY

The primary goal of the Apparel Design program is to prepare students for entry-level positions in the apparel and textile industries in design, production, and management. Sequential course offerings provide basic and upper-level skill development and knowledge of the design field. The common body of knowledge is taught not only through studio classes but also in art and design history courses. The experience students gain during their tenure provides an excellent foundation for professional and educational development. The Fashion Retailing program is planned for students interested in preparing for merchandising and management careers in retailing and related fashion fields. Supervised internships are offered for students who have successfully completed 86 semester hours. Students may have an international retailing focus and may complete additional coursework for a general business minor.

FACILITIES

Facilities include three computer labs in buildings in central campus and one at the new Child Development Research Center which are equipped with usual printers and several color plotters. Two clothing laboratories have sewing machines and sergers with cutting tables, pressing equipment, and standard Wolf and PGMpro dressforms.

ONLINE / DISTANCE LEARNING

The apparel design program is not offered online.

COURSES OF INSTRUCTION

- Applied Design
- Apparel Construction
- Textiles
- Apparel Manufacturing
- Flat Pattern
- Draping
- Textile Design
- Visual Merchandising
- History of Costume or History of Textile Design
- International Trade
- Quality Control for Textiles
- Advanced Apparel Design
- Drawing I
- Principles of Microeconomics
- Marketing

INTERNSHIPS

Not required. Design Interns have been placed at Calvin Klein–dress division, Tibi, Betsy Johnson, Donna Karan, *Vanity Fair*, Anna Sui, Lilli Rose, Eli Tahari, Michael Kors, Hunter Dixon, LeonaFashion Retailing Interns -required: *Vanity Fair*, Calvin Klein, Liz Clairborne, Eli Tahari, Tibi,Tory Burch, Coach, BCBG, DVF, Bergdorf Goodman, Loro Pianna, French Connection, Deri Kroeil, *Seventeen* magazine, *W*.

STUDY ABROAD

The university study abroad program has summer studies in Italy, Japan, and China. We also accept credits with advance planning with the departmental adviser from other international programs, such as American International University.

NOTABLE ALUMNI

Anthony L. Williams–7th Season Project Runway, Michael Spoors–Merchandising Manager for Fruit of the Loom, Hunter Lingle–Owner of Hunter Dixon, Smith Sinrod–just recognized as upcoming young designer in southeast; Janet Gurwich–CEO Laura Mercier Cosmetics; Lauren Leonard–Leona; Michael Blackwell–head designer for denim at Sean John; Beth Hubbard–Burda Patterns-USA Division until the late 90s

STUDENT ACTIVITIES AND ORGANIZATIONS

The student organization for the Apparel and Textiles concentrations of Fashion Retailing and Apparel design is Fashion, Inc. This group sponsors a fashion show of student collections once a year called "Rock the Runway" presented to the campus in collaboration with Creative Campus and a spring event, called "Tee-Time," where the students deconstruct a T-shirt into original designs which are shown by a fashion show and then offered for sale to the public by silent auction. This group also sponsors fieldtrips to fashion cities of Atlanta, Dallas, and Chicago. Students may also belong to the Mable Adams Society, which encompasses students from all majors within the College of Human Environmental Sciences.

FACULTY SPECIALIZATIONS AND RESEARCH

Dr. Marcy Koontz specializes in computer design applications for the betterment of human society; Dr. Michelle Tong investigates the marketing behavior of consumers across cultures–China and the United States and e-commerce; Drs. Amanda Thompson and Virginia Wimberley research in material culture of Native Americans with emphasis on what can be learned from surviving textiles about social organization and behavior.

Harding University

Family and Consumer Sciences Department

Box 12233, Searcy, AR 72149 | 501-279-4472 | www.harding.edu/fcs

UNIVERSITY PROFILE
Private
Suburban
Residential
Semester Schedule
Co-ed

STUDENT DEMOGRAPHICS
Undergraduate: 4,086
Graduate: 2,398

Male: 40%
Female: 60%

Full-time: 67%
Part-time: 33%

EXPENSES
Tuition: $13,140
Room & Board: $5,814

ADMISSIONS
Box 12255
Searcy, AR 72149-2255
501-279-4129
admissions@harding.edu

DEGREE INFORMATION

Major / Degree / Concentration	Enrollment	Requirements for entry	Graduation rate
Fashion Merchandising Bachelor of Science	24	Acceptance to Harding University	98%
Interiors Merchandising Bachelor of Science	7	Acceptance to Harding University	98%

TOTAL PROGRAM ENROLLMENT
Undergraduate: 31
Graduate: Not reported

Male: 0%
Female: 100%

Full-time: 94%
Part-time: 6%
Online: Not reported

International: 3%
Minority: 10%

Job Placement Rate: 75-80%

SCHOLARSHIPS / FINANCIAL AID
Several scholarships are offered within the department for Juniors and Seniors.

Students receiving Scholarships or Financial Aid: 97%

TOTAL FACULTY: 8
Full-time: 6
Part-time: 2

FASHION ADMINISTRATION
Dr. Beth Wilson, Department Chair

PROFESSIONAL / ACADEMIC AFFILIATIONS
Not reported

PROGRAM DESCRIPTION AND PHILOSOPHY

Our program is dedicated to empowering individuals, by preparing Christian professionals to assume leadership roles that support the mission of their potential companies or private endeavors. We use current educational techniques, as well as hands-on experience to provide the best possible learning environment for fashion and interiors merchandising.

FACILITIES

Computer lab, sewing and construction lab, historical clothing archive

ONLINE / DISTANCE LEARNING

Not available

COURSES OF INSTRUCTION

- Clothing Concepts
- Textiles
- Visual Merchandising and Display
- Introduction to Retailing
- Fashion Merchandising
- Apparel Analysis
- Marketing
- Principles of Sales
- Consumer Behavior
- Interiors Styles and Trends
- Housing Technology
- Fabrications
- Home Furnishings

INTERNSHIPS

Required of majors by Junior or Senior year. Interns are typically placed at companies such as Nordstrom, Dillard's, Crate and Barrel, showrooms at regional apparel markets, and privately owned boutiques.

STUDY ABROAD

Harding has six international programs, including Florence, Italy, Athens, Greece, London, England, France, Latin America, Zambia.

NOTABLE ALUMNI

Not reported

STUDENT ACTIVITIES AND ORGANIZATIONS

American Association of Family and Consumer Sciences Student Section, Harding and Arkansas Chapters, American Marketing Association

FACULTY SPECIALIZATIONS AND RESEARCH

Extensive personal experience in women's specialty retail, full-service interior design, visual merchandising (both clothing and home furnishings), home furnishings buyer

The Art Institute of Tucson

Departments of Fashion Design & Fashion Marketing

5099 E Grant Rd., Suite 100, Tucson, AZ 85745 | 520-318-2716 | www.artinstitutes.edu/tucson

UNIVERSITY PROFILE
Private
Suburban
Commuter
Quarter Schedule
Co-ed

STUDENT DEMOGRAPHICS
Undergraduate: 393
Graduate: 0

Male: 48%
Female: 52%

Full-time: 75%
Part-time: 25%

EXPENSES
Tuition: $29,875
Room & Board: n/a

ADMISSIONS
Not reported

DEGREE INFORMATION

Major / Degree / Concentration	Enrollment	Requirements for entry	Graduation rate
Fashion Design Bachelor of Arts	26	2.0 gpa Portfolio review in quarters 3, 6, 9, and final review at graduation	Not reported
Fashion Marketing Bachelor of Arts	19	2.0 gpa Portfolio review in quarters 3, 6, 9, and final review at graduation	Not reported

TOTAL PROGRAM ENROLLMENT
Undergraduate: 393
Graduate: n/a

Male: 48%
Female: 52%

Full-time: 75%
Part-time: 25%
Online: n/a

International: 2%
Minority: 45%

Job Placement Rate: Not reported

SCHOLARSHIPS / FINANCIAL AID
See opposite page for more info.

TOTAL FACULTY: 45
Full-time: 30%
Part-time: 70%

FASHION ADMINISTRATION
Elizabeth Heuisler, Academic
   Department Director Fashion Design &
   Fashion Marketing
Arthur Tsai, Full-time Faculty

PROFESSIONAL / ACADEMIC AFFILIATIONS
Fashion Group International

PROGRAM DESCRIPTION AND PHILOSOPHY

The Bachelor of Arts in Fashion Design degree program helps students attain a fundamental grounding in fashion design, including the theory and practice of tailoring, draping, pattern drafting, construction and sewing, fashion illustration, and creative design. These skills are enhanced through computerized patternmaking and design hardware and software systems. The more advanced courses focus on surface design and the creative process. The Fashion Marketing students acquire in-depth knowledge of the apparel industry and fashion cycles. Areas of study include fashion history, textiles, marketing and advertising for the industry. Other focal points for the students are trend forecasting, consumer behavior, visual display design, catalog design as well as business development and management.

FACILITIES

Students have use of a PC and MAC lab, a sewing lab, drafting and drawing rooms. Library has periodicals and other industry-related publications and texts available to the students six days a week. Students have access to cameras and video equipment to complete projects. Continuously changing art shows in our lobby gallery and several local and regional museums are also available.

ONLINE / DISTANCE LEARNING

Selected courses in Fashion Design and Fashion Marketing bachelor's degree programs are available online through a third-party consortium agreement with The Art Institute of Pittsburgh Online Division.

COURSES OF INSTRUCTION

Fashion Design Majors:
- Draping
- Fundamentals of Construction
- Fashion illustration
- Fashion History
- Textiles
- Fundamentals of Patternmaking
- Computerized Patternmaking
- Current Designers
- Costume Specialties

Fashion Marketing Majors:
- Fundamentals of Advertising
- Fundamentals of Marketing
- Apparel Evaluation & Construction
- Global Marketing
- Principals of Market Research
- Visual Techniques & Design
- In-House Promotion
- Retail Store Management

INTERNSHIPS

Required of majors at Junior and Senior levels. Fashion Marketing students work in management offices in larger department stores or local malls. Depending on their area of interest they may be placed in the visual display department or in retail sales positions.

Fashion Design externs typically work under an independent designer or boutique with design room.

STUDY ABROAD

Not available

NOTABLE ALUMNI

Not reported

STUDENT ACTIVITIES AND ORGANIZATIONS

The Fashion Club includes fashion design and Fashion Marketing Students.

FACULTY SPECIALIZATIONS AND RESEARCH

Costume design, ashion show production, market research, retail store management

COMMUNITY COLLEGE TRANSFERS

Students may transfer to any of 46 Art Institutes nationwide.

SCHOLARSHIPS / FINANCIAL AID

Passion for Fashion Competition provides local and national scholarships for high school seniors. EDMC Education Foundation scholarships are available annually to support students interested in continuing their education in the creative arts. Eligible students may apply for financial assistance under various federal and state programs including but not limited to: Federal Pell Grant, Federal Academic Competitive Grant, Federal Supplemental Educational Opportunity Grant, the Federal Direct Loan Program Subsidized Stafford Loan, Unsubsidized Stafford Loan and PLUS (Parent) Loan Program, Federal Work-Study, Vocational Rehabilitation Assistance, Veteran's Administration Benefits, and Bureau of Indian Affairs.

Students receiving Scholarships or Financial Aid: 90%

Collins College

Department of Fashion Design & Merchandising

4750 S. 44th Pl, Phoenix, AZ 85040 | 1-800-876-7070 | www.collinscollege.edu

UNIVERSITY PROFILE

Public
Urban
Commuter
Semester Schedule
Co-ed

STUDENT DEMOGRAPHICS

Undergraduate: Not reported
Graduate: Not reported

Male: Not reported
Female: Not reported

Full-time: Not reported
Part-time: Not reported

EXPENSES

Tuition: $12,600
Room & Board: n/a

ADMISSIONS

4750 S. 44th Pl.
Phoenix, AZ 85040
1-800-876-7070
http://contact.collinscollege.
edu/

DEGREE INFORMATION

Major / Degree / Concentration	Enrollment	Requirements for entry	Graduation rate
Fashion Design & Merchandising Bachelor of Fine Arts	37	Application for Admission; HS Diploma or Equivalent; Enrollment Agreement; Payment of Application Fee; Disclosure Form	Not reported

TOTAL PROGRAM ENROLLMENT

Undergraduate: 37
Graduate: 0

Male: Not reported
Female: Not reported

Full-time: Not reported
Part-time: Not reported
Online: Not reported

International: Not reported
Minority: Not reported

Job Placement Rate: Not reported

SCHOLARSHIPS / FINANCIAL AID

Financial Aid is available for those who qualify. Collins College participates in a variety of financial aid programs for the benefit of students. Students must meet the eligibility requirements of these programs in order to participate. Collins College administers its financial aid programs in accordance with prevailing federal and state laws and its own institutional policies.

TOTAL FACULTY: NOT REPORTED

Full-time: Not reported
Part-time: Not reported

FASHION ADMINISTRATION

Nicole Bissing, Department Chair

PROFESSIONAL / ACADEMIC AFFILIATIONS

International Textile and Apparel Association
Fashion Group International

PROGRAM DESCRIPTION AND PHILOSOPHY

The combined Bachelor of Fine Arts program of Fashion Design and Merchandising teaches both the design and business side of fashion. Students graduate understanding the entire industry which makes them more valuable and marketable in the workplace.

FACILITIES

Brand new sewing lab, Library, Fashion Snoops Membership

ONLINE / DISTANCE LEARNING

All General Education Courses, Intro to Business, and Evolution of Fashion are available online.

COURSES OF INSTRUCTION

- Intro to Fashion
- Fashion Sketching I & II
- Clothing Construction I & II
- Evolution of Fashion
- Textiles for Fashion
- Intro to Business
- Computer Graphics for Fashion Design
- Visual Merchandising
- Pattern Drafting I & II
- Retail Management
- Draping I & II
- Electronic Marketing
- Business Law
- Pricing Strategies
- Apparel Production I
- Merchandise Planning and Inventory Control
- Fashion Design I
- Salesmanship
- Textile Design
- Special Topics in Fashion Design and Merchandising I & II
- Fashion Publicity and Promotion
- Senior Fashion Merchandising Portfolio
- Fashion Merchandising Internship
- Entrepreneurship

INTERNSHIPS

Required of majors at the Senior level

STUDY ABROAD

Not reported

NOTABLE ALUMNI

Not reported

STUDENT ACTIVITIES AND ORGANIZATIONS

Fashion club "Collins Runway," Phoenix Costume Institute Events, volunteer work at both "Scottsdale Fashion Week" and "Phoenix Fashion Week"

FACULTY SPECIALIZATIONS AND RESEARCH

Fashion Design Construction, Merchandising, and Fashion Show Production

Mesa Community College

Fashion Merchandising & Design Department

1833 W. Southern Ave., Mesa, AZ 85202 | 480-461-7140 | www.mc.maricopa.edu/fashion

UNIVERSITY PROFILE
Public
Urban
Commuter
Semester Schedule
Co-ed

STUDENT DEMOGRAPHICS
Undergraduate: 16,000
Graduate: 0

Male: Not reported
Female: Not reported

Full-time: Not reported
Part-time: Not reported

EXPENSES
Tuition: $2,000
Room & Board: n/a

ADMISSIONS
1833 W. Southern Ave.
Mesa, AZ 85202
480-461-7200
ebowling@mesacc.edu

DEGREE INFORMATION

Major / Degree / Concentration	Enrollment	Requirements for entry	Graduation rate
Fashion Merchandising & Design **Associate of Applied Science** Fashion Merchandising	180	Open enrollment	70%
Fashion Merchandising & Design **Associate of Applied Science** Fashion Design	130	Open enrollment	75%
Fashion Merchandising & Design **Associate of Applied Science** Retailing	25	Open enrollment	New program

TOTAL PROGRAM ENROLLMENT
Undergraduate: 350
Graduate: 0

Male: 20%
Female: 80%

Full-time: 75%
Part-time: 25%
Online: 0%

International: 5%
Minority: 35%

Job Placement Rate: 100%

SCHOLARSHIPS / FINANCIAL AID
MCC Fashion Program raises over $5,000 each year through its annual fashion show of student work. 100% goes to 10 scholarships. Other Financial Aid available on website.

Receiving Scholarships or Financial Aid: 65%

TOTAL FACULTY: 20
Full-time: 2%
Part-time: 18%

FASHION DESIGN ADMINISTRATION
Evonne Bowling, Program Director

PROFESSIONAL / ACADEMIC AFFILIATIONS
Fashion Group International

PROGRAM DESCRIPTION AND PHILOSOPHY

Mesa Community College's Fashion Programs are open to all interested students with the goal of training the next generation of fashion professionals. Mesa Community College incorporates the merchandising and design programs to successful complete the teaching of the real fashion industry. All faculty have years of real industry experience and keep current with industry standards. We use service learning working in the fashion industry in our community.

FACILITIES

CAD Lab with new Lectra/ Freeboarders/Tukatek, computer study lab, sewing/design room with industrial equipment

ONLINE / DISTANCE LEARNING

Not reported

COURSES OF INSTRUCTION

- Textiles
- Intro to Fashion Merchandising
- Fashion Design
- CAD for Fashion Design
- History of Fashion
- Clothing & Culture
- Illustration
- Sales Management
- Retail Merchandising
- Visual Display
- Draping
- Patternmaking

INTERNSHIPS

Required of majors at any level. Our retail industry recruits from our students and even in recessionary times our students find acceptable work. As a two-year college we place well at our level and above. All majors represented in the Phoenix/Scottsdale Metro area.

STUDY ABROAD

NYC, London, and Paris 2-week trips available for credit

NOTABLE ALUMNI

Not yet

STUDENT ACTIVITIES AND ORGANIZATIONS

Fashion Focus Club (produces annual show and volunteers in fashion community with models, designers and dressers)
Phi Kappa Theta Honor Society
Business Societies

FACULTY SPECIALIZATIONS AND RESEARCH

Our goals are to place graduates in careers or transfer to finish a Bachelor's degree

COMMUNITY COLLEGE TRANSFERS

Mesa Community College students transfers to all public and private universities with the fashion major. Program Director works closely with the receiving college.

Northern Arizona University

School of Communication

P.O. Box 5619, Flagstaff, AZ 86011-5619 | 928-523-2232 | www.nau.edu/sbs/communication/

UNIVERSITY PROFILE
Public
Rural
Residential
Semester Schedule
Co-ed

STUDENT DEMOGRAPHICS
Undergraduate: 25,719
Graduate: 8,166

Male: 38%
Female: 62%

Full-time: 91%
Part-time: 9%

EXPENSES
Tuition: $6,964 (resident)
$19,364 (non-resident)
Room & Board: $8,072

ADMISSIONS
P.O. Box 4084
Flagstaff, AZ 86011-4084
1-888-628-2968
undergraduate.admissions@
nau.edu

DEGREE INFORMATION

Major / Degree / Concentration	Enrollment	Requirements for entry	Graduation rate
Merchandising Bachelor of Science	Not reported	2.5 gpa in major classes required for graduation	Not reported

TOTAL PROGRAM ENROLLMENT
Undergraduate: 100%
Graduate: 0

Male: <5%
Female: 95%

Full-time: 87%
Part-time: 13%
Online: 0%

International: 0%
Minority: 22%

Job Placement Rate: Not reported

SCHOLARSHIPS / FINANCIAL AID
Merchandising Leaders of the 21st
Century Scholarship
Moller Scholarship
School of Communication Alumni
Scholarship

TOTAL FACULTY: 2
Full-time: 100%
Part-time: 0%

FASHION DESIGN ADMINISTRATION
Mark Neumann, Professor and Director
of the School of Communication

PROFESSIONAL / ACADEMIC AFFILIATIONS
International Textile and Apparel
Association
Fashion Group International
American Collegiate Retailing
Association

PROGRAM DESCRIPTION AND PHILOSOPHY

Northern Arizona University's School of Communication offers one of the most unique four-year programs in merchandising in the western United States. Students preparing to work in the textile, apparel, accessory, cosmetic, retail, and related industries have the opportunity to study all of the activities involved in merchandising products and services in addition to obtaining a solid foundation in communication skills. Merchandising encompasses all of the activities necessary to have the right merchandise at the right time, in the right quantities, at the right price to meet customer satisfaction. Classes in the merchandising program help students gain competence in analyzing products and consumer demand; buying and presenting merchandise through a variety of retail outlets; and preparing advertising, promotional and special event campaigns to promote sales of products to consumers. Graduates earn a Bachelor of Science degree in Merchandising. Students select a minor from programs in the School of Communication (advertising, electronic media and film, journalism, photography, public relations, speech communication, visual communication) or the College of Business Administration.

FACILITIES

Open computer labs are available in our building. We have a historic costume collection. Mannequins and other props are available for students who construct window displays on campus and in the community.

ONLINE / DISTANCE LEARNING

Not available

COURSES OF INSTRUCTION

- Merchandising Fundamentals
- Evaluating Apparel Quality
- Merchandise Buying
- Textiles
- Promotional Communication
- Merchandise Planning & Control
- Merchandising Promotion
- Visual Merchandising
- Professional Practices in Merchandising
- History of Clothing
- 20th Century Dress
- Social, Psychological, and Cultural Aspects of Dress
- Trends and Research in Merchandising
- Fashion Show Production
- Cooperative Education or Internship

INTERNSHIPS

Not required, but available between Junior and Senior year. Interns are typically placed at companies such as Neiman Marcus, Nordstrom, Dillards, DKNY, Buckle, Basement Marketplace, Forest Highlands Golf Club, Follett Higher Education Group.

STUDY ABROAD

We have several opportunities through our International office. Students have traveled to Italy, London, Paris, and the Netherlands.

NOTABLE ALUMNI

Trina Manning, Managing Director for Hermes of Paris; Debbie Nichols, Buyer and Manager of Basement Marketplace; Leah Stephens, Chanel Specialist at Neiman Marcus; Sheree Hartwell, Owner/Director FORD/ Robert Black Agency; Reah Norman, West Coast Style Editor, *PLUS Model* magazine.

STUDENT ACTIVITIES AND ORGANIZATIONS

Northern Arizona Merchandising Association (NAMA) is a student society created for the advancement of professionalism in the merchandising program. Students meet with professionals in the field, participate in field trips and sponsor fund-raising events. Trips have included visits to design houses, major retailers, fashion publications, fashion forecasters, museums, and major market centers. Previously students have traveled to MAGIC, the men's apparel trade show held in Las Vegas, Dallas Apparel Mart, and New York City.

FACULTY SPECIALIZATIONS AND RESEARCH

Tourism retailing and merchandise promotion

Academy of Art University

School of Fashion

180 New Montgomery St., 7th Fl., San Francisco, CA 94105-3410 | 415-618-3826
www.academyart.edu/fashion-school

UNIVERSITY PROFILE
Private
Urban
Residential & Commuter
Semester Schedule
Co-Ed

STUDENT DEMOGRAPHICS
Undergraduate: 11,277
Graduate: 4,963

Male: 47%
Female: 53%

Full-time: 57%
Part-time: 43%

EXPENSES
Tuition: $17,760
Room & Board: $13,500

ADMISSIONS
79 New Montgomery St., 4th Fl.
San Francisco, CA 94105-3410
415-274-2200 (International)
800-544-2787 (US Only)
admissions@academyart.edu

DEGREE INFORMATION

Major / Degree / Concentration	Enrollment	Requirements for entry	Graduation rate
Fashion **Associate of Arts** **Specialty Tracks:** **Fashion Design, Knitwear, Menswear, Merchandising, Textiles, Visual Merchandising**	193	Open enrollment policy.	Not reported
Fashion **Bachelor of Fine Arts** **Fashion Design, Knitwear, Merchandising, Textile Design, Visual Merchandising**	1,474	Open enrollment policy.	Not reported
Fashion **Master of Fine Arts** **Fashion Design, Knitwear, Merchandising, Textile Design**	670	Resume describing educational and professional experience.; Official college transcripts.; Portfolio/reel for placement in the MFA program.	Not reported

*Academy of Art University requires all students in degree-seeking programs to have a high school diploma, a GED, or may be admitted by passing a Department of Education approved "ability to benefit test" if beyond the age of compulsory attendance.

TOTAL PROGRAM ENROLLMENT
Undergraduate: 1,754
Graduate: 683

Male: 12%
Female: 88%

Full-time: 61%
Part-time: 39%
Online: 37%

International: 25%
Minority: Not reported

Job Placement Rate: Not reported

SCHOLARSHIPS / FINANCIAL AID
See opposite page for more information.

TOTAL FACULTY: 137
Full-time: 16%
Part-time: 84%

FASHION ADMINISTRATION
Melissa Lai, Fashion Administrator

PROFESSIONAL / ACADEMIC AFFILIATIONS
Western Association of Schools and
   Colleges (WASC)
NASAD
Council for Interior Design Accreditation
   (BFA-IAD)
NAAB (M-ARCH)

PROGRAM DESCRIPTION AND PHILOSOPHY

The School of Fashion provides the instruction, resources, and opportunities that encourage students to excel. Curriculum is updated regularly and includes classroom, studio, one-on-one directed-studies, and online education. Sustainable design has been layered into the curriculum since 1998, and is integrated into on-site and online class education. The School of Fashion publishes its own magazine "One Eighty," created by a student staff responsible for producing shoots, interviewing designers, and writing articles on the intersection of fashion and culture. Merchandising students create window and retail displays, and engage in the business of managing a boutique (the university's "Gallery Store").

Fashion students have opportunities to collaborate with industry companies on projects, competitions and sponsorships, as well as, connect with international brands and recruitment agencies for internships and job placement.

Since 2005, Academy of Art University has been the first and only school to present graduate collections during Mercedes-Benz New York Fashion Week. The university also hosts an annual Graduation Fashion Show and Awards Ceremony in San Francisco. Each show attracts press from major publications, top designers, and industry executives.

FACILITIES

In addition to industry-standard equipment for sewing, textiles, silk screens, pattern drafting, and more, the department also provides two Stoll America Industrial Knitting production machines, 16 single-bed and 10 double-bed knitting machines, two industrial linkers, and two domestic linkers. Students also have use of the library, computer labs, and textile labs.

ONLINE / DISTANCE LEARNING

The online School of Fashion currently offers Associate of Arts, Bachelor of Fine Arts, and Master of Fine Arts degree programs. The Fashion curriculum refines and focuses the student's individual vision, offering online courses in design, merchandising, textiles, and knitwear. Studio courses hone the student's mastery of industry standards in design and construction.

COURSES OF INSTRUCTION

- Fashion Design
- Fashion Merchandising
- Fashion Marketing Merchandising
- Fashion Journalism
- Menswear Design
- Knitwear Design
- Textile Design
- Active Sportswear Design
- Visual Merchandising & Store Design
- History of Beauty and Fashion
- Cosmetics and Fragrance Industry
- Sustainable and Green Design
- Fashion Illustration
- Fashion Figure & Rendering Techniques
- Fashion Sewing Techniques
- Consumer Motivation in Fashion
- Costume Design for Film
- Fabric & Fiber Technology

INTERNSHIPS

Not required

STUDY ABROAD

Since 1998, through the Sister City Scholarship Exchange Program, the University awards scholarships to fashion students to study at two of the best fashion schools in Paris: Studio Berçot and L'Ecole de la Chambre Syndicale de la Couture Parisienne.

NOTABLE ALUMNI

Hanii Yoon (Y & Kei); Jill Giordano (gr. dano); Sara Shepherd (Sara Shepherd)

STUDENT ACTIVITIES AND ORGANIZATIONS

The student fashion club, "Beyond the Front Row," promotes community service, provides social activities, and functions as a professional network for all university students interested in fashion, the fashion industry, and linking fashion to community service/charity.

FACULTY SPECIALIZATIONS AND RESEARCH

Gladys Perint Palmer (GPP), Executive Director of Fashion, is a working journalist and illustrator. In 1998, The Fashion Book (Phaidon Press) named GPP one of 500 people of influence in fashion since 1860.

Simon Ungless, Director of Fashion, graduated from Central St. Martins School of Art and Design in 1992 and was awarded the prestigious MA Degree in Fashion with Distinction. Ungless collaborated with Alexander McQueen on the first 10 collections shown in London and New York.

Sharon Murphy, Director of Fashion Merchandising, held management positions in product development, sourcing, manufacturing, and fashion retailing. She worked for Esprit de Corp on domestic and international levels with a focus on the development of fabrics and apparel for contemporary, junior, and children's markets.

Ellen Sears, Director of Online Fashion, has experience in store operations, merchandising, profitability improvement and team building at such companies as Macy's, Burberry, The Limited, and Jones Apparel Group.

SCHOLARSHIPS / FINANCIAL AID

Academy of Art University offers financial aid packages consisting of grants, loans, and work-study to eligible students with a demonstrated need. Explore which aid packages are available to you to help make your dreams come true, options include: federal and state aid, Federal Work Study, Veterans Affairs/Yellow Ribbon education benefits, private lenders' loans, scholarships, and tax credits. Low-interest loans are available to all eligible students, regardless of need.

The Art Institute of California—Inland Empire

Department of Fashion Design & Fashion Retail Management

674 E. Brier Dr., Suite 221, San Bernardino, CA 92408 | 909-915-2189 | www.artinstitutes.edu/inland-empire/

UNIVERSITY PROFILE
Private
Urban
Commuter
Quarter Schedule
Co-ed

STUDENT DEMOGRAPHICS
Undergraduate: 1,450
Graduate: n/a

Male: Not reported
Female: Not reported

Full-time: Not reported
Part-time: Not reported

EXPENSES
Tuition: $29,000
Room & Board: Not reported

ADMISSIONS
674 E. Brier Dr.
San Bernardino, CA 92408
909-915-2100

DEGREE INFORMATION

Major / Degree / Concentration	Enrollment	Requirements for entry	Graduation rate
Fashion & Retail Management Bachelor of Science	Not reported	Not reported	Not reported
Fashion Design Bachelor of Fine Arts	Not reported	Not reported	Not reported

TOTAL PROGRAM ENROLLMENT
Undergraduate: Not reported
Graduate: Not reported

Male: Not reported
Female: Not reported

Full-time: Not reported
Part-time: Not reported
Online: Not reported

International: Not reported
Minority: Not reported

Job Placement Rate: Not reported

SCHOLARSHIPS / FINANCIAL AID
Not reported

TOTAL FACULTY: NOT REPORTED
Full-time: Not reported
Part-time: Not reported

FASHION ADMINISTRATION
Sherry W., Academic Director Fashion Programs (Chair)
Jonathan DeAscentis, Dean of Academic Affairs
Emam El Hout, President

PROFESSIONAL / ACADEMIC AFFILIATIONS
International Textile and Apparel Association
Fashion Group International

PROGRAM DESCRIPTION AND PHILOSOPHY

The Bachelor of Science degree program in Fashion & Retail Management is a twelve-quarter program that will offer experience across disciplines in business, fashion, and design, covering both soft and hard lines. This cross-functional focus is designed to allow students to expand beyond traditional fashion design positions and choose among entry-level options in manufacturing, design, and retailing. The content of the curriculum includes fashion industry trends and manufacturing, general business management, operations and compliance, retailing, marketing, advertising, and design. Students will have the opportunity to learn how to effectively bridge the gap between designers and the retail market. They will be required to both identify and anticipate fashion trends, as well as to develop the decision-making skills needed to insure that the preferred consumer goods are in stock at the appropriate time.

The Bachelor of Fine Arts degree program in Fashion Design is designed to emphasize innovation and creativity in fashion. Courses are designed to prepare students to take an idea from the planning stage through the construction process to the finished garment. Students move on to the development of collections with opportunities to present their creativity in fashion shows and competitions. Students critique their ideas and creations as art, as a fashion statement, and as a marketable garment. An objective of the Bachelor of Fine Arts in Fashion Design degree program is to help students obtain a fundamental grounding in fashion design, an introduction to the theory and practice of draping, pattern drafting, construction and sewing, fashion illustration, and creative design. These skills are enhanced through computerized patternmaking and design hardware and software systems. Advanced courses provide students with the opportunity to focus on surface design and select a professional direction in men's, women's, children's, or accessory design. The program is designed to introduce professional skills as well as technical knowledge.

FACILITIES

Computer labs, fashion sewing labs, Gerber Technology room, Wet rooms for printing, lecture rooms, life drawing rooms, outstanding art library, art gallery.

ONLINE / DISTANCE LEARNING

Not reported

COURSES OF INSTRUCTION

- Fashion Illustration
- Early History of Fashion Trends & Forecasting
- Technical Design
- Fit Analysis
- Draping
- Textiles
- Sales and Event Promotion
- Elements of Retail Operations and Technology
- Store Planning and Lease Management
- Introduction to Manufacturing
- Business & Copyright Law
- Principles of Accounting
- International Marketing and Buying
- Media Planning and Buying
- Leadership and Team Building
- Web Marketing for Fashion and Retail Management

INTERNSHIPS

Required of majors at Junior level.

STUDY ABROAD

Available

NOTABLE ALUMNI

Not reported

STUDENT ACTIVITIES AND ORGANIZATIONS

Fashion clubs, department newsletters, and community fashion shows for scholarship fundraisers

FACULTY SPECIALIZATIONS AND RESEARCH

Costume, design, patternmaking, CAD, Visual Merchandising, Marketing, Fashion Design, Apparel Construction, Manufacturing and Product Development

The Art Institute of California—San Francisco

Department of Fashion Design & Department of Fashion Marketing & Management

1170 Market St., San Francisco, CA 94102 | 415-276-6793 | www.artinstitutes.edu/sanfrancisco

UNIVERSITY PROFILE
Private
Urban
Commuter
Quarter Schedule
Co-ed

STUDENT DEMOGRAPHICS
Undergraduate: 1,500
Graduate: 25

Male: 51%
Female: 49%

Full-time: Not reported
Part-time: Not reported

EXPENSES
Tuition: Not reported
Room & Board: Not reported

ADMISSIONS
Office of Admissions
1170 Market St.
San Francisco, CA 94102
415-276-1078

DEGREE INFORMATION

Major / Degree / Concentration	Enrollment	Requirements for entry	Graduation rate
Fashion Design Associate of Applied Science	25	Not reported	Not reported
Fashion Design Bachelor of Fine Arts Fashion Marketing Associate of Applied Science	100	Not reported	Not reported
Fashion Marketing & Management Bachelor of Arts		Not reported	Not reported

TOTAL PROGRAM ENROLLMENT
Undergraduate: Not reported
Graduate: Not reported

Male: 51%
Female: 49%

Full-time: Not reported
Part-time: Not reported
Online: Not reported

International: Not reported
Minority: Not reported

Job Placement Rate: 90%

SCHOLARSHIPS / FINANCIAL AID
We have a student financial services
staff of 16 full-time people who do
nothing else but help our students
with financial aid. We offer some
scholarships, some competitive, and we
help students identify others.

TOTAL FACULTY: 134
Full-time: 35%
Part-time: 99%

FASHION ADMINISTRATION
Bo Breda, Academic Director Fashion
  Design
Angella Hoffman, Academic Director
  Fashion Marketing and Management

PROFESSIONAL / ACADEMIC AFFILIATIONS
International Textile and Apparel
  Association
Fashion Group International

PROGRAM DESCRIPTION AND PHILOSOPHY

Our focus is on the skills necessary for entry-level employment in today's clothing industry. We cover technical, design, and life skills needed for good communication in a world-wide business.

FACILITIES

We are a technically focused school, so state of the art equipment and software of all kinds is available to students. The fashion labs are modeled on industry design rooms, so all of the equipment is the same as is used by professionals. We have a fine library on campus with a great deal of specialized collections for our major areas and we are next door to the San Francisco Public Library, one of the best on the west coast. Also we are close to the DeYoung Museum which has a spectacular textiles and fashion collection. It is the base for the Textile Arts Council. We are near the Rock and Roll Museum, the Yerba Buena Center, MOMA, and many other internationally known cultural institutions.

ONLINE / DISTANCE LEARNING

Not available

COURSES OF INSTRUCTION

Fashion Design BFA:
- Fundamentals of Observational Drawing
- Fundamentals of Design
- Fundamentals of Construction
- Introduction to the Fashion Industry
- Color Theory
- Textiles
- Fundamentals of Patternmaking
- Apparel Marketing
- Computer Applications
- Fashion Illustration
- History of Fashion I
- Intermediate Construction
- Manufacturing Concepts
- Advanced Fashion Illustration
- History of Fashion II
- Draping
- Intermediate Patternmaking
- Visual Language and Culture
- Technical Drawing
- Basic Bodice
- Pattern Details
- Trends and Concepts
- Computerized Patternmaking
- Applied Construction
- Production Processes
- Career Development
- Computerized Grading/Markers
- Portfolio Prep
- Surface Design
- Current Designers
- Advanced Draping
- Line Development
- Fashion Show Production
- Screen Printing
- Computer Design
- Costume Construction
- Production Systems
- Wovens
- Knits
- Couture
- Applied Computer Design
- Costume Design
- Product Development
- Portfolio

INTERNSHIPS

Required of majors. We have a Career Services staff of seven people who work full-time placing our students in both internships and regular employment. The list of companies is too long and changes all the time. We place people both in our city and in other major fashion centers around the country. In San Francisco, Byer USA and Nordstrom are two companies that regularly use many of our students at the same time.

STUDY ABROAD

We offer a variety of opportunities, some are full-quarter study trips where courses are taken for credit at the city visited. Some are shorter trips often given during the breaks between quarters. Some are in Europe, some in the Far East.

NOTABLE ALUMNI

Not reported

STUDENT ACTIVITIES AND ORGANIZATIONS

We have a string of student clubs in all majors. For our students in particular, the Fashion Marketing club is very active and both design and marketing majors are members. Our annual fashion show is the best in this city and we also partner with various non-profits in the area during the year to create other smaller shows.

FACULTY SPECIALIZATIONS AND RESEARCH

Costume design, contemporary fiber art including using light sources in textiles, African textiles and beadwork, industrial practice in textiles and knit construction, ecologically sensitive textile manufacturing and dyeing practice, recycled materials, etc.

The Art Institute of California—Sunnyvale

Department of Fashion Marketing & Management

1120 Kifer Rd., Sunnyvale, CA 94086 | 408-962-6400 | 1-866-583-7961 | www.artinstitutes.edu/sunnyvale

UNIVERSITY PROFILE
Private
Suburban
Residential & Commuter
Quarter Schedule
Co-ed

STUDENT DEMOGRAPHICS
Undergraduate: 650+
Graduate: n/a

Male: Not reported
Female: Not reported

Full-time: Not reported
Part-time: Not reported

EXPENSES
Tuition: Not reported
Room & Board: Not reported

ADMISSIONS
1120 Kifer Rd.
Sunnyvale, CA 94086
408-962-6400
1-866-583-7961

DEGREE INFORMATION

Major / Degree / Concentration	Enrollment	Requirements for entry	Graduation rate
Fashion Marketing & Management Bachelor of Science	100	Not reported	Not reported

TOTAL PROGRAM ENROLLMENT
Undergraduate: >100
Graduate: n/a

Male: Not reported
Female: Not reported

Full-time: Not reported
Part-time: Not reported
Online: Not reported

International: Not reported
Minority: Not reported

Job Placement Rate: Not reported

SCHOLARSHIPS / FINANCIAL AID
Not reported

TOTAL FACULTY: 10
Full-time: Not reported
Part-time: Not reported

FASHION ADMINISTRATION
Jinah Oh, Academic Director

PROFESSIONAL / ACADEMIC AFFILIATIONS
Fashion Group International

PROGRAM DESCRIPTION AND PHILOSOPHY

The Fashion Marketing & Management Bachelor's degree program at The Art Institute of California – Sunnyvale combines business practices with creativity to prepare students for a wide variety of entry-level management positions. Emphasis is placed on the applied approach of providing practical experiences through team and individual projects while maintaining contact with current industry standards and instilling ethical and professional standards of behavior within the fashion industry.

FACILITIES

Computer labs, state-of-the-art software and equipment

ONLINE / DISTANCE LEARNING

Not reported

COURSES OF INSTRUCTION

- Retail Buying
- Brand Marketing
- Entrepreneurship
- Visual Merchandising
- Specialty Merchandise
- Retailing
- Product Development

INTERNSHIPS

Opportunities available after 2nd year.

STUDY ABROAD

Available

NOTABLE ALUMNI

Not reported

STUDENT ACTIVITIES AND ORGANIZATIONS

Not reported

FACULTY SPECIALIZATIONS AND RESEARCH

Not reported

California College of the Arts

Fashion Design Program

1111 Eighth St., San Francisco, CA 94107 | 415-703-9563 | www.cca.edu/academics/fashion-design

UNIVERSITY PROFILE
Private
Urban
Commuter
Semester Schedule
Co-ed

STUDENT DEMOGRAPHICS
Undergraduate: 1,400
Graduate: 425

Male: 39%
Female: 61%

Full-time: n/a
Part-time: Not reported

EXPENSES
Tuition: $32,000
Room & Board: $6,800

ADMISSIONS
80 Carolina
San Francisco, CA 94107
800.447.1ART
enroll@cca.edu

DEGREE INFORMATION

Major / Degree / Concentration	Enrollment	Requirements for entry	Graduation rate
Fashion Design Bachelor of Fine Arts	70+	3.1 gpa and portfolio review	80%

TOTAL PROGRAM ENROLLMENT
Undergraduate: 70
Graduate: n/a

Male: 10%
Female: 90%

Full-time: 95%
Part-time: 5%
Online: n/a

International: 25%
Minority: 20%

Job Placement Rate: Not reported

SCHOLARSHIPS / FINANCIAL AID
The college gives approximately 75% of its students some level of financial aid, need scholarship and merit scholarships. Scholarships are awarded through the financial aid offices. Merit Scholarships are awarded through price competition programs.

Students receiving Scholarships or Financial Aid: 40%

TOTAL FACULTY: 14
Full-time: 4
Part-time: 10

FASHION ADMINISTRATION
Amy Williams, Chair
Kerry Gould, Program Manager
Leslie Becker, Director of Design Programs

PROFESSIONAL / ACADEMIC AFFILIATIONS
International Textile and Apparel Association
Fashion Group International

PROGRAM DESCRIPTION AND PHILOSOPHY

California College of the Art's Fashion Design Program's sustainable design practice, innovative conceptual development, and interdisciplinary curriculum spark new approaches to an established profession. The college's program inspires young designers who will ignite change in the global fashion industry.

FACILITIES

Computer labs -MAC + PC, all with wacom tablets, rapid prototyping lab, knit studios, textile dye/weave studios, industrial sewing machinery, cutting tables, and seam bonding machinery

ONLINE / DISTANCE LEARNING

Not available

COURSES OF INSTRUCTION

- Sustainable Seminar
- Sustainable Design
- Conceptual Design
- Fashion Illustration 1-3
- History of Fashion
- Fashion Studio 1-5
- Introduction to Knitwear
- Fashion Textiles
- Elements of Business

INTERNSHIPS

Not required, but students have interned at companies such as outerwear manufacturers, contemporary women's and children's design houses.

STUDY ABROAD

Mobility semesters are offered in Paris, Geneva, Mexico, Guatemala, Tokyo

NOTABLE ALUMNI

Amy Sarabi, Andrew Hague, Caroline Preibe, Karina Michel, James Edwards, Sam Formo

STUDENT ACTIVITIES AND ORGANIZATIONS

Fraternal organization, international student organizations, gay alliance

FACULTY SPECIALIZATIONS AND RESEARCH

Costume/textile curation, personal tailoring, knitwear design, sustainable practice professor/author, fashion designer/entrepreneurs

California State University, Fresno

Department of Child, Family & Consumer Sciences

5300 N. Campus Dr., M/S FF12, Fresno, CA 93740 | 559-278-2283 | http://cfcs.jcast.csufresno.edu/

UNIVERSITY PROFILE
Public
Urban
Commuter
Semester Schedule
Co-ed

STUDENT DEMOGRAPHICS
Undergraduate: 18,216
Graduate: 2,424

Male: 41%
Female: 59%

Full-time: 81%
Part-time: 19%

EXPENSES
Tuition: $11,160
Room & Board: $3,822

ADMISSIONS
5150 North Maple
Fresno, CA 93740
559-278-2261
graduateadmissions@listserv.
csufresno.edu

DEGREE INFORMATION

Major / Degree / Concentration	Enrollment	Requirements for entry	Graduation rate
Family & Consumer Sciences Bachelor of Arts Fashion Merchandising	60	Not reported	Not reported

TOTAL PROGRAM ENROLLMENT
Undergraduate: 60
Graduate: 0

Male: 1%
Female: 99%

Full-time: 95%
Part-time: 5%
Online: 0%

International: 0%
Minority: 50%

Job Placement Rate: Not reported

SCHOLARSHIPS / FINANCIAL AID
Not reported

TOTAL FACULTY: 2
Full-time: 100%
Part-time: 0%

FASHION ADMINISTRATION
Not reported

PROFESSIONAL / ACADEMIC AFFILIATIONS
International Textile and Apparel
Association

PROGRAM DESCRIPTION AND PHILOSOPHY

The fashion merchandising program focuses on preparing students with basic knowledge and skills for a wide variety of careers related with buying and selling fashion goods.

FACILITIES

Textile lab; display windows

ONLINE / DISTANCE LEARNING

Not available

COURSES OF INSTRUCTION

- Textile Science
- Fashion Merchandising Fundamentals
- Social and Psychological Aspects of Clothing
- Fashion Merchandising
- Fashion Retail Buying
- Textile/Apparel Economics
- Visual Display
- History of Costume
- Global Perspectives on Fashion
- Career Development and Preparation
- Fashion Study Tours

INTERNSHIPS

Not required

STUDY ABROAD

Available

NOTABLE ALUMNI

Not reported

STUDENT ACTIVITIES AND ORGANIZATIONS

Fashion Merchandising student club: Fashion Inc.

FACULTY SPECIALIZATIONS AND RESEARCH

Some of the faculty research interests include consumer perceived value (CPV), shopping behavior, as well as social and cultural aspects of consumption.

California State University, Long Beach

Department of Family & Consumer Sciences

1250 Bellflower Blvd., Long Beach, CA 90840 | 562-985-4404 | www.csulb.edu/colleges/chhs/departments/fcs/

STUDENT DEMOGRAPHICS
Undergraduate: 35,000
Graduate: 10,000

Male: 45%
Female: 55%

Full-time: 90%
Part-time: 10%

EXPENSES
Tuition: $3,392
Room & Board: Varies

ADMISSIONS
1250 Bellflower Blvd
Long Beach, CA 90840
562-985-5471
csulb.edu/administration

DEGREE INFORMATION

Major / Degree / Concentration	Enrollment	Requirements for entry	Graduation rate
Family & Consumer Sciences Bachelor of Arts Fashion Merchandising & Design	450	Not reported	95%
Family & Consumer Sciences Bachelor of Arts Textiles & Clothing	150	Not reported	95%

TOTAL PROGRAM ENROLLMENT
Undergraduate: 600
Graduate: 10

Male: 10%
Female: 90%

Full-time: 95%
Part-time: 5%
Online: 0%

International: 10%
Minority: 70%

Job Placement Rate: 70%

SCHOLARSHIPS / FINANCIAL AID
Mary Kefgen FMD scholarship and others through the university

Students receiving Scholarships or Financial Aid: 30%

TOTAL FACULTY: 10
Full-time: 5
Part-time: 5

FASHION ADMINISTRATION
Dr. Wendy Reiboldt, Chair
Dr. Suzanne Marshall, Fashion Merchandising and Design Director

PROFESSIONAL / ACADEMIC AFFILIATIONS
International Textile and Apparel Association
American Collegiate Retailing Association

PROGRAM DESCRIPTION AND PHILOSOPHY

Fashion show each spring with over 200 designs. New York Fashion Tours in January, Europe in summer.

FACILITIES

Various labs

ONLINE / DISTANCE LEARNING

Not reported

COURSES OF INSTRUCTION

- Global Sourcing for the Fashion Industry
- Fashion Promotion
- Buying 1 & 2
- Internship

INTERNSHIPS

Required of majors at the Senior level. Interns are typically placed at companies such as Orange County surf companies and LA design companies, plus the California Mart.

STUDY ABROAD

Available

NOTABLE ALUMNI

Phillip Lim

STUDENT ACTIVITIES AND ORGANIZATIONS

Students in Fashion

FACULTY SPECIALIZATIONS AND RESEARCH

3D imaging, consumer behavior, women's leadership

California State University, Sacramento

Department of Family & Consumer Sciences

6000 J St., Sacrameto, CA 95819-6053 | 916-278-6393 | www.asn.csus.edu/facs/

UNIVERSITY PROFILE

Public
Urban
Residential & Commuter
Semester Schedule
Co-ed

STUDENT DEMOGRAPHICS

Undergraduate: Not reported
Graduate: Not reported

Male: Not reported
Female: Not reported

Full-time: Not reported
Part-time: Not reported

EXPENSES

Tuition: $2,483
Room & Board: $3,000

ADMISSIONS

6000 J. St.
Sacramento, CA 95819
916-278-6011
jbrenner@csus.edu

DEGREE INFORMATION

Major / Degree / Concentration	Enrollment	Requirements for entry	Graduation rate
Family & Consumer Sciences Bachelor of Arts Apparel Marketing & Design	145	2.0 gpa	95%

TOTAL PROGRAM ENROLLMENT

Undergraduate: 145
Graduate: 0

Male: 10%
Female: 90%

Full-time: 95%
Part-time: 5%
Online: 0%

International: 1%
Minority: 40%

Job Placement Rate: 65%

SCHOLARSHIPS / FINANCIAL AID

M. Catherine Starr Scholarship $500
The Textiles, Clothing, and
Merchandising Scholarship $500
The Gail Landes Scholarship $500
The Shalita and Helen Blackburn
Scholarship $500

TOTAL FACULTY: 3

Full-time: 67%
Part-time: 33%

FASHION ADMINISTRATION

Judi Brenner, Administrative Support
Coordinator
Carolann Forseth, Instructional Support
Assistant

PROFESSIONAL / ACADEMIC AFFILIATIONS

International Textile and Apparel
Association

PROGRAM DESCRIPTION AND PHILOSOPHY

The Apparel Marketing and Design concentration prepares students for careers in the field of apparel, including design, manufacturing, distribution, marketing, and consumption. The program emphasizes the contemporary and historical ways of meeting the economic, physiological, psychological, and sociological needs of consumers relative to apparel and textile products.

FACILITIES

Sewing lab, costume collection gallery, computer labs

ONLINE / DISTANCE LEARNING

Not available

COURSES OF INSTRUCTION

- Textiles
- Fundamentals of Apparel Production
- Quality Analysis: Apparel
- History of Fashion
- Creative Principles of Apparel Design
- Introduction to Fashion Marketing
- Merchandise Buying
- Fashion Retailing
- Clothing, Society, and Culture

INTERNSHIPS

Not required, but students have placed at companies such as Nordstrom, Anthropologie, Macy's, Disney Land, Target, etc.

STUDY ABROAD

Available

NOTABLE ALUMNI

Not reported

STUDENT ACTIVITIES AND ORGANIZATIONS

Student fashion association (SFA)

FACULTY SPECIALIZATIONS AND RESEARCH

Cross-culture studies on consumer behavior and consumer psychology, international trade; post-purchase consumer behavior, mood regulatory consumption, retail environments, customer loyalty, and social psychological aspects of dress

City College of San Francisco

Fashion Department

50 Phelan Ave., L131, San Francisco, CA 94112 | 415-239-3224 | www.ccsf.edu/fashion

UNIVERSITY PROFILE
Public
Urban
Commuter
Semester Schedule
Co-ed

STUDENT DEMOGRAPHICS
Undergraduate: 36,000
Graduate: 0

Male: 47%
Female: 53%

Full-time: 15%
Part-time: 85%

EXPENSES
Tuition: $0
Room & Board: $11,683

ADMISSIONS
50 Phelan Ave., E107
San Francisco, CA 94112
415-239-3285

DEGREE INFORMATION

Major / Degree / Concentration	Enrollment	Requirements for entry	Graduation rate
Fashion Merchandising Certificate of Achievement	400	Open enrollment	95%
Fashion Design Certificate of Achievement	200	Open enrollment	90%

TOTAL PROGRAM ENROLLMENT
Undergraduate: 36,000
Graduate: 0

Male: 47%
Female: 53%

Full-time: 15%
Part-time: 85%
Online: 3%

International: 2%
Minority: 80%

Job Placement Rate: 95%

SCHOLARSHIPS / FINANCIAL AID
Student Financial Resources are available through Financial Aid, CalWorks and EOPS. Together they serve students who need assistance in meeting the basic cost of their education.

Students receiving Scholarships or Financial Aid: 30%

TOTAL FACULTY: 2,000
Full-time: 40%
Part-time: 60%

FASHION ADMINISTRATION
Diane Green, Fashion Department Chair

PROFESSIONAL / ACADEMIC AFFILIATIONS
Fashion Group International

PROGRAM DESCRIPTION AND PHILOSOPHY

The Fashion Department offers both credit and non-credit courses in Fashion Merchandising and Fashion Design for students who plan to transfer, or enrich their professional and/or personal lives. The Fashion Program is a comprehensive, professional program that prepares students for careers in the exiting field of fashion. Real-world industry projects and work-based learning are emphasized to ensure students develop marketable skills using the most current technology.

Throughout the program, theoretical and technical knowledge is integrated with skill development in communication, problem solving and team work to provide the necessary skills for success in the changing global fashion environment. Students gain real world experience through industry internships and develop a professional portfolio and resume to assist in the transition from school to work.

Courses are available in the day and evening, rotating each semester, enabling students to complete a certificate or degree while working part or full-time. The Program is not limited to direct vocational training.

FACILITIES
All of the above

ONLINE / DISTANCE LEARNING
Not available

COURSES OF INSTRUCTION
- Introduction to the Fashion Industry
- Textiles
- Fashion Illustration

INTERNSHIPS
Required of majors. Interns are typically placed at companies such as Gap, Levi Strauss, Saks Fifth Ave., Gucci, Prada, Chanel

STUDY ABROAD
Semester in Paris available in general education class

NOTABLE ALUMNI
Durard Guion, Men's fashion director, Macy's
Theresa Spiers, GM, Neiman Marcus
Natalie Smith, Manager, Macy's special productions

STUDENT ACTIVITIES AND ORGANIZATIONS
Not reported

FACULTY SPECIALIZATIONS AND RESEARCH
All faculty are currently working in the fashion field

COMMUNITY COLLEGE TRANSFERS
Merchandising students successfully transfer to both private and public four-year school where they may pursue a Bachelor's degree. Students typically transfer to private design schools like Otis, Parsons, and the Academy of Art University, which articulates our fashion design certificate so that students may enter as juniors.

Typical public educational institutions include the Fashion Institute of Technology, San Francisco State University, and the University of California.

College of Alameda

Apparel Design & Merchandising Program

555 Ralph Appezzato Memorial Parkway, Alameda, CA 94501 | 510-748-2102 | http://adamcoa.com

UNIVERSITY PROFILE
Public
Urban
Commuter
Semester Schedule
Co-ed

STUDENT DEMOGRAPHICS
Undergraduate: 5,500
Graduate: n/a

Male: 44%
Female: 56%

Full-time: 21%
Part-time: 79%

EXPENSES
Tuition: $1,144
Room & Board: n/a

ADMISSIONS
College of Alameda
555 Ralph Appezzato
Memorial Parkway
Alameda, CA 94501
510-466-7368

DEGREE INFORMATION

	Enrollment	Requirements for entry	Graduation rate
Apparel Design & Merchandising Associate of Arts	175	High school graduate or equivalent	90%
Apparel Design & Merchandising Certificate of Completion	Not reported	High school graduate or equivalent	Not reported

TOTAL PROGRAM ENROLLMENT
Undergraduate: 125
Graduate: 50

Male: 5%
Female: 95%

Full-time: 64%
Part-time: 36%
Online: n/a

International: 2%
Minority: 75%

Job Placement Rate: 50%

SCHOLARSHIPS / FINANCIAL AID
Fees at all California Community Colleges have risen, but there are many aid programs to fit a variety of circumstances. Students are encouraged to stop by a Financial Aid Office located on campus to obtain information and necessary application forms to receive student Financial Assistance. The ADAM Program has small scholarship awards given to second-year students according to academic achievement.

Students receiving Scholarships or Financial Aid: 40%

TOTAL FACULTY: 4
Full-time: 50%
Part-time: 50%

FASHION ADMINISTRATION
OJ Roundtree, Department Chair
Derek Piazza, Contract Faculty

PROFESSIONAL / ACADEMIC AFFILIATIONS
Not reported

PROGRAM DESCRIPTION AND PHILOSOPHY

Apparel Design and Merchandising (ADAM) courses offer basic and advanced technical skills training which reflects current industry technology and changing fashion trends. Individual ADAM courses are complete units of instruction in each subject area and may be taken either for credit or for non credit by a student interested in a single subject. Students interested in pursuing a career focused on design and manufacturing may earn a Two Year Certificate of Completion in Apparel Design and Merchandising. Students may also obtain an Associate in Arts Degree which requires additional liberal arts courses and may be taken concurrently with the certificate courses. The ADAM Program provides students with a stable curriculum that offers some flexibility in scheduling and is cost affordable. ADAM offers a day program which can be completed in a two-year period with full-time attendance. In addition, the class schedule allows students with jobs/careers and family obligations to pursue and achieve their educational goals. ADAM offers computer training in the areas of technical pattern design/modification, size-grading, and marker-making with the aid of the Gerber Computer System. Additional computer courses include instruction using Adobe Illustrator CS3 Suite for concept development and portfolio presentation. This computer/software training gives ADAM students a competitive edge over other apparel design programs which lack courses and technical equipment in this area as well as meets the current trends of the apparel industry and future career opportunities.

FACILITIES

- ADAM Program courses using Gerber and Adobe CS3 technology/software
- San Francisco Garment District/Mart
- Various Museums/San Fransico/Oakland / Berkeley
- Various Apparel Design and Production Companies
- Various Retail Businesses

ONLINE / DISTANCE LEARNING
Not available

COURSES OF INSTRUCTION

- Apparel Design
- Apparel Sketching
- Pattern Drafting
- Pattern Draping
- Apparel Construction
- Sample Making
- Costing Analysis
- Marketing
- Size Grading
- Marker Making
- Textile Identification
- History of Apparel
- Production Operations
- Computer Design/Production

INTERNSHIPS
Not required, but students have placed at companies such as:
- Levi Strauss, Inc.
- Gymboree
- The Northface Company
- Two Star Dog
- Erica Tanov
- Byer Company
- Jessica Mcclintock
- Biscotti
- Mountain Hardwear
- Verrieres & Sako
- San Francisco Opera
- Ocelot Clothing

STUDY ABROAD
Not available

NOTABLE ALUMNI
Stella Carakasi, Designer/Owner Two Star Dog/Berkeley, CA Women's Casual Wear/Multi Million Dollar Global Business

STUDENT ACTIVITIES AND ORGANIZATIONS
College of Alameda campus clubs and organizations

FACULTY SPECIALIZATIONS AND RESEARCH
Not reported

COMMUNITY COLLEGE TRANSFERS
Currently six courses are university certified for UCA transfer credit: Apparel Textiles; Apparel History; Design and Sketching I; Design and Sketching II; Apparel Construction I; Apparel Construction II

Cuesta College

Department of Fashion Design & Merchandising

Highway 1, San Luis Obispo, CA 93401 | 805-546-3100 ext. 2762 | www.cuesta.edu

UNIVERSITY PROFILE
Public
Suburban
Commuter
Semester Schedule
Co-ed

STUDENT DEMOGRAPHICS
Undergraduate: 10,500
Graduate: Not reported

Male: Not reported
Female: Not reported

Full-time: Not reported
Part-time: Not reported

EXPENSES
Tuition: depends on units
Room & Board: Not reported

ADMISSIONS
PO Box 8106
San Luis Obsipo, CA 93401
805-546-3140

DEGREE INFORMATION

Major / Degree / Concentration	Enrollment	Requirements for entry	Graduation rate
Fashion Design Associate of Arts	Varies	High school graduate	Varies
Fashion Associate of Arts Merchandising	Varies	High school graduate	Varies
Fashion Design Certificate of Achievement	Varies	High school graduate	Varies
Fashion Merchandising Certificate of Achievement	Varies	High school graduate	Varies

TOTAL PROGRAM ENROLLMENT
Undergraduate: 200
Graduate: Not reported

Male: Not reported
Female: Not reported

Full-time: 10%
Part-time: 90%
Online: Not reported

International: Not reported
Minority: Not reported

Job Placement Rate: Unknown

SCHOLARSHIPS / FINANCIAL AID
Cuesta College has an on-campus
financial aid department available to all
students.

TOTAL FACULTY: 7
Full-time: Not reported
Part-time: 100%

FASHION ADMINISTRATION
Ginger Behnke, Lead Faculty

PROFESSIONAL / ACADEMIC AFFILIATIONS
Not reported

PROGRAM DESCRIPTION AND PHILOSOPHY

The Department of Fashion Design and Merchandising is a small but very dedicated department that is proud of our long history. We are always adapting classes to meet the changes in our industry and strongly encourage a hands-on learning experience. Because of our small class sizes, we give individualized attention to our students. We continue to make Cuesta Collge a fun and exciting place to learn.

FACILITIES

Clothing construction and pattern drafting lab, design, and merchandising classroom. Computer labs and library available on campus.

ONLINE / DISTANCE LEARNING

Not reported

COURSES OF INSTRUCTION

- Introduction to Fashion
- Textiles
- Design Analysis
- Apparel Evaluation
- Fashion Analysis
- Fashion Illustration
- Fashion Design 1 and 2
- Visual Merchandising
- History of Fashion
- Fashion Promotion
- Apparel Product Development
- Clothing Construction 1 and 2
- Pattern Development
- Fashion Buying

INTERNSHIPS

Not required. Interns are typically placed at local apparel manufacturers and designers.

STUDY ABROAD

Not available

NOTABLE ALUMNI

Not reported

STUDENT ACTIVITIES AND ORGANIZATIONS

Fashion Showcase Annual Event and Fashion Student Club

FACULTY SPECIALIZATIONS AND RESEARCH

Not reported

COMMUNITY COLLEGE TRANSFERS

Most classes offered are CSU and US transferrable

El Camino College

Fashion & Related Technologies

16007 Crenshaw Blvd., Torrance, CA 90506 | 831-646-4138 | www.elcamino.edu/academics/indtech/fashion/

STUDENT DEMOGRAPHICS
Undergraduate: 27,271
Graduate: 0

Male: 47.5%
Female: 52.5%

Full-time: 31.4%
Part-time: 68.5%

EXPENSES
Tuition: $26 per unit (CA residents)
Room & Board: n/a

ADMISSIONS
16007 Crenshaw Blvd.
Torrance, CA 90506
310-660-3593 x 3414
www.elcamino.edu/admissions

DEGREE INFORMATION

Major / Degree / Concentration	Enrollment	Requirements for entry	Graduation rate
Fashion Design & Production Associate of Science	Not reported	Not reported	Not reported
Fashion Merchandising Associate of Science	Not reported	Not reported	Not reported
Computer Patternmaking Technician Certificate of Achievement	Not reported	Not reported	Not reported
Costume Technician Certificate of Achievement	Not reported	Not reported	Not reported
Fashion Design & Production Certificate of Achievement	Not reported	Not reported	Not reported
Fashion Merchandising Certificate of Achievement	Not reported	Not reported	Not reported

TOTAL PROGRAM ENROLLMENT
Undergraduate: 335
Graduate: 0

Male: Not reported
Female: Not reported

Full-time: Not reported
Part-time: Not reported
Online: Not reported

International: Not reported
Minority: Not reported

Job Placement Rate: Not reported

SCHOLARSHIPS / FINANCIAL AID
General scholarships available to the entire campus.

TOTAL FACULTY: 11
Full-time: 1%
Part-time: 99%

FASHION ADMINISTRATION
Dr. Stephanie Rodriguez, Industry & Technology Dean
Dr. Tom Jackson, Industry & Technology Assistant Dean
Dr. Vera Bruce Ashley, Full-time fashion instructor

PROFESSIONAL / ACADEMIC AFFILIATIONS

International Textile and Apparel Association

PROGRAM DESCRIPTION AND PHILOSOPHY

The Fashion Department of El Camino College is an integral program in the Industry & Technology Division. Our primary goal is student success. We strive to achieve the following objectives:

- To exceed the educational needs of students entering the Fashion Department for a "first look around" or as declared Fashion Majors.
- To provide support through campus counseling and networking with industry professionals.
- To encourage teamwork and student awareness of the changing and fast-paced Fashion Industry through the campus club, "Tailor Made."
- To graduate students ready for entry-level positions within the fashion industry job market.

FACILITIES

Computer labs, classrooms with industrial sewing machines

ONLINE / DISTANCE LEARNING

Not available

COURSES OF INSTRUCTION

- Career Opportunities in Fashion
- Presentation Techniques for Fashion
- Fashion Introduction to Macintosh
- Computer Fashion Illustration
- Clothing Construction
- Clothing Construction II
- Pattern Grading
- Fashion Sketching
- Fashion Illustrating
- Decorative Textiles
- Textiles
- Fitting and Alterations
- Tailoring
- Basic Design and Patternmaking
- Basic Dress Design Through
- Draping Process
- Fashion Merchandising
- Visual Merchandising
- Computer Pattern Design/ Patternmaking
- Fashion 31
- History of Costume
- Applied Color Theory
- Advanced Apparel Pattern Making and Draping Design
- Fashion Analysis and Selection
- Fashion Show Production and Promotion
- Cooperative Career Education

INTERNSHIPS

Required of majors. Interns are typically placed at retail stores, apparel manufacturers, and costumers.

STUDY ABROAD

Not available

NOTABLE ALUMNI

Not available

STUDENT ACTIVITIES AND ORGANIZATIONS

Tailor Made Fashion Club

FACULTY SPECIALIZATIONS AND RESEARCH

Dr. Vera Bruce Ashley specializes in using Internet videoconferencing to connect fashion students to apparel industry professionals.

COMMUNITY COLLEGE TRANSFERS

We have articulation agreements with California State University campus

Fashion Careers College

1923 Morena Blvd., San Diego, CA 92110 | 619-275-4700 | www.fashioncareerscollege.com

UNIVERSITY PROFILE
Private
Urban
Commuter
Quarter Schedule
Co-ed

STUDENT DEMOGRAPHICS
Undergraduate: 110
Graduate: n/a

Male: 16%
Female: 84%

Full-time: 100%
Part-time: Not reported

EXPENSES
Tuition: $19,900
Room & Board: n/a

ADMISSIONS
1923 Morena Blvd.
San Diego, CA 92110
619-275-4700 ext.328
Info@fashioncareerscollege.
com

DEGREE INFORMATION

Major / Degree / Concentration	Enrollment	Requirements for entry	Graduation rate
Fashion Design & Technology Specialized Associate Degree	38	Completion of Application Form, Typed Essay, High School Transcript, or GED with graduation date, minimum score of 19 on the Wonderlic test, $25 non-refundable application fee	82.5%
Fashion Business & Technology Specialized Associate Degree	28	Same as above	80%
Fashion Business & Technology Hybrid-Online Certficiate Program	16	Same as above	New program
Fashion Design & Technology Certficiate Program	18	Same as above	88.9%

TOTAL PROGRAM ENROLLMENT
Undergraduate: 110
Graduate: n/a

Male: 16%
Female: 84%

Full-time: 100%
Part-time: n/a
Online: 13%

International: 1%
Minority: 30%

Job Placement Rate: 80%

SCHOLARSHIPS / FINANCIAL AID
FCC has been certified by the U.S. Department of Education for participation in the following programs: Federal Pell Grant; CAL Grant; the Federal Supplemental Educational Opportunity Grant (FSEOG); Federal

Work Study (FWS); Subsidized and Unsubsidized Stafford Loans; PLUS Loans; Direct Loans; VA Loans; and Meritorious Scholarships. FCC awards private scholarships for perfect attendance and Grade Point Average.

TOTAL FACULTY: 17
Full-time: n/a
Part-time: 100%

FASHION ADMINISTRATION
Pat O'Connor, CEO/Founder/Chairman of the Board
Judy Thacker, President/CAO
Andrew Bisaha, Vice President/CFO
Susan Suarez, Director of Education/COO

PROFESSIONAL / ACADEMIC AFFILIATIONS
Fashion Group International

PROGRAM DESCRIPTION AND PHILOSOPHY

Fashion Careers College offers a Specialized Associates Degree in both Fashion Design and Technology and Fashion Business and Technology. Both of these degree programs include general education courses. The degree programs last about 18 months and contain approximately 95 quarter credits with 15 of the credits in general education. The programs' objectives are to provide students with a fundamental grounding in fashion design and fashion business including an introduction to theory and practice. FCC also offers certificates in Fashion Design and Technology and Fashion Business and Technology Hybrid-Online. These certificate programs last approximately 16 months and contain approximately 50 quarter credits. FCC seeks to impart a large body of fashion-related theory and information augmented by general education skills and knowledge from the students' participation in special workshops, elective tracks, courses, fashion tours, internships, volunteer work, and counseling. Students should expect that their FCC education will equip them with skills for adult life and a fashion career.

FACILITIES

FCC has an on-campus library, a computer lab with Photoshop & Illustrator programs, a Lectra Systems Patternmaking CAD Center, two design studio labs with industrial design-room equipment and machines, and campus-wide WIFI.

ONLINE / DISTANCE LEARNING

FCC offers a Certificate in Fashion Business and Technology Hybrid-Online that combines a selection of first- and second-year courses from the Degree program. The certificate program lasts approximately 16 months and contains 46.5 quarter credits required for completion. 50% of the courses are offered online with the other 50% offered in FCC's residential classrooms.

COURSES OF INSTRUCTION

Fashion Business Major:
- Principles of Merchandise Math
- Textile Science
- Fashion Forecasting
- Contemporary Buying
- Advertising and Promotion Essentials
- Import/Export

Fashion Design Major:
- Fashion Drawing for Design
- Creative Draping
- Patternmaking 1 & 2
- Apparel Construction 1 & 2
- Fashion Portfolio
- CAD Patternmaking
- CAD Grading

INTERNSHIPS

Required of degree majors at the 2nd year of study. Internships are available at: Disguise Costumes, InCharacter Costumes, Nordstrom, Charlotte Russe, Zandra Rhodes Studio, House of Brands, Inc., Reef, DC Shoes, Bloomingdales, Saks 5th Ave., Lambs Players Theatre, San Diego Repertory Theatre, Old Globe Theatre, Ashworth Golf, No Fear, and Barbara Fields Buying Office.

STUDY ABROAD

Every other year, FCC takes a study tour to Europe which is offered as an enrichment/extracurricular opportunity and a look at fashion in various countries. Zandra Rhodes "Studies in Textiles Workshop" in London.

NOTABLE ALUMNI

Jesus Estrada/Project Runway Season 7 Contestant, Jessica Young/Copyright Editor for Macy's New York City, Tasha Beckman/Patternmaker BCBG, David Souza/Paragon Model Management (in top 3 of Mexico City's modeling agencies), Jacob McCabe/Head Designer for Commune, Chris Sachs/ Guess? Inc. Training and Development Manager, Tessa Phillips/Head Designer Japan Market J.Crew

STUDENT ACTIVITIES AND ORGANIZATIONS

FCC offers community involvement such as assisting models and cueing backstage at local fashion shows, or working as a production assistant for freelance fashion show producers. FCC offers the annual Golden Hanger Fashion Awards which is a showcase for student work and local designers. The Art of Fashion which is held in conjunction with Balboa Parks' Timken Museum of Art is an annual fundraising event in which selected design students create modern costumes to interpret the clothing worn in the Timken's collection of fine art. Twice a year, FCC holds a design competition called "Project Fashion," in which applicants compete for scholarship awards to attend FCC's degree and certificate programs. The college also offers trips to the California Market Center to visit buyer showrooms, buying offices, and the Los Angeles Garment District.

FACULTY SPECIALIZATIONS AND RESEARCH

Andrew Clausen–BA San Diego State University, Online Faculty Santa Monica Online College; Christie Dunning–BA & MFA San Diego State University, Mingei International Museum, La Jolla Fiber Arts; Wrena Mathews–AA FIDM, Patternmaker La Belle Fashions, Rampage Clothing Co; Shady Mickhail–BS Cal State Univ LA, IT Consultant, Web Communications Analyst; Marina Myers–AA FIDM, Senior Trainer Lectra Systemes; Luca Perez–BFA Pratt Inst., Graphic Web Designer; Jeanne Reith–AA SD Mesa College, Resident Costume Designer for Lambs Players Theatre; Patti O'Connor–MBA Thunderbird School of Global Management, Sr Product Manager Levi Strauss and Company; Meme Snell–BS Texas A&M University, Senior Designer Ashworth Golf, Designer/Merchandiser Reef.

Fashion Institute of Design & Merchandising

919 S. Grade Ave., Los Angeles, CA 90015 | 213-624-1200 | www.fidm.edu

UNIVERSITY PROFILE
Private
Urban
Commuter
Quarter Schedule
Co-ed

STUDENT DEMOGRAPHICS
Undergraduate: 7,500
Graduate: 0

Male: 10%
Female: 90%

Full-time: 88%
Part-time: 12%

EXPENSES
Tuition: $25,011
Room & Board: n/a

ADMISSIONS
919 S. Grand Ave
Los Angeles. CA 90015
800.624.1200
info@fidm.edu

OTHER CAMPUSES
San Francisco
San Diego
Orange County

DEGREE INFORMATION

Major / Degree / Concentration	Enrollment	Requirements for entry	Graduation rate
Apparel Industry Management Associate of Arts	Not reported	High School Diploma or GED; 3 recommendations; admissions essay	Not reported
Fashion Design Associate of Arts	604	Same as above	52.9%
Fashion Knitwear Design Associate of Arts	Not reported	Same as above	Not reported
Merchandise Marketing Associate of Arts	625	Same as above	60.5%
Merchandise Product Development Associate of Arts	600	Same as above	60.7%
Advanced Fashion Design Associate of Arts	Not reported	Prior FIDM degree in a related discipline	Not reported
International Manufacturing & Product Development Associate of Arts	Not reported	Same as above	Not reported

Also avaiable: Beauty Industry Merchandising & Marketing (A.A.); Jewelry Design (A.A.); Film & TV Costume Design (A.A.); Theatre Costume Design (A.A.); Footwear Design (A.A.); Business Management (B.S.)

TOTAL PROGRAM ENROLLMENT
Undergraduate: 7,500
Graduate: 0

Male: 10%
Female: 90%

Full-time: 88%
Part-time: 12%
Online: 1%

International: 6.6%
Minority: 38%

Job Placement Rate: Not reported

SCHOLARSHIPS / FINANCIAL AID
See opposite page for more info.

TOTAL FACULTY: 438
Full-time: 20%
Part-time: 80%

FASHION ADMINISTRATION
Tonian Hohberg, President
Barbara Bundy, Vice President of Education
Vivien Lowy, Vice President of Marketing

PROFESSIONAL / ACADEMIC AFFILIATIONS
International Textile and Apparel Association
American Apparel and Footwear Association
Fashion Group International

PROGRAM DESCRIPTION AND PHILOSOPHY

The Fashion Institute of Design and Merchandising's curriculum is intense, concentrated, and rewarding. Its purpose: preparing students for careers in the Fashion, Visual Arts, Interior Design, and Entertainment industries. FIDM challenges you to live up to your greatest potential. Our graduates enter the global market as highly trained professionals ready to make a contribution. Our curriculum has been developed, and is continually updated, to reflect the needs of each industry served by our majors. FIDM Students study real-world scenarios related to their career choices.

FACILITIES

FIDM has the largest fashion library on the West Coast with access to thousands of books, periodicals, trade publications, newspaper clipping files, trends reports, fabric swatch archives, fashion videos, and non-print reference material. The FIDM Museum and Galleries Permanent and Study Collection encompasses over 12,000 costumes, accessories, and textiles from the 18th century to the present. The museum features top designers such as Chanel, Christian Dior, and Yves St. Laurent, to name a few.

ONLINE / DISTANCE LEARNING

Merchandise Marketing Associate of Arts (Professional Designation) is offered online.

COURSES OF INSTRUCTION

Depending on the major, student take courses in Adobe Photoshop and Illustrator, Perspective Drawing, Color Theory, Creative Process, Pattern-drafting and Draping, Industrial Sewing, Technical Sketching, Textiles Science, Merchandise Strategies, Branding, and Trend Forecasting.

INTERNSHIPS

Not required but available to 2nd year students. Interns are typically placed at retail stores such as Lisa Kline Stores, Armani, and Saks Fifth Ave., Anthropologie, Burberry, local prop houses, film companies, interior design firms such as Kelly Wearstler, fashion apparel companies such as Poleci, and beauty industry companies such as Stila and Smashbox.

STUDY ABROAD

Study Tours in New York City, Rome, Paris, London, and Milan.

NOTABLE ALUMNI

Monique Lhuiller, Fashion Designer; Vani Kumar, Business Owner; Jeff Poulin, Graphic Designer; Nichols Kreglow & Stephanie Bodnar, Fashion Designers; Althea Lim, Beauty Product Developer; Michele Rose Coseo, Interior Designer; Joie Rucker, Creative Director and Line Co-Owner.

STUDENT ACTIVITIES AND ORGANIZATIONS

FIDM's unique industry connections provide a valuable network for guest speakers and field trips. Through the FIDM network, Career Connections, there is an annual opportunity for FIDM students on all four campuses to meet and interact with FIDM Alumni. Building a global network, FIDM's study tours to New York City, Rome, Paris, London, and Milan allow students to meet with top industry professionals, tour major companies, and gather inspiration from some of the world's most exciting architecture and art.

FACULTY SPECIALIZATIONS AND RESEARCH

FIDM instructors are working professionals with invaluable industry connections.

COMMUNITY COLLEGE TRANSFERS

Students who wish to explore their transfer options should consult FIDM's Articulation Officer on the Los Angeles campus for assistance. Students graduating from FIDM must complete the graduation requirements for their specific degree. FIDM requirements, however, do not necessarily meet all lower division or general education requirements for other colleges. FIDM currently maintains articulation agreements with selected colleges with the intent of enhancing a student's transfer opportunities.

SCHOLARSHIPS / FINANCIAL AID

FIDM is committed to helping students seek out all the kinds of financial aid for which they may be eligible. Various scholarships are available to students who qualify, in addition to loans and/or grants. Some are FIDM's Annual National Scholarship Competition, DECA/DEX, Distributive Education Clubs of America, FBLA/Future Business Leaders of America, FHA-HERO/Future Homemakers of America, FCCLA/Family, Career & Community Leaders of America, California Academic Decathlon, ROP/ROCP/Regional Occupational (Centers &) Programs, Phi Theta Kappa, Mentor Program, Cotton Incorporated, Fashion Club.com, PromAdvice.com, Federal Pell & SEOG Grants, Federal Perkins & Stafford Loans, Federal Plus Loan, and Cal Grants.

Students receiving Scholarships or Financial Aid: 53%

Monterey Peninsula College

Department of Fashion

980 Fremont St., Monterey, CA 93940　|　831-646-4138　|　**www.mpc.edu**

UNIVERSITY PROFILE
Public
Suburban
Commuter
Semester Schedule
Co-ed

STUDENT DEMOGRAPHICS
Undergraduate: 14,587
Graduate: n/a

Male: 48%
Female: 52%

Full-time: 16%
Part-time: 84%

EXPENSES
Tuition: $780
Room & Board: n/a

ADMISSIONS
980 Fremont St.
Monterey, CA 93940
831-646-4002
vcoleman@mpc.edu

DEGREE INFORMATION

Major / Degree / Concentration	Enrollment	Requirements for entry	Graduation rate
Fashion Design Associate of Science	25	Open enrollment	Not reported
Fashion Merchandising Associate of Science	20	Open enrollment	Not reported
Fashion Production Associate of Science	15	Open enrollment	Not reported
Fashion Costuming Associate of Science	10	Open enrollment	Not reported

TOTAL PROGRAM ENROLLMENT
Undergraduate: 70
Graduate: n/a

Male: 15%
Female: 85%

Full-time: 20%
Part-time: 80%
Online: 0%

International: 10%
Minority: 31.5%

Job Placement Rate: 25%

SCHOLARSHIPS / FINANCIAL AID
See opposite page for more info.

TOTAL FACULTY: 3
Full-time: 0%
Part-time: 100%

FASHION DESIGN ADMINISTRATION
Sunshine Giesler, Department Chair
Julie Bailey, Division Office Manager

PROFESSIONAL / ACADEMIC AFFILIATIONS
Not reported

PROGRAM DESCRIPTION AND PHILOSOPHY

The Fashion Design major at Monterey Peninsula College prepares students for entry-level positions in apparel design, fashion design, or freelance design. The program emphasizes basic principles of design, knowledge of the fashion business, presentation techniques, and computer-aided design.

The Fashion Merchandising major prepares students to enter the retail or wholesale fashion business and progress toward buying, sales, or merchandising positions. Fashion product knowledge, career pathways, and business operations are stressed in the program.

The Fashion Production major prepares students to enter the retail or wholesale fashion business with the ability to produce salable, quality merchandise. Custom design and production, as well as the business aspects of working from home as an entrepreneur, are included as topics in the program.

Costuming is an interdisciplinary program in fashion, drama, and art designed to provide students with design and sewing skills applied to costuming for the stage, film and television, and period or theme parks. Students will experience actual costume design and production for the MPC Theater.

FACILITIES

PC lab with patternmaking and design software, historic textiles collection catalogued using Past Perfect software, production lab with commercial and domestic machines.

ONLINE / DISTANCE LEARNING

Not available

COURSES OF INSTRUCTION

- Textiles
- Clothing Construction
- Apparel Analysis
- History of Fashion
- Introduction to Fashion
- Flat Pattern Design
- Couture Techniques
- Sewing Specialty Fabrics
- Tailoring
- Fitting and Pattern Alteration
- Fashion Illustration

INTERNSHIPS

Required of majors at 2nd-year level. Interns are typically placed at local custom clothiers and retail shops.

STUDY ABROAD

Not available

NOTABLE ALUMNI

Not reported

STUDENT ACTIVITIES AND ORGANIZATIONS

Student Fashion Club

FACULTY SPECIALIZATIONS AND/ OR RESEARCH

Costume and textiles history

COMMUNITY COLLEGE TRANSFERS

The transfer program enables the student to complete the first two years in preparation for transfer to a baccalaureate-granting institution. MPC courses parallel those offered to Freshman and Sophomore students at the University of California, California State University, and private colleges and universities.

SCHOLARSHIPS / FINANCIAL AID

- Federal Pell Grant: Applicants who meet all requirements will receive a Federal Pell Grant based on need and number of units in which they are enrolled. Maximum Pell Grant for 2009-2010 = $5,350.
- Federal Supplemental Educational Opportunity Grant (SEOG): Student who qualify for additional assistance may be offered an SEOG if eligible for the Pell Grant. Funds are awarded based on priority and need.
- Cal Grants: Cal Grant recipients must be California residents. The Cal Grant application is separate from the FAFSA. To apply, the FAFSA and Cal Grant GPA Verification Form must be postmarked by March 2nd or September 2rd. The Cal Grant is a competitive Grant and not all applicants receive funds. For more information, see www.csac.ca.gov.
- District Grant in Aid (DGIA): Monterey Peninsula College provides institutional grants (while funds are available) to undergraduate students who have completed less then 48 college units.
- Orr Estate Grant: Monterey Peninsula College provides institutional grants (while funds are available) to students who have completed 12 units, are enrolled full-time, and have at least a 2.0 gpa.

Students receiving Scholarships or Financial Aid: 40%

Otis College of Art & Design

Department of Fashion

110 E. 9th St., Suite C201, Los Angeles, CA 90079 | 310-665-6875 | www.otis.edu

UNIVERSITY PROFILE
Private
Urban
Commuter
Semester Schedule
Co-ed

STUDENT DEMOGRAPHICS
Undergraduate: 1,153
Graduate: 68

Male: Not reported
Female: Not reported

Full-time: Not reported
Part-time: Not reported

EXPENSES
Tuition: $31,360
Room & Board: Not reported

ADMISSIONS
9045 Lincoln Blvd.
Los Angeles, CA 90045
310-665-6826
admissions@otis.edu

DEGREE INFORMATION

Major / Degree / Concentration	Enrollment	Requirements for entry	Graduation rate
Fashion Design Bachelor of Fine Arts	200	2.5 gpa Portfolio approval	53.9%

TOTAL PROGRAM ENROLLMENT
Undergraduate: 200-225
Graduate: 0

Male: 5%
Female: 95%

Full-time: 100%
Part-time: 0%
Online: 0%

International: 64 from 14 countries
Minority: 54%

Job Placement Rate: 60%

SCHOLARSHIPS / FINANCIAL AID
Financial Aid provides assistance to all matriculated US citizen and permanent residents in financing their education. Grants, Scholarships, campus employment, loans, and Internet resources are among the methods by which students may cover all or a portion of the cost of attendance. Financial Aid awards are applied towards tuition & registration fees, material fees, parking, etc. Institutional grants & some named scholarship awards can be used to pay tuition only. Students may apply for Federal Pell Grant & Supplemental Education Opportunity Grants, Cal Grant from State of California, the Otis Institutional Grand, Federal Stafford Loans and plus (Pernt) Loans & Federal and Institutional work-study.

Students receiving Scholarships or Financial Aid: 75%

TOTAL FACULTY: 43
Full-time: 19
Part-time: 24

FASHION DESIGN ADMINISTRATION
Rosemary Brantley, Chair of Fashion Design
Jill Higashi, Assistant Chair, Design
MariBeth Baloga, Assistant Academic Chair

PROFESSIONAL / ACADEMIC AFFILIATIONS
Fashion Group International

PROGRAM DESCRIPTION AND PHILOSOPHY

Fashion students, working with professional faculty and guest design mentors, are trained in all aspects of the design process. Working in teams, they create clothing for several mentors simultaneously, emulating the fashion design studio, and following the industry's seasonal schedule. The program focuses on preparing students for professional entry into American design houses and markets as Assistant Designers. Curriculum emphasizes a practical application to fashion design rather than a theoretical and conceptual one. Students receive the necessary curricular components offered at similar leading fashion design undergraduate programs; these courses include fashion design, fashion drawing, sewing, draping, patternmaking, textile knowledge, survey of fashion history, digital studies, and business studies.

FACILITIES

Computer labs; Drawing, studio, and design labs; Fashion theatre with runway for fittings; Cutting room; On campus, Richard Martin Fashion library with extensive forecasting services and trend periodicals; Los Angeles County Central Library; Los Angeles County Museum of Art (extensive costume collection and Doris Stein Research Center), Museum of Contemporary Art, Fowler Museum; California Market Center showrooms and sponsored markets; 250 fabric and trim jobbers within walking distance; fashion shows; Proximity to manufacturers and finishers; Online demos developed by instructors; Fashion Department's working relationship with design professionals and representative of industry; Mentorships with professional designers

ONLINE / DISTANCE LEARNING

Not available

COURSES OF INSTRUCTION

- Studio
- Illustration
- Model Drawing
- Textiles
- Pattern Drafting
- Design
- Digital Design
- Marketing
- Costume History
- Apparel Manufacturing Practices
- English
- Art History
- Liberal Studies

INTERNSHIPS

Not required.

Interns are typically placed at companies such as Guess? Abercrombie & Fitch, Mattel, La Blanca/Warnaco, Lunada Bay, Nordstrom, Nike

STUDY ABROAD

Foundation level–Paris trip

NOTABLE ALUMNI

Steve McSween, 2004, Director at Sean John; Heather Brown, class of 2003, Assistant Designer at Abercrombie & Fitch, Dana Schnitman, Class of 2007, Assistant Designer, Michael Kors Collection; Tae Kim, Class of 2007, Guess?; Evelyn Choi, Class of 1996, owner of Skinny Minnie

STUDENT ACTIVITIES AND ORGANIZATIONS

Fabric fund available for students with financial need; Annual juried fashion show; The "Scholarship Benefit Show "which raises scholarship money for all majors; Portfolio Day held on campus; Student Placement Office." Inside the Designer's Studio" lecture series; "Adopt a Sophomore" program to support new students in the department"; Student Services; National Competitions

FACULTY SPECIALIZATIONS AND RESEARCH

Members of our faculty are actively involved in the fashion industry and have expertise in draping, patternmaking, design, and fashion illustration. They have years of experience in design for apparel manufacturing and retail; many of our faculty exhibit locally and internationally; freelance design for television and film; interior design and window designs for Saks, et al.; and private couture labels; draping, technical drawing.

Saddleback College

Fashion Department

28000 Margurite Parkway, Mission, CA 92692-3635 | 949-582-4949 | www.saddleback.edu/atas/Fashion

UNIVERSITY PROFILE
Public
Suburban
Commuter
Semester Schedule
Co-ed

STUDENT DEMOGRAPHICS
Undergraduate: 39,772
Graduate: 0

Male: 40%
Female: 60%

Full-time: Not reported
Part-time: Not reported

EXPENSES
Tuition: $26 per unit in state
Room & Board: n/a

ADMISSIONS
28000 Margurite Parkway
Mission Viejo, CA 92692-3635
949-582-4555

DEGREE INFORMATION

Major / Degree / Concentration	Enrollment	Requirements for entry	Graduation rate
Fashion Design Associate of Arts Associate of Science Certificate	775	Application/High School Diploma or GRE	90%
Advanced Fashion Design & Apparel Manufacturing Associate of Arts Associate of Science Certificate	19	Application/High School Diploma or GRE	84%
Fashion Merchandisng Associate of Arts Associate of Science Certificate	247	Application/High School Diploma or GRE	82%
Visual Fashion Merchandising Associate of Arts Associate of Science Certificate	23	Application/High School Diploma or GRE	87%

Also available: Basic Costume Construction & Sourcing Skills aware and Sustainable Fashion and Social Entrepreneurship Skills Award

TOTAL PROGRAM ENROLLMENT
Undergraduate: 1,064
Graduate: 0

Male: 14%
Female: 86%

Full-time: 32%
Part-time: 68%
Online: 0%

International: 6%
Minority: 51%

Job Placement Rate: 87%

SCHOLARSHIPS / FINANCIAL AID
See opposite page for more info.

TOTAL FACULTY: 15
Full-time: 20%
Part-time: 80%

FASHION DESIGN ADMINISTRATION
Lindsay Smith Fox, Fashion Department Chair

PROFESSIONAL / ACADEMIC AFFILIATIONS
International Textile and Apparel Association
Fashion Group International

PROGRAM DESCRIPTION AND PHILOSOPHY

Saddleback College is located in the heart of the surf industry, film industry, and is near Disney Land. Many of our students go on to work in the action sports area of design, manufacturing, or merchandising. Our students are also very successful in the areas of costume design and construction for both film and theater. We provide students with skills necessary to start own businesses and we are among the first programs to offer green fashion classes and certificates. With the strong support of our advisory board, internship program and excellent teachers, many of our students go on to find success in the fashion industry. Our goal is to provide students an education that rivals private fashion schools at a fraction of the price.

FACILITIES

Professional, fully-outfitted fashion design and construction labs with industrial sewing machines, specialty industrial machines, vacuum irons, cutting tables, and full-scale Wolf and Superior Dress forms. Costume Study Collection of garments and accessories from 1770's-1990's as well as a Textile Collection. Dye Lab, laundry room and fitting room. Merchandising lab, 6 visual display store windows, visual prop collection. Shared computer labs offering Illustrator, Photoshop, and CAD classes. College Library.

ONLINE / DISTANCE LEARNING

Some General Education classes are offered online.

COURSES OF INSTRUCTION

- Intro to Fashion and Careers
- Sewing Basic–Advanced
- Textiles
- Fashion Illustration
- Fashion Trends and Cultural Costumes
- Flat Pattern
- Draping
- Fashion Apparel and Professional Techniques
- Fashion Image
- Apparel Selection

INTERNSHIPS

Required of majors at all levels.

Interns are typically placed at companies such as Oakley, Quiksilver, Billabong, Element, Paul Frank, St. John Knits, Trina Turk, Disney, Ambiguous, Rip Curl, Fashion Business Inc., Hoffman Fabrics, Robert Kauffman Fabrics, Anthopologie, Fox Sports, Hurley, Volcom, S. Coast Repatory, *Surfboarder* magazine, *Damsel* magazine, Sushi A La Mode, Cach Cach, Tra La La, Produce Company, California Market Center, New Market Center, California Apparel News, Harvey Seat Bag Co., Royal Underground and misc. student and award-winning film projects.

STUDY ABROAD

Saddleback College offers many study aboard opportunities annually - none are exclusive to fashion at this time.

NOTABLE ALUMNI

Karen Mamont–former Director of Marketing for the California Market Center, Dusty Smith of Dusty Doll Clothing, Malia Hill–Nordsrom Product Group/Disney Costume, Kristopherm Hamms–Black Ribbon Society, Brandi Bochard–Bonsoir, Bella!, Amy Paris -Sushi A La Mode, Tracy West–Cach Cach Kids, Joseph Morris, Marrissa K and Seven Jeans

STUDENT ACTIVITIES AND ORGANIZATIONS

Fashion Club, Guest Lecture Series of Industry Professionals, Portfolio Review Days, Annual Fashion Show in Spring, A"wear"ness day in Fall, Student Chapter of Fashion Business Inc., collaborations with student film projects and school theater. Fashion Department Blog, Twitter and Facebook pages: www.saddlebackcollegefashion.blogspot.com

FACULTY SPECIALIZATIONS AND RESEARCH

Fashion Design, Action Sports Design, Apparel Manufacturing, Accessory Design, Formal/Bridal Design, Children's Wear Design and Manufacturing, Textile Design, Textile Science, Fiber Arts, Flat-Pattern, Couture Sewing, Costume Design, Costume History, Millinery, Corsetry and Underpinning Design and Construction, Visual Display and Merchandising

COMMUNITY COLLEGE TRANSFERS

Students who are interested in transfer go to CSU Long Beach, CAL Poly Pamona, as well as many private colleges such as FIT, FIDM, Parsons, Otis, and Central St. Martin's College of Art and Design.

SCHOLARSHIPS / FINANCIAL AID

Financial aid is available through the financial aid office for those who qualify. In addition, there are academic excellence awards/scholarships awarded by the department and work study opportunities.

Students receiving Scholarships or Financial Aid: 23%

San Joaquin Delta College

Department of Fashion

5151 Pacific Ave., Stockton, CA 95207 | 209-954-5573 | www.deltacollege.edu/div/finearts/fashion/fashion.html

UNIVERSITY PROFILE
Public
Suburban
Residential
Semester Schedule
Co-ed

STUDENT DEMOGRAPHICS
Undergraduate: 22,000
Graduate: n/a

Male: 40%
Female: 60%

Full-time: 62%
Part-time: 38%

EXPENSES
Tuition: $11 per unit
Room & Board: n/a

ADMISSIONS
5151 Pacific Ave.
Stockton, CA 95207
209-954-5151

DEGREE INFORMATION

Major / Degree / Concentration	Enrollment	Requirements for entry	Graduation rate
Fashion Merchandising Associate of Science	119	Open enrollment	92%
Apparel Design Associate of Art	126	Open enrollment	88%

TOTAL PROGRAM ENROLLMENT
Undergraduate: 100%
Graduate: Not reported

Male: 40%
Female: 60%

Full-time: 62%
Part-time: 38%
Online: Not reported

International: Not reported
Minority: 69%

Job Placement Rate: Not reported

SCHOLARSHIPS / FINANCIAL AID
Students receiving Scholarships or
Financial Aid: 52%

TOTAL FACULTY: 7
Full-time: 1
Part-time: 6

FASHION DESIGN ADMINISTRATION
Dr. Raul Rodriguez, Superintendent/
President
Dr. Kathy Hart, President
Dr. Hazel Hill, Dean of Economic and
Workforce Development

PROFESSIONAL / ACADEMIC AFFILIATIONS
Fashion Group International

PROGRAM DESCRIPTION AND PHILOSOPHY

The Fashion Program prepares students for careers in the fashion industry and/or transfer to a four-year university.

FACILITIES

Computer labs, sewing labs, and library resources

ONLINE / DISTANCE LEARNING

Not Reported

COURSES OF INSTRUCTION

- Introduction to Fashion Merchandising
- Fashion Product Analysis
- History of Fashion to the 20th Century
- History of Fashion from the 20th Century
- Clothing and Culture
- Textiles
- Beginning Industry Sewing
- Intermediate Industry Sewing
- Flat Pattern
- Draping
- Collection Design
- Trend Forecasting
- Fashion Retailing
- Fashion Illustration

INTERNSHIPS

Required of majors. Interns are typically placed at local retailer and independent fashion designers in Northern CA.

STUDY ABROAD

Not available

NOTABLE ALUMNI

Jennavave Barbero–designer in Milan, Italy; Riley John-Donnell–publisher and co-founder of *Surface* magazine; Billy Hutchinson–Manager of Gump's (SF) and independent Calligrapher; Jennifer Rocha–merchandiser for Ugg's

STUDENT ACTIVITIES AND ORGANIZATIONS

Fashion Club; Industry Tours to SF, NY, LA, Paris, London

FACULTY SPECIALIZATIONS AND RESEARCH

Several Fashion Design faculty have their own independent design businesses and all have years of experience in the industry. Merchandising faculty are retail store owners, buyers, visual directors, etc.

West Valley College

Department of Fashion Design & Apparel Technologies

14000 Fruitvale Ave., Saratoga, CA 95070 | 408-741-4039 | www.westvalley.edu/fd/

UNIVERSITY PROFILE
Public
Suburban
Commuter
Semester Schedule
Co-ed

STUDENT DEMOGRAPHICS
Undergraduate: 12,000
Graduate: n/a

Male: 43%
Female: 57%

Full-time: 30%
Part-time: 70%

EXPENSES
Tuition: $26 per unit (CA residents)
Room & Board: n/a

ADMISSIONS
14000 Fruitvale Ave.
Saratoga, CA 95070
408-741-2001
askwvc@westvalley.edu

DEGREE INFORMATION

Major / Degree / Concentration	Enrollment	Requirements for entry	Graduation rate
Apparel Design Associate of Science & Certificate	Not reported	Open enrollment	Not reported
Apparel Production Associate of Science & Certificate	Not reported	Open enrollment	Not reported

TOTAL PROGRAM ENROLLMENT
Undergraduate: 500
Graduate: n/a

Male: Not reported
Female: Not reported

Full-time: Not reported
Part-time: Not reported
Online: Not reported

International: Not reported
Minority: Not reported

Job Placement Rate: Not reported

SCHOLARSHIPS / FINANCIAL AID
West Valley College offers variety of scholarships and financial aid such as BOG Fee Waiver, Cal and Pell Grants, Federal Work Study program, etc. For more information, please contact the Financial Aid Office directly: Call 408-741-2024 or visit: www.westvalley.edu/financialaid/links.html

TOTAL FACULTY: 6
Full-time: 50%
Part-time: 50%

FASHION DESIGN ADMINISTRATION
Tina Keller, Department Chair

PROFESSIONAL / ACADEMIC AFFILIATIONS
Not reported

PROGRAM DESCRIPTION AND PHILOSOPHY

The West Valley College Fashion Design and Apparel Technology department offers an Associate of Science degree and certificate options in Apparel Design and Apparel Production. We are a part of an accredited California Community College and our Associate Degrees are transferable to California State Universities. We are also accredited by ACCJC, a division of WASC Western Association of Schools and Colleges.

The program's strength is in a comprehensive curriculum of design and production courses based on industry standard methods. These courses are designed to meet the different experience levels of students from beginner to advanced, as well as assist industry professionals seeking to upgrade their skills. To insure industry experience, students are required to complete an internship in the apparel or related industry.

FACILITIES

West Valley College is located on the west side of Silicon Valley, in the foothills of the Santa Cruz Mountains, 50 miles south of San Francisco. Continuing a nearly 40-year tradition, West Valley College offers 18 dynamic career programs, professional certificates, and degree programs with exceptional preparation for transfer to four-year colleges and universities.

West Valley College offers several computer labs, Writing labs, ESL labs, Library, TV Studio, Theater, etc. Department operates and maintains a Production Lab and a Technology Lab with Gerber AccuMark system.

ONLINE / DISTANCE LEARNING
Not available

COURSES OF INSTRUCTION
- Intro to Fashion
- History of Fashion
- Fashion Drawing
- Fabric Analysis
- Apparel Manufacturing
- Patternmaking
- Draping

INTERNSHIPS

Required of majors for the Associate of Science Degree.

Fashion Design and Apparel Technology program offers wide variety of internship opportunities around the Greater Bay area with companies such as Gap, Marian Clayden, Levi's, Fox Racing, Illusions Sportswear, Effie's Heart, etc.

STUDY ABROAD
Not available

NOTABLE ALUMNI
Joseph Domingo, Joseph Domingo Studio in San Francisco
Cris Applegate, designer at Maximum Clothing and faculty at Academy of Arts University in San Francisco
Terry O'Connor, designer at Illusions Sportswear in Campbell
Cindy Lee, patternmaker at Fox Racing in Morgan Hill

STUDENT ACTIVITIES AND ORGANIZATIONS

West Valley College is home to 42 Inter-Club Council 08-09 Chartered Clubs. Fashion Design and Apparel Technology department has a very active Fashion Club. The Fashion Club was awarded the Student Club of the Year in Spring 2010.

FACULTY SPECIALIZATIONS AND RESEARCH

Members of the faculty are working professionals who understand industry requirements. Courses are taught by a variety of instructors who bring unique and current perspectives to the classroom environment.

COMMUNITY COLLEGE TRANSFERS

Fashion Design and Apparel Technology program at West Valley College is fully-accredited by the State of California and upon graduation, students can transfer to the University of California and California State University. Some have transferred in the past to universities such as Fashion Institute of Technology in New York and Academy of Art University in San Francisco.

Woodbury University

Department of Fashion Design

School of Media, Culture, & Design, 7500 Glenoaks Blvd., Burbank, CA 91510 | 818-252-5239

http://mcd.woodbury.edu/fashiondesign/

UNIVERSITY PROFILE
Private
Suburban
Commuter
Semester Schedule
Co-ed

STUDENT DEMOGRAPHICS
Undergraduate: 1,269
Graduate: 306

Male: 46.8%
Female: 53.1%

Full-time: 84.7%
Part-time: 15.2%

EXPENSES
Tuition: $27,635
Room & Board: $8,978

ADMISSIONS
7500 Glenoaks Blvd.
Burbank, CA 91510-7846
info@woodbury.edu
818-767-0888

DEGREE INFORMATION

Major / Degree / Concentration	Enrollment	Requirements for entry	Graduation rate
Fashion Design Bachelor of Fine Arts	70	Not reported	36.3%

TOTAL PROGRAM ENROLLMENT
Undergraduate: 70
Graduate: 0

Male: 7.1%
Female: 92.8%

Full-time: 88.5%
Part-time: 11.4%
Online: Not reported

International: 8.5%
Minority: 50%

Job Placement Rate: Not reported

SCHOLARSHIPS / FINANCIAL AID
Merit Scholarships based on test scores
and GPA are available.

TOTAL FACULTY: NOT REPORTED
Full-time: Not reported
Part-time: Not reported

FASHION DESIGN ADMINISTRATION
Louise Coffey-Webb, Chair, Department of Fashion

PROFESSIONAL / ACADEMIC AFFILIATIONS
International Textile and Apparel Association
Fashion Group International

PROGRAM DESCRIPTION AND PHILOSOPHY

Woodbury University offers a Bachelor of Fine Arts degree program with a major in Fashion Design. The program is tailored to meet the needs of students wishing to enter the challenging and exciting world of the fashion professional. The curriculum emphasizes research, critical and creative thinking, and strong technical skills. Freshman students may enter with no previous training; transfer students should submit samples of their work for placement evaluation.

FACILITIES

The Woodbury University Fashion Study Collection, consisting of over 6,000 garments and accessories which represent the clothing history of the past 200 years, is available as a hands-on resource to students and faculty. The Judith Tamkin Fashion Center houses rotating exhibitions of items from the Fashion Study Collection, as well as student work. Students may intern with the curator, working on displays and management of the collection.

ONLINE / DISTANCE LEARNING

Not available

COURSES OF INSTRUCTION

Courses are taught by fashion design educators and industry professionals, and the curriculum is enhanced with internationally renowned visiting lecturers. Fundamental skill areas include drawing, pattern drafting, draping, apparel construction, as well as fashion history and textiles. Studio classes include leading categories of women's wear, men's wear, knitwear, active wear, and swimwear. Courses are offered in millinery, shoe design, costume design, textile design and weaving, and other specialized areas. Computer-assisted design is integrated into the curriculum. The creative work of the fashion design students is showcased at the university's annual Gala.

INTERNSHIPS

Not reported

STUDY ABROAD

Not reported

NOTABLE ALUMNI

Not reported

STUDENT ACTIVITIES AND ORGANIZATIONS

Not reported

FACULTY SPECIALIZATIONS AND RESEARCH

Not reported

Woodbury University

Department of Marketing

School of Business, 7500 Glenoaks Blvd., Burbank, CA 91510 | 818-252-5131 | www.woodbury.edu

UNIVERSITY PROFILE
Private
Suburban
Commuter
Semester Schedule
Co-ed

STUDENT DEMOGRAPHICS
Undergraduate: 1,269
Graduate: 306

Male: 46.8%
Female: 53.1%

Full-time: 84.7%
Part-time: 15.2%

EXPENSES
Tuition: $27,635
Room & Board: $8,978

ADMISSIONS
7500 Glenoaks Blvd.
Burbank, CA 91510
818.252.5221
info@woodbury.edu

DEGREE INFORMATION

Major / Degree / Concentration	Enrollment	Requirements for entry	Graduation rate
Fashion Marketing Bachelor of Business Administration	53	2.5 gpa; IGETSI articulation agreements with over 100 California Community Colleges	Not reported

TOTAL PROGRAM ENROLLMENT
Undergraduate: 53
Graduate: 0

Male: 3.7%
Female: 96.2%

Full-time: 94.3%
Part-time: 5.6%
Online: n/a

International: 15%
Minority: 33.9%

Job Placement Rate: 75%

SCHOLARSHIPS / FINANCIAL AID
Merit Scholarships based on test scores and GPA; National and state need-based financial aid; Private scholarships.

Students receiving Scholarships or Financial Aid: 90%

TOTAL FACULTY: 4
Full-time: 50%
Part-time: 50%

FASHION DESIGN ADMINISTRATION
Karen Kaigler-Walker, Ph.D., Assistant Dean, School of Business, Chair, Department of Marketing

PROFESSIONAL / ACADEMIC AFFILIATIONS
International Textile and Apparel Association
Fashion Group International

PROGRAM DESCRIPTION AND PHILOSOPHY

Located in the heart of the Los Angeles media/entertainment industry Fashion Marketing program at Woodbury University provides the opportunity to learn from professionals who work in the most exciting field possible–fashion. But, we offer more than just the glamour of our proximity to Hollywood. We hold high academic standards, knowing that fashion professionals need to be business savvy as well as fashion savvy. We are housed in the School of Business and fully prepare our graduates to enter the demanding world of the fashion business. We require students to take courses in management, accounting, and finance that are taught by business professors in those fields. In these times of high unemployment among recent college graduates, having this strong background in business puts our graduates ahead of the pack. We are unique in that our program is accredited by the Association of Collegiate Business Schools and Programs (ACBSP). Currently, we are in candidacy to be accredited by AACSB, the most prestigious business accrediting body of business programs. No other university or college worldwide offers a fashion program that is accredited by either of these two agencies. In summary, we are the place of choice for those who want a solid career in fashion marketing.

FACILITIES

On-campus computer labs; major museums in the Los Angeles area; field trips to and on-campus activities with professionals from major studios, fashion forecasting companies, fashion corporate headquarters, fashion manufacturers, and studio services.

ONLINE / DISTANCE LEARNING

Not available

COURSES OF INSTRUCTION

- Fashion Fundamentals
- Trend Analysis
- Retail Buying
- Los Angeles Field Experience
- Internship
- Consumer Behavior
- Market Research and Analysis
- Fashion Promotion
- Fashion Journalism
- Styling for the Media
- Fashion Production and Wholesaling
- Field Experience: Europe
- Field Experience: China

INTERNSHIPS

Required of majors by the 4th year. Interns are typically placed at all major media/entertainment studios such as Warner Bros., NBC, and Fox; all major retailers, such as Bloomingdale's and Macy's; designer retailers, such as Armani; high-end specialty corporate offices, such as BCBG and Juicy Couture; major publications, such as *California Daily News*.

STUDY ABROAD

NYC, Europe, Asia

NOTABLE ALUMNI

List available on request.

STUDENT ACTIVITIES AND ORGANIZATIONS

National social sororities; Collegiate Entrepreneur Organization (national organization); BPWOW (national business women's organization); Delta Mu Delta (national business honor society); Woodbury Association of Student Government ; Woodbury MBA Association; Threads (fashion association)

FACULTY SPECIALIZATIONS AND RESEARCH

Professor Wendy K. Bendoni, trend analysis, fashion journalism, social marketing, international travel; Professor Emily Davis, special events, retailing; Professor Kevin Keele, advertising, promotion; Dr. Karen Kaigler-Walker, fashion consumer behavior, fashion market research and analysis; Asian fashion

The Art Institute of Colorado

Departments of Fashion Design & Fashion Retail Management

1200 Lincoln St., Denver, CO 80203 | 303-837-0825 | www.artinstitutes.edu/denver/

UNIVERSITY PROFILE
Private
Urban
Commuter
Quarter Schedule
Co-ed

STUDENT DEMOGRAPHICS
Undergraduate: 1,800
Graduate: 0

Male: Not reported
Female: Not reported

Full-time: Not reported
Part-time: Not reported

EXPENSES
Tuition: Not reported
Room & Board: Not reported

ADMISSIONS
1200 Lincoln St.
Denver, CO 80203
303-837-0825

DEGREE INFORMATION

Major / Degree / Concentration	Enrollment	Requirements for entry	Graduation rate
Fashion Design Bachelor of Arts	70	Not reported	Not reported
Fashion Retail Management Bachelor of Arts	110	Not reported	Not reported

TOTAL PROGRAM ENROLLMENT
Undergraduate: 170
Graduate: Not reported

Male: 10%
Female: 90%

Full-time: Not reported
Part-time: Not reported
Online: Not reported

International: Not reported
Minority: Not reported

Job Placement Rate: 100%

SCHOLARSHIPS / FINANCIAL AID
Not reported

TOTAL FACULTY: 6
Full-time: Not reported
Part-time: Not reported

FASHION ADMINISTRATION
Rosalind Grenfell, Academic
Department Chair, Fashion Design and
Fashion Retail Management

PROFESSIONAL / ACADEMIC AFFILIATIONS
International Textile and Apparel
Association
American Apparel and Footwear
Association
Fashion Group International
American Collegiate Retailing
Association

PROGRAM DESCRIPTION AND PHILOSOPHY

The Bachelor's degree program in Fashion Design at The Art Institute of Colorado in Denver takes a well-rounded approach to the fashion industry. It offers an expanded curriculum that allows students to develop the knowledge and skills in business, design, fashion, technology, and marketing to be competitive in today's market. Technological trends in fashion design are also reflected in the curriculum. To maintain a balance between technology and creativity, students take such courses as accessory design, knitting and weaving, and life drawing to better understand design and their craft. The Fashion Design program prepares graduates to seek career-entry positions such as assistant designer, stylist, visual display artist, and fashion illustrator. More technical career options might include manufacturing production assistant, computer marking and grading technician, patternmaker, and technical designer.

In the Fashion Retail Management degree program, students begin with a solid foundation that includes an introduction to retailing and fashion history. Coursework then allows the opportunity to learn drawing and design, apparel evaluation and construction, retail operations, and manufacturing. Students can then delve into event and show production, marketing, advertising, promotions principles, store planning and lease management, sales management, leadership, and teambuilding concepts. Graduates are prepared to seek such entry-level career opportunities as assistant manager, sales associate, special event coordinator, and visual merchandiser.

FACILITIES

Computer labs, library, career services

ONLINE / DISTANCE LEARNING

Not reported

COURSES OF INSTRUCTION

- Fashion History
- Current Designers
- Trends and Concepts in Fashion

INTERNSHIPS

Required of majors

STUDY ABROAD

Not reported

NOTABLE ALUMNI

Not reported

STUDENT ACTIVITIES AND ORGANIZATIONS

Not reported

FACULTY SPECIALIZATIONS AND RESEARCH

All faculty have a Master's degree and industry experience.

Colorado State University

Department of Design & Merchandising

1574 Campus Delivery, Fort Collins, CO 80523 | 970-491-1629 | www.dm.cahs.colostate.edu

UNIVERSITY PROFILE
Public
Urban
Residential
Semester Schedule
Co-ed

STUDENT DEMOGRAPHICS
Undergraduate: 21,204
Graduate: 4,209

Male: 49%
Female: 51%

Full-time: 87%
Part-time: 13%

EXPENSES
Tuition: $6,500 (in-state)
Room & Board: $8,318

ADMISSIONS
1062 Campus Delivery
Fort Collins, CO 80523
970-491-6909
www.admissions.colostate.edu

DEGREE INFORMATION

Major / Degree / Concentration	Enrollment	Requirements for entry	Graduation rate
Design & Merchandising Bachelor of Science Apparel Design and Production	80	2.5 gpa with portfolio review at end of fall semester to select a cohort of 25 students to continue in the program	90%
Design & Merchandising Bachelor of Science Merchandising	320	Same requirements as entry into Colorado State University	90%
Design & Merchandising Master of Science Apparel and Merchandising	37	3.00 gpa undergraduate, GRE scores, and strong recommendations	80%

TOTAL PROGRAM ENROLLMENT
Undergraduate: 400
Graduate: 37

Male: 5%
Female: 95%

Full-time: Not reported
Part-time: Not reported
Online: 0

International: Not reported
Minority: 15%

Job Placement Rate: Varies with years since graduation.

SCHOLARSHIPS / FINANCIAL AID
In addition to the usual government loans, there are a wide variety of scholarships available to students through the department and college.

TOTAL FACULTY: 17
Full-time: 88%
Part-time: 12%

FASHION ADMINISTRATION
Mary A. Littrell, Ph.D., Professor and Department Head, Design and Merchandising

PROFESSIONAL / ACADEMIC AFFILIATIONS
International Textile and Apparel Association
Fashion Group International
American Collegiate Retailing Association

PROGRAM DESCRIPTION AND PHILOSOPHY

Fashion students identify concentrations in Appare Design and Production or in Merchandising. Social responsibility and sustainability permeate all courses. Both concentrations include capstone integrative courses. International study and service learning are integral to student learning. The department conducts international study tours to Guatemala, Hong Kong and Thailand, and India and also has a biannual study tour to New York.

FACILITIES

The department has state of the art computer labs with over $5 million in Lectra-donated software, as well as other industry focused software. All students take an introductory computer course that introduces them to the department's apparel and merchandising focused software at the beginning of their academic programs. The newly opened Avenir Museum of Design and Merchandising offers students opportunities to work with a collection of over 12,000 artifacts from the US and abroad. Major concentrations in the collection exist for 19th- and 20th- century US, Asia, and Central America.

ONLINE / DISTANCE LEARNING

Colorado State University participates in the multi state GPIDEA Master's degree program in Merchandising that is offered online (see Web site). We offer some undergraduate online courses but not a full major/program.

COURSES OF INSTRUCTION

The undergraduate core includes courses in fashion industries, design foundations, textiles, clothing and human behavior, merchandising, consumer behavior, and product development. In addition to upper division courses, many students also pursue a minor in business.

INTERNSHIPS

Required of majors, Junior/Seniors with at least a 2.5 gpa. Students intern with major retailers, apparel manufacturers, advertising and promotions, and publication firms across the country, including Denver, New York, Los Angeles, Chicago, and Dallas.

STUDY ABROAD

The department offers three of our own international study tours to Guatemala, Hong Kong and Thailand, and India. A number of students also study at semester long programs in France, Great Britain, and Italy.

NOTABLE ALUMNI

Graduates have risen to upper-level management positions at companies such as Pearl Azumi, Target, Inc., and Nike to name a few. A number of graduates have initiated and grown their highly successful own businesses.

STUDENT ACTIVITIES AND ORGANIZATIONS

The department has an active student chapter of Fashion Group International-Denver. FGI meets bi weekly with a number of professional speakers and sponsors a highly successful and well-attended annual recycled fashion show on campus.

FACULTY SPECIALIZATIONS AND RESEARCH

All faculty programs of research support the department emphasis on social responsibility and sustainability. Examples include research on sustainable natural dyes for biomedical usage, body image, socially responsible promotions and advertising, international retailing, fair trade, recycled apparel design, and hospital gown design, to name a few.

University of Bridgeport

Department of Fashion Merchandising and Retailing

230 Park Ave., Bridgeport, CT 06604 | 203-576-4098 | www.bridgeport.edu

UNIVERSITY PROFILE
Private
Urban
Residential
Semester Schedule
Co-ed

STUDENT DEMOGRAPHICS
Undergraduate: 2,248
Graduate: 2,855

Male: 43%
Female: 57%

Full-time: 59%
Part-time: 41%

EXPENSES
Tuition: $23,400
Room & Board: $11,400

ADMISSIONS
126 Park Ave.
Bridgeport, CT 06604
203-576-4552
bgross@bridgeport.edu

DEGREE INFORMATION

Major / Degree / Concentration	Enrollment	Requirements for entry	Graduation rate
Fashion Merchandising and Retailing Associate of Arts	2	2.5 gpa	Not reported
Fashion Merchandising and Retailing Bachelor of Science	84	2.5 gpa	Not reported

TOTAL PROGRAM ENROLLMENT
Undergraduate: 2,248
Graduate: 2,855

Male: 43%
Female: 57%

Full-time: 59%
Part-time: 41%
Online: 353

International: 33.8%
Minority: 30.4%

Job Placement Rate: 95%

SCHOLARSHIPS / FINANCIAL AID
Students receiving Scholarships or
Financial Aid: 96.5%

TOTAL FACULTY: 493
Full-time: 125
Part-time: 368

FASHION DESIGN ADMINISTRATION
Provost Michael Spitzer
Dean Paul Lerman
Program Director Patricia Rigia

PROFESSIONAL / ACADEMIC AFFILIATIONS
Not reported

PROGRAM DESCRIPTION AND PHILOSOPHY

Both two-year and four-year programs in fashion merchandising and retailing consist of a university core of classes that give the student a well-rounded education which includes fine arts, social sciences, and lab sciences. Located 50 miles from New York City, students may commute to job sites locally or in Manhattan. Field trips into the New York fashion markets and museums fit into individual classes. A highly international population of undergraduate and graduate students provides fashion inspiration and business possibilities on a global scale. Campus is located along the shore of Long Island Sound in Fairfield county Connecticut.

FACILITIES

Computer labs in all classroom buildings and in Library. Wireless Access, Smart Classrooms, and access to local museums and large Manhattan based museums

ONLINE / DISTANCE LEARNING

Not available

COURSES OF INSTRUCTION

- Fundamentals of Fashion
- Fashion Accessories
- Textiles, Textile Design
- History of Costume
- History of Textiles
- Strategies of Selling
- Buying, Mass Merchandising and Marketing
- Home Furnishings
- Human Resource Management
- Retail Management
- Fashion show production

INTERNSHIPS

Required of majors at the Sophomore level and available for Junior and Senior years, but not required. Locally, students are placed in major department, chain, and discount apparel stores such as Lord & Taylor, Macy's, Saks Fifth Ave., Nordstrom, T.J. Maxx, Marshall's, and Target. Students may also participate in internships with manufacturers, retailers, and magazines in Manhattan such as Ax, Tommy Hilfiger, Applebottoms, Lord & Taylor, Macy's, Bloomigdale's, Saks Fifth Ave., and Seventeen.

STUDY ABROAD

London, Paris, and through Global Learning Systems

NOTABLE ALUMNI

Karen Kaplin Newitts–American Museum of Natural History, Wendy Wagner–PLMA, Barbara Simmons Lomie–Liz Claiborne, Tanya Hine-Perry Ellis, Nicole Jacques–9West, Gary Fischer–Loehmann's, Mary Jean Basileo-Salomon Bros

STUDENT ACTIVITIES AND ORGANIZATIONS

Over 45 student organizations are available on campus.

FACULTY SPECIALIZATIONS AND RESEARCH

Technology in Fashion, Student internships

Delaware State University

Department of Human Ecology

1200 N. Dupont Highway, Dover, DE 19901 | 302-857-6440 | www.desu.edu

UNIVERSITY PROFILE
Public
Suburban
Residential
Semester Schedule
Co-ed

STUDENT DEMOGRAPHICS
Undergraduate: 3,000
Graduate: 750

Male: Not reported
Female: Not reported

Full-time: 81%
Part-time: 19%

EXPENSES
Tuition: $6,146 (in-state)
$13,000 (out-of-state)
Room & Board: $9,000

ADMISSIONS
1200 N. DuPont Hwy
Dover, DE 19901
302-857-6351

DEGREE INFORMATION

Major / Degree / Concentration	Enrollment	Requirements for entry	Graduation rate
Textile & Apparel Studies **Bachelor of Science**	Not reported	Not reported	Not reported

TOTAL PROGRAM ENROLLMENT
Undergraduate: 50
Graduate: Not reported

Male: 5%
Female: 95%

Full-time: 100%
Part-time: Not reported
Online: Not reported

International: 2%
Minority: 95%

Job Placement Rate: 95%

SCHOLARSHIPS / FINANCIAL AID
Not reported

TOTAL FACULTY: 2
Full-time: 100%
Part-time: Not reported

FASHION ADMINISTRATION
Dr. Besong, Chair

PROFESSIONAL / ACADEMIC AFFILIATIONS
Not reported

PROGRAM DESCRIPTION AND PHILOSOPHY

Textiles & Apparel Studies focuses on developing professional skills, such as communications, analytical thinking, and ethical behavior that sustain graduates as they apply management and marketing theory and business principles to the global fashion industry. Students in the fashion merchandising program have opportunities to develop knowledge of retail functions, merchandising principles, forecasting trends, and textile selection and evaluation.

FACILITIES

Not reported

ONLINE / DISTANCE LEARNING

Not available

COURSES OF INSTRUCTION

- Apparel Construction
- Apparel Production & Evaluations
- Introduction to the Fashion Industry
- Textiles
- Quantitative Merchandising
- Merchandising Assortment
- Planning & Buying
- Textiles & Apparel in the Global Economics
- Social Psychology of Clothing
- Flat Pattern

INTERNSHIPS

Required of majors

STUDY ABROAD

Not available

NOTABLE ALUMNI

Not reported

STUDENT ACTIVITIES AND ORGANIZATIONS

Not reported

FACULTY SPECIALIZATIONS AND RESEARCH

Not reported

University of Delaware

Department of Fashion & Apparel Studies

Room 211 Alison W., Newark, DE 19716 | 302-831-8714 | www.udel.edu/fash

UNIVERSITY PROFILE
Public
Suburban
Residential
Semester Schedule
Co-ed

STUDENT DEMOGRAPHICS
Undergraduate: 16,521
Graduate: 3,634

Male: 42%
Female: 58%

Full-time: 96%
Part-time: 4%

EXPENSES
Tuition: $23,186
Room & Board: $9,066

ADMISSIONS
210 S. College Ave.
Newark, DE 19716
302-831-8123
admissions@udel.edu

DEGREE INFORMATION

Major / Degree / Concentration	Enrollment	Requirements for entry	Graduation rate
Fashion Merchandising Bachelor of Science	280	see www.udel.edu/admissions/for/freshmen.html	Not reported
Apparel Design Bachelor of Science	80	see www.udel.edu/admissions/for/freshmen.html	Not reported
Fashion Studies Master of Science	10	see www.udel.edu/fash/graduate/masters/masters_admis_requir.html	Not reported
Socially Responsible and Sustainable Apparel Business Online graduate certificate	10	see www.udel.edu/fash/graduate/certificate/admis_requir.html	Not reported

TOTAL PROGRAM ENROLLMENT
Undergraduate: 400
Graduate: 20

Male: 3%
Female: 97%

Full-time: 95%
Part-time: 5%
Online: 1%

International: 2%
Minority: 23%

Job Placement Rate: 85%

SCHOLARSHIPS / FINANCIAL AID
Please see www.udel.edu/admissions/finance/

TOTAL FACULTY: 17
Full-time: 12
Part-time: 5

FASHION DESIGN ADMINISTRATION
Dr. Marsha Dickson, Professor and Chair
Dr. Belinda Orzada, Professor and Associate Chair
Patricia Brinley, Assistant to the Chair

PROFESSIONAL / ACADEMIC AFFILIATIONS
International Textile and Apparel Association
American Apparel and Footwear Association
Fashion Group International
American Collegiate Retailing Association

PROGRAM DESCRIPTION AND PHILOSOPHY

The Mission of the Department of Fashion & Apparel Studies is to prepare professionals with essential knowledge and critical skills to influence fashion and apparel-related fields in creative ways. Our graduates are aware of and able to act with accountability toward issues of social responsibility and sustainability. We teach, conduct research and creative scholarship, and interact with local and global communities in ways that are innovative and collaborative. We value work that is student centered, relevant to business and society, built upon international and cultural diversity, and which contributes to continuous learning.

FACILITIES

CAD Design laboratory, Historic Costume and Textile Collection, Pattern Development and Fashion Rendering Lab, and Design and Preproduction Lab

ONLINE / DISTANCE LEARNING

The Department of Fashion & Apparel Studies offers a graduate certificate in Socially Responsible and Sustainable Apparel Business that addresses labor and environmental problems in the global supply chains for the apparel, textile, and footwear industries.
The certificate is comprised of nine, one-credit courses that are offered through the Internet. Students select a Labor or Environment track. A set of seven core courses are taken by all students and two specialized courses are taken for each selected track. If students wish, they may pursue both tracks by taking all four specialized courses in addition to the seven core courses. The graduate certificate provides a foundation of knowledge needed to manage design, product development, buying, promotion, sourcing, and production of apparel, textiles, and footwear in ways that are socially responsible and sustainable.

COURSES OF INSTRUCTION

Fashion Merchandising:
- Apparel Brand Management and Marketing
- Merchandise Planning
- Assortment Planning and Sourcing and Buying
- International Fashion Consumers and Retailers

Apparel Design:
- Apparel Design by Flat Pattern
- Product Development & Management Studio
- Fashion Forecasting and Design
- Fashion Drawing and Rendering

Both Apparel Design and Fashion Merchandising:
- Seminar on Fashion Sustainability
- Global Apparel and Textile Trade and Sourcing
- Multimedia Fashion Presentations
- Fundamentals of Textiles I and II

Master's in Fashion Studies:
- Global Fashion Consumer
- Apparel Supply Chains & Social Responsibility
- Research Analysis in Fashion Studies
- Interdisciplinary Approaches to Creative Problem Solving

Graduate Certificate in Socially Responsible and Sustainable Apparel Business:
- Apparel Consumers and Social Responsibility
- Worker-Centric Social Responsibility for Apparel Industry
- Redesigning Green Apparel-Design, Sourcing, Packaging
- Producing Environmentally Responsible Apparel

INTERNSHIPS

Not required. Interns are placed at companies that are widely varied: Macy's, Kohl's, Liz Claiborne, Jones New York, *Glamour* magazine, QVC, Anthropologie, Phillips-van Heusen, Donna Karan, Under Armour, Escada, Marc Jacobs, Polo Ralph Lauren, Miss Sixty, Kenneth Cole, many others

STUDY ABROAD

Paris, China, others not focused on fashion in every continent

NOTABLE ALUMNI

Not reported

STUDENT ACTIVITIES AND ORGANIZATIONS

UDress Club publishes a fashion magazine, Synergy Club produces the annual fashion show featuring Senior design collections, Fashion Merchandising Club produces annual UD Fashion Week and other events, and Garment District combines fashion designing, art, and merchandising.

FACULTY SPECIALIZATIONS AND RESEARCH

Faculty research focuses on three key intellectual areas: social responsibility and sustainability, fashion consumer behavior, apparel innovation and technology–international content crosses all areas.

International Academy of Design & Technology— Orlando

Fashion Design & Merchandising

6039 S. Rio Grande Ave., Orlando, FL 32765 | 407-857-2300 | www.iadt.edu

UNIVERSITY PROFILE

Private
Urban
Commuter
Quarter Schedule
Co-ed

STUDENT DEMOGRAPHICS

Undergraduate: 1,000
Graduate: 0

Male: Not reported
Female: Not reported

Full-time: Not reported
Part-time: Not reported

EXPENSES

Tuition: $16,800
Room & Board: n/a

ADMISSIONS

6039 S. Rio Grande Ave
Orlando, FL 32765
407 857 2300
igill@iadt.edu

DEGREE INFORMATION

Major / Degree / Concentration	Enrollment	Requirements for entry	Graduation rate
Fashion Design & Merchandising	380	High School Degree or GED	Not reported

TOTAL PROGRAM ENROLLMENT
Undergraduate: 390
Graduate: 0

Male: 42%
Female: 58%

Full-time: 80%
Part-time: 10%
Online: 10%

International: 5%
Minority: 50%

Job Placement Rate: Not reported

SCHOLARSHIPS / FINANCIAL AID

Title IV is available for students that
qualify. Scholarships available to
students are listed in the school catalog.
Scholarships include, High School
Scholarship, Presidential Scholarship
and an Art & Design Grant is available
for those that qualify

Students Receiving Scholarships or
Financial Aid: 95%

TOTAL FACULTY: 11
Full-time: 40%
Part-time: 60%

FASHION ADMINISTRATION

Sara Miller, chair, Fashion Design &
  Merchandising
Caroline Zebrowski, Director of
  Education

PROFESSIONAL / ACADEMIC AFFILIATIONS

Not reported

PROGRAM DESCRIPTION AND PHILOSOPHY

Students can learn about fashion illustration, pattern drafting, design, draping, clothing construction, textiles, fashion history, fashion merchandising, and production techniques. All of the instruction is presented using industrial grade equipment in spacious and comfortable facilities built for optimum fashion designing. A balanced curriculum provides students with the expertise to design and communicate their ideas combining theoretical elements of design with creative and practical approaches to the solution of problems pertaining to the functional quality of marketable products.

FACILITIES

Classrooms are equipped with Mac and PC computers with programs such as Visual Retailing 4, Gerber Accumark, NedGraphics Fashion Studio, Adobe Creative Suite and Microsoft. The machinery in the sewing labs includes industrial Juki straight stitch, walking foot and serger machines. The Student Success Center at IADT Orlando is a central location where students benefit from academic advising, assessments and tutoring. Our campus bookstore offers textbooks, software and class supplies. A student lounge is also available. Local museums include Orlando Museum of Art, Morse Museum of American Art and Cornell Fine Art Museum.

ONLINE / DISTANCE LEARNING

All General Education courses are offered online and a limited number Program Core classes are offered online.

COURSES OF INSTRUCTION

We offer a hybrid program, with core classes that are both Fashion Design related and Merchandising focused. Examples of Fashion Design classes include Fashion Sketching, Textiles for Fashion, Clothing Construction, Computer Graphics for Fashion and Pattern Drafting. Examples of Merchandising classes include Visual Merchandising, Salesmanship, Merchandise Planning and Inventory Control.

INTERNSHIPS

Not reported

STUDY ABROAD

American Continental University in Europe

NOTABLE ALUMNI

Not reported

STUDENT ACTIVITIES AND ORGANIZATIONS

Our Fashion Club offers students a range of fashion and merchandising based activities including domestic and international trips to fashion design and merchandising studios, production and manufacturing facilities, workshops and fashion events. TrendWave Magazine is a fashion publication run by students with an interest in fashion journalism, styling and layout design.

FACULTY SPECIALIZATIONS AND RESEARCH

Not reported

International Academy of Design & Technology—Tampa

Fashion Design & Merchandising

5104 Eisenhower Blvd., Tampa, FL 33634 | 813-881-0007 | 1-800-ACADEMY | www.academy.edu

UNIVERSITY PROFILE
Private
Urban
Commuter
Quarter Schedule
Co-ed

STUDENT DEMOGRAPHICS
Undergraduate: 2,561
Graduate: 29

Male: 41
Female: 59

Full-time: 87
Part-time: 13

EXPENSES
Tuition: $19,080
Room & Board: $8,547

ADMISSIONS
5104 Eisenhower Blvd.
Tampa, FL 33634
813-881-0007 or
1-800-ACADEMY
evega@academy.edu

DEGREE INFORMATION

Major / Degree / Concentration	Enrollment	Requirements for entry	Graduation rate
Fashion Design Bachelor of Fine Arts	225	High School Graduation / GED	Not reported
Fashion Merchandising Bachelor of Arts	80	High School Graduation / GED	Not reported

TOTAL PROGRAM ENROLLMENT
Undergraduate: 305
Graduate: 0

Male: 30%
Female: 70%

Full-time: 80%
Part-time: 20%
Online: 0%

International: 10%
Minority: 40%

Job Placement Rate: Not reported

SCHOLARSHIPS / FINANCIAL AID
Financial Aid is available for those who qualify. The Academy participates in a variety of financial aid programs for the benefit of students. Students must meet the eligiblity requirements for these programs in order to participate. The Academy administrates its financial aid programs in accordance with prevailing federal and state laws and its own institutional policies. Financial Aid includes: Academic Competitiveness Grant, Pell Grant, Federal Supplemental Educational Opportunity Grant, Florida Student Assistant Grant, The National Science and Mathematics Access to Retain Talent Grant, Veteran's Educational Benefits, Yellow Ribbon Grant, Federal Stafford Loans, Federal Direct Parent Loans, Federal Direct Graduate, and Private Loans.

Students Receiving Scholarships or Financial Aid: 75%

TOTAL FACULTY: 20
Full-time: 30%
Part-time: 70%

FASHION ADMINISTRATION
Dr. Alexxis Avalon, Chair, Fashion Design and Merchandising
Mr. Phil Bulone, Dean of Academics
Ms. Michele Lurch, Faculty, Fashion Design and Merchandising

PROFESSIONAL / ACADEMIC AFFILIATIONS
International Textile and Apparel Association
American Apparel and Footwear Association
Fashion Group International
American Collegiate Retailing Association

PROGRAM DESCRIPTION AND PHILOSOPHY

The Fashion Design program engages students in the process of apparel conceptualization, illustration, construction, production, and marketing. Students will experiment with lines, colors, patterns, textures, functions, and style in the design and creation of original garments. The Fashion Design program provides students with the opportunity to enhance their creative skills and to develop technical competencies for employment in the field.

The Fashion Merchandising program allows students to partner their interest in the world of fashion with the development of key business competencies critical to employment in today's global market place. While students develop skills in merchandising, management, marketing, and buying, they will also have the opportunity to explore the integration of conceptual and creative abilities with business practices.

FACILITIES

The International Academy of Design and Technology is located in a convenient suburban setting, just minutes from the Tampa International Airport. This location is adjacent to major thoroughfares and is accessible from all of west-central Florida. Affordable housing, public transportation, and nearby shopping malls allow the students to live, commute, and work near the college. Classrooms are equipped with Mac and PC computers, with programs such as Gerber, Ned Graphics, Microsoft, and Adobe software. There is a Learning Resource Center that contains books, periodicals, databases, and audio-visual materials. The campus bookstore offers books, software, and supplies. There is a student lounge and designated centralized areas that serve as information centers for information. There are numerous museums located in the Tampa Bay area such as the Salvador Dali Museum, The Museum of Fine Art in St. Petersburg, and the Tampa Museum of Art.

ONLINE / DISTANCE LEARNING

Students have the option to complete a portion of their Fashion or General Education courses through the study of various online courses. The online courses are supported through services provided by the International Academy of Design and Technology Online, based in Tampa, Florida.

COURSES OF INSTRUCTION

- Introduction to Fashion
- Textiles for Fashion
- Evolution of Fashion
- Trend Forecasting
- Computer Graphics for Fashion
- Fashion Marketing
- Consumer Behavior

Fashion Majors:
- Clothing Construction
- Draping
- Drafting
- Apparel Production
- Fashion Design Studio

Merchandising Majors:
- Buying
- Retail Management
- Visual Merchandising
- Fashion Product Development

INTERNSHIPS

Required of majors at the Senior level. The Academy's Internship Program allows students to participate in various businesses and programs that engage their skills and make them ready for a competitive work environment in the Fashion Industry.

STUDY ABROAD

Available with the American InterContinental University (AIU) Study Abroad programs

NOTABLE ALUMNI

Not reported

STUDENT ACTIVITIES AND ORGANIZATIONS

The Fashion Club provides students a network of opportunities to meet and share ideas about the fashion industry. The Student Ambassadors group is a select group of students who work closely with the Department Chairs and assist with various duties on campus and off campus while building skills necessary for their futures.

FACULTY SPECIALIZATIONS AND RESEARCH

Specializations of faculty skills include: GERBER software programs and AccuMark V8, Ned Graphics, Adobe Photoshop and Illustrator, Fashion Sketching, Design Production, Pattern and Drafting, Couture Techniques, and Portfolio development.

COMMUNITY COLLEGE TRANSFERS

Students who previously attended an accredited college or university recognized by the U.S. Department of Education may be granted transfer credit, at the sole discretion of the Academy. Courses taken at previous institutions must be determined by the Academy to be sufficiently equivalent courses offered at the Academy. The Academy must determine that those courses are applicable to their program of study. Only courses in which the student earned a grade of C or above will be considered for transfer. Students are responsible for having official transcripts forwarded from the granting institution to the Academy for review. Students may also be required to submit a school catalog and/or course syllabus.

Brenau University

Fashion Design

500 Washington St. SE, Gainesville, GA 30501 | 770-534-6240 | www.brenau.edu

UNIVERSITY PROFILE
Private
Suburban
Residential
Semester Schedule
Co-ed

STUDENT DEMOGRAPHICS
Undergraduate: 18
Graduate: n/a

Male: Not reported
Female: Not reported

Full-time: Not reported
Part-time: Not reported

EXPENSES
Tuition: Contact Admissions
Room & Board: Contact Admissions

ADMISSIONS
500 Washington St. SE
Gainesville, GA 30501
1-800-252-5119
lgann-smith@brenau.edu

DEGREE INFORMATION

Major / Degree / Concentration	Enrollment	Requirements for entry	Graduation rate
Fashion Design Bachelor of Fine Arts	18	Not reported	Not reported

TOTAL PROGRAM ENROLLMENT
Undergraduate: Not reported
Graduate: Not reported

Male: Not reported
Female: Not reported

Full-time: Not reported
Part-time: Not reported
Online: Not reported

International: Not reported
Minority: Not reported

Job Placement Rate: Not reported

SCHOLARSHIPS / FINANCIAL AID
Not reported

TOTAL FACULTY: NOT REPORTED
Full-time: Not reported
Part-time: Not reported

FASHION ADMINISTRATION
Not reported

PROFESSIONAL / ACADEMIC AFFILIATIONS
Not reported

PROGRAM DESCRIPTION AND PHILOSOPHY

The Fashion Design program offers a Bachelor of Fine Arts degree, as well as a Minor in Fashion Design. The curriculum provides a solid liberal arts base, while allowing a student to focus on an area of interest in the fashion field. Graduates may pursue careers in product development, manufacturing, sourcing, or fashion styling.

FACILITIES
Not reported

ONLINE / DISTANCE LEARNING
Not reported

COURSES OF INSTRUCTION
- The Fashion Industry
- Two-Dimensional Design
- Three-Dimensional Design
- Drawing I
- Apparel Construction
- Patterning and Draping
- Practicum
- Digital Graphic Design LE
- Fashion Textiles
- History of Fashion LE
- Life Drawing
- Art History I
- Art History II
- Apparel I: Women's Wear
- Apparel II: Men's Wear
- Merchandise Promotion & Communication
- Illustration Techniques
- Apparel III: Children's Wear
- Professional Development
- Fashion Collection Research
- Fashion Collection
- Internship

INTERNSHIPS
Not reported

STUDY ABROAD
Not reported

NOTABLE ALUMNI
Not reported

STUDENT ACTIVITIES AND ORGANIZATIONS
Not reported

FACULTY SPECIALIZATIONS AND RESEARCH
Not reported

Savannah College of Art & Design

School of Fashion

Savannah Campus: 115 W. Henry St., Savannah, GA 31401 | 915-525-6650 | www.scad.edu/programs/fashion/index.cfm Atlanta
Campus: 1600 Peachtree St., Atlanta, GA 30309 | 912-525-5700 | www.scad.edu/programs/fashion/index.cfm

UNIVERSITY PROFILE
Private
Urban
Residential & Commuter
Quarter Schedule
Co-ed

STUDENT DEMOGRAPHICS
Undergraduate: Not reported
Graduate: Not reported

Male: Not reported
Female: Not reported

Full-time: Not reported
Part-time: Not reported

EXPENSES
Tuition: $29,070
Room & Board: Not reported

ADMISSIONS
SCAD Admissions
Department
P.O. Box 2072
Savannah, GA 31402
800-869-7223
admissions@scad.edu

DEGREE INFORMATION

Major / Degree / Concentration	Enrollment	Requirements for entry	Graduation rate
Fashion Design Bachelor of Fine Arts Master of Arts Master of Fine Arts	Not reported	Not reported	Not reported
Accessory Design Bachelor of Fine Arts Master of Arts Master of Fine Arts	Not reported	Not reported	Not reported
Fashion Marketing and Management Bachelor of Fine Arts	Not reported	Not reported	Not reported
Luxury & Fashion Management Master of Arts Master of Fine Arts	Not reported	Not reported	Not reported
Menswear Design Minor	Not reported	Not reported	Not reported

TOTAL PROGRAM ENROLLMENT
Undergraduate: Not reported
Graduate: Not reported

Male: Not reported
Female: Not reported

Full-time: Not reported
Part-time: Not reported
Online: Not reported

International: Not reported
Minority: Not reported

Job Placement Rate: Not reported

SCHOLARSHIPS / FINANCIAL AID
Not reported

TOTAL FACULTY: NOT REPORTED
Full-time: Not reported
Part-time: Not reported

FASHION DESIGN ADMINISTRATION
Michael Fink, Dean of the School of Fashion
Anthony S. Miller, Interim Chair of Fashion
Linda Hinkle, Administrative Assistant

PROFESSIONAL / ACADEMIC AFFILIATIONS
Not reported

PROGRAM DESCRIPTION AND PHILOSOPHY

Accessory Design:
At SCAD, accessory design students develop an awareness of this specialized industry and its various markets. Students learn to think and design in the realms of both 2D and 3D, allowing them to direct creativity into functional innovation. Students learn to design and construct marketable 3D accessory items at a high level of craftsmanship.

Fashion Design:
SCAD offers one of the largest and most comprehensive fashion programs in the United States with a balanced curriculum of design and construction. Fashion students are encouraged to develop creative and intellectual thinking, inventive design skills, and practical expertise necessary to succeed in careers in the global fashion industry.

Fashion Marketing and Management:
The Fashion Marketing and management program prepares students for cross-functional careers in a global marketplace comprised of fashion, business, and marketing sectors. With a focus on the business trends of hard and soft line goods, students are prepared to address the demands of an innovative, competitive, and changing industry. Students acquire the decision-making skills and professionalism necessary to enter and thrive in a global industry.

Luxury and Fashion Management:
Through a dynamic curriculum driven by innovation and current trends, Luxury and Fashion Management addresses the various facets of a fast-paced, constantly evolving industry. Students develop analytical and decision-making skills and explore the future role of luxury and fashion management. Graduates have a full understanding of the luxury fashion sector and have the knowledge necessary to become successful professionals in a high-end, complex market.

FACILITIES

Sewing studios are equipped with professional sewing machines, industry-standard dress forms, cutting tables, specialty finishing equipment, and specialized equipment including a selection of women's and men's shoe lasts, a shoe finishing machine, and cylinder industrial sewing machines. Computer labs offer an Infinity Plus plotter for patternmaking, Mimaki textile printer, software including Kaledo, Vision Fashion Studio, Gerber Suite, Lectra U4ia, Lectra Romans CAD software, Virtual Fashion Pro, and online or print trends including WGSN, here & there, and Peclers.

ONLINE / DISTANCE LEARNING
Not reported

COURSES OF INSTRUCTION
Accessory Design:
- Sewing Technology
- Sketching and Rendering
- Introduction to Accessory Design
- Computer-aided Design
- Millinery Design
- Handbag Design I & II
- Footwear Design I & II
- Belt Design
- Senior Collection
- Design I, II, & III

Fashion Design:
- Fashion Technology
- Introduction to Textiles
- Introduction to Fashion Design
- Advanced Fashion Technology
- Apparel Development I, II, III, & IV
- Introduction to Fashion Sketching
- Advanced Fashion Sketching
- History of Fashion
- Computer-aided Fashion Design
- The Business of Fashion
- CAD Patternmaking
- Fashion Illustration
- Knitwear Design for Fashion
- Decorative Surfaces
- Menswear Design I & II
- Active Sportswear
- Menswear Construction
- Childrenswear Design
- Special Topics in Fashion Design
- Menswear Patternmaking I & II
- New York City Fashion Seminar
- Evening Wear
- Current Trends and Forecasting
- Senior Collection I, II & III
- Advanced Computer Applications
- Fashion Portfolio Presentation
- Computer-aided Fashion Manufacturing

Fashion Marketing and Management:
- Fashion Aesthetics and Style
- Fashion Merchandising, Planning, and Control
- Retail Buying Simulation
- Private Label Product Development
- Contemporary Issues in Fashion Merchandising
- Retail Management
- Nontraditional Retailing
- Global Sourcing and Import Buying
- Visual Merchandising

INTERNSHIPS
Not required

STUDY ABROAD
Study abroad programs are offered at SCAD's campus in Lacoste, France. Frequent intensive programs are offered in a variety of other worldwide locations including London, Paris, Milan, Tokyo, Berlin, Barcelona, and Florence.

NOTABLE ALUMNI
Not reported

STUDENT ACTIVITIES AND ORGANIZATIONS
Through the Style Lab mentorship program, selected students receive direction and inspiration for their Senior collections through one-on-one critiques and guidance from concept through production. Mentors have included Zac Posen, Catherine Malandrino, Bryan Bradley, Angel Sanchez, Lars Nilsson, and Yigal Azrouël.

During the annual SCAD fashion show, juried collections of undergraduate and graduate student work are showcased in a major production, covered by national and international media and streamed live over the Internet.

FACULTY SPECIALIZATIONS AND RESEARCH
Not reported

University of Georgia

Department of Textiles, Merchandising, & Interiors

School of Family & Consumer Sciences, Dawson Hall, Athens, GA 30602 | 706-542-7861 | www.fcs.uga.edu/tmi

DEGREE INFORMATION

Major / Degree / Concentration	Enrollment	Requirements for entry	Graduation rate
Fashion Merchandising Bachelor of Science in Family & Consumer Sciences	252	Enter as freshmen	Not reported
Fashion Merchandising Bachelor of Science in Family & Consumer Sciences Global Soft Goods Emphasis	Not reported	Not reported	Not reported
Furnishings and Interiors Bachelor of Science in Family & Consumer Sciences	64	Portfolio Review	Not reported

TOTAL PROGRAM ENROLLMENT
Undergraduate: 316
Graduate: 20

Male: 4%
Female: 96%

Full-time: 99%
Part-time: 1%
Online: 1%

International: 3%
Minority: 16%

Job Placement Rate: Not reported

SCHOLARSHIPS / FINANCIAL AID
See opposite page for more info.

TOTAL FACULTY: 15
Full-time: 87%
Part-time: 13%

FASHION DESIGN ADMINISTRATION
Laura D. Jolly, Dean
Jan M. Hathcot, Associate Dean for
   Academic Affairs and Research
Patricia Hun-Hurst, Department Head,
   Textiles, Merchandising and Interiors

PROFESSIONAL / ACADEMIC AFFILIATIONS
International Textile and Apparel
   Association
American Collegiate Retailing
   Association

PROGRAM DESCRIPTION AND PHILOSOPHY

The faculty members in the department have teaching and research expertise in many areas. We offer a diverse undergraduate program which covers all aspects of fashion merchandising and residential interior design, including kitchen and bath design. The Global Soft Goods undergraduate emphasis offers our students the opportunity to gain knowledge and experience in global sourcing, logistics, and production. Undergraduate and Graduate students may also enroll in classes that engage them in the creation and installation of historic dress and textile exhibits at the university and surrounding Athens community.

FACILITIES

Computer labs, Textile labs, Historic Costume Collection

ONLINE / DISTANCE LEARNING

Not available

COURSES OF INSTRUCTION

Fashion Merchandising required courses:
- Retail Planning and Buying
- Global Retailing
- Textiles
- Textile Testing
- Dress, Society, and Culture
- History of Dress and Fashion
- Apparel and Textile Economics

- Apparel Line Development and Presentation
- Fashion Promotion
- Visual Merchandising

Students enroll in approximately nine hours of courses in the Terry College of Business.

The Global Soft Goods emphasis includes the following courses:
- Product Development
- Computer-Aided Design for Apparel Design and Production
- International Textiles
- Apparel Quality Analysis

Fashion Merchandising majors must complete the following prerequisites for major required courses:
- Statistics
- Elementary Chemistry/Chemistry Lab
- Economics, Psychology
- Sociology
- Computer Science
- Accounting

INTERNSHIPS

Not required. Interns are typically placed at companies such as Neiman Marcus, Macy's, David Yurman, Marc Jacobs, Nordstrom, Target, AmericasMart-Atlanta, Escada, Nicole Miller, Armani Exchange, and Harper's Bazaar.

STUDY ABROAD

Textiles, Merchandising, and Interiors faculty-led trips to Japan, Ghana, London, and China.

NOTABLE ALUMNI

Not reported

STUDENT ACTIVITIES AND ORGANIZATIONS

Fashion Design Student Association, Student Merchandising Association, Little Red Book

FACULTY SPECIALIZATIONS AND RESEARCH

Not reported

SCHOLARSHIPS / FINANCIAL AID

The University of Georgia participated in several federal financial aid programs. In addition, the College of Family and Consumer Sciences administers over $100,000 in competitive scholarships. Outstanding Georgia residents are eligible for HOPE scholarship that pays tuition and book fees for those students graduating from a Georgia high school with a qualifying 3.0 gpa. Contact financial aid for additional information.

University of Hawaii

Department of Apparel Product Design & Merchandising

2515 Campus Rd., Honolulu, HI 96822 | 808-956-6133 | www.hawaii.edu

UNIVERSITY PROFILE
Public
Urban
Residential & Commuter
Semester Schedule
Co-ed

STUDENT DEMOGRAPHICS
Undergraduate: 18,000
Graduate: 5,000

Male: 48%
Female: 52%

Full-time: 85%
Part-time: 15%

EXPENSES
Tuition: Not reported
Room & Board: Not reported

ADMISSIONS
University of Hawaii at Manoa
2600 Campus Rd., Rm. 001
Honolulu, HI 96822-2385
808-956-8975
uhmanoa.admissions@hawaii.edu

DEGREE INFORMATION

Major / Degree / Concentration	Enrollment	Requirements for entry	Graduation rate
Apparel Product Design & Merchandising Bachelor of Science	200	2.5 gpa Portfolio at Senior year	100%

TOTAL PROGRAM ENROLLMENT
Undergraduate: 200
Graduate: 2

Male: 5%
Female: 95%

Full-time: 90%
Part-time: 10%
Online: 0%

International: 20%
Minority: 45%

Job Placement Rate: Not reported

SCHOLARSHIPS / FINANCIAL AID
Two college-scholarships and some
university scholarships are available.

Students receiving Scholarships or
Financial Aid: 15%

TOTAL FACULTY: 9
Full-time: 50%
Part-time: 50%

FASHION DESIGN ADMINISTRATION
Barabra Yee, Professor and Chair

PROFESSIONAL / ACADEMIC AFFILIATIONS
International Textile and Apparel
  Association
Fashion Group International

PROGRAM DESCRIPTION AND PHILOSOPHY

The mission of the instruction program in Apparel Product Design and Merchandising is to provide students with appropriate knowledge and skills for career positions in apparel and fashion-related industries; to promote understanding of the effects of global social, economic, and political issues on apparel and fashion-related industries and on modes of dress; to foster appreciation of the role of dress and appearance as these reflect and shape individual behavior, social and economic exchange, and cultural conditions; to nurture intellectual growth and creativity, and to support the mission of the College of Tropical Agriculture & Human Resources by fostering student acquisition of problem-solving, analytic, and communication skills.

FACILITIES

CAD computer lab, historic costume collection, textile lab, and sewing lab

ONLINE / DISTANCE LEARNING

Not reported

COURSES OF INSTRUCTION

- Textiles I & II
- Aesthetics
- Culture, Gender, & Appearance
- Fashion Promotion
- Basic Construction
- Fashion Illustration I
- Fashion History
- Retailing Buying & Merchandising
- Merchandise Planning & Control
- Boot Camp for Entrepreneurs
- International Trade Issues
- Internship

INTERNSHIPS

Required of majors at the Senior level. Interns are typically placed at design firms, retailers, as buying office assistants, and/or events organizers.

STUDY ABROAD

Available

NOTABLE ALUMNI

Not reported

STUDENT ACTIVITIES AND ORGANIZATIONS

Senior fashion show

FACULTY SPECIALIZATIONS AND RESEARCH

Design theory, textiles, trade

Iowa State University

Apparel, Educational Studies, & Hospitality Department

31 MacKay Hall, Ames, IA 50011-1121 | 515-294-7474 | www.aeshm.hs.iastate.edu/students/

UNIVERSITY PROFILE
Public
Rural
Residential
Semester Schedule
Co-ed

STUDENT DEMOGRAPHICS
Undergraduate: 22,521
Graduate: 5,424

Male: 56.3%
Female: 43.7%

Full-time: 88.5%
Part-time: 11.5%

EXPENSES
Tuition: $6,102
(undergraduate, resident)
$17,668 (undergraduate, non-resident)
$7,120 (graduate, resident)
$18, 548 (graduate, non-resident)
Room & Board: $6,600–$11,456

ADMISSIONS
100 Enrollment Services Center
Ames, IA 50011-2011
515-294-5836
admissions@iastate.edu

DEGREE INFORMATION

Major / Degree / Concentration	Enrollment	Requirements for entry	Graduation rate
Bachelor of Science Merchandising Option	240	Enrollment at Iowa State University	71%
Bachelor of Science Creative Design Option	160	Passing of Design Review after Sophomore year	71%
Bachelor of Science Technical Design Option	22	Passing of Design Review after Sophomore year	71%
Bachelor of Science Product Development Option	48	Enrollment at Iowa State University	71%
Bachelor of Science Production and Sourcing Management	12	Enrollment at Iowa State University	71%

TOTAL PROGRAM ENROLLMENT
Undergraduate: 240
Graduate: 20

Male: 7%
Female: 93%

Full-time: 100%
Part-time: 0

International: 10%
Minority: 6%

Job Placement Rate: 100%

SCHOLARSHIPS / FINANCIAL AID
Financial aid and scholarships are available through the Office of Student Financial Aid at ISU for both merit and need (see www.financialaid.iastate.edu), as well as a large number of scholarships through the College of Design that apply specificially to Design students, and even more available to assist in the cost of study abroad in our Rome Program.

TOTAL FACULTY: 8
Full-time: 7
Part-time: 1
Online: 0

NCIDQ Certified: 3
Licensed Interior Designers: 1
LEED Certified: 3

INTERIOR DESIGN ADMINISTRATION
Lee Cagley, Director of Interior Design
Linda Galvin, Admistrative Specialist

PROFESSIONAL / ACADEMIC AFFILIATIONS
American Society of Interior Designers
International Interior Design Association
Interior Design Educators Council

CIDA ACCREDITATION
Bachelor of Fine Arts in Interior Design (2009, 2015)

PROGRAM DESCRIPTION AND PHILOSOPHY

The Apparel, Merchandising, and Design undergraduate program is one of 13 programs endorsed by the American Apparel and Footwear Association Education Foundation for having an integrated program offering. All students must complete a selection of classes providing a broad understanding of the industry, including an introduction to the industry, dress and diversity, textiles, computer applications, aesthetics, merchandising, manufacturing, global issues, an internship, and a selection of a field study to NY, LA, Chicago, or Mexico. Future program emphasis will include creativity and service learning.

The program is designed to allow the student to mix and match a primary option with their core depending on their interests. The program allows the student enough elective credits for a minor, typically in Journalism, Business, Entrepreneurship, Art and Design, or Foreign Languages. A portfolio is not required of design students; however, after completion of a set of Sophomore-level courses design students have two attempts to pass a design review.

The Textiles and Clothing graduate program offers the Doctor of Philosophy and Master of Science. In addition to the five program specializations in the undergraduate major, the graduate program adds consumer behavior and history and conservation to the program list of specializations and research.

FACILITIES

The Textile and Clothing Museum houses nearly 9,500 pieces of historic and cultural garments and textiles. The production technology lab includes 50 industrial machines, a fuser, and industry pressing equipment. The digital printing lab allows students to print their designs on fabrics using a Mimaki TX 2 printer and Optitex software. Computer labs feature VR (visual retailing), PDM/PLM, Sourcing Simulator, Stylesight and the Adobe Creative Suite package.

The quality assurance lab exposes students to product development and evaluation of product quality using a variety of equipment and industry standards. A (TC)2 3D body scanner is used for research and outreach.

ONLINE / DISTANCE LEARNING

Individual classes are offered on-line

COURSES OF INSTRUCTION

Clothing & Textiles:
- Overview of the Fashion Industry
- Dress & Diversity in Society
- Textile Science I & II
- Computer Applications in Textiles & Clothing
- Patternmaking I & II
- Aesthetics & Brand Image
- Museum Studies
- Fashion Illustration
- Quality Assurance of Textiles & Apparel
- Creative Design Processes
- History of European & North American Dress
- History of 20th Century Fashion
- Cultural Perspectives in Dress
- Sourcing & Global Issues
- Merchandise Planning & Control
- Brand Management & Promotions
- Technical Design Processes
- Apparel Production Management
- Consumer Behavior
- Retail Information Analysis
- Senior Design Studio
- Fashion Forecasting & Product Development

INTERNSHIPS

Required of majors at Sophomore, Junior, and/or Senior level. Internships are supervised by faculty and graded. Interns are typically placed at companies like: Adidas, Anthropologie, Armani Exchange, BCBG, Chicos, Disney, Donna Karen, Elie Tahari, Glamour, Guess, J Brand, Lacoste, Lands' End, Macys, Michael Kors, Nanette LePore, Nordstrom, Obey, Ralph Lauren, Taiwanese Textile Federation, Target, Tobe Report, Tommy Hilfiger, Trachtenberg PR, Tulle, Volcom, Vogue, Zac Posen.

STUDY ABROAD

The Textiles and Clothing program partners with four international institutions: London College of Fashion, Paris American Academy, Accademia Italiana in Florence, Italy, and Lorenzo de Medici in Florence. Semester-long and summer programs are both offered. Approximately 25-30% of our students in the major will study abroad. A field trip to Mexico is offered. Exchange opportunities are being developed with Textiles and Clothing programs at Universities in China and South Africa.

NOTABLE ALUMNI

Carol Anderson, CAbi: Todd Snyder (former VP of Men's Design at J. Crew), Jim Ryan, Creative Director/Brand Strategist for U.S. Polo Association/Jordache; Linda and Kim Renk, owners - Sequin Jewelry; Laurie Beja Miller, Senior Vice President/General Manager North America at Bare Escentuals; Michael McBreen, President of Global Operations, Wolverine World Wide; Elle Thompson, Head Technical Designer, Marc Jacobs; Merry Mathes, Vice President of Sales, Delta Galil USA; Lisa Hendrickson, Chief Merchandising Officer, Destination Maternity Corporation; Beth Teggatz, Technical Design Manager, Lands' End; Kristin Hunziker, owner, Ju-Ju-Be

STUDENT ACTIVITIES AND ORGANIZATIONS

The juried ISU Fashion Show is student-produced by the Event Management class and sells more than 2,200 tickets. The learning community, Common Threads, enhances the freshmen year experience. Additional clubs include MODA Fashion Club, Closets Collide, and Toms offering students experiences in green retailing and philanthropy. The entrepreneurship showcase and Main Street Iowa projects provide community consulting experiences.

FACULTY SPECIALIZATIONS AND RESEARCH

Current faculty have written numerous textbooks.

College of DuPage

Department of Fashion Merchandising & Design

425 Fawell Blvd., Glen Ellyn, IL 60137 | 630-942-2619 | www.cod.edu/fashion/

DEGREE INFORMATION

Major / Degree / Concentration	Enrollment	Requirements for entry	Graduation rate
Fashion Design Associate of Applied Science	100	Interest in program	Not reported
Fashion Design Certificate	Not reported	Interest in program	Not reported
Fashion Merchandising Associate of Applied Science	Not reported	Interest in program	Not reported
Fashion Merchandising Certificate	Not reported	Interest in program	Not reported
Fashion Entrepreneurship Certificate	Not reported	Interest in program	Not reported

TOTAL PROGRAM ENROLLMENT
Undergraduate: Not reported
Graduate: Not reported

Male: Not reported
Female: Not reported

Full-time: Not reported
Part-time: Not reported
Online: Not reported

International: Not reported
Minority: Not reported

Job Placement Rate: Not reported

SCHOLARSHIPS / FINANCIAL AID
At this point, there are no scholarships
specific to our department.

TOTAL FACULTY: 5
Full-time: 20%
Part-time: 80%

FASHION ADMINISTRATION
Sharon M. Scalise, Coordinator, Fashion
 Merchandising and Design

PROFESSIONAL / ACADEMIC AFFILIATIONS
Not reported

PROGRAM DESCRIPTION AND PHILOSOPHY

The goal of the Fashion Design program at College of DuPage is to provide students with an environment in which they can learn the skills of fashion design, develop creativity, and understand the aesthetic, intellectual, and professional aspects of the field. Students gain these skills through classes in clothing construction, pattern-making, draping, tailoring and CAD. Classes in design principles, fashion illustration, motivation, marketing and merchandising, the history of costume, and principles of textiles enhance the students' grasp of the broad scope of fashion and its impact. Elective classes include bridal couture, millinery, machine-knitting a,nd fiber arts.

FACILITIES
Not reported

ONLINE / DISTANCE LEARNING
Not available

COURSES OF INSTRUCTION
- Clothing Construction
- Flat Pattern Design
- Fashion Illustration
- History of Costume
- Fashion for Business

INTERNSHIPS
Not reported

STUDY ABROAD
Not reported

NOTABLE ALUMNI
Not reported

STUDENT ACTIVITIES AND ORGANIZATIONS
Student-produced fashion show

FACULTY SPECIALIZATIONS AND RESEARCH
Not reported

Columbia College Chicago

Fashion Studies & Fashion Retail Management

600 S. Michigan Ave., Chicago, IL 60605 | 312-369-6280 | www.colum.edu/Academics/

UNIVERSITY PROFILE
Public
Rural
Residential
Semester Schedule
Co-ed

STUDENT DEMOGRAPHICS
Undergraduate: 3,052
Graduate: 985

Male: 63%
Female: 37%

Full-time: 69%
Part-time: 31%

EXPENSES
Tuition: $4,450
Room & Board: $5,778

ADMISSIONS
600 S. Michigan Ave.
Chicago, IL 60605
312-369-7130
www.colum.edu/Admissions/
visit.php

DEGREE INFORMATION

Major / Degree / Concentration	Enrollment	Requirements for entry	Graduation rate
Fashion Design Bachelor of Fine Arts	450	Generous Admission	Not reported
Fashion Retail Management Bachelor of Arts	450	Generous Admission	Not reported

TOTAL PROGRAM ENROLLMENT
Undergraduate: 160
Graduate: 0

Male: 3%
Female: 97%

Full-time: 70%
Part-time: 20%
Online: 10%

International: 2%
Minority: 50%

Job Placement Rate: Not reported

SCHOLARSHIPS / FINANCIAL AID
Two fashion scholarships available in addition to college-wide scholarship opportunities.

Students Receiving Scholarships or Financial Aid: 80%

TOTAL FACULTY: 7
Full-time: 72%
Part-time: 28%

FASHION ADMINISTRATION
Michael Olszweski, Department Chair

PROFESSIONAL / ACADEMIC AFFILIATIONS
International Textile and Apparel Association
American Collegiate Retailing Association

PROGRAM DESCRIPTION AND PHILOSOPHY

The Fashion Design and Fashion/Retail Management programs integrate studies in fashion design, fashion/retail management, fashion photography, fashion journalism, entrepreneurship, all within the context of a liberal arts education. The program is designed to allow flexibility, collaborative, and experiential learning.

FACILITIES

Fashion Columbia Study Collection, design studios, CAD computer labs, all that Chicago has to offer.

ONLINE / DISTANCE LEARNING

Some classes offered online, but not full program.

COURSES OF INSTRUCTION

Fashion Design:
- Fundamentals of Fashion Design
- Garment Construction I and II
- Flat Pattern and Draping
- Art & Design foundation classes

Fashion/Retail Management:
- Introduction to Fashion Business
- Fashion Product Evaluation
- Retail Management
- Merchandise Management
- Fashion Marketing
- Management Core Classes

INTERNSHIPS

Required of majors at the Junior or Senior level. Interns are typically placed at companies such as Bloomingdale's, Macy's, Neiman Marcus, Nordstrom, Chanel, Michael Kors, Ford Model Agency, Ralph Lauren, Escada, Vera Wang, Express, Kate Spade, *Modern Luxury* magazine, Chicago Fashion Incubator.

STUDY ABROAD

Florence, AIU

NOTABLE ALUMNI

Lana Fertelmesiter/Lana Jewelry, Beth Morgan/Emmy Award, Winning Costume Designer

STUDENT ACTIVITIES AND ORGANIZATIONS

Columbia College Fashion Association; Fashion Columbia Fundraising Fashion Show; Launch, student fashion show; Spring Break New York City Tour; annual International Fashion Tours

FACULTY SPECIALIZATIONS AND RESEARCH

Service-Learning, Textile Surface Design, Small Business Consulting, Cultural Dress

Dominican University

Department of Apparel Design & Merchandising

7900 W. Division St., River Forest, IL 60305 | 708-524-6633 | www.dom.edu

UNIVERSITY PROFILE
Private
Suburban
Residential
Semester Schedule
Co-ed

STUDENT DEMOGRAPHICS
Undergraduate: 1,904
Graduate: 2,005

Male: 31%
Female: 69%

Full-time: 98%
Part-time: 2%

EXPENSES
Tuition: $25,560
Room & Board: $8,000

ADMISSIONS
7900 W. Division St.
River Forest, IL 60305
708-524-6800
domadmis@dom.edu

DEGREE INFORMATION

Major / Degree / Concentration	Enrollment	Requirements for entry	Graduation rate
Apparel Design Bachelor of Arts Options: Fashion Development Surface Design Dress & Textile Studies	40	Admission to the university	Not reported
Apparel Merchandising Bachelor of Arts	60	Admission to the university	Not reported

TOTAL PROGRAM ENROLLMENT
Undergraduate: 100
Graduate: 0

Male: 4%
Female: 96%

Full-time: 98%
Part-time: 2%
Online: Not reported

International: 3%
Minority: 38%

Job Placement Rate: Not reported

SCHOLARSHIPS / FINANCIAL AID
Dominican's Recognition, Achievement, University Honor, Dean's, and Presidential Scholarships start at $6,000. These are awarded automatically upon admission based upon ACT/SAT score, class rank, and gpa. Additional scholarships are available based upon students' academic interests and history. Institutional need-based aid is available and depended upon the results of the FAFSA.

Students Receiving Scholarships or Financial Aid: 98%

TOTAL FACULTY: 7
Full-time: 43%
Part-time: 57%

FASHION ADMINISTRATION
Tracy Jennings, Apparel Design and Merchandising Department Chair

PROFESSIONAL / ACADEMIC AFFILIATIONS
International Textile and Apparel Association
Fashion Group International
American Collegiate Retailing Association

PROGRAM DESCRIPTION AND PHILOSOPHY

The mission of the Apparel Design and Merchandising department is to provide students with an environment in which they can develop and nurture creativity, gain aesthetic, intellectual, and professional competence in both the knowledge and skills of the apparel field and cultivate a humanistic and ethical understanding of apparel as a business and an art form.

A strength of the program is that it is situated within a liberal arts university which encourages students to draw inspiration and insight from a breadth of disciplines.

FACILITIES

Computer Labs, PAD Computer-aided design, Ned Graphics Design Suite, Fashion Design Lab

ONLINE / DISTANCE LEARNING

Not reported

COURSES OF INSTRUCTION

- Textile Science
- Cultural Perspectives of Dress
- History of Dress
- Design Applications
- Retail Buying
- Flat Pattern
- Apparel Design
- Fashion Markets

INTERNSHIPS

Required of majors at the Junior or Senior level. Interns are typically placed at companies such as Nordstrom, Macy's, Gucci, Chicago History Museum, Penney Textile Arts, and Merchandise Mart Properties.

STUDY ABROAD

Paris, London, Ghana, Rome, Milan, Florence, China

NOTABLE ALUMNI

Not reported

STUDENT ACTIVITIES AND ORGANIZATIONS

Not reported

FACULTY SPECIALIZATIONS AND RESEARCH

Tracy Jennings: Creativity in apparel design; Susan Strawn: Historical/cultural aspects of dress and textiles, Artisan sustainability, History of hand knitting; Melissa Carr: Social networking within creative industries

Illinois State University

Family & Consumer Sciences

Campus Box 5060, Normal, IL 61790 | 309-438-2517 | http://fcs.illinoisstate.edu

UNIVERSITY PROFILE
Public
Suburban
Residential
Semester Schedule
Co-ed

STUDENT DEMOGRAPHICS
Undergraduate: 18,344
Graduate: 2,512

Male: 43%
Female: 57%

Full-time: 94%
Part-time: 6%

EXPENSES
Tuition: $2,795
Room & Board: $2,118

ADMISSIONS
See Web site

DEGREE INFORMATION

Major / Degree / Concentration	Enrollment	Requirements for entry	Graduation rate
Family & Consumer Sciences Bachelor of Arts Apparel Design	2	Application to University or application to major if already admitted	Not reported
Family & Consumer Sciences Bachelor of Science Apparel Merchandising	102	Application to University or application to major if already admitted	Not reported
Family & Consumer Sciences Bachelor of Arts Apparel Merchandising	3	Application to University or application to major if already admitted	Not reported
Family & Consumer Sciences Bachelor of Science Apparel Design	35	Application to University or application to major if already admitted	Not reported

TOTAL PROGRAM ENROLLMENT
Undergraduate: 142
Graduate: 2

Male: 2.8%
Female: 97.2%

Full-time: 94.4%
Part-time: 5.6%
Online: 0%

International: 0%
Minority: 17.6%

Job Placement Rate: Not reported

SCHOLARSHIPS / FINANCIAL AID
11 departmental scholarships available after Freshman year is completed, ranging in value from $350 to $2000. College and university scholarships also available, as well as student on-campus jobs, federal work study, and other traditional financial aid.

TOTAL FACULTY: 21
Full-time: 95%
Part-time: 5%

FASHION ADMINISTRATION
Dr. Randy Winter, Acting Department Chair
Dr. Tricia Widner Johnson, Apparel Merchandising & Design Sequence Coordinator
Mr. Richard Kane, Departmental Academic Advisor

PROFESSIONAL / ACADEMIC AFFILIATIONS
International Textile and Apparel Association

PROGRAM DESCRIPTION AND PHILOSOPHY

The Apparel, Merchandising, and Design (AMD) sequence in the Department of Family and Consumer Sciences is a competitive admission program. The sequence prepares students for employment in the forecasting, product development, promotion, distribution, wholesale, and retail sectors of the global textile and apparel industries. Students study the flow of apparel through trend analysis, design and product development, production, marketing, and retail. Within the AMD sequence, students can select either the Apparel Merchandising option or the Apparel Design and Product Development option.

The AMD program houses the Lois Jett Historic Costume Collection, a textiles laboratory, apparel design studio, and computer laboratories with Adobe Photoshop and Illustrator, AutoCAD, and Visual Retailing software packages.

AMD students have the opportunity to participate in study tours both inside and outside the US. Students have travelled to New York and Los Angeles as well as Florence, London, and Paris. The tours provide students the opportunity to learn about various firms within the textiles and apparel industry.

Faculty in AMD are productive scholars who received their educations from some of the most outstanding graduate programs in the field including Iowa State University, Oklahoma State University, and Oregon State University.

FACILITIES

PC Computer labs for use of AutoCAD, Adobe, and Visual Retailing. Apparel construction lab with industrial equipment. Textile lab with textile science testing equipment including Instron, Elmendorf tear tester, and Solar UV simulator. Lois Jett Historic Costume Collection, a teaching collection that houses approximately 2500 artifacts of historic clothing and accessories dating from c 1870-2000.

ONLINE / DISTANCE LEARNING

Not available

COURSES OF INSTRUCTION

- Textiles
- Fashion Trend & Industry Analysis
- Clothing & Behavior
- Economics of Fashion
- Apparel Product Analysis
- Fashion History
- Fashion Promotion
- Draping & Design

INTERNSHIPS

Required of majors at Junior or Senior level. Interns are typically placed at companies such as Nordstrom, Buckle, Ann Taylor Loft, Express, and a growing number are participating in the Internship of Dreams Program.

STUDY ABROAD

Bi annual study tour to Europe visiting London, Paris, and Florence. Domestic study tours to New York and Los Angeles on other years.

NOTABLE ALUMNI

Donsia Strong-Hill, Kim & Jen Gennace

STUDENT ACTIVITIES AND ORGANIZATIONS

Student led Apparel Merchandising & Design Association has meetings and activities throughout the year, culminating in an annual fashion show each spring.

FACULTY SPECIALIZATIONS AND RESEARCH

- Personality as it relates to appearance
- Management and consumer behavior
- Compulsive clothing buying
- Fast fashion consumerism
- Social responsibility
- Services marketing
- Research methods
- Sustainability in the apparel and textile industry
- Apparel product development
- Consumers' eco-friendly purchasing behavior

International Academy of Design & Technology— Chicago

Fashion Design Department

One N. State St., Suite 500, Chicago, IL 60602 | 312-980-9200 | www.iadtchicago.edu

UNIVERSITY PROFILE
Private
Urban
Commuter
Quarter Schedule
Co-ed

STUDENT DEMOGRAPHICS
Undergraduate: 1,451
Graduate: 0

Male: Not reported
Female: Not reported

Full-time: Not reported
Part-time: Not reported

EXPENSES
Tuition: $19,440
Room & Board: n/a

ADMISSIONS
One N. State St.,
Suite 500
Chicago, IL 60602
312-980-9200
www.iadtchicago.edu

DEGREE INFORMATION

Major / Degree / Concentration	Enrollment	Requirements for entry	Graduation rate
Fashion Design Bachelor of Fine Arts Associate of Applied Science	320	High school diploma or equivalent; assessment for reading comprehension, writing and/or math	Not reported
Merchandising Management Bachelor of Arts Associate of Applied Science	260	High school diploma or equivalent; assessment for reading comprehension, writing and/or math	Not reported

TOTAL PROGRAM ENROLLMENT
Undergraduate: 1,451
Graduate: 0

Male: 43%
Female: 57%

Full-time: 83%
Part-time: 17%
Online: 0%

International: 1%
Minority: 75%

Job Placement Rate: Not reported

SCHOLARSHIPS / FINANCIAL AID
Financial Aid is available for those who qualify. Students are eligible to apply for a number of scholarships such as Outstanding Senior, Portfolio Review, Presidential, Outstanding Fashion Design; Academic Success; and the New Student Academy Scholarship. Students can apply and may be eligible for Stafford Loans, Federal Pell Grants, Academic Competitive Grant, National Smart, Federal SEOG and other grant or loan assistance authorized by Title IV of the HEA.

Students Receiving Scholarships or Financial Aid: 90%

TOTAL FACULTY: 113
Full-time: 12%
Part-time: 88%

FASHION ADMINISTRATION
Robert Nachtsheim, President
Kathleen Embry, Vice President of Academic Affairs
Nancy Plummer, Program Chair - Fashion Design

PROFESSIONAL / ACADEMIC AFFILIATIONS
International Textile and Apparel Association
Fashion Group International

PROGRAM DESCRIPTION AND PHILOSOPHY

The Fashion Design curriculum is a demanding and comprehensive program taught by qualified industry professionals and specialists. Students follow their original work from start to finish–sketching, pattern making, draping, construction–from fabric to consumer. The Merchandising Management curriculum is a general business program with a focus on fashion merchandising that can prepare students to pursue career opportunities in merchandising, management, or a business.

FACILITIES

Dedicated computer-generated pattern drafting labs, sewing labs, textiles lab, pattern drafting and draping labs, vintage costume collection, fashion resource room, educational resource lab, portfolio enrichment resource lab.

ONLINE / DISTANCE LEARNING

Assorted classes are offered online for Fashion Design and Merchandising Management are available such as: Introduction to Fashion, Introduction to Business, Evolution of Fashion, Entrepreneurship, Business Law, Textiles for Fashion and General Education courses.

COURSES OF INSTRUCTION

- Clothing Construction I and II
- Patternmaking I and II
- Pattern Draping I and II
- Fashion Marketing & Consumer Behavior
- Couture Techniques
- Computer Generated Apparel Design
- Fashion Manufacturing & Appraisal
- Visual Merchandising
- Global Sourcing & Product Development
- Merchandising Planning & Inventory Control
- Fashion Journalism
- Fashion Trend Analysis

INTERNSHIPS

Required of majors at the Senior level.

STUDY ABROAD

Currently Study Abroad opportunities are available for earned credit at American Intercontinental University which has campuses in London and Paris.

NOTABLE ALUMNI

Not reported

STUDENT ACTIVITIES AND ORGANIZATIONS

Behind-the-Scenes (Merchandising focus), Fashion Council (Fashion Design focus), Image Consulting (open to all students)

FACULTY SPECIALIZATIONS AND/ OR RESEARCH

Fashion Design Construction, Merchandising, and Fashion Show Production

COMMUNITY COLLEGE TRANSFERS

Not reported

International Academy of Design & Technology— Schaumburg

Fashion Design Department

915-A National Pkwy., Schaumburg, IL 60173 | 1-877-464-4238 | www.iadtschaumburg.com

UNIVERSITY PROFILE
Private
Suburban
Residential
Quarter Schedule
Co-ed

STUDENT DEMOGRAPHICS
Undergraduate: 250
Graduate: 0

Male: Not reported
Female: Not reported

Full-time: Not reported
Part-time: Not reported

EXPENSES
Tuition: Not reported
Room & Board: Not reported

ADMISSIONS
915A National Pkwy.
Schaumburg, IL 60173
1-877-464-4238
www.iadtschaumburg.com

DEGREE INFORMATION

Major / Degree / Concentration	Enrollment	Requirements for entry	Graduation rate
Fashion Design Bachelor of Fine Arts	Not reported	High School diploma or GED	Not reported

TOTAL PROGRAM ENROLLMENT
Undergraduate: 250
Graduate: Not reported

Male: Not reported
Female: Not reported

Full-time: Not reported
Part-time: Not reported
Online: Not reported

International: Not reported
Minority: Not reported

Job Placement Rate: Not reported

SCHOLARSHIPS / FINANCIAL AID
Financial Aid is available for those who qualify.

TOTAL FACULTY: NOT REPORTED
Full-time: Not reported
Part-time: Not reported

FASHION ADMINISTRATION
Polly Lamers, Program Chair of Fashion Design

PROFESSIONAL / ACADEMIC AFFILIATIONS
International Textile and Apparel Association
Fashion Group International

PROGRAM DESCRIPTION AND PHILOSOPHY

The Bachelor of Fine Arts program in Fashion Design takes students beyond the basis of design and construction providing them with a broader business foundation and more complex design courses including designing and construction with specialty fabrics, manufacturing and quality assurance, developing entrepreneurial skills, and designing original collections. Students also have the opportunity to develop a proficiency in computer generated apparel design, computer generated pattern drafting and product data management using industry-standard computer software. Students are allowed to customize their program with a diverse selection of fashion design special topic courses.

FACILITIES

Computer Labs, Pattern Drafting Lab, Construction Lab, Display Windows, and Gerber Lab

ONLINE / DISTANCE LEARNING

The general education courses are available online.

COURSES OF INSTRUCTION

- Fashion Design I
- Draping
- Pattern Making
- Couture Techniques
- Computer Generated Pattern Drafting
- Computer Graphics for Fashion Design
- Fashion Sketching
- Theory and History of Fashion Design

INTERNSHIPS

Required of majors at the Senior level

STUDY ABROAD

Available through American InterContinental University (AIU) study abroad program

NOTABLE ALUMNI

Not reported

STUDENT ACTIVITIES AND ORGANIZATIONS

Fashion Club, school news letter, Travel Club

FACULTY SPECIALIZATIONS AND RESEARCH

Fashion Design Construction, Merchandising, and Fashion Show Production

Northern Illinois University

School of Family, Consumer, & Nutrition Sciences

DeKalb, IL 60115-2854 | 815-753-1543 | www.chhs.niu.edu/

UNIVERSITY PROFILE
Public
Urban
Residential
Semester Schedule
Co-ed

STUDENT DEMOGRAPHICS
Undergraduate: 24,424 (both undergrad and grad)
Graduate: Not reported

Male: 48%
Female: 52%

Full-time: Not reported
Part-time: Not reported

EXPENSES
Tuition: $9,390
Room & Board: $8,112

ADMISSIONS
1425 W. Lincoln Hwy.
DeKalb, IL 60115
815-753-0681
admissions@niu.edu

DEGREE INFORMATION

Major / Degree / Concentration	Enrollment	Requirements for entry	Graduation rate
Textiles, Apparel & Merchandising Bachelor of Science	117	2.0 gpa	Not reported
Family and Consumer Sciences Master of Science Apparel Studies	2	Completed baccalaureate degree from an accredited U.S. college or university, or equivalent degree from a recognized foreign institution, with a minimum 2.75 gpa. Applicants are required to have a minimum of 9 semester hours of undergrad courses in a textiles and apparel-related curriculum, three of which must be at the upper-division level. Alternately, students may complete undergraduate deficiency coursework by the end of the second semester of enrollment and/or prior to enrolling in certain major courses.	Not reported

TOTAL PROGRAM ENROLLMENT
Undergraduate: 117
Graduate: 2

Male: 6%
Female: 94%

Full-time: Not reported
Part-time: Not reported
Online: Not reported

International: Not reported
Minority: 38.5%

Job Placement Rate: Not reported

SCHOLARSHIPS / FINANCIAL AID
See opposite page for more info.

TOTAL FACULTY: 4
Full-time: 4
Part-time: 0

FASHION DESIGN ADMINISTRATION
Dr. Laura Smart - Chair of School of FCNS

PROFESSIONAL / ACADEMIC AFFILIATIONS
International Textile and Apparel Association

PROGRAM DESCRIPTION AND PHILOSOPHY

This Textile, Apparel, and Merchandising program is designed to prepare students to enter fashion merchandising positions in the apparel/textile industry. The program provides students with the product knowledge of textiles and apparel as well as an understanding of socioeconomic influences and the business skills relevant to merchandising fashion products.

FACILITIES

The Textiles, Apparel and Merchandising program at Northern Illinois University is supported by computer laboratory facilities housed in the College of Health and Human Sciences. In addition, the program has a textile and apparel laboratory and a historic costume collection with items of dress dating from the 19th and 20th centuries, including several designer pieces. A vast number of the collection items are donations from the Fashion Institute of Technology Museum in New York.

ONLINE / DISTANCE LEARNING

Not available

COURSES OF INSTRUCTION

- Fiber and Fabric Analysis
- Fashion Industries
- Design Trends in Western Costume
- Apparel Product Analysis
- Economics of Apparel and Textiles Industries
- Consumer Behavior Related to Apparel
- Fashion Merchandising
- TAM Internship or Co-operative Education Experience

INTERNSHIPS

Required of majors at Junior/Senior level. Interns are typically placed at companies such as Students typically secure positions in the Chicagoland area, though some students secure positions out of state or abroad. Some of the work sites for student interns and co-ops from Summer 2009 include Anastasia Chatzka, American Eagle, Discovery Clothing (Sydney, Australia), Forever 21, Gilly Hicks, Kohl's Department Stores, Lorenzo Relli Fashion (Italy), Michael Kors (New York), Nordstrom, Nordstrom Rack, Target.

STUDY ABROAD

Available through the Northern Illinois University Study Abroad Program

NOTABLE ALUMNI

Not reported

STUDENT ACTIVITIES AND ORGANIZATIONS

The student organization for the Textiles, Apparel and Merchandising program at NIU is the Fashion Industries Organization which is open to any NIU student who has an interest in the field of fashion.

FACULTY SPECIALIZATIONS AND RESEARCH

Dr. Sarah Cosbey–Dress, gender roles and the media in the 19th century through the present; visual analysis methods
Dr. Hyun-Mee Joung–Older consumers, shopping behavior and appearance management; textile recycling; online shopping
Dr. Seahee Lee–Social responsibility in the textiles and apparel industry; small rural business; luxury market; visual merchandising; e-commerce

SCHOLARSHIPS / FINANCIAL AID

One endowed scholarship, variable amount (2010-2011 $2400) for student in School of FCNS (including the Textiles, Apparel, and Merchandising program). One $500 scholarship available alternate years to undergrad honor society member. One endowed scholarship for members of Fashion Industries Organization. Additional scholarships for Textiles, Apparel, and Merchandising students may be available, subject to funding.

Southern Illinois University Carbondale

Fashion Design & Merchandising, School of Architecture

875 S. Normal Ave., Carbondale, IL 62901 | 618-453-3734 | http://architecture.siuc.edu/

UNIVERSITY PROFILE
Public
Rural
Residential
Semester Schedule
Co-ed

STUDENT DEMOGRAPHICS
Undergraduate: 15,551
Graduate: 4,113

Male: 57%
Female: 43%

Full-time: 88%
Part-time: 12%

EXPENSES
Tuition: $7,290
Room & Board: $8,082

ADMISSIONS
425 Clocktower Dr.
Carbondale, IL 62901
618-536-4405
www.siuc.edu/admissions/

DEGREE INFORMATION

Major / Degree / Concentration	Enrollment	Requirements for entry	Graduation rate
Fashion Design & Merchandising Bachelor of Science Fashion Design	44	Freshman applicants: Composite ACT 23 or above + class rank upper 75%; Composite ACT 21 or 22 + class rank upper 50% Transfer students: gpa 2.6 or above with 26 semester hours completed.	Not reported
Fashion Design & Merchandising Bachelor of Science Fashion Merchandising	70	Composite ACT 23 or above + class rank upper 75%; Composite ACT 21 or 22 + class rank upper 50% Transfer students: gpa 2.6 or above with 26 semester hours completed.	Not reported

TOTAL PROGRAM ENROLLMENT
Undergraduate: 114
Graduate: 0

Male: 3%
Female: 97%

Full-time: 100%
Part-time: 0%
Online: 0%

International: 4%
Minority: 30%

Job Placement Rate: Not reported

SCHOLARSHIPS / FINANCIAL AID
There are four scholarships available to students: The Fashion Design and Merchandising Scholarship (2 awarded every year), the Pitkin Scholarship, the Rendleman Scholarship, and the Ridley Scholarship.

Students Receiving Scholarships or Financial Aid: 90+%

TOTAL FACULTY: 4.5
Full-time: 89%
Part-time: 11%

FASHION DESIGN ADMINISTRATION
Walter V. Wendler, Director, School of Architecture
Jane E. Workman, Program Director, Fashion Design and Merchandising

PROFESSIONAL / ACADEMIC AFFILIATIONS
International Textile and Apparel Association

PROGRAM DESCRIPTION AND PHILOSOPHY

From the 2010-2011 Undergraduate Catalog (p. 234): "The four-year curriculum in fashion design and merchandising offers the beginning level of education for those who intend to pursue a career in fashion. There are two specializations in the Fashion Design and Merchandising major: Fashion Design and Fashion Merchandising. Within each specialization a structured sequencing of courses is included which provides for a gradual interactive development of required knowledge and skills. This preparation is combined with the University Core Curriculum courses to provide a comprehensive scholarly foundation for advancement. A fast-paced atmosphere is created by the amount of information to be covered, the frequency of assignments, and the pressure of due dates. Successful students must be able to handle multiple projects simultaneously and manage their time wisely."

FACILITIES

Fashion design studios, historic costume collection, resource library, computer graphics lab, Gerber Technology PDS2000, wireless and high-speed Internet

ONLINE / DISTANCE LEARNING

Not available

COURSES OF INSTRUCTION

Fashion Design students are expected to take Fashion Production I, II, and III, Fashion Illustration, Flat Patternmaking and Drafting, Draping, Computer-Aided Apparel Design, Experimental Design, Advanced Patternmaking, Senior Fashion Design Studio I and II.

Fashion Merchandising students are expected to take Fashion Promotional Strategies I and II, Fashion Merchandising Mathematics I and II, Personnel Issues in Fashion Retailing, and Internship. Students in both specializations are expected to take Basic Principles of Clothing Design, Careers in Fashion, Textiles I and II, Fashion Product Analysis, Fashion History (3 classes), Fashion Motivation, and Apparel & Textile Economics.

INTERNSHIPS

Required of majors for Fashion Merchandising undergraduates.

Interns are typically placed at companies such as Abercrombie & Fitch, American Eagle, Buckle, Express, Gap, JCPenney, Kohls, Macy's, and Victoria's Secret, among others.

STUDY ABROAD

Available

NOTABLE ALUMNI

Not reported

STUDENT ACTIVITIES AND ORGANIZATIONS

Fashion Design and Merchandising Organization

FACULTY SPECIALIZATIONS AND RESEARCH

Faculty conduct research in the areas of dress codes and uniforms, spatial visualization, history of fashion, consumer behavior, branding strategies, human resource management, and creativity.

Western Illinois University

Department of Dietetics, Fashion Merchandising & Hospitality

One University Circle, Knoblauch Hall 140, Macomb, IL 61455 | 309-298-1085 | www.wiu.edu/dfmh

UNIVERSITY PROFILE
Public
Rural
Residential
Semester Schedule
Co-ed

STUDENT DEMOGRAPHICS
Undergraduate: 11,000
Graduate: Not reported

Male: 49%
Female: 51%

Full-time: Not reported
Part-time: Not reported

EXPENSES
Tuition: $6,778
Room & Board: $7,642

ADMISSIONS
One University Circle,
Sherman Hall 110
Macomb, IL 61455
309-298-1891

DEGREE INFORMATION

Major / Degree / Concentration	Enrollment	Requirements for entry	Graduation rate
Fashion Merchandising Bachelor of Science	80	Meet university requirements	Not reported

TOTAL PROGRAM ENROLLMENT
Undergraduate: Not reported
Graduate: n/a

Male: 5%
Female: 95%

Full-time: Not reported
Part-time: Not reported
Online: Not reported

International: Not reported
Minority: Not reported

Job Placement Rate: 90%

SCHOLARSHIPS / FINANCIAL AID
The University gives over 1,000 scholarships yearly to students; the Department gives approx. l5 scholarships during the Spring Semester. Average amount of award is from $500 -$1,500.

TOTAL FACULTY: 6
Full-time: 4
Part-time: 2

FASHION DESIGN ADMINISTRATION
Dr. Karen Greathouse, Department Chairperson

PROFESSIONAL / ACADEMIC AFFILIATIONS
International Textile and Apparel Association
Fashion Group International

PROGRAM DESCRIPTION AND PHILOSOPHY

The job market is more accessible for fashion students specializing in the Fashion Merchandising area rather than in the Fashion Design area. Students are not always able to assess their own level of creativity in the design area.

FACILITIES

Vignettes, Textile Laboratory, Computer Labs, Costume Museum (development in progress), Bulletin Boards for design, Display windows for design projects on campus and downtown

ONLINE / DISTANCE LEARNING

Not available

COURSES OF INSTRUCTION

- Intro to Fashion
- Intro to Design
- Textiles 1 and 2
- Social/Psych Aspects of Apparel
- History of Costume
- Visual Merchandising
- Diversity of Dress
- Fashion Computer Technologies
- Fashion Global Issues
- Buying

INTERNSHIPS

Required of majors at the Senior level.

Interns are typically placed at bridal stores, Buckle, Maurice's, Nordstrom's, Cato, boutiques, shoe stores, Disney, the Limited, Victoria's Secret, vintage shops, Vera Wang, Oscar de la Renta, Armani, Wings, Ford Modeling Agency, *Marie Claire* magazine, and Claire's.

STUDY ABROAD

We have Study Abroad advisors at our university who work with students in planning trip details and determining courses that would be transferable. We also have a Fashion Study class in our department; this year, students visited five cities in Italy.

NOTABLE ALUMNI

Not reported

STUDENT ACTIVITIES AND ORGANIZATIONS

Visual and Apparel Merchandising Organization (VAMO): honor society for students with gpa over 3.0. Department Ambassadors represent the department at university functions Chicago Fashion Tours and Career Day (CGIF).

FACULTY SPECIALIZATIONS AND RESEARCH

One faculty member has owned her own business and specializes in retail/marketing/entrepreneurship; another has a textile degree with specialization in that area; other faculty teach in the major classes.

William Rainey Harper College

Fashion Department

1200 W. Algonquin Rd., H119, Palatine, IL 60067 | 847-925-6788 | www.harpercollege.edu

DEGREE INFORMATION

Major / Degree / Concentration	Enrollment	Requirements for entry	Graduation rate
Fashion Design Associate of Arts Certificate	Not reported	Not reported	Not reported
Fashion Merchandising Associate of Arts Certificate	Not reported	Not reported	Not reported

TOTAL PROGRAM ENROLLMENT
Undergraduate: Not reported
Graduate: Not reported

Male: 44%
Female: 56%

Full-time: 44%
Part-time: 56%
Online: 12%

International: >1%
Minority: 33%

Job Placement Rate: Not reported

SCHOLARSHIPS / FINANCIAL AID
Students Receiving Scholarships or
Financial Aid: 32%

TOTAL FACULTY: 853
Full-time: 23%
Part-time: 77%

FASHION DESIGN ADMINISTRATION
Sally Griffith, Asst. Vice Pres and Dean
  of Career and Technical Programs
Dr. John Smith, Assoc. Dean Career and
  Technical Programs

**PROFESSIONAL / ACADEMIC
AFFILIATIONS**
Fashion Group International

PROGRAM DESCRIPTION AND PHILOSOPHY

The Fashion Department offers Associates Degrees and Certificates in both Fashion Design and Merchandising. The curriculum emphasizes developing the creative as well as the technical side of the industry. Design offerings include Industrial Sewing Methods, Weaving, Patternmaking, Illustration, CAD, Textiles, and Fashion Arts. Offerings for Merchandising include Promotions, Forecasting, Visual Merchandising, Marketing, Retail Merchandising, among others.

FACILITIES

We are located in the northwest suburbs of Chicago, close to train and have all the advantages of the City. Computer labs are located throughout campus and accessible through week from 9:00am-11:00pm. Sat-Sun 9:00am-6:00pm. Fashion Department holds open labs for use of dress forms and cutting tables. Industrial sewing machines such as sergers, coverlock, straight stitch, buttonhole, knitting machines, and weaving looms. Vacuum table, light table.

ONLINE / DISTANCE LEARNING

Not reported

COURSES OF INSTRUCTION

Not reported

INTERNSHIPS

Required of majors. Interns are typically placed at manufacturing and design firms in the Chicago area.

STUDY ABROAD

Available through American Intercontinental University as well as individualized departmental trips.

NOTABLE ALUMNI

This is a Community College with transfer capability to FIT, and articulated schools. Students complete their degrees elsewhere.

STUDENT ACTIVITIES AND ORGANIZATIONS

Approximately 50 different clubs and organizations around campus. The Harper's Bizarre Fashion Club is actively involved in the production of the annual fashion show with Industry professionals. Students from different classes provide graphics, art, and other diverse projects for the show. Students compete successfully regionally, nationally, and internationally.

FACULTY SPECIALIZATIONS AND RESEARCH

Each faculty member has specialty, Illustration Instructor is prof. illustrator. Design Instructors specialize in patternmaking and design, Textiles Instructor with fabrication, and/or Fiber Art, Sewing Instructors wrote textbook, Fashion Arts Instructor holds MFA in Fiber Art.

COMMUNITY COLLEGE TRANSFERS

Both Design and Merchandising students transfer to FIT, Columbia College, Chicago, Mount Mary College, Milwaukee, and Northern Illinois University.

Ball State University

Fashion Merchandising, Department of Family & Consumer Sciences

150 AT Building, Muncie, IN 47306 | 765-285-5931 | www.bsu.edu/fcs/

UNIVERSITY PROFILE
Public
Suburban
Residential
Semester Schedule
Co-ed

STUDENT DEMOGRAPHICS
Undergraduate: 17,737
Graduate: 3,664

Male: 45.9%
Female: 54.1%

Full-time: 82.7%
Part-time: 17.3%

EXPENSES
Tuition: $7,508 (in-state)
$20,960 (out-of-state)
Room & Board: $7,932

ADMISSIONS
Lucina Hall
Muncie, IN 47306
1-800-482-4278
askus@bsu.edu

DEGREE INFORMATION

Major / Degree / Concentration	Enrollment	Requirements for entry	Graduation rate
Family & Consumer Sciences Bachelor of Science Bachelor of Arts Fashion Merchandising	168	2.0 gpa	77%
Family & Consumer Sciences Bachelor of Science Bachelor of Arts Fashion Design	107	2.0 gpa	77%
Fashion Minor	168	2.0 gpa	n/a
Family & Consumer Sciences Master of Science Master of Arts Fashion	47	2.75 gpa	n/a

TOTAL PROGRAM ENROLLMENT
Undergraduate: 773
Graduate: 63

Male: Not reported
Female: Not reported

Full-time: Not reported
Part-time: Not reported
Online: Not reported

International: Not reported
Minority: Not reported

Job Placement Rate: Not reported

SCHOLARSHIPS / FINANCIAL AID
University provides financial aid through
government programs; department
has scholarships, including the Moore
Scholarship program.

TOTAL FACULTY: 10
Full-time: 70%
Part-time: 30%

FASHION ADMINISTRATION
Dr. Alice Spangler, Chair and Professor

PROFESSIONAL / ACADEMIC AFFILIATIONS
International Textile and Apparel
Association

PROGRAM DESCRIPTION AND PHILOSOPHY

The Fashion Merchandising program focuses on preparing students for the ever-changing retail industry as well as manufacturing, distribution, and other related fashion areas. Study includes courses in dimensions of clothing, textiles, clothing construction (including the use of CAD), evolution of costume, visual merchandising, fashion product analysis, designers and forecasting, fashion buying and merchandising, apparel manufacturing and wholesaling, international apparel markets, and fashion promotion.

Students in Apparel Design are prepared for positions in the ever-changing, but exciting fashion global marketplace as designers, illustrators, pattern makers, textile designers, fabric and notions buyers, sample makers, apparel manufacturers' managers, sewers, retail custom clothiers, and other related positions in the fashion industry. Students selecting the Apparel Design Option in Family and Consumer Sciences will complete the Family and Consumer Scisnces common core.

FACILITIES

Lectra System, Beeman Historic Costume Collection, Computer Labs

ONLINE / DISTANCE LEARNING

Merchandising Mathematics and Designers classes are offered online.

COURSES OF INSTRUCTION

- Fashion industry
- Construction
- Fit and Construction
- Tailoring, Draping
- Grading and Marking
- Studio
- Portfolio
- Buying and E-Commerce
- Textiles for Apparel
- Fashion Product Analysis
- Flat Pattern
- Designers
- Fashion Trend Analysis
- Merchandising Mathematics
- CAD
- Fashion Illustration

INTERNSHIPS

Required of majors at Junior and Senior levels. Interns are placed all over the country at many companies, local examples include Petticoat Junction in Anderson, Kicky Couture in Indianapolis, Minnestra in Muncie; non-local include Baby Phat, Beau & Earas in California, Sweetface Fashion Co., Betsey Johnson, and Ulla-Maija in NY; Mira Couture, Superficial in Chicago.

STUDY ABROAD

University Programs Available to London, Italy, etc.

NOTABLE ALUMNI

Angela Arhendts

STUDENT ACTIVITIES AND ORGANIZATIONS

Clubs, Fashion Merchandising Association, Fashion Design Society, and honors club Phi Upsilon Omicron

FACULTY SPECIALIZATIONS AND RESEARCH

Dr. Leahy, Buying, Technology; Dr. Nam, Fit and Design, Dr. Saiki Costume History

Harrison College

Fashion Merchandising, School of Business

550 E. Washington St., Indianapolis, IN 46204 | 317-264-5656 | www.harrison.edu

UNIVERSITY PROFILE
Private
Urban
Commuter
Quarter Schedule
Co-ed

STUDENT DEMOGRAPHICS
Undergraduate: 600
Graduate: 0

Male: Not reported
Female: Not reported

Full-time: Not reported
Part-time: Not reported

EXPENSES
Tuition: Not reported
Room & Board: n/a

ADMISSIONS
550 E. Washington St.
Indianapolis, IN 46204
317-264-5656

DEGREE INFORMATION

Major / Degree / Concentration	Enrollment	Requirements for entry	Graduation rate
Apparel Merchandising Associate of Applied Science	45	Not reported	85%

TOTAL PROGRAM ENROLLMENT
Undergraduate: 45
Graduate: 0

Male: 5%
Female: 95%

Full-time: 80%
Part-time: 20%
Online: 0%

International: Not reported
Minority: Not reported

Job Placement Rate: 70%

SCHOLARSHIPS / FINANCIAL AID
Not reported

TOTAL FACULTY: 1
Full-time: 100%
Part-time: 0

FASHION ADMINISTRATION
Penny Rosenthal, Chair and Instructor

PROFESSIONAL / ACADEMIC AFFILIATIONS
Fashion Group International

PROGRAM DESCRIPTION AND PHILOSOPHY

The Fashion Merchandising program provides students with a combination of highly creative, fashion-oriented courses as well as a solid business background. By including management classes, students are prepared for such positions as merchandise manager, buying assistant, fashion coordinator, and retail store manager.

FACILITIES

Computer Labs; Libraries; Learning Resource Centers; Museums; Fabric Stores; Art Centers; Malls; Retailers

ONLINE / DISTANCE LEARNING

Not available

COURSES OF INSTRUCTION

- Textile Science
- Display Design
- Apparel Merchandising
- Historical Costume
- Fashion Show Planning
- Psychology of Dress
- Retail Management
- Ready-to-Wear Evaluation
- Introduction to Fashion

INTERNSHIPS

Required of majors. Interns are typically placed with fashion designers and retailers.

STUDY ABROAD

Not available

NOTABLE ALUMNI

Not reported

STUDENT ACTIVITIES AND ORGANIZATIONS

Midwest Fashion Week; Market Week

FACULTY SPECIALIZATIONS AND RESEARCH

Master's Degree

Purdue University

Consumer Sciences & Retailing

812 W. State St., Matthews Hall, W. Lafayette, IN 47907 | 765-494-8317 | www.cfs.purdue.edu/csr

UNIVERSITY PROFILE
Public
Suburban
Residential
Semester Schedule
Co-ed

STUDENT DEMOGRAPHICS
Undergraduate: 31,145
Graduate: 7,639

Male: 57.6%
Female: 42.4%

Full-time: 95%
Part-time: 5%

EXPENSES
Tuition: $9,100 (in-state)
$26,250 (out-of-state)
Room & Board: $9,125

ADMISSIONS
Schleman Hall
W. Lafayette, IN 47907
765-494-1776
admissions@purdue.edu

DEGREE INFORMATION

Major / Degree / Concentration	Enrollment	Requirements for entry	Graduation rate
Apparel Design & Technology Bachelor of Science	101	Core 40; 2.0 gpa	99%

TOTAL PROGRAM ENROLLMENT
Undergraduate: 102
Graduate: n/a

Male: 1%
Female: 99%

Full-time: 100%
Part-time: Not reported
Online: Not reported

International: 0%
Minority: Not reported

Job Placement Rate: 50%

SCHOLARSHIPS / FINANCIAL AID
Financial assistance is available through the Purdue University Division of Financial Aid, Schlemann Hall, West Lafayette, IN 47907.

TOTAL FACULTY: 2
Full-time: 2
Part-time: 1

FASHION DESIGN ADMINISTRATION
Christine Ladisch, Dean
Sugato Chakravarty, Department Head
Nancy Strickler, Associate Clinical Professor & Program Director

PROFESSIONAL / ACADEMIC AFFILIATIONS
International Textile and Apparel Association
Fashion Group International

PROGRAM DESCRIPTION AND PHILOSOPHY

Students have the opportunity to earn a Bachelor of Science 4-year degree at a Big Ten university. The students will develop a good foundation in the science and technology of pattern making, creative design and rendering, consumer business, the creative arts of drawing, and 2D and 3D design.

FACILITIES

Not reported

ONLINE / DISTANCE LEARNING

Not available

COURSES OF INSTRUCTION

- Design I & II
- Drawing I & II
- Life Drawing
- Introduction to the Apparel Industry
- Apparel Construction
- Apparel Design I–draping and flat pattern
- Apparel Design II–draping and flat pattern
- Apparel Design III–line development/production
- CAD for Apparel Pattern Design– Grading, Marking and Pattern Design Systems

- Fashion Illustration
- Apparel Portfolio Development
- Textile Science
- History of Fashion
- Marketing
- Financial Accounting
- Economics
- Selected business courses in buying
- Customer Relations Management
- Interviewing
- Business Writing
- Advertising
- Leadership
- Visual Merchandising
- Consumer Behavior
- Cross-Cultural Marketing
- Personal Finance

INTERNSHIPS

Required of majors at the Sophomore/ Junior level. Students select their own internship locations. They may work in bridal shops, boutiques, or large and small designer houses including, but not limited to: Anna Sui, Zac Posen, Richard Simonton, Guess?, Ralph Lauren, Abercrombie & Fitch, and Liz Claiborne.

STUDY ABROAD

London and Sydney Internship programs are available. Other popular sites of study include Hong Kong and Italy. There are also 3-week study tours to Western European cities.

NOTABLE ALUMNI

Not reported

STUDENT ACTIVITIES AND ORGANIZATIONS

Purdue Fashion Association; Purdue Retail Organization; Professional Development Council, and any student organization offered in a large 4-year resident university.

FACULTY SPECIALIZATIONS AND RESEARCH

Faculty are focused on full-time teaching responsibilities. The professors offer a closely supervised, hands-on opportunity to learn in a very friendly and professional environment.

Vincennes University

Department of Family & Consumer Sciences

1002 N. First St., SH 15, Vincennes, IN 47591 | 812-888-5304 | www.vinu.edu

DEGREE INFORMATION

Major / Degree / Concentration	Enrollment	Requirements for entry	Graduation rate
Fashion Merchandising Associate of Science Associate of Applied Science	40	Program has open admissions policy.	Not reported
Interior Design Associate of Science Associate of Applied Science	40	Program has open admissions policy	Not reported

TOTAL PROGRAM ENROLLMENT
Undergraduate: 4,824
Graduate: 0

Male: Current info on VU Web site www.vinu.edu
Female: Not reported

Full-time: Not reported
Part-time: Not reported
Online: Not reported

International: Not reported
Minority: Not reported

Job Placement Rate: Not reported

SCHOLARSHIPS / FINANCIAL AID
Vincennes University scholarships can be located through the VU Foundation Office Web site at www.vinu.edu/cms/opencms/alumni_foundation/foundation/#found.

TOTAL FACULTY: NOT REPORTED
Full-time: Not reported
Part-time: Not reported

FASHION DESIGN ADMINISTRATION
Lou Ann Lindsey, Prof. & Department Chair
Dr. Charles Reinhart, Dean of Humanities

PROFESSIONAL / ACADEMIC AFFILIATIONS
Not reported

PROGRAM DESCRIPTION AND PHILOSOPHY

Vincennes University's Fashion Merchandising program leads to A.S. or A.A.S. degree and is designed to meet the needs of individuals entering the industry or transferring to a four-year school to continue their studies.

FACILITIES

At Vincennes University you will have the advantage of small classes and labs, free tutoring and excellent course transferability.   Students have the opportunity to visit fashion markets and fashion businesses. Hands-on instructional activities in visual merchandising, fashion wholesaling, and clothing construction are provided.   Internships in the field are available to students who qualify.

ONLINE / DISTANCE LEARNING

Multiple courses for each major are available online

COURSES OF INSTRUCTION

- Survey of Family & Consumer Sciences
- Clothing I & II
- Art Appreciation
- Buying in Fashion
- Tailoring

- History of Costume

- Psychology
- Textiles
- Visual Merchandising

- Economics

INTERNSHIPS

Available

STUDY ABROAD

Not reported

NOTABLE ALUMNI

Not reported

STUDENT ACTIVITIES AND ORGANIZATIONS

Not reported

FACULTY SPECIALIZATIONS AND RESEARCH

Not reported

Johnson County Community College

Fashion Merchandising & Design
Box #37, Overland Park, KS 66210 | 913-469-8500 ext. 3357 | www.jccc.edu/home/depts/1201

UNIVERSITY PROFILE
Public
Suburban
Commuter
Semester Schedule
Co-ed

STUDENT DEMOGRAPHICS
Undergraduate: 20,401
Graduate: n/a

Male: Not reported
Female: Not reported

Full-time: Not reported
Part-time: Not reported

EXPENSES
Tuition: $75 per credit hour
Room & Board: n/a

ADMISSIONS
Box 41
Overland Park, KS 66210
913-469-3803
jcccadmissions@jccc.edu

DEGREE INFORMATION

Major / Degree / Concentration	Enrollment	Requirements for entry	Graduation rate
Fashion Merchandising Associate of Applied Science	55	Open enrollment	21% (many transfer)
Fashion Design Associate of Applied Science	51	Undergraduate degree in Interior Design or related area	19% (many transfer)

TOTAL PROGRAM ENROLLMENT
Undergraduate: 20,401
Graduate: n/a

Male: 46.8%
Female: 53.2%

Full-time: 51.4%
Part-time: 48.6%
Online: 18%

International: 10%
Minority: 16%

Job Placement Rate: 100%

SCHOLARSHIPS / FINANCIAL AID
See opposite page for more info.

TOTAL FACULTY: 901
Full-time: 36%
Part-time: 64%

FASHION ADMINISTRATION
Dr. Terry Callaway, President
Dr. Marilyn Rhinehart, Executive Vice President, Instruction/Chief Academic Officer
Lindy Robinson, Dean, Business Division

PROFESSIONAL / ACADEMIC AFFILIATIONS
Fashion Group International

PROGRAM DESCRIPTION AND PHILOSOPHY

The Fashion Merchandising and Design program at Johnson County College is committed to proving a program of quality academic coursework and on-the-job training for employment in the fashion industry.

The Fashion Merchandising and Design program is designed to provide maximum flexibility to meet the needs of a diverse student body. Honors options are available to qualified students. Quick Step and vocational transfer agreements provide early for talented high school students. Transfer agreements are arranged with several institutions for students who desire a baccalaureate degree.

FACILITIES

- Construction Laboratory
- Computer Lab with Adobe Suite and Gerber
- Store-like windows for visual merchandising
- Large library of mannequins and props
- Large historical costume collection
- Digital historical costume collection
- Textile Library
- Smart classrooms
- *Women's Wear Daily WWD* Online and in classroom
- Retail and Franchise Library
- Apparel Construction and Tailoring Laboratory
- Nerman Museum of Contemporary Art

ONLINE / DISTANCE LEARNING

Textiles, History of Costume, Fashion Fundamentals

COURSES OF INSTRUCTION

Fashion Fundamentals, Apparel Construction I and II, Visual Merchandising, Aesthetics, Career Options, Capstone: Industry Topics, CAD: Apparel Design, The Market Center, Image Management, Marketing Communication, Consumer Product Evaluation, Textiles, Merchandising Planning and Control, Internship l-IV, Flat Pattern Development, Fashion Illustration, Computer Aided Apparel Design, Fashion Product Development, History of Costume, Computer Aided Pattern Development, Fashion Portfolio Development, and 16 credits in general education.

INTERNSHIPS

Required of majors at the Freshman and Sophomore level. Interns are typically placed at companies such as Nordstrom, Gap, Maurices, Gear for Sports, Dillard's, Macy's, American Apparel, Macy's, Halls, Imagery, Guess, Kate Spade, Fossil, Peggy Noland, Jessica McClintock, Abercrombie & Fitch, Forever 21, American Eagle Outfitter, Justice, Addie Rose, Ella Klara, Victoria Secret, and TomBoy.

STUDY ABROAD

Through JCCC's Study Abroad Program, you can receive college credit while studying in any one of over 30 countries for a summer, semester or a year. Programs are offered in Europe, Asia, Latin America, Africa, and Australia. In addition to studying the country's language, you'll take other courses taught in English.

NOTABLE ALUMNI

Valisha Lasker, past manager of alliances Mark and Avon Beauty

STUDENT ACTIVITIES AND ORGANIZATIONS

Employer/Employee Appreciation Breakfast, Annual Fashion Show in the Polsky Theater, Fashion Group International Career Day

FACULTY SPECIALIZATIONS AND RESEARCH

Textile Science, Product Development, Apparel Design, Personal Branding, Illustration, Computer Aided Pattern Making, Computer Aided Design, Visual Merchandising, Store Planning, Retail Management, Professional Selling, Alterations, Event Planning, Tailoring, Costume Curator

COMMUNITY COLLEGE TRANSFERS

Chicago School of Art, Fashion Institute of Technology–New York, Fashion Institute of Design and Merchandising–Los Angeles Articulations: Stephens College, Kansas State University, Missouri State University, University of Missouri

SCHOLARSHIP / FINANCIAL AID

To be considered for financial aid, you must:

- Be enrolled in a program that leads to an Associate's degree or an eligible vocational certificate or be in a transfer program that leads to a Bachelor's degree at another institution.
- Be a U.S. citizen, an eligible noncitizen or a permanent resident of the United States.
- Maintain satisfactory academic progress according to the JCCC student financial aid policy.
- Not be in default on a student loan or owe a repayment on a grant.
- Register with the selective service (if required) and sign a statement of selective service status (www.sss.gov).

FM+D Scholarships $5,000+ annually: Every spring scholarships are awarded to students that have demonstrated outstanding leadership skills. FM+D program is very active. There are many activities that offer opportunities for students to take the lead. Original designs modeled in the annual fashion show are judged by professionals in the industry. Scholarships are awarded to the top designers.

Dollars for Scholars Auction: Dollars for Scholars is an annual fundraiser for student scholarships. The event features a live and a silent auction, buffet dinner, beverages, a raffle, games of chance and entertainment. This event is hosted by JCCC friends, alumni, faculty, staff, and students. In past years, this event has raised over $50,000 for 30 scholarships and program funds. Fashion Merchandising and Design participate to raise money for their scholarships.

Receiving Scholarships or Financial Aid: 60%

Kansas State University

Apparel, Textiles & Interior Design

225 Justin Hall, Manhattan, KS 66506-1405 | 785-532-6993 | www.humec.k-state.edu/atid/

UNIVERSITY PROFILE
Public
Suburban
Residential
Semester Schedule
Co-ed

STUDENT DEMOGRAPHICS
Undergraduate: 19,000
Graduate: 4,800

Male: 52%
Female: 48%

Full-time: 88%
Part-time: 12%

EXPENSES
Tuition: $6,456
Room & Board: $6,752

ADMISSIONS
Kansas State University,
119 Anderson Hall
Manhattan, KS 66506-0102
1-800-432-8270
k-state@k-state.edu

DEGREE INFORMATION

Major / Degree / Concentration	Enrollment	Requirements for entry	Graduation rate
Apparel & Textiles Bachelor of Science Specialization in Apparel Design and Production;	25	Admission to KSU Selective Advancement testing after second year	90%
Apparel & Textiles Bachelor of Science Specialization in Apparel Marketing	210	Admission to KSU	87%
Apparel & Textiles Master of Science	11	Bachelor of Science Graduate School application Application fee GRE score Three letters of recommendation Statement of Goals and Objectives Transcripts of all university coursework (International students must also have TOEFL Score and Financial Support)	96%
Apparel & Textiles Master of Science Merchandising GP-IDEA	30	Same as above	98%
Doctorate of Philosophy in Human Ecology	6	Master of Science Graduate School application Application fee GRE score Three letters of recommendation Statement of Goals and Objectives Transcripts of all university coursework (International students must also have TOEFL Score and Financial Support)	95%

TOTAL PROGRAM ENROLLMENT
Undergraduate: 235
Graduate: 47

Male: 5%
Female: 95%

Full-time: 87%
Part-time: 13%
Online: 10%

International: 4%
Minority: 8%

Job Placement Rate: Not reported

SCHOLARSHIPS / FINANCIAL AID
There are multiple endowed scholarships for students in the ATID department and additional scholarships and aid available at the college and university level.

Students Receiving Scholarships or Financial Aid: 75%

TOTAL FACULTY: 9
Full-time: 78%
Part-time: 22%

FASHION ADMINISTRATION
Dr. Jana Hawley, Department Head and Professor

PROFESSIONAL / ACADEMIC AFFILIATIONS
International Textile and Apparel Association
Fashion Group International
American Collegiate Retailing Association

PROGRAM DESCRIPTION AND PHILOSOPHY
The Department of Apparel, Textiles, and Interior Design encompasses disciplines that study the interaction of humans and their environment. Faculty members specialize in apparel design, apparel marketing, and textile and product development. They share a commitment to excellence in scholarship in its many diverse forms including discovery, integration, application, and teaching. ATID programs share a common responsibility to teach within a human ecological framework and to give considerable attention to environmental ethics and social responsibility within the disciplines and professions represented.

FACILITIES
Design studios, printing and plotting, body scanner for fit studies, extensive equipment for natural dye research, historic textiles and costume collection housed in a climate-controlled storage facility, K-State's Beach Museum of Art, excellent Library services, WGSN, Lectra software, digitizer.

ONLINE / DISTANCE LEARNING
ATID is a member of the Great Plains Interactive Distance Education Alliance (GP-IDEA) offering an online graduate degree in merchandising. The program offers a 36-hour Master's degree distance program. The inter-institutional program draws on the knowledge and expertise of graduate faculty and graduate courses from five universities: Colorado State University, Kansas State University, North Dakota State University, Oklahoma State University, and South Dakota State University. Students completing the Master's degree program from KSU will earn a M.S. in Apparel and Textiles with a specialization in Merchandising.

COURSES OF INSTRUCTION
- Apparel and Textile Industry
- Aesthetics of Apparel and Textiles
- Textiles
- Apparel Consumers and Society
- Aesthetics of Apparel and Textiles
- History of Apparel Fashion: Renaissance to Present
- Professional Development
- Apparel and Textile Evaluation
- Global Apparel and Textile Product and Distribution
- Private Label Apparel Product Development
- Apparel Design and Production Specialization
- Fashion Illustration
- Apparel Production I and II
- Computer-Aided Design of Apparel
- Apparel Pattern Development I and II
- Apparel Marketing Specialization
- Apparel and Textile Store Operation
- Principles of Forecasting
- Principles of Buying
- Apparel and Textile Business Strategy

INTERNSHIPS
Required of majors. Interns are typically placed at companies such as Dillards, Gap, Fossil, Nordstrom, Hot Topic, Walmart, Nolan Glove Co., American Eagle Outfitters, Zotics, Hollister, GTM Sportswear, J.Crew, JCPenney, Nike, Abercrombie, Payless Shoesource

STUDY ABROAD
Students who choose to study abroad for a summer or a semester receive guidance from the faculty advisors. Many students choose American Intercontinental University.

NOTABLE ALUMNI
Mary Ellen Vernon, Linda Lee, Sherry Maxwell, Lana Irish, Linda Leeper, Janice Hamilton

STUDENT ACTIVITIES AND ORGANIZATIONS
Apparel Marketing Design Alliance (AMDA)
Advocates 4 Artisans
Apparel and Textiles Graduate Student Organization (ATGSO)
Collaboration with Marketplace India

FACULTY SPECIALIZATIONS AND RESEARCH
The Apparel and Textile faculty members have diverse areas of expertise including: disciplines that study the interaction of humans and their environment, textile and product development, textile surface design, thermal and barrier properties of fabrics and protective clothing systems, sustainable consumer behavior and consumption, textile recycling, retail strategies, creative and functional

University of Kentucky

Department of Merchandising, Apparel, & Textiles

318 Erikson Hall, Lexington, KY 40506-0050 | 859-257-4917 | www.ca.uky.edu/hes/?p=27

UNIVERSITY PROFILE
Public
Urban
Residential
Semester Schedule
Co-ed

STUDENT DEMOGRAPHICS
Undergraduate: Not reported
Graduate: Not reported

Male: Not reported
Female: Not reported

Full-time: Not reported
Part-time: Not reported

EXPENSES
Tuition: $8,122
Room & Board: $6,139

ADMISSIONS
100 W.D. Funkhouser Building
Lexington, KY 40506-0054
859-257-2000
admissions@uky.edu

DEGREE INFORMATION

Major / Degree / Concentration	Enrollment	Requirements for entry	Graduation rate
Merchandising, Apparel & Textiles Bachelor of Arts	250	Not reported	Not reported

TOTAL PROGRAM ENROLLMENT
Undergraduate: 250
Graduate: 14

Male: Not reported
Female: Not reported

Full-time: Not reported
Part-time: Not reported
Online: Not reported

International: Not reported
Minority: Not reported

Job Placement Rate: Not reported

SCHOLARSHIPS / FINANCIAL AID
Not reported

TOTAL FACULTY: 7
Full-time: 100%
Part-time: 0%

FASHION DESIGN ADMINISTRATION
Dr. Ann Vail, Director School of Human Environmental Sciences
Dr. Ann Vail, Interim Chair, Merchandising, Apparel and Textiles
Dr. Vanessa Jackson, Director of Undergraduate Studies

PROFESSIONAL / ACADEMIC AFFILIATIONS
International Textile and Apparel Association
American Collegiate Retailing Association

PROGRAM DESCRIPTION AND PHILOSOPHY

The Department of Merchandising, Apparel, and Textiles is committed to excellence as it prepares students for merchandising, apparel, and textiles positions in an increasingly diverse and technological world. Teaching, research, and service programs support student development and contribute to the economic and social well-being of the Commonwealth, the nation, and the world. The department offers the Bachelor of Science in Merchandising, Apparel, and Textiles. The graduate program offers either a Master of Science in Merchandising, Apparel, and Textiles. There are currently 7 full-time faculty.

FACILITIES

Computer labs with Illustrator CS4, SnapFashun, Plaid software, Betty D. Eastin Historic Costume Collection, textile testing lab

ONLINE / DISTANCE LEARNING

The following courses are offered online: Dress and Culture, International Retailing, and E-tailing.

COURSES OF INSTRUCTION

- Introduction to Merchandising
- Textile Science
- Aesthetics in Merchandising
- Dress and Culture
- Planning and Organization
- Research Methods
- History of Costume
- Brand Management
- Retail Entrepreneurship

INTERNSHIPS

Required of majors between Junior and Senior year.

STUDY ABROAD

Available

NOTABLE ALUMNI

Not reported

STUDENT ACTIVITIES AND ORGANIZATIONS

MAT Club (Merchandising, Apparel and Textiles)

FACULTY SPECIALIZATIONS AND RESEARCH

Laundry fundamentals, social/psych and cultural aspects of dress, gender differences within dress and costume, sustainability, green textiles, rural retailing, cross-cultural retailing studies, online shopping, consumer behavior

Western Kentucky University

Department of Family & Consumer Sciences

1906 College Heights Blvd., #11037, Bowling Green, KY 42101 | 270-745-4352 | www.wku.edu/Dept/Academic/chhs/cf

UNIVERSITY PROFILE
Public
Urban
Residential
Semester Schedule
Co-ed

STUDENT DEMOGRAPHICS
Undergraduate: 1,900
Graduate: 3,000

Male: 40%
Female: 60%

Full-time: Not reported
Part-time: Not reported

EXPENSES
Tuition: $7,200
Room & Board: Not reported

ADMISSIONS
1906 College Heights Blvd.
Bowling Green, KY 42101
270-745-0111
western@wku.edu

DEGREE INFORMATION

Major / Degree / Concentration	Enrollment	Requirements for entry	Graduation rate
Textiles & Apparel Merchandising Bachelor of Science	90	2.0 gpa	80%

TOTAL PROGRAM ENROLLMENT
Undergraduate: 90
Graduate: Not reported

Male: 10%
Female: 90%

Full-time: 90%
Part-time: 10%
Online: Not reported

International: 5%
Minority: 10%

Job Placement Rate: 90%

SCHOLARSHIPS / FINANCIAL AID
- Marie Adams–Home Economics Alumni Association Scholarship
- Beta Delta–Phi Upsilon Omicron Scholarships
- Bernice King Doublas Scholarship
- Evadine Parker–Phi Upsilon Omicron Scholarship
- Fashion, Inc., Scholarship
- Susie Pate Scholarship
- Warren County Homemakers Association–Melissa Bohannon Clemmons Scholarship

TOTAL FACULTY: 4
Full-time: 3
Part-time: 1

FASHION DESIGN ADMINISTRATION
Dr. Doris Sikora, Department Head

PROFESSIONAL / ACADEMIC AFFILIATIONS
International Textile and Apparel Association
Fashion Group International

PROGRAM DESCRIPTION AND PHILOSOPHY

The Textiles and Apparel Merchandising major at Western Kentucky University is comprised of 76 hours in the major. The central purpose of this program is to prepare graduates who can successfully fulfill focal roles as managers, merchandisers, and problem solvers in the textile and apparel industry.

FACILITIES

Not reported

ONLINE / DISTANCE LEARNING

Not reported

COURSES OF INSTRUCTION

- Perspectives of Dress
- Textiles
- Basic Apparel Construction
- Merchandising
- Creative Problem Solving
- Textile Design and Performance

INTERNSHIPS

Required of majors at the Senior level. Interns are typically placed at companies such as Fruit of a Loom, Russell Athletics, *Vanity Fair*.

STUDY ABROAD

Yearly interior design trip to Australia or Europe through Department and opportunities with KIIS, CSSA, and Semester at Sea.

NOTABLE ALUMNI

Not reported

STUDENT ACTIVITIES AND ORGANIZATIONS

Not reported

FACULTY SPECIALIZATIONS AND RESEARCH

Not reported

Framingham State College

Fashion Design & Retailing, Consumer Sciences Department

100 State St., Hemenway Hall, Framingham, MA 01701 | 508-626-4700 | www.framingham.edu/fashion

UNIVERSITY PROFILE
Public
Suburban
Residential & Commuter
Semester Schedule
Co-ed

STUDENT DEMOGRAPHICS
Undergraduate: 3,847
Graduate: 2,142

Male: 34%
Female: 66%

Full-time: 72%
Part-time: 28%

EXPENSES
Tuition: $6,540 (in-state)
$12,620 (out-of-state)
$7,025 (New England Regional)
Room & Board: $8,018

ADMISSIONS
100 State St.
Framingham, MA 01701
508-626-4500
admissions@framingham.edu.

DEGREE INFORMATION

Major / Degree / Concentration	Enrollment	Requirements for entry	Graduation rate
Fashion Design & Retailing Bachelor of Science Apparel Design	56	MA State college requirements	Not reported
Fashion Design & Retailing Bachelor of Science Merchandising	150	MA State college requirements	Not reported
Graduate Certificate in Fashion Design Apparel Design	3	Bachelor degree	Not reported
Merchandising Graduate Certificate	New program in 2010	Bachelor degree	Not reported

TOTAL PROGRAM ENROLLMENT
Undergraduate: 3,847
Graduate: 2,142

Male: 34%
Female: 66%

Full-time: 72%
Part-time: 28%
Online: unknown

International: <1%
Minority: 19%

Job Placement Rate: Not reported

SCHOLARSHIPS / FINANCIAL AID
Federal and State
Institutional: Endowed scholarships, annual gifts and tuition funded grants, awarded by the college, excluding athletic aid and tuition waivers
Scholarships/grants from external sources (e.g., Kiwanis, National Merit) not awarded by the college
College Alumni Association scholarships, grants, and loans
Also specific scholarships, loans, and awards to Fashion Design and Retailing students

TOTAL FACULTY:
Full-time: Not reported
Part-time: Not reported

FASHION ADMINISTRATION
Dr. Timothy J. Flanagan, President of Framingham State College
Professor Janet Schwartz, Consumer Sciences Department Chair
Dr. Irene M. Foster, Fashion Design and Retailing Program Coordinator

PROFESSIONAL / ACADEMIC AFFILIATIONS
International Textile and Apparel Association
Fashion Group International
American Collegiate Retailing Association

PROGRAM DESCRIPTION AND PHILOSOPHY

Why choose Framingham State College?

- Bachelor of Science degree with a major in Fashion Design and Retailing
- Business and industry partnerships
- State-of-the-art computer technology
- Professional curriculum combined with strong Liberal Arts
- Located in suburban Boston
- Dynamic merchandising and design opportunities
- Seven full-time faculty
- Small classes and individual attention
- Individual advising
- Career counseling
- Diverse student body

FACILITIES

Wireless Internet campus, laptop computer technology, computer labs and printers, Costume Collection and Archives, located less than 20 miles from Boston, MA

ONLINE / DISTANCE LEARNING

Some courses are offered online

COURSES OF INSTRUCTION

Fashion Design and Retailing Major requirements:

- Principles of Apparel Construction
- Fashion: Designer to Consumer
- Consumer Textiles
- History of Costume or History of Textiles
- Research Methods for the Fashion Industry
- Fashion Merchandising: Theory and Distribution
- World Market: Textiles to Retailing
- Introduction to Statistics

Merchandising Concentration requirements:

- Field Study in Merchandising (no credit)
- Retailing and Consumer Behavior
- Fashion Promotion
- Fashion Merchandising: Planning, Policies, and Implementation
- Internship in Merchandising (credit– two courses)
- Apparel Design Concentration requirements:
- Advanced Apparel Construction
- Flat Pattern Design
- Draping
- Fabric Structure and Design
- Apparel Industry Methods
- Functional Clothing Design
- Apparel Design Portfolio
- Drawing I
- Introduction to Drawing
- Color Theory
- Fashion Illustration

INTERNSHIPS

Required of Merchandising majors at Senior level; optional for Apparel Design majors. Interns are typically placed at companies such as Reebok, Int., Collective Brands (StrideRite Corp.), TJX, Co., US Army Natick Soldier Systems Center, Boston Apparel Group (Chadwick's), J.Jill Group, Boston Ballet, Amari Bridal, Bennett and Company.

STUDY ABROAD

Available through American Inter-Continental University, Paris Fashion Institute, Paris American Academy, more

NOTABLE ALUMNI

Nancy Atchue, AVP Merchandising, TJX; David Ambach, Buyer TJX, Co.; Ellen DiBattista, Buyer, Reebok, Int.; Kristine Modugno, AVP Manager of Corporate Brands, BJ's Wholesale Club; Michele Simmarano, Buyer, Filene's Basement; Heather Cumming-Rowell, Clothing Designer, US Army Natick Soldier Systems

STUDENT ACTIVITIES AND ORGANIZATIONS

Fashion Club, Design and Development Club, Phi Upsilon Omicron National Honor Society

FACULTY SPECIALIZATIONS AND RESEARCH

Merchandising, Promotion, Retail Technology, Apparel Design and Construction, Computer Applications in Design (Adobe Illustrator CS), Wearable Art, Historic Costume Reproduction, Flat Sketching, Historic Textiles, Museum Studies, Social Aspects of Dress, Product Development, Technical Design, Theater Costuming, Bridal Eveningwear.

COMMUNITY COLLEGE TRANSFERS

All Massachusetts Community Colleges–state transfer; other colleges university must meet College requirements for State College system; transfer study abroad courses

Lasell College

Fashion Department

1844 Commonwealth Ave., Newton, MA 02466 | 617-243-2042 | www.lasell.edu/fashion

DEGREE INFORMATION

Major / Degree / Concentration	Enrollment	Requirements for entry	Graduation rate
Fashion Design & Production Bachelor of Arts	146	Not reported	Not reported
Fashion & Retail Merchandising Bachelor of Science	256	Not reported	Not reported
Fashion Communication & Promotion Bachelor of Science	New in 2010	Not reported	Not reported

TOTAL PROGRAM ENROLLMENT
Undergraduate: 402
Graduate: 0

Male: 6.2%
Female: 93.8%

Full-time: 99.3%
Part-time: 0.7%
Online: 0%

International: 0.7%
Minority: 10.0%

Job Placement Rate: Not reported

SCHOLARSHIPS / FINANCIAL AID
Financial aid and scholarships at Lasell
are available across all majors.

Receiving Scholarships or Financial Aid:
96.5%

TOTAL FACULTY: 18
Full-time: 44.4%
Part-time: 55.6%

FASHION ADMINISTRATION
Mary Ruppert-Stroescu, Chair

PROFESSIONAL / ACADEMIC AFFILIATIONS
International Textile and Apparel
  Association
Fashion Group International

PROGRAM DESCRIPTION AND PHILOSOPHY

The Fashion department offers three majors: Fashion Retail & Merchandising, Fashion Design & Production, and Fashion Communication & Promotion. Fashion majors at Lasell have a unique opportunity to combine a Liberal Arts education with industry knowledge to succeed in a variety of professional areas. Coursework builds on an Arts and Science base while developing proficiency in product knowledge and contemporary business practices. Through application of Lasell's Connected Learning philosophy, Fashion students have ongoing opportunities to apply theoretical concepts through industry-oriented assignments and by working in the field with recognized leaders in the fashion industry. The upper-level professional courses are oriented toward a critical thinking and decision-making environment that graduates will face when making the transition from college to middle- and upper-management positions. Students learn how to plan strategically, organize for profitability, and cultivate creativity.

FACILITIES

Computer labs in both Mac and PC formats. Industry software for both design and merchandising. The Lasell Fashion Collection of historic garments. On-site gallery that exhibits work of students and professionals.

ONLINE / DISTANCE LEARNING

Not available

COURSES OF INSTRUCTION

Core:
- Fashion History
- Apparel Product Development
- Textiles
- 20th Century Fashion History

Fashion & Retail Merchandising:
- Contemporary Issues in Fashion Merchandising
- Financial Accounting
- Marketing
- Organizational Behavior
- Merchandise Planning & Control
- Retail Management
- Visual Merchandising
- Fashion and Society
- Visual Promotion
- Retail Operations Analysis
- Interior Display & Design
- Trend Forecasting
- Fashion Promotion

Fashion Design and Production:
- Clothing Construction I & II
- Pattern Generation I & II
- Fashion Illustration
- Fashion Design Concepts
- Flat Pattern Design I & II
- Digital Design for Apparel
- Professional Presentation Methods
- Draping
- Accessories Design
- Technical Patterns
- Tailoring/Couture Detail
- CAD I & II–Lectra
- Senior Thesis Development
- Senior Thesis Production

Fashion Communication & Promotion:
- Fashion Styling and Photography
- Fashion Communication
- Understanding Mass Media
- Writing for the Media
- Introduction to Public Relations
- Introduction to Advertising

INTERNSHIPS

Required of majors at Junior/Senior level. Interns are typically placed at companies such as Marc Jacobs Design, NYC, TJX Corporate, Converse Corporate, New Balance Corporate, Talbots Corporate, *Women's Wear Daily*, *Marie Claire*, *Bride's Magazine*, Berghdorf Goodman, Macy's Corporate, Natick Military Research

Labs: Textile & Clothing division, J. Jill Corporate, Blue Man Group costuming, Priscilla of Boston, X-Hale Boutique, Creative Events, Levi Jeans, Chanel Boutique, Steve Marsel Studio, Yolanda, Gucci, Lucky Magazine, Eloie, Anthropologie, The Red Wagon, City Sports, IMG, Click Models, Metropark, Lord & Taylor, Forever 21, Juicy Couture, The Melting Pot, Pink, Matt Reimer Sales Agency, Martin & Osa, Classic Threads, Simply Inviting Weddings, Panssofurs Bridal Shop, Fashion Feng Shui.

STUDY ABROAD

Junior-year study abroad programs are available in nearly every country worldwide. Fashion majors often select continental European countries as their destinations.

NOTABLE ALUMNI

Isabelle Miller, Designer, Little Marc by Marc Jacobs, Wendy Tarfano, Merchandising/Operations Manager for all Retail Brand Alliance eCommerce businesses, Stacey Scarcella, Senior Art Buyer for TJX Companies.

STUDENT ACTIVITIES AND ORGANIZATIONS

Polished Magazine, a student-generated Boston fashion, art, music and culture published twice a year and online: www.polishedfashion.com. Student organizations: The Fashion Connection does outreach and networking with the fashion industry. Fashion Service Society incorporates fashion into service projects.

FACULTY SPECIALIZATIONS AND RESEARCH

Faculty all have industry and teaching experience. Research regarding creativity in fashion is a strong focus.

Massachusetts College of Art & Design

Fashion Design Department

621 Huntington Ave., Boston, MA 02115 | 617-879-7650 | www.massart.edu/Academic_Programs/Fashion_Design

UNIVERSITY PROFILE
Public
Urban
Residential
Semester Schedule
Co-ed

STUDENT DEMOGRAPHICS
Undergraduate: 1,684
Graduate: 175

Male: 34%
Female: 66%

Full-time: 94%
Part-time: 6%

EXPENSES
Tuition: $9,000 (MA resident)
$15,700 (New England Resident)
$25,400 (non-resident)
Room & Board: $10,880-$12,590

ADMISSIONS
621 Huntington Ave.
Boston, MA 02116
617-879-7222
admissions@massart.edu

DEGREE INFORMATION

Major / Degree / Concentration	Enrollment	Requirements for entry	Graduation rate
Fashion Design Bachelor of Fine Arts	153	Students must meet general admission standards for entry to the college; no additional requirements for fashion majors.	68%

TOTAL PROGRAM ENROLLMENT
Undergraduate: 153
Graduate: 92

Male: 8%
Female: 92%

Full-time: 75%
Part-time: 15%

International: 4%
Minority: 33%

Job Placement Rate: Not reported

SCHOLARSHIPS / FINANCIAL AID
All BFA students, including Fashion majors, are eligible for merit- and need-based MassArt scholarships. See our Web site for details

Students Receiving Scholarships or Financial Aid: 75%

TOTAL FACULTY: 12
Full-time: 42%
Part-time: 58%

FASHION DESIGN ADMINISTRATION
Sondra Grace, Professor, Chairperson, Fashion Design Department

PROFESSIONAL / ACADEMIC AFFILIATIONS
International Textile and Apparel Association
Fashion Group International

PROGRAM DESCRIPTION AND PHILOSOPHY

The Massachusetts College of Art and Design has offered Fashion Design for 100 years. The study of fashion at MassArt trains students to create fashion as art and develop an understanding of the fundamentals needed to be a designer in the fashion industry.

MassArt Fashion students design, research and construct both couture and ready-to-wear garments. Traditional methods of foundation and shape are developed for couture and bespoke clothing. Trend forecasting and fabric innovations are explored for ready-to-wear line production. Computer knowledge in Adobe Photoshop and Illustrator along with U4ia CAD and Gerber CAM are incorporated into the curriculum.

MassArt Fashion Design students combine in their studies the worlds of fine arts high couture and of commerce, learning to create both one-of-a-kind and ready-to-wear garments as well as accessory design and theatrical costume, using traditional and nontraditional materials. Students in the program learn to design and construct garments for women, men, and children. They are encouraged to explore their individual interests and to develop their own style as they master detailing techniques, design, and pattern making. Program faculty members teach traditional design methods, along with cutting-edge computer design technology. Students are trained to consider issues of marketability, cost, care, and function.

Students organize and produce an annual show of their work. They work with lighting and sound, design sets, engage models, choose make-up and accessories, and write copy and promotional materials.

In the Senior year, each student undertakes a degree project consisting of the creation of a signature line of garments. The degree project draws on independent research, and students are encouraged here, especially, to explore their individual aesthetic. Some recent projects have included African-inspired millinery, costumes derived from the Sámi culture, and a line of sportswear inspired by the history of aviation.

MassArt students have designed for the Chadwick's division of Redcats USA, Radici Spandex, Levi Strauss, Sommers Plastic, Stride Rite, and Go-Pak Outerwear and the Italian Trade Commission. Fashion Design students have won major design competitions including: GenArt, CFDA, Air France Design, Fashion Group International of Boston, and IACDE Scholarship Competition. Fashion Design graduates are in every area of the industry—from designing to manufacturing and product development; as well as theater costuming and retail merchandising—Michael Kors, DKNY, Karl Lagerfeld, Victoria's Secret, Boston Apparel Group, Nautica, Puma, Tory Burch, Betsy Johnson, Tommy Hilfiger, Reebok, Phillip Van Heusen, Josie Natori, Talbots, Fossil, Vera Wang, Nicole Miller, the Kellwood Group, J.Jill, Appleseed, and Andrew Harmon.

FACILITIES

MassArt has nearly one million square feet of studio, workshop, classroom, and exhibition space. There also are nine galleries on campus.

ONLINE / DISTANCE LEARNING

Not available

COURSES OF INSTRUCTION

- Fashion Illustration I & II
- Pattern Drafting I, II, & III
- Creative Fashion I, II, III & IV
- CAD courses in Textiles & U4ia
- Digital Tools—Photoshop & Illustrator
- Gerber PDS
- Fashion History I & II
- Art History
- Literary Traditions
- Marketing
- Couture Techniques
- Specialized Fashion Degree Project I & II

INTERNSHIPS

Required of majors.

MassArt Fashion Design students have the opportunity to intern for credit during their Junior and Senior years. A broad range of experiences are offered through internships with Boston Ballet, Karmaloop. com, Reebok, Puma and Boston Conservatory to name a few. New York internships during the summers include Armani, Marc Jacobs, Zac Posen, and Michael Kors.

STUDY ABROAD

Travel courses and study aboard opportunities include Paris Fashion Institute; Paris & Antwerp; Central Saint Martin; and Brazil

NOTABLE ALUMNI

Andrew Harmon, Tunji Dada, Dayanne Danier, Maya Luz, Rebecca Turbow, Alison Kelly, Jane Marie Henry

STUDENT ACTIVITIES AND ORGANIZATIONS

MassArt has an active student body with clubs and activities of all kinds. In addition, it is a member of the Colleges of the Fenway (COF), a consortium of six colleges with a student population totaling nearly 12,000. COF offers intramural athletics, performing arts, and other student activities, as well as cross-registration among the six campuses.

FACULTY SPECIALIZATIONS AND RESEARCH

Fashion faculty represent diverse areas of fashion expertise and research including global design and sustainability, historical costume research; working with artisans in Fortaleza, Brazil, and Lyon, France along with curating and producing apparel collections.

Baltimore City Community College

Fashion Design Program

2901 Liberty Heights Ave., Baltimore, MD 21215 | 410-462-8300 | www.bccc.edu

UNIVERSITY PROFILE
Public
Urban
Commuter
Semester Schedule
Co-ed

STUDENT DEMOGRAPHICS
Undergraduate: 6,953
Graduate: n/a

Male: 29%
Female: 71%

Full-time: 40%
Part-time: 60%

EXPENSES
Tuition: $1,231 (in-state)
$2,695 (out-of-state)
Room & Board: n/a

ADMISSIONS
See Web site

DEGREE INFORMATION

Major / Degree / Concentration	Enrollment	Requirements for entry	Graduation rate
Fashion Design Associate of Applied Arts	60	High School Diploma	95%
Fashion Design Certificate	40	High School Diploma	85%
Fashion Retailing Associate of Applied Arts	27	High School Diploma	95%

TOTAL PROGRAM ENROLLMENT
Undergraduate: Not reported
Graduate: n/a

Male: 10%
Female: 90%

Full-time: 60%
Part-time: 40%
Online: /a

International: 25%
Minority: 75%

Job Placement Rate: 90%

SCHOLARSHIPS / FINANCIAL AID
Students enrolled in the Fashion Design program can apply for the following scholarships and/or financial aid.
1. Damon Gibson Memorial Scholarship
2. Payless ShoeSource Scholarship (Up to $500.00 awarded to two to three students each semester who apply and demonstrate academic excellence in fashion design. The students must prove that they are in need of financial assistance and that they are not receiving any other type of financial aid).
3. Pell Grants (Eligibility is based on financial need and family income).

Students Receiving Scholarships or Financial Aid: 75%

TOTAL FACULTY: 11
Full-time: 20%
Part-time: 80%

FASHION ADMINISTRATION
Dr. Katana Hall, Department Chairperson, English Speech, Visual and Performing Arts
Ted Along, Division Dean, Liberal Arts, Education, and Applied Arts

PROFESSIONAL / ACADEMIC AFFILIATIONS
International Textile and Apparel Association
Fashion Group International

PROGRAM DESCRIPTION AND PHILOSOPHY

Baltimore City Community College's Fashion Design program was inaugurated in 1975 with forty-five students majoring in Fashion Designing. Today, 127 students, full and part-time, have the opportunity to pursue the Fashion Design AAS Degree or Certificate Options, and the Fashion Retailing AAS Degree Option. It is the only program of its kind in any institution of higher learning in the State of Maryland. Students from beyond the boundaries of Baltimore City enroll from areas as far away as Annapolis, Delaware, Pennsylvania, Virginia, and Washington, D.C. The American Textile Manufacturers Institute cited the program for innovative curriculum design and teaching excellence.

The program's commitment to career education is reinforced with state-of-the-art equipment, a faculty made up of working professionals, and an industry-driven Advisory Committee. As a result, students are exposed to the latest technical advancements in the field and are prepared to compete and work in the global marketplace. In addition, to studying fashion, fine arts, and business, students can take part in annual New York trips, and European Study Tours to cultural and fashion centers in Brussels, England, France, Greece, Ireland, Italy, Sicily, and Spain. Students take part in national and international competitions and shows, they produce the College's Annual Fashion Show, and they join their peers in exploring fashion-related activities via the Fashion Club. The program boasts a roster of illustrious alumni who lend support by serving as guest lecturers and mentoring the students.

FACILITIES

Technical classrooms and laboratories are equipped with the most advanced educational and industrial technology available thus enabling students to learn the latest practices and techniques (Juki industrial machines, dress forms, specialty machines, pressing systems, and cutting tables). Computer labs equipped with Gerber Technology Accumark software. A study collection of haute couture original garments from the top design houses and designers such as Chanel that dominated the fashion industry between the 1950 to 1970. An admirable collection of historical and current fashion-related books is housed in the College's library.

ONLINE / DISTANCE LEARNING

None at this time.

COURSES OF INSTRUCTION

- Apparel Technology
- Advanced Apparel Technology
- Flat Pattern Design
- Computer Assisted Pattern Design
- Design by Draping I
- Design by Draping II
- Fashion Illustration
- Fashion Entrepreneurship
- Tailoring Techniques
- Visual Merchandising
- Survey of Textiles
- Apparel Buying and Retailing
- Survey of Apparel Retailing
- Fashion Show Production
- Fashion Design Concepts
- Historic Costume and Textile Development

INTERNSHIPS

Not required

STUDY ABROAD

Not available

NOTABLE ALUMNI

Notable local alumni:
Linda Savar, Buyer, Nordstrom; Blondell Howard, started the only Sewing Lounge in the State of Maryland; Katarina Kozarova and Erika Yuille, faculty, Baltimore City Community College; Susan Lenderking, design work frequently featured in *Threads* magazine; Sarah Veblin, frequently writes articles for *Threads* magazine; Aaron Neely, Freelance Designer to the stars in California; Damon Gibson (deceased), designed costumes for country stars Loretta Lynn and Tammy Wynette; Dermaine Johnson produces a successful line of casual clothing under the "Madison Walker" label; Alena Kankova frequently works with the costume designers of Brodway plays such as *Cats*.

STUDENT ACTIVITIES AND ORGANIZATIONS

Students have the option of participating in yearly study tours to New York City and Europe. The Baltimore-Washington area serves as a laboratory for the students. The students are assigned projects that integrate the areas many cultural resources such as museums, libraries, industrial, and retailing locations. Fashion design research projects whereby students undertake the creation of new and innovative ideas for specific local companies.

FACULTY SPECIALIZATIONS AND RESEARCH

BCCC's faculty is made up of working professionals.

COMMUNITY COLLEGE TRANSFERS

Students are eligible to transfer to any College or University that offers fashion design or a related area of concentration. Locally, students transfer to Morgan State University's School of Human Ecology, Maryland Institute College of Art, Marymount University, and the University of Maryland at the Eastern Shore. Other transfer options nearby are schools in the Philadelphia area. Over the years, numerous students have transferred to LIM, FIT, and Parsons in New York City.

University of Maryland Eastern Shore

Department of Human Ecology

2100 Richard A. Henson Center, Princess Anne, MD 21853 | 410-651-6055 | http://umes.edu/HE

UNIVERSITY PROFILE
Public
Rural
Residential
Semester Schedule
Co-ed

STUDENT DEMOGRAPHICS
Undergraduate: 3,697
Graduate: 433

Male: 39%
Female: 61%

Full-time: 99%
Part-time: 1%

EXPENSES
Tuition: $6,082
Room & Board: $7,230

ADMISSIONS
University of Maryland
Eastern Shore
Princess Anne, MD 21853
410-651-8410

DEGREE INFORMATION

Major / Degree / Concentration	Enrollment	Requirements for entry	Graduation rate
Human Ecology Bachelor of Science Fashion Merchandising Option	80	2.5	90%

TOTAL PROGRAM ENROLLMENT
Undergraduate: Not reported
Graduate: Not reported

Male: Not reported
Female: Not reported

Full-time: Not reported
Part-time: Not reported
Online: Not reported

International: Not reported
Minority: Not reported

Job Placement Rate: 95%

SCHOLARSHIPS / FINANCIAL AID
Human Ecology Alumni Scholarship
Aletheia Elps Scholarship
Retia Scott Walker Scholarship
The James W. & Anne Taylor Endowment
  Fund
The Brenda Eaton Edwards Scholarship
  Fund
The Holden Scholarship Fund
The Julia Carter Lacy Endowed
  Scholarship Fund University
  scholarships, financial and state aid

TOTAL FACULTY: 174
Full-time: Not reported
Part-time: Not reported

FASHION DESIGN ADMINISTRATION
Dr. Nina Bennet, Acting Chair

PROFESSIONAL / ACADEMIC AFFILIATIONS
International Textile and Apparel
  Association
American Collegiate Retailing
  Association

PROGRAM DESCRIPTION AND PHILOSOPHY

The mission of the Department of Human Ecology is to prepare students for careers, graduate study, and leadership roles in Fashion Merchandising, Child Development, Family and Consumer Sciences, and Food and Nutrition. The department challenges faculty and students to make contributions that will enhance the quality of life of individuals and families in diverse societies. Our focus is to empower individuals to cope with change, explore new technologies, and manage resources wisely. The philosophical tenets and programmatic focus remain central to the mission of the 1890-land grant university. This mission is carried out through teaching, research, and community service.

FACILITIES

Computer labs, library, university shoppe

ONLINE / DISTANCE LEARNING

Not reported

COURSES OF INSTRUCTION

- Introduction to Fashion Industry
- Foundations of Early Childhood Education
- Elements of Nutrition
- Human Development
- Introduction to Contemporary Education
- Scientific Principles of Food

INTERNSHIPS

Required of majors at Junior year.

Interns are typically placed at companies such as Nordstrom, Macys, small business, hospitals, and schools

STUDY ABROAD

2-weeks in London and Paris and 6 weeks study abroad in London during the summer

NOTABLE ALUMNI

Not reported

STUDENT ACTIVITIES AND ORGANIZATIONS

Human Ecology club

FACULTY SPECIALIZATIONS AND RESEARCH

Textiles testing/pesticide; student retention; curriculum and service learning enhancement; dress and material culture; housing

Central Michigan University

Department of Human Environmental Studies

Wightman Hall 205, Mt. Pleasant, MI 48859 | 989-774-5486 | www.ehs.cmich.edu/hev

UNIVERSITY PROFILE
Public
Rural
Residential
Semester Schedule
Co-ed

STUDENT DEMOGRAPHICS
Undergraduate: 18,542
Graduate: 1,902

Male: 45.6%
Female: 54.4%

Full-time: 93%

EXPENSES
Tuition: $10,170 (in-state)
$23,670 (out-of-state)
Room & Board: $7,835

ADMISSIONS
Undergraduate Admissions
Warriner Hall 102
Mt. Pleasant, MI 48859
989-774-3076
cmuadmit@cmich.edu

DEGREE INFORMATION

Major / Degree / Concentration	Enrollment	Requirements for entry	Graduation rate
Apparel Merchandising & Design Bachelor of Arts Bachelor of Applied Arts Apparel Design	108	Student must have a minimum gpa of 2.0	98%
Apparel Merchandising & Design Bachelor of Arts Bachelor of Applied Arts Merchandising	183	Student must have a minimum gpa of 2.0	98%

TOTAL PROGRAM ENROLLMENT
Undergraduate: 267
Graduate: 9

Male: 7%
Female: 93%

Full-time: 99%
Part-time: 1%
Online: Not reported

International: 2.3%
Minority: 10%

Job Placement Rate: 98%

SCHOLARSHIPS / FINANCIAL AID
There are undergraduate scholarships and financial aid available through the Office of Scholarships and Financial Aid (OSFA) at CMU. Additionally, privately funded endowments from the department provide supplemental funding to students based on need, academic merit, career aspirations or other specfic criteria. For the graduate students, assistantships may be available through the department of Human Environmental Studies; various university fellowships, scholarships and awards are available.

TOTAL FACULTY: 9
Full-time: 78%
Part-time: 22%

FASHION ADMINISTRATION
Kathy Koch, Interim Dean
Tanya Domina, Professor
Maureen MacGillivray, Professor

PROFESSIONAL / ACADEMIC AFFILIATIONS
International Textile and Apparel Association
Fashion Group International

PROGRAM DESCRIPTION AND PHILOSOPHY

Graduates are uniquely prepared by an academic program with a strong core of courses which integrate design and merchandising in a way that closely reflects industry trends and competencies necessary for job success across a variety of careers. As an Apparel Merchandising & Design program, we provide students with the newest in merchandising and design theory and technology to simulate real-world applications. The program incorporates technology in both the design and merchandising courses. Industry projects are integrated into the classroom and company executives help to evaluate student work.

FACILITIES

Textile Testing Laboratory that provides students with a variety of textile testing equipment including several pieces of ASTM and AATCC standardized equipment for performance testing. Human Environment Lab houses a 3D body scanner, walk-in environmental chamber, Sweating Guarded Hot Plate (SGHP) and Bio feed Back System for Human Bio physical analysis, and a and thermal mannikin for testing of garment prototypes. CAD Lab has both PCs and Macs, laser printers and large-scale color plotter. Students can utilize industry standardized software including: CAD design and technical design software, 3D visualization software, a product data management system, color matching software, and a variety of web creation software. Apparel Construction Laboratory houses sewing machines, sergers, dress forms, and other professional equipment necessary to apparel design. There is ample workspace for pattern development and manipulation.

ONLINE / DISTANCE LEARNING

Not available

COURSES OF INSTRUCTION

Design:
- Advanced construction
- Fashion illustration
- Computer aided design
- Functional design
- Product development

Merchandising:
- Visual merchandising
- Multi channel retailing
- Fashion advertising & promotion
- Buying

INTERNSHIPS

Required of majors at the Junior level. Interns are typically placed at companies such as Abercrombie & Fitch, Lululemon Athletica, Federated Department Stores, Nordstroms, Victoria's Secret, Nautica, Sears, JC Penney, Adidas, Barney's New York, Beall's Department Store, Forever 21, Target, True Religion, The Buckle, Chan Lu, White House Black Market, Champs Sports, Oakley

STUDY ABROAD

Both semester and summer study and internship opportunities are available. Students are placed throughout Europe, Asia and Australia. Additionally, a summer faculty led study tour to Paris is available.

NOTABLE ALUMNI

Not reported

STUDENT ACTIVITIES AND ORGANIZATIONS

Fashion Association of Merchandising & Design, the pre professional student organization. Threads–the annual fashion show featuring student designers, completely student run and produced.

FACULTY SPECIALIZATIONS AND RESEARCH

The faculty are actively involved in several research areas encompassing our core competencies. Internet shopping, consumer behavior, Functional Apparel Design Database Development, Mass Customization of next-to-skin apparel, 2D/3D thermal mapping for functional apparel design, Human Centered Design analysis of Functional Clothing, and Bio sensory analysis of textiles are some of the research currently being conducted in the program.

Finlandia University

International School of Art and Design

200 Michigan St., Hancock, MI 49930 | 906-487-7376 | www.finlandia.edu

UNIVERSITY PROFILE
Private
Rural
Residential
Semester Schedule
Co-ed

STUDENT DEMOGRAPHICS
Undergraduate: 560
Graduate: 0

Male: 35%
Female: 65%

Full-time: Not reported
Part-time: Not reported

EXPENSES
Tuition: $18,474
Room & Board: $6,154

ADMISSIONS
601 Quincy St.
Hancock, MI 49930
906-487-7274
877-202-5491
admissions@finlandia.edu.

DEGREE INFORMATION

Major / Degree / Concentration	Enrollment	Requirements for entry	Graduation rate
Fiber & Fashion Design Bachelor of Fine Arts	14	2.0 gpa Portfolio review after Sophomore year	72.2%

TOTAL PROGRAM ENROLLMENT
Undergraduate: 14
Graduate: n/a

Male: 15%
Female: 85%

Full-time: 100%
Part-time: 0%
Online: 0%

International: 0%
Minority: 0%

Job Placement Rate: Not reported

SCHOLARSHIPS / FINANCIAL AID
Students receive federal, state, and local grants, an institutional grant is available to most, and 100% of our students who applied have received the Barbara Kuhlman Foundation grant since 2006. There are annual merit awards available institutionally including one for Freshman women.

Students Receiving Scholarships or Financial Aid: 100%

TOTAL FACULTY: 1
Full-time: 100%
Part-time: Not reported

FASHION ADMINISTRATION
Phyllis Fredendall, Associate Professor, Fiber and Fashion Design

PROFESSIONAL / ACADEMIC AFFILIATIONS
Not reported

PROGRAM DESCRIPTION AND PHILOSOPHY

Finlandia University was founded as Suomi College by Finnish immigrants in 1896. The BFA program was established in 1996 as the International School of Art and Design in parnership with the Kuopio Academy of Design in Kuopio, Finland which was begun as a weaving school in the 1870s. Fibers, Textiles, and Garment Design are our three areas of study. Students have the opportunity to explore materials and processes in all three areas giving a broad base from which to specialize. The studio philosophy is one of openness and exploration. We encourage interdisciplinary collaborations. Students may work in concert with the ceramic, wood, metal, studio arts areas to accomplish their visions. We are in a rural setting, near Lake Superior in a former copper-mining area.

FACILITIES

Mac and PC labs, EAT software for upholstrey design with yardage woven for students in mills, pattern drafting software, AVL and Cranbrook looms, Juki industrial sewing machines comprehensive dye studio; fiber studio open until midnight seven days a week/ Finnish-American Historical Archives with extensive textile collection. Two University galleries with opportunities for students to exhibit there and in local galleries.

ONLINE / DISTANCE LEARNING

Not available

COURSES OF INSTRUCTION

- Surface Design
- Weaving and Off-Loom Structures
- Flat-Pattern Drafting and Draping
- Jacquard Design
- Studio Practices of Fiber and Fashion
- Technical Aspects of Fiber and Fashion Design
- Art and Design Project Management
- Business for Artists and Designers
- Web Portfolio
- Chemistry of Artists Materials
- Color and Composition
- Human Factors
- Professional Drawing
- Noetic Skills
- Art History
- History of Design
- Design Research Skills

INTERNSHIPS

Internships are encouraged but not required. Students have had internships with companies in Chicago and New York, as well as with local garment designers.

STUDY ABROAD

We have partnerships with universities in Finland. Students have the opportunity to study for one or two semesters there.

NOTABLE ALUMNI

Not reported

STUDENT ACTIVITIES AND ORGANIZATIONS

Active Young Women's Caucus for Art chapter, local fiber guild, annual trips to urban centers.

FACULTY SPECIALIZATIONS AND RESEARCH

Felt-making, textiles in Finland, local history and mapping.

Michigan State University

Art & Art History

113 Kresge Art Center, E. Lansing, MI 48824 | 517-355-7610 | www.art.msu.edu/

UNIVERSITY PROFILE
Public
Suburban
Residential
Semester Schedule
Co-ed

STUDENT DEMOGRAPHICS
Undergraduate: Not reported
Graduate: Not reported

Male: Not reported
Female: Not reported

Full-time: Not reported
Part-time: Not reported

EXPENSES
Tuition: Not reported
Room & Board: Not reported

ADMISSIONS
See Web site

DEGREE INFORMATION

Major / Degree / Concentration	Enrollment	Requirements for entry	Graduation rate
Apparel & Textile Design Bachelor of Arts Bachelor of Fine Arts	140	Not reported	Not reported

TOTAL PROGRAM ENROLLMENT
Undergraduate: Not reported
Graduate: Not reported

Male: Not reported
Female: Not reported

Full-time: Not reported
Part-time: Not reported
Online: Not reported

International: Not reported
Minority: Not reported

Job Placement Rate: Not reported

SCHOLARSHIPS / FINANCIAL AID
See www.msu.edu

TOTAL FACULTY: NOT REPORTED
Full-time: Not reported
Part-time: Not reported

FASHION DESIGN ADMINISTRATION
Thomas Berding, Chair

PROFESSIONAL / ACADEMIC AFFILIATIONS
International Textile and Apparel
 Association
Fashion Group International

PROGRAM DESCRIPTION AND PHILOSOPHY

The program offers a holistic approach to analysis, integration of knowledge, and creative problem-solving. The core of the program emphasizes aesthetics and creativity; two and three-dimensional design skills; design technology; textile materials; the historical and cultural aspects of apparel; and the role of apparel and textiles in a global context.

FACILITIES

Two apparel design studios; one weaving studio (20+ looms); one knitwear studio; one textile design studio; one Senior design studio

ONLINE / DISTANCE LEARNING

See www.msu.edu

COURSES OF INSTRUCTION

- Design Approaches and Methods
- Knitwear
- History of Dress
- Textile Design
- Design Studio

INTERNSHIPS

Not required. Interns are typically placed at companies such as Macy's, Vera Wang, Target, *Vogue* magazine, Peckam, American Apparel

STUDY ABROAD

Available

NOTABLE ALUMNI

Jillian Granz (2010 Oscar Dress—Suzy Amis Cameron)

STUDENT ACTIVITIES AND ORGANIZATIONS

Student Apparel Design Association

FACULTY SPECIALIZATIONS AND/ OR RESEARCH

Historic Dress, Textile Design, Subcultural Dress and Design; Cultural Aspects of Dress and Knitwear

The Art Institutes International Minnesota

Department of Fashion & Retail Management

15 S. 9th St., Minneapolis, MN 55402 | 000-000-0000 | www.artinstitutes.edu/minneapolis

UNIVERSITY PROFILE
Private
Urban
Commuter
Quarter Schedule
Co-ed

STUDENT DEMOGRAPHICS
Undergraduate: 2,008
Graduate: n/a

Male: 40%
Female: 60%

Full-time: 55%
Part-time: 45%

EXPENSES
Tuition: $22,416
Room & Board: $6,480

ADMISSIONS
15 S. 9th St.
Minneapolis, MN 55402
800-777-3643
aimadm@aii.edu

DEGREE INFORMATION

Major / Degree / Concentration	Enrollment	Requirements for entry	Graduation rate
Fashion & Retail Management Bachelor of Science	207	2.0 gpa	Not reported

TOTAL PROGRAM ENROLLMENT
Undergraduate: 207
Graduate: n/a

Male: 2%
Female: 98%

Full-time: 60%
Part-time: 40%
Online: 13%

International: 0%
Minority: Not reported

Job Placement Rate: Not reported

SCHOLARSHIPS / FINANCIAL AID
Passion for Fashion Tuition Scholarship
To learn more, visit: www.artinstitutes.edu/competitions/PassionforFashion.aspx.

The Art Institutes International Minnesota Merit and Need Scholarship
Student Success Scholarship
EDMC Education Foundation Scholarship

Students Receiving Scholarships or Financial Aid: 94%

TOTAL FACULTY: 4
Full-time: 50%
Part-time: 50%

FASHION ADMINISTRATION
John Schulz, Fashion & Retail Management Academic Director

PROFESSIONAL / ACADEMIC AFFILIATIONS
Not reported

PROGRAM DESCRIPTION AND PHILOSOPHY

The mission of the Fashion & Retail Management program is to ensure that graduates will be capable of implementing professional communication and presentation. Graduates will demonstrate effective leadership skills reflective of the curriculum. Emphasis on the role of management in inspiring groups of staff members and supervisors will prepare graduates for challenging roles in the industry. Graduates will be able to effectively and creatively manage groups of staff and supervisors using innovative and original theory and practice.

FACILITIES

Several computer labs, library, Academic Achievement Center which offers tutoring, Career Services Department

ONLINE / DISTANCE LEARNING

Some of the program's courses and general education courses are available online, but the majority of this program is in a traditional classroom setting.

COURSES OF INSTRUCTION

- Fashion History I and II
- Textiles and Fiber
- Introduction to Retailing
- Apparel Evaluation and Construction
- Retail Mathematics
- Introduction to Manufacturing
- Merchandise Management
- Visual Merchandising

INTERNSHIPS

Required of majors at upper division levels.

STUDY ABROAD

Not reported

NOTABLE ALUMNI

Not reported

STUDENT ACTIVITIES AND ORGANIZATIONS

Fashion Forward is our student organization.

FACULTY SPECIALIZATIONS AND RESEARCH

Not reported

Minneapolis Community and Technical College

Apparel Technologies

1501 Hennepin Ave., Room T5000, Minneapolis, MN 55403 | 612-659-6000 | www.minneapolis.edu

UNIVERSITY PROFILE
Public
Urban
Commuter
Semester Schedule
Co-ed

STUDENT DEMOGRAPHICS
Undergraduate: 13,484
Graduate: n/a

Male: 46%
Female: 54%

Full-time: 41%
Part-time: 59%

EXPENSES
Tuition: $6,074
Room & Board: n/a

ADMISSIONS
1501 Hennepin Ave. Room
T2200
Minneapolis, MN 55403
612-659-6000 ext 6213
Sandra.Castro-pearson@
minneapolis.edu

DEGREE INFORMATION

Major / Degree / Concentration	Enrollment	Requirements for entry	Graduation rate
Apparel Design Technical Design Diploma	120	High school diploma or post secondary option (PSO) and MCTC math and reading requirements	95.5
Apparel Design Technical Design Advanced Certificate	20	Completion of MCTC Apparel Technologies Diploma or similar program	Not reported

TOTAL PROGRAM ENROLLMENT
Undergraduate: 120
Graduate: n/a

Male: 10%
Female: 90%

Full-time: 65%
Part-time: 35%
Online: n/a

International: 2%
Minority: 25.7%

Job Placement Rate: 66.7%

SCHOLARSHIPS / FINANCIAL AID
The following scholarships are available to qualifying students; National Science Foundation S-Stem Scholarship and a variety of MCTC Foundation scholarships are offered each year. The following grants are available to qualifying students; Perkins Grant, Federal Pell Grant, F.S.E.O. Grant, MN State Grant, Post Secondary Childcare Grant. In addition, Stafford Loans and Plus Loans are available to qualifying students.

Receiving Scholarships or Financial Aid: 60%

TOTAL FACULTY: 5
Full-time: 0
Part-time: 100%

FASHION DESIGN ADMINISTRATION
Phillip L. Davis, President
Lois Bollman Ph.D, Vice President
Irene Kovala Ed.D, Vice President
 Academic & Student Affairs

PROFESSIONAL / ACADEMIC AFFILIATIONS
International Textile and Apparel
 Association
Fashion Group International

PROGRAM DESCRIPTION AND PHILOSOPHY

MCTC's Apparel Technologies program is committed to providing a comprehensive hands-on education that is driven by the demands of the sewn products industry. It is the program's goal to inspire students and to help them realize their potential in an environment that is personally and professionally fulfilling.

FACILITIES

Facilities include a complete sewing lab including 40 industrial straight stitch and specialty machines, industrial cutting equipment, professional dress forms, fitting rooms, CAD lab (OptiTex), multi-media smart rooms equipped for projected on-camera demos. Apparel Technologies also has access to the University of MN's Goldstein Museum of Design's extensive costume collection and archives and the MN Historical Society's costume collection.

ONLINE / DISTANCE LEARNING

Not reported

COURSES OF INSTRUCTION

- Industrial Sewing Methods
- Textiles
- Pattern Development
- Garment Construction
- Draping

INTERNSHIPS

Not required. Internship is an elective course and interns are placed in a variety of apparel and costume production companies including Vee Corporation, Travel Products Inc., Kelly Company, Christopher and Banks, Satin Stitches, Bloomington Civic Theater, Minnesota Opera, Guthrie Theater.

STUDY ABROAD

Not available

NOTABLE ALUMNI

Not reported

STUDENT ACTIVITIES AND ORGANIZATIONS

Apparel Technologies students have an active student and alumni organization. In addition to publishing a newsletter, the club brings in speakers, arranges field trips, holds fundraisers, and produces fashion exhibits.

FACULTY SPECIALIZATIONS AND RESEARCH

Apparel Technologies' faculty, most of whom are currently working in the industry, come from a broad range of specializations including apparel design, technical design (CAD), textile sciences, product development, fit analysis, and couture sewing.

COMMUNITY COLLEGE TRANSFERS

MCTC's Apparel Technologies and Metro State University have an articulation agreement in place. In addition, many Apparel Technologies students have gone on to complete their baccalaureate at U of M College of Design, College of St. Catherine MN, F.I.T. NY, and F.I.D.M. CA.

St. Catherine University

Department of Family, Consumer, & Nutritional Sciences

2004 Randolph Ave., St. Paul, MN 55105 | 651-690-6669 | www.stkate.edu/academic/

UNIVERSITY PROFILE
Private
Urban
Residential & Commuter
Semester Schedule
Women Only

STUDENT DEMOGRAPHICS
Undergraduate: 3,797
Graduate: 1,480

Male: 4.4%
Female: 95.6%

Full-time: 64.5%
Part-time: 35.5%

EXPENSES
Tuition: $30,000
Room & Board: $7,650

ADMISSIONS
2004 Randolph Ave.
St. Paul, MN 55105
651-690-8850
admissions@stkate.edu

DEGREE INFORMATION

Major / Degree / Concentration	Enrollment	Requirements for entry	Graduation rate
Fashion & Apparel Bachelor of Arts Bachelor of Science Apparel Design	32	Criteria for university acceptance	95%
Fashion & Apparel Bachelor of Arts Bachelor of Science Fashion Merchandising	58	Criteria for university acceptance	95%

TOTAL PROGRAM ENROLLMENT
Undergraduate: 90
Graduate: n/a

Male: 0%
Female: 100%

Full-time: 100%
Part-time: 0%
Online: 0%

International: 1%
Minority: 10%

Job Placement Rate: 60%

SCHOLARSHIPS / FINANCIAL AID
Once students are accepted into the department they may apply for one of four department scholarships. These scholarships are in addition to scholarships and financial aid available from the university. Local chapters of Fashion Group International and American Association of Family and Consumer Sciences also offer scholarship opportunities.

Students Receiving Scholarships or Financial Aid: 92%

TOTAL FACULTY: 6
Full-time: 50%
Part-time: 50%

FASHION DESIGN ADMINISTRATION
Debra Barone Sheats, Department Chair
Mary Galvin, Department Assistant

PROFESSIONAL / ACADEMIC AFFILIATIONS
International Textile and Apparel Association
Fashion Group International

PROGRAM DESCRIPTION AND PHILOSOPHY

The department builds on the strong liberal arts tradition of the University to create a program that has substantially more liberal arts courses than most similar programs at land grant universities. It strives to offer education of the highest quality to its students and supports a belief in the importance of religious and ethical values in preparation for living. This learning environment strengthens the ability of students to understand and reflect upon the multifaceted issues facing fashion and apparel industries today, and empowers graduates to advocate in a socially responsible manner. The faculty continues to emphasize the potential of women in society. The department encourages critical thinking, writing proficiency, technical skills in information management, intellectual inquiry, the development of leadership qualities, and a sense of professionalism.

St. Kate's fashion and apparel major prepares students for careers in the fashion and apparel industry, in the areas of both design and merchandising. Students select a concentration area to reflect their interests and career aspirations. A student may choose a minor in art, business, journalism, communications or psychology in order to prepare for careers in design, product development, merchandising, buying, management, fashion writing, or fashion consulting.

FACILITIES

Computer lab with CAD, Illustrator, Photoshop, & Textiles Unraveled; Costume Collection; Minneapolis Institute of Arts, Minnesota History Center, Goldstein Gallery at the University of Minnesota, Minnesota Textile Center, Science Museum of Minnesota

ONLINE / DISTANCE LEARNING

Not available

COURSES OF INSTRUCTION

- Sociocultural Aspects of Dress
- Textiles
- Apparel Construction & Analysis
- History of Costume
- History of Fashion

INTERNSHIPS

Required of majors at the Junior/ Senior level. Interns are typically placed at companies such as Target, JV Company, Trendlab, Gander Montain, Junonia, American Girl, Mall of America, Christopher & Banks, Minneapolis Institute of Arts, Minnesota History Center, *Cosmopolitan*, L'atelier (Couture Bridal), Nordstrom, Ralph Lauren Polo, Banana Republic, and Shop NBC.com

STUDY ABROAD

London School of Fashion, UK; Acadia University, Florence, Italy

NOTABLE ALUMNI

Not reported

STUDENT ACTIVITIES AND ORGANIZATIONS

FCNS Club, Fashion Group International, MNFashion, Annual Katwalk

FACULTY SPECIALIZATIONS AND RESEARCH

Sustainability within fashion and apparel; AfroBrazilian Dress

University of Minnesota

Department of Design, Housing & Apparel

1985 Buford Ave., Saint Paul, MN 55108 | 612-624-2750 | http://dha.design.umn.edu

UNIVERSITY PROFILE

Public
Urban
Commuter
Semester Schedule
Co-ed

STUDENT DEMOGRAPHICS

Undergraduate: 29,978
Graduate: 21,738

Male: 47%
Female: 53%

Full-time: 82%
Part-time: 28%

EXPENSES

Tuition: $11,542 (in-state undergrad)
Room & Board: $7,280

ADMISSIONS

231 Pillsbury Dr. S.E.
Minneapolis, MN 55455
612-625-2008

DEGREE INFORMATION

Major / Degree / Concentration	Enrollment	Requirements for entry	Graduation rate
Apparel Design Bachelor of Science	88	Portfolio review at end of first year as a pre-Apparel Design student Overall gpa of at least 2.50. Minimum of C- in six required courses	86%
Retail Merchandising Bachelor of Science	169	Overall academic record	72%
Design - Apparel Studies Track Master of Arts Master of Science Ph.D.	22	Overall academic record GRE scores Goal statement Letters of reference Also could require TOEFL scores, portfolio, writing sample	

TOTAL PROGRAM ENROLLMENT

Undergraduate: 257
Graduate: 22

Male: 6%
Female: 94%

Full-time: 92%
Part-time: 8%
Online: 0%

International: 9%
Minority: 14%

Job Placement Rate: 82%

SCHOLARSHIPS / FINANCIAL AID

Incoming Freshman scholarships based on need and merit; continuing student scholarships based on merit.

TOTAL FACULTY: 10

Full-time: 8
Part-time: 2

FASHION DESIGN ADMINISTRATION

Becky Yust, Department Head
Elizabeth Bye, Apparel Studies Program Director
Kim Johnson, Retail Merchandising Program Director
Stephanie Zollinger, Director of Graduate Studies

PROFESSIONAL / ACADEMIC AFFILIATIONS

International Textile and Apparel Association
Fashion Group International
American Collegiate Retailing Association

PROGRAM DESCRIPTION AND PHILOSOPHY

The Apparel Design program emphasizes and integrates creative thinking and technical skill. Students become proficient in manual and computer methods of pattern development and implement apparel structuring methods appropriate for custom design or industry production. Courses cover costume history, social and cultural meanings of apparel, the textile and apparel consumer, and aesthetics. Students take six sequential apparel design studio courses.

Students in Retail Merchandising learn merchandising principles that are applied across a broad spectrum of U.S. and global retail businesses. Students apply these principles in a variety of formats including store, Internet, and catalog. Outstanding instructional opportunities are offered students including travel to domestic and international retail centers and opportunities to study aboard. Today's employers are seeking individuals with leadership abilities along with the ability to innovate. Students complete internships that offer examination of retail careers and enhance a student's job competitiveness upon graduation. One of the few four-year undergraduate retailing programs in the nation offered through a college of Design, the program features courses that address creativity, innovation, and analytical skills. Students can elect an apparel emphasis or a general retail emphasis

FACILITIES

PC and Mac computer labs with unique software related to apparel design and retail merchandising; Goldstein Museum of Design; Human Dimensioning Lab

ONLINE / DISTANCE LEARNING

Not available

COURSES OF INSTRUCTION

For undergraduate degree in Apparel Design: Six sequential apparel design studio courses; Drawing & Design; Color & Design; Textile Analysis; Fashion Illustration; Fashion Trends & Visual Analysis; Dress, Society & Culture; Product Development—Softlines

For undergraduate degree in Retail Merchandising: Economics; Management; Marketing; Accounting; Multichannel Retailing; Softlines Analysis; Design & Visual Presentation; Textile Analysis; Retail Promotion & Consumer Decision Making; International Retail Markets; Visual Merchandising; Retail Buying; Retail Environments & Human Behavior

For graduate degrees: Quantitative and/or Qualitative & Mixed Research Methods; Human Factors in Design; Design Theory and Criticism; Innovation Theory and Analysis; Retailing–Strategic Perspectives; History of Costume; Aesthetics; Product Development; Research Ethics

INTERNSHIPS

Required of majors at the upper division level (jr/sr).

Interns are typically placed at numerous companies in the Minneapolis-Saint Paul area and in New York City.

STUDY ABROAD

Yes, students are encouraged to study abroad for a semester and faculty have identified appropriate international programs related to the major; faculty also lead short-term study abroad trips.

NOTABLE ALUMNI

Not reported

STUDENT ACTIVITIES AND ORGANIZATIONS

Apparel Design Student Club; annual Apparel Design Fashion Runway Show; mentor program

FACULTY SPECIALIZATIONS AND/OR RESEARCH

Clothing design; apparel and textile product development; sizing and fit; apparel technology; aesthetics; apparel history; cross-cultural influences on design; socio-psychological aspects of clothing; functional apparel; smart clothing/wearable technology; merchandising; consumer behavior; retail design; mass customization and co-design

Fontbonne University

Human Environmental Sciences

6800 Wydown Blvd., St. Louis, MO 63105 | 314-889-1415 | www.fontbonne.edu

UNIVERSITY PROFILE
Private
Suburban
Commuter
Semester Schedule
Co-ed

STUDENT DEMOGRAPHICS
Undergraduate: 1,943
Graduate: 920

Male: 30%
Female: 70%

Full-time: 75%
Part-time: 25%

EXPENSES
Tuition: $19,500
Room & Board: $7,200

ADMISSIONS
6800 Wydown Blvd.
St. Louis, MO 63105
314-889-1400
fadmiss@fontbonne.edu

DEGREE INFORMATION

Major / Degree / Concentration	Enrollment	Requirements for entry	Graduation rate
Fashion Merchandising Bachelor of Science	65	2.5 gpa	Not reported

TOTAL PROGRAM ENROLLMENT
Undergraduate: 202
Graduate: 20

Male: 7.9%
Female: 92.1%

Full-time: 80.7%
Part-time: 19.3%
Online: 0%

International: 1.3%
Minority: 21%

Job Placement Rate: 90%

SCHOLARSHIPS / FINANCIAL AID
Some classes in each specific major on offered online but not any program is offered entirely online.

Students Receiving Scholarships or Financial Aid: 20%

TOTAL FACULTY: 15
Full-time: 8
Part-time: 7

FASHION ADMINISTRATION
Kimberly Edmunds, Administrative Assistant

PROFESSIONAL / ACADEMIC AFFILIATIONS
International Textile and Apparel Association
Fashion Group International

PROGRAM DESCRIPTION AND PHILOSOPHY

The Fashion Merchandising program at Fontbonne University offers students a curriculum which provides a thorough understanding of the textile and apparel industries. Built upon a foundation of liberal arts studies to prepare students for a wide range of careers within the global marketplace, the core curriculum encompasses the principles and elements of design, production, manufacturing, buying, merchandising, and distribution of textiles, apparel, and accessories. An academic internship during the Junior or Senior year provides an opportunity to apply classroom experiences to specific career positions. Students earn credit toward their degree by fulfilling an internship at diverse sites including major department and specialty stores, small boutiques, apparel manufacturers, market showrooms, shopping center marketing offices, and talent, model, and public relations agencies. An essential part of the educational experience is professional growth and development. Participation in professional organizations, attendance at extracurricular events, and experiential learning allow students to interact with professionals in organizations such as The Fashion Group International and the International Textile and Apparel Association. Trips to regional and national markets and career days allow students to witness the importance of professionalism, effective communication, critical thinking, and career planning required to be successful in this competitive environment. Career opportunities for graduates are distinct and varied. Graduates have found positions as retail managers and buyers, product developers, market and sales representatives, visual merchandisers, fashion promoters, and entrepreneurs.

FACILITIES

Computer/technology labs, Apparel labs, Visual Merchandising labs, WGSN, Worth Global Style Network is also accessible for Fashion Merchandising students.

ONLINE / DISTANCE LEARNING

Some classes in each specific major on offered online but not any program is offered entirely online.

COURSES OF INSTRUCTION

- The Fashion Industry
- Apparel Product Development
- Apparel Production and Evaluation;
- Textiles
- History of Costume
- Fashion Behavior and Forecasting
- Personal, Professional, and Cultural Dress
- Visual Merchandising
- Promotion in the Merchandising Environment
- Fashion Merchandising and Management
- Merchandising Buying: Planning and Control
- Fashion Merchandising Internship

INTERNSHIPS

Required of majors at the Junior or Senior level. Interns are typically placed at Retail Stores, Manufacturers; Product Developers; Mall Marketing Offices; Boutique/ Small store owners; Corporate Offices; Specific examples would be: Nordstrom, Dillard's, The Gap, Marc Jacobs (corporate), Neiman Marcus, Aquarius; Bronx-Diba Shoes, The Limited, JCrew, etc.

STUDY ABROAD

Students may study abroad in London or Paris for fashion merchandising classes. They may also participate in trips to China, Costa Rica, etc.

NOTABLE ALUMNI

Not reported

STUDENT ACTIVITIES AND ORGANIZATIONS

Students may join our departmental organization, SHESA-Student Human Environmental Sciences Association. In addition, students may join a number of other organizations such as the Student Government Association; Student Ambassadors, and a variety of sports teams.

FACULTY SPECIALIZATIONS AND RESEARCH

Joyce Starr Johnson, Ph.D., is an Associate Professor in Fashion Merchandising. Her areas of specialization include fashion history and cultural perspectives on appearance. Her research has focused on contemporary needle workers.

Rogene Nelsen is an Assistant Professor and Director of the Fashion Merchandising program. She coordinates and supervises the Internship program. Her areas of interest are professional development and fashion marketing. She is a generalist and teaches courses in all areas of the curriculum.

Angie Dowel, instructor, is concurrently obtaining her Ph.D. in the University of Kansas American Studies Program. Her areas of specialization are in the areas of cultural dress studies, mid-20th century U.S. women's history, and gender theory. In particular, she is interested in the study of gendered dress and appearances.

Metropolitan Community College—Penn Valley

Apparel & Textiles Program

3201 Southwest Trafficway, Humanities 203, Kansas City, MO 64111 | 816-604-4272 | www.mcckc.edu/aptx

UNIVERSITY PROFILE
Public
Urban
Commuter
Semester Schedule
Co-ed

STUDENT DEMOGRAPHICS
Undergraduate: Not reported
Graduate: Not reported

Male: 50%
Female: 50%

Full-time: 25%
Part-time: 75%

EXPENSES
Tuition: $1,230 - $2925
Room & Board: Not reported

ADMISSIONS
3201 Southwest Trafficway
Kansas City, MO 64111
816.604.4623
PV.Admissions@MCCKC.edu

DEGREE INFORMATION

Major / Degree / Concentration	Enrollment	Requirements for entry	Graduation rate
Apparel & Textiles Associate of Applied Science Product Development & Design	45	Open application process. Portfolio review upon graduation.	89%
Apparel & Textiles Associate of Applied Science Marketing and Merchandising	20	Open application process.	95%

TOTAL PROGRAM ENROLLMENT
Undergraduate: 50-75
Graduate: Not reported

Male: 20%
Female: 80%

Full-time: 25%
Part-time: 75%
Online: Not reported

International: Not reported
Minority: 70%

Job Placement Rate: 90%

SCHOLARSHIPS / FINANCIAL AID
Residency determines the amount charged per credit hour. Significant funding is available for both in-state and out-of-state students. See the MCC financial web pages at www.mcckc.edu for details and deadlines for application.

Students Receiving Scholarships or Financial Aid: 80%

TOTAL FACULTY: 5
Full-time: 25%
Part-time: 75%
Online: %

FASHION DESIGN ADMINISTRATION
Sheryl Farnan Leipzig, MBA, Ph.D., Program Coordinator
Vicki Raine, Humanities Division Chair

PROFESSIONAL / ACADEMIC AFFILIATIONS
International Textile and Apparel Association
Fashion Group International

PROGRAM DESCRIPTION AND PHILOSOPHY

Our challenging curriculum combines disciplines of art, business, and technology to prepare students for entry-level opportunities in this competative, global industry. Students study design and merchandising in an exciting urban environment and our facility features state of the industry computer lab, design lab, and exhibit areas. Each year students showcase 2D and 3D work in PANACHE – a professional, juried fashion showcase.

FACILITIES

Computer labs equipped with Gerber AccuMark8, Adobe, Illustration. State of the industry design lab and cut and spread studio. Exhibit space. Rebecca Maude Owens Historic Clothing Collection.

ONLINE / DISTANCE LEARNING

Some individual courses are offered in online sections.

COURSES OF INSTRUCTION

- Introduction to Apparel and Textiles Studies
- Aesthetics
- Clothing Construction
- Advanced Clothing Construction
- Merchandising I
- Merchandising II-Global Issues
- Costume History
- Pattern Design-Flat Pattern
- Pattern Design-Draping
- Textiles
- 20th Century Costume History
- Pattern Design-CAD (Gerber AccuMark8)
- Computer Aided Fashion Illustration
- Portfolio Presentation

INTERNSHIPS

Required of majors for students in Marketing and Merchandising. Interns are typically placed at companies such as Macy's, Limited, Walmart, JCPenney and others.

STUDY ABROAD

Domestic and international opportunities through partnership with area universities.

NOTABLE ALUMNI

Not reported

STUDENT ACTIVITIES AND ORGANIZATIONS

Fashion Group International

FACULTY SPECIALIZATIONS AND RESEARCH

Design process, 20th century fashion industry history, history of design as a profession for American women, design and pattern development for plus and petite sizes

COMMUNITY COLLEGE TRANSFERS

We have a formal articulation agreement with the University of Missouri-Columbia Textile and Apparel Management program for both concentration areas. In addition, our program is fully accredited and students successfully transfer to area schools such as Stephen's College, Missouri State University, Kansas State University, University of Nebraska-Lincoln, Iowa State University, Colorado State University, and other. In addition, students have successfully transferred from our program to national programs such at Fashion Institute of Technology in New York and FIDM in Los Angeles.

Missouri State University

Department of Fashion & Interior Design

901 S. National Ave., Springfield, MO 65897 | 417-836-5136 | www.missouristate.edu/fid

UNIVERSITY PROFILE
Public
Urban
Residential
Semester Schedule
Co-ed

STUDENT DEMOGRAPHICS
Undergraduate: 12,908
Graduate: 2,600

Male: Not reported
Female: Not reported

Full-time: Not reported
Part-time: Not reported

EXPENSES
Tuition: Not reported
Room & Board: Not reported

ADMISSIONS
901 S. National Ave.
Springfield, MO 65897
417-836-5517
info@missouristate.edu

DEGREE INFORMATION

Major / Degree / Concentration	Enrollment	Requirements for entry	Graduation rate
Fashion Design & Product Development Bachelor of Science	50	open enrollment	90%
Fashion Merchandising & Management Bachelor of Science	140	open enrollment	90%

TOTAL PROGRAM ENROLLMENT
Undergraduate: 190
Graduate: 0

Male: 5%
Female: 95%

Full-time: Not reported
Part-time: Not reported
Online: Not reported

International: Not reported
Minority: Not reported

Job Placement Rate: 85%

SCHOLARSHIPS / FINANCIAL AID
University scholarships are many and are listed at the University Web site. Program scholarships are through Fashion Group International, Inc.

TOTAL FACULTY: 6
Full-time: 4
Part-time: 2

FASHION DESIGN ADMINISTRATION
Dr. Paula Kemp, Acting Department. Head

PROFESSIONAL / ACADEMIC AFFILIATIONS
International Textile and Apparel Association
Fashion Group International

PROGRAM DESCRIPTION AND PHILOSOPHY

The Department of Fashion and Interior Design (FID), located in the Park Central Office Building on Park Central Square, houses three different programs. Students receive knowledge and training that enable them to seek gainful employment in challenging and satisfying careers, while gaining a strong general education foundation.

Our curriculum combines a formal classroom setting with faculty-supervised projects to provide the personal, professional, and technological skills necessary to compete in our modern competitive business environment.

Qualified, dedicated, student-oriented faculty, a balanced curriculum, and knowledgeable and approachable student support services provide the perfect environment for students.

FACILITIES

Computer labs, CAD, Kaledo, Illusrator, Photoshop; design lab; costume collection, interior design lab and materials resource room

ONLINE / DISTANCE LEARNING

A Fashion Entrepreneurship class will be offered as a blended course (part online) Spring 2011

COURSES OF INSTRUCTION

- Survey of the Global Fashion Industry
- Product Development I & II
- History of Costume
- Textiles
- Pre-internship Seminar
- Senior Seminar
- Fashion Entrepreneurship
- Marketing
- Fashion Merchandising Strategies
- Clothing construction I & II
- Patternmaking I & II
- Draping
- Senior Collections

INTERNSHIPS

Required of majors between Junior and Senior year. Interns are typically placed at companies such as Missoni, Zac Posen, Glamour, Showroom Seven, Michael Kors.

STUDY ABROAD

Paris, China, and Italy offered alternating summers

NOTABLE ALUMNI

Not reported

STUDENT ACTIVITIES AND ORGANIZATIONS

Association of Fashion and Design, Interior Design student organizations (2); Study Abroad Tours to Paris, Italy, and China; Study Abroad semesters via AIU, etc.; Missouri-London semester abroad program; summer internship program; annual NYC Fashion Industry tour; Los Angeles annual tour in planning stage; annual juried fashion show featuring original student designs, show produced by students in one of the required courses.

FACULTY SPECIALIZATIONS AND RESEARCH

Internship, entrepreneurship, and product development

Stephens College

School of Design & Fashion

1200 E. Broadway, Box 2042, Columbia, MO 65215 | 573-876-7233 | www.stephens.edu/academics/programs/fashion

UNIVERSITY PROFILE
Private
Suburban
Residential
Semester Schedule
Women Only

STUDENT DEMOGRAPHICS
Undergraduate: 760
Graduate: 426

Male: 2%
Female: 98%

Full-time: 99%
Part-time: 1%

EXPENSES
Tuition: $25,400
Room & Board: $8,680

ADMISSIONS
1200 E. Broadway, Box 2121
Columbia, MO 65215
800.876.7207
apply@stephens.edu

DEGREE INFORMATION

Major / Degree / Concentration	Enrollment	Requirements for entry	Graduation rate
Fashion Communication Bachelor of Fine Arts	55	2.5 gpa, 19 or above ACT, 1500 or above SAT C- or better required in each class in the major to move onto the next course	75%
Fashion Design & Product Development Bachelor of Fine Arts	75	2.5 gpa, 19 or above ACT, 1500 or above SAT C- or better required in each class in the major to move onto the next course	65%
Fashion Marketing and Management Bachelor of Science	65	2.5 gpa, 19 or above ACT, 1500 or above SAT C- or better required in each class in the major to move onto the next course	80%

TOTAL PROGRAM ENROLLMENT
Undergraduate: Not reported
Graduate: 0

Male: 0%
Female: 100%

Full-time: Not reported
Part-time: Not reported
Online: Not reported

International: Not reported
Minority: Not reported

Job Placement Rate: 100%

SCHOLARSHIPS / FINANCIAL AID
Fashion students are considered for merit and need based institutional aid, federal and state aid. A select number of selective scholarship opportinities exsist in the Fashion Department.

Students Receiving Scholarships or Financial Aid: 95%

TOTAL FACULTY: 111
Full-time: 53%
Part-time: 47%

FASHION DESIGN ADMINISTRATION
Dr. Dianne Lynch, President
Dr. Mary Hassigner, VPAA
Monica McMurry, Dean School of Design and Fashion

PROFESSIONAL / ACADEMIC AFFILIATIONS
International Textile and Apparel Association
Fashion Group International

PROGRAM DESCRIPTION AND PHILOSOPHY

School of Design and Fashion Mission Statement: By recognizing and developing individual potential, the School of Design and Fashion educates and challenges students to negotiate the dynamic global marketplace as distinctive, creative, ethical professionals. We are committed to providing a respectful, supportive, collaborative community that cultivates intellectual agility, marketable creativity, technical excellence, and a passion for a life of learning and leading. Fashion Department Mission Statement: The Fashion Department programs educated students to become accomplish, versatile fashion professionals. Students learn by doing via industry-assessed projects, a required internship, and a cumulative Senior capstone project. Our curriculum emphasizes exceptional technical sills, marketable creativity, analytical and critical thinking, creative problem solving, and professional communication.

FACILITIES

Three large art-painting, drawing, fabric-design labs; six large fully equipped fashion design studios (2 for Senior fashion design students only); two large computer classrooms (PC and Mac) and one Mac studio for upper-class use; one dedicated 50 seat technology accessible lecture classroom with other large and small "smart" classrooms for lecture based classes. Also available to students are large seating venues for fashion show and other events, each sitting about 300. The Costume Museum and Research library houses approx. 13,000 garments dating back to the early 1700s. This facility includes a gallery with three yearly shows, archival storage areas, a research room with photo studio and an online museum development space. In addition, we have the Davis Art Gallery where five shows/year feature international and regional artists, plus yearly BFA student art show. The campus library has a very large collection of fashion magazines and books for research.

ONLINE / DISTANCE LEARNING

None of the fashion degrees are offered exclusively online. General education and some lecture fashion and business classes are available online.

COURSES OF INSTRUCTION

- Current Issues in the Global Fashion Industry
- Draping and Patternmaking I & II
- Beg. & Adv. Computer Aided Design
- Product Development
- Post Internship
- Senior Collection: Line Development and Studio
- Portfolio Development
- Applied Fashion Marketing and Management Project
- Fashion Show Production and Coordination
- Fashion Industry Strategies and Decision Making
- Art Direction & Photo Styling
- Fashion Journalism
- Fashion Communication
- Digital Photography
- Creating Online Media

INTERNSHIPS

Required of majors at the Junior level. Interns are typically placed at companies such as Under Armour, Gear for Sports, Michael Kors, Burberry, *WWD*, California Apparel News, Baby Phat, Dillard's, Armani Exchange, Elie Tahari, Ralph Lauren, Coldwater Creek, Hermes, Fratelli Rosetti, Anthropologie, Lee Jeans, The Hemp Trading Company, Nanett Lepore, and Bergdorf Goodman.

STUDY ABROAD

Trips each year to NYC and every other year to MAGIC in Las Vegas. Other travel study options to London (AIU, LCF and others) and Paris (AIU, and others). Stephens has a travel study office to help students find the right school in a large number of countries. We have articulation agreements with AIU.

NOTABLE ALUMNI

Jeannene Booher, founder/designer, Maggie London

STUDENT ACTIVITIES AND ORGANIZATIONS

Student club–Innovative Fashion Association. Fashion honorary club–Pi Phi Rho (for members of IFA with a 3.5 gpa and above, designated at graduation with the wearing of honor cords)

FACULTY SPECIALIZATIONS AND RESEARCH

All faculty have significant experience working in the fashion industry. Specialties include: jewelry, millinery, surface design and beading, textile design, leather garments, buying for the luxury market, couture and bespoke tailoring, product and line development, sales rep, costume historian, visual merchandise and display

Stevens Institute of Business and Arts

Department of Retail Management & Fashion Merchandising

1521 Washington Ave., Saint Louis, MO 63101 | 314-421-0949 | www.siba.edu

UNIVERSITY PROFILE

Private
Urban
Commuter
Quarter Schedule
Co-ed

STUDENT DEMOGRAPHICS

Undergraduate: 186
Graduate: 0

Male: 7%
Female: 93%

Full-time: 61%
Part-time: 39%

EXPENSES

Tuition: Not reported
Room & Board: Not available

ADMISSIONS

1521 Washington Ave.
Saint Louis, MO 63101
314-421-0949

DEGREE INFORMATION

Major / Degree / Concentration	Enrollment	Requirements for entry	Graduation rate
Retail Management/ Fashion Merchandising Bachelor of Arts Associate of Applied Science	74	High School Diploma with 2.5 gpa or GED	83%

TOTAL PROGRAM ENROLLMENT

Undergraduate: 74
Graduate: 0

Male: 5%
Female: 95%

Full-time: 72%
Part-time: 28%
Online: 0%

International: 0%
Minority: 65%

Job Placement Rate: 100%

SCHOLARSHIPS / FINANCIAL AID

Federal Pell Grant and Federal Student Loans

Students Receiving Scholarships or Financial Aid: 88%

TOTAL FACULTY: 6

Full-time: 33%
Part-time: 67%

FASHION DESIGN ADMINISTRATION

Lynne Wasson-Department Head

PROFESSIONAL / ACADEMIC AFFILIATIONS

Fashion Group International

PROGRAM DESCRIPTION AND PHILOSOPHY
Small classes, individualized attention, hands-on experience.

FACILITIES
Computer Labs, CAD Lab, School Library, St. Louis City Library, St. Louis Art Museum, St. Louis History Museum & Archives

ONLINE / DISTANCE LEARNING
Not available

COURSES OF INSTRUCTION
Textiles
- History of Costume
- Merchandising Math
- Retail Buying
- Apparel Product Development
- Fashion Forecasting
- Visual Merchandising
- Retailing
- Clothing and Design
- Advanced Retail profitability

INTERNSHIPS
Not required

STUDY ABROAD
Not available

NOTABLE ALUMNI
Not reported

STUDENT ACTIVITIES AND ORGANIZATIONS
Not reported

FACULTY SPECIALIZATIONS AND RESEARCH
Not reported

Delta State University

Division of Family & Consumer Sciences

Ewing 112, P.O. Box 3273, DSU, Cleveland, MS 38733 | 662-846-4315 | www.deltastate.edu/pages/444.asp

UNIVERSITY PROFILE
Public
Rural
Residential
Semester Schedule
Co-ed

STUDENT DEMOGRAPHICS
Undergraduate: 3,052
Graduate: 985

Male: 63%
Female: 37%

Full-time: 69%
Part-time: 31%

EXPENSES
Tuition: $4,450
Room & Board: $5,778

ADMISSIONS
Kent Wyatt Hall 117, DSU
Cleveland, MS 38733
662-846-4020
admissions@deltastate.edu

DEGREE INFORMATION

Major / Degree / Concentration	Enrollment	Requirements for entry	Graduation rate
Family & Consumer Sciences Bachelor of Science	20	2.5 gpa overall or 3.0 in FCS classes	85%

TOTAL PROGRAM ENROLLMENT
Undergraduate: 160
Graduate: 0

Male: 3%
Female: 97%

Full-time: 70%
Part-time: 20%
Online: 10%

International: 2%
Minority: 50%

Job Placement Rate: 50%

SCHOLARSHIPS / FINANCIAL AID
Federal financial aid is the primary source of financial aid.

Students Receiving Scholarships or Financial Aid: 80%

TOTAL FACULTY: 7
Full-time: 72%
Part-time: 28%

FASHION ADMINISTRATION
Janice B. Haynes, Division Chair

PROFESSIONAL / ACADEMIC AFFILIATIONS
International Textile and Apparel Association
American Collegiate Retailing Association

PROGRAM DESCRIPTION AND PHILOSOPHY

The concentration in Fashion Merchandising is an interdisciplinary program developed by the faculty in the Division of Family & Consumer Sciences, the Department of Art, and the Division of Management, Marketing and Business Administration. Students are prepared to enter the broad-based fashion industry on a variety of levels and in a variety of capacities. A number of courses are offered that do not have prerequisites and are excellent choices for electives.

FACILITIES

Students have access to computer labs in their main building and in the library. There is Adobe CS4 software on 5 stations for them to utilize.

ONLINE / DISTANCE LEARNING

Not available

COURSES OF INSTRUCTION

- The Fashion Industry
- Dress & Identity
- Apparel Analysis
- Fashion Merchandising
- Consumers in the Marketplace
- Fashion Promotion
- Interior Environmental Design
- Historic Costume
- Textiles
- Fashion Internship
- Professional Development

INTERNSHIPS

Required of majors at the Senior level; Interns are typically placed at retail companies or in Sales Positions with assorted companies.

STUDY ABROAD

Not available

NOTABLE ALUMNI

Not reported

STUDENT ACTIVITIES AND ORGANIZATIONS

Fashion Study Tours are available every 2-3 years to New York. Every year students have the opportunity to go to Fashion Career Day in Dallas. They may register for one or 2 semesters before to design garments to submit to the Design Competition. They also may submit trend boards.

The Fashion Promotion class coordinates a large campus wide fashion show every two years.

Students are invited to learn apparel design on an independent study basis. Many students take Fiber Arts classes in the Art Department, and utilize those skills in their original design work.

FACULTY SPECIALIZATIONS AND RESEARCH

Design work in wearable art; sustainability through repurposing; apparel sizing; surface design

East Carolina University

Department of Interior Design & Merchandising

249 Rivers Building, Greenville, NC 27858 | 252-328-6929 | www.ecu.edu/che/idmr/

UNIVERSITY PROFILE

Public
Suburban
Residential & Commuter
Semester Schedule
Co-ed

STUDENT DEMOGRAPHICS

Undergraduate: 21,400
Graduate: 6,000

Male: 40%
Female: 60%

Full-time: 76%
Part-time: 24%

EXPENSES

Tuition: $4,327 (residents)
$15,161 (non-resident)
Room & Board: $3,500 to
$3,700 per semester

ADMISSIONS

106 Whichard Building
East Carolina University
Greenville, NC 27858-4353
252.328.6640
admis@ecu.edu

DEGREE INFORMATION

Major / Degree / Concentration	Enrollment	Requirements for entry	Graduation rate
Merchandising Bachelor of Science	180	2.5 gpa to declare major	90%

TOTAL PROGRAM ENROLLMENT

Undergraduate: 180
Graduate: Not yet

Male: 9%
Female: 91%

Full-time: 100%
Part-time: Not reported
Online: Not reported

International: 3%
Minority: 15%

Job Placement Rate: 85%

SCHOLARSHIPS / FINANCIAL AID

See opposite page for more info.

TOTAL FACULTY: 5

Full-time: 100%
Part-time: 0%

FASHION ADMINISTRATION

Katherine Swank, Department Chair
Runying Chen, Merchandising Program
   Coordinator
Judy Siguaw, Dean of College of Human
   Ecology

PROFESSIONAL / ACADEMIC AFFILIATIONS

International Textile and Apparel
   Association
American Apparel and Footwear
   Association
Fashion Group International
American Collegiate Retailing
   Association

PROGRAM DESCRIPTION AND PHILOSOPHY

Our merchandising program is small in terms of student numbers but not in terms of full-time faculty numbers compared to other big programs. All five merchandising faculties are full-time, either tenure track or tenured. This means that our students get more attention and feedback from our faculties who are all committed to excellence in teaching, research and service; and students also have more opportunities to interact with faculties either inside or outside the classroom. Our merchandising curriculum allows students to develop diverse career paths in either fashion or interiors industries, depending on their personal strength and interest, such as being a buyer, store manager, visual merchandising manager, style director, planning and sourcing manager, wholesale manager, store owner, showroom manager, account executive, regional manager, or director. Our faculty members have diverse professional training and cultural backgrounds, which is extremely important when preparing professionals who will work in the merchandising field. We have an excellent Merchandising Advisory Board which consists of leaders from a variety of sectors in the fashion and interiors industry, and these board members provide our students and faculties with valuable guidance and resources towards industry network development, merchandising program marketing, fund raising, and more.

FACILITIES
- Computer CAD Lab
- Textile Analytical Lab
- Costume Collection (19th and 20th century)
- Interiors Material Resource Room

ONLINE / DISTANCE LEARNING
Some courses are available online, especially during Summer semesters.

COURSES OF INSTRUCTION
- Merchandising Principles
- Merchandising Strategies
- Preprofessional Merchandising Seminar
- Consumer Behavior
- Merchandising Analysis (math)
- Visual Merchandising
- Global Economics: Textiles, Apparel, and Interior Furnishings Industry
- Merchandising Planning, Buying and Sourcing
- Merchandising Internship
- Merchandising Capstone
- Apparel Quality Analysis
- 19th and 20th Century Fashion History
- Green Fashion
- Fashion Branding
- Global Fashion Merchandising

INTERNSHIPS
Required of majors at the Senior level. Our students intern with retailers, manufacturers, fashion magazines, fashion show rooms, design houses, and independent boutiques, including: Nordstrom; Crate & Barrel; J.Crew; H&M; Burberry; Lily Pulitzer; Gap; Kate Spade; Valentino, Natori; Jessica McClintock; Joey Showroom; Juicy Couture; DKNY; A/X Armani Exchange; Overton's Inc.; Stuart Peter Ltd.; Peter Millar; *Marie Claire*; Chico's FAS Inc.; Coffman's Menswear

STUDY ABROAD
Students have traveled to China, Italy, England, France, and Spain. Study abroad is offered every year, alternating between Asia and other areas of the world.

NOTABLE ALUMNI
Not reported

STUDENT ACTIVITIES AND ORGANIZATIONS
AIMO is our merchandising program student organization, but open to all students who are interested in fashion. AIMO's main activities include annual fashion show in Spring semester, T-shirt design, industry network field tirp to New York City, fundraising activities, community service projects, and social activities. Officers will join the Advisory Board Meeting each semester to report AIMO activities and also seek support from the board members.

Other student activities include field trips for learning and industry network, such as visiting High Point Furniture Market, working at the apparel mart, and meeting industry professionals and alumni.

FACULTY SPECIALIZATIONS AND/ OR RESEARCH
Application of 3D body scanning in the apparel industry; analyzing textile materials to explore underwater textile degradation of ship wrecked artifacts; niche marketing, branding, competitive strategies of the US textile and apparel industry, and international trade and marketing; domestic and international textiles and apparel; Web site design and consumer behavior related to fashion products.

SCHOLARSHIPS / FINANCIAL AID
Merchandising program has two established scholarships: The endowed Belk scholarship, and Merchandising Alum and Friends Scholarship. We usually offer several $1,000 scholarships each academic year. We also have a Merchandising Advisory Board which helps us to raise funds for special scholarships such as study abroad. Our student organization, AIMO, does a lot of fund-raising to help student members' professional field trips, such as trips to New York City and apparel trade shows. In the year of 2009-2010, AIMO raised over $5,500. Our college and university have a number of other scholarship opportunities available to our students. Financial aid is available to students who meet the standard–see ECU Web site.

Receiving Scholarships or Financial Aid: Two to four students receive Merchandising Scholarship during each academic year. ECU has about 75% students on financial aid.

Mars Hill College

Fashion & Interior Merchandising

P.O. Box 6685, Mars Hill, NC 28754 | 828-689-1150 | www.mhc.edu/academics/majors/fim

UNIVERSITY PROFILE
Private
Rural
Residential
Semester Schedule
Co-ed

STUDENT DEMOGRAPHICS
Undergraduate: 1,237
Graduate: n/a

Male: 55%
Female: 45%

Full-time: 81%
Part-time: 19%

EXPENSES
Tuition: $21,997
Room & Board: $7,623

ADMISSIONS
P.O. Box 370
Mars Hill, NC 28754
828-689-1201
admissions@mhc.edu

DEGREE INFORMATION

Major / Degree / Concentration	Enrollment	Requirements for entry	Graduation rate
Fashion and Interior Merchandising Bachelor of Science	20	Acceptance to the College	80%

TOTAL PROGRAM ENROLLMENT
Undergraduate: 22
Graduate: 0

Male: 1%
Female: 99%

Full-time: 100%
Part-time: Not reported
Online: Not reported

International: 1%
Minority: 1%

Job Placement Rate: 80%

SCHOLARSHIPS / FINANCIAL AID
Federal and state grants are available based on financial need. Numerous academic and service learning scholarships are available through the Financial Aid Office. Majors who qualify for federal work study funds are recruited to work in the Fashion and Interior Merchandising Department.

Students Receiving Scholarships or Financial Aid: 99%

TOTAL FACULTY: 2
Full-time: 100%
Part-time: Not reported

FASHION ADMINISTRATION
Becky Cody, Associate Professor of Fashion & Interior Merchandising and Department Chair

PROFESSIONAL / ACADEMIC AFFILIATIONS
International Textile and Apparel Association

PROGRAM DESCRIPTION AND PHILOSOPHY

The Department of Fashion and Interior Merchandising provides a broad-based education in apparel and interiors with emphasis on fashion, business, technology, and design. The curriculum promotes the importance of conceptual thinking, analytical problem solving, and creative development. This program of study enables students to develop attributes, skills, and abilities to become effective contributors to businesses and organizations.

FACILITIES

Fashion and Interior Merchandising majors are given priority in the campus computer lab which houses the Adobe Creative Suite, AutoCad and color printer. Use of technology is required throughout the Fashion and Interior Merchandising curriculum. Trips to the High Point Furniture Market, and Americas Mart are integrated into the curriculum. The surrounding community is a mecca for small design studios and galleries which provide numerous opportunities for interaction with professionals in the field.

ONLINE / DISTANCE LEARNING

Not available

COURSES OF INSTRUCTION

- Fashion Study Tour
- Introduction to Apparel and Interiors
- Fashion Designers
- The Interior Environment
- Interiors in Retrospect
- Apparel Analysis and Evaluation
- Markets and Visual Merchandising
- Environmental Design Applications
- Textile Fundamentals
- The Fashion Industry
- Apparel Design
- Merchandising Practices

INTERNSHIPS

Required of majors. Securing an internship placement is viewed as a learning experience. In preparation for the experience students enroll in the Professional Seminar course, develop a resume, interview skills and target a specific career direction. Students then identify companies of interest and are assisted during the application and interview process. In conjunction with the internship supervisor, students then develop a personalized learning contract with the company.

STUDY ABROAD

Available

NOTABLE ALUMNI

Not required

STUDENT ACTIVITIES AND ORGANIZATIONS

Current majors are members of numerous sororities, fraternities, student organizations, and the national championship clogging team. Majors assume leadership positions on campus, including but not limited to, student government, student life staff and academic preceptors. Students actively engage in service learning opportunities, and are encouraged to spend at least one semester in a study abroad experience.

FACULTY SPECIALIZATIONS AND RESEARCH

Faculty actively encourage and support undergraduate research and presentation of results in local, regional, state, and national venues.

North Carolina State University

Department of Textile & Apparel Technology & Management, College of Textiles

2401 Research Dr., Box 8301, Raleigh, NC 27695 | 919-515-6632 | www.tx.ncsu.edu/departments/tatm/

UNIVERSITY PROFILE
Public
Suburban
Residential
Semester Schedule
Co-ed

STUDENT DEMOGRAPHICS
Undergraduate: 950
Graduate: 150

Male: 25%
Female: 75%

Full-time: Not reported
Part-time: Not reported

EXPENSES
Tuition: $5,500 (in-state)
$18,000 (out-of-state)
Room & Board: $9,000

ADMISSIONS
Box 8301
Raleigh, NC 27695-8301
919-515-0030
liz_moran@ncsu.edu

DEGREE INFORMATION

Major / Degree / Concentration	Enrollment	Requirements for entry	Graduation rate
Fashion & Textile Management Bachelor of Science Fashion Development and Product Management	219	2.8 Transfer gpa Freshmen Admission Averages: 1170 (Math + Verbal) SAT, 4.0 weighted gpa, 3.27 unweighted	~75% 6yr graduation rate for entire College of Textiles
Fashion & Textile Management Bachelor of Science Brand Management and Marketing	278	Same as above	Same as above
Fashion & Textile Management Bachelor of Science Retail and Supply Chain	31	Same as above	Same as above
Textile Technology Bachelor of Science Design	24	Same as above	Same as above

TOTAL PROGRAM ENROLLMENT
Undergraduate: 540
Graduate: 72

Male: 14%
Female: 86%

Full-time: 95%
Part-time: 5%
Online: Not reported

International: 1% undergraduate, 28% graduate
Minority: 23%

Job Placement Rate: 60%

SCHOLARSHIPS / FINANCIAL AID
See opposite page for more info.

TOTAL FACULTY: 38
Full-time: Not reported
Part-time: Not reported

FASHION DESIGN ADMINISTRATION
Dr. Nancy Cassill, Department Head for TATM
Dr. William Oxenham, Associate Dean of Academic Programs
Dr. Blanton Godfrey, Dean of College of Textiles

PROFESSIONAL / ACADEMIC AFFILIATIONS
International Textile and Apparel Association
American Apparel and Footwear Association
American Collegiate Retailing Association

PROGRAM DESCRIPTION AND PHILOSOPHY

The Department of Textile and Apparel Technology, & Management at North Carolina State University educates undergraduate and graduate students for a career in the fiber, textile, apparel, and retail industries, The mission of the department is accomplished by offering Bachelor of Science, Master of Science, and Ph.D. degree programs that seek to develop leadership and promote academic excellence in both the student and the faculty. These programs are designed to provide the student with a thorough background in fundamental concepts of scientific, technological, and management principles, and an ability to define and solve challenging technological and managerial problems. An essential component of the department's mission is the development of new knowledge through research and the subsequent transfer of this knowledge to both the textile complex and society.

FACILITIES
Not reported

ONLINE / DISTANCE LEARNING
There are a few introductory textile courses offered online, but not core coursework.

COURSES OF INSTRUCTION
- Intro to Textile Technology
- Intro to the College of Textiles
- The Textile Industry
- Intro to Fiber Science
- Principles of Retail & Supply Chain
- Yarn Production & Properties
- Formation & Structure of Textile Fabrics
- Intro to Textile Brand Mgt/Mkt
- Fashion & the Consumer
- Entrepreneurship in Textiles
- Intermediate Textile Brand Mgt/Mkt
- The Fashion Industry

Fashion Development & Product Management
- Fashion Product Analysis
- Computer-Aided Textile Brand Mgt/Mkt
- Fashion Product Design
- CAD for Fashion
- Fashion Development Processes
- Fashion Product Development
- Senior Collection Studio
- Brand Management & Marketing
- Textile Brand Communication
- Visual Merchandising Textile Products
- Textile Market Research
- Textile & Apparel Labor Management
- Global Textile Trade & Sourcing

Retail & Supply Chain Management
- Product Costing for Textiles
- Management Control Textile Apparel Systems
- Retail Buying in Fashion & Textiles
- Supply Chain Management for Textiles

INTERNSHIPS
Not required. Interns are typically placed at companies such as Polo Ralph Lauren, Belk's, Nordstrom, Cotton, Inc., Diane von Furstenberg, Kohl's, Victoria's Secret, Target, Lilly Pulitzer, Chanel, Perry Ellis, Li & Fung, Disney, Versace, and many other fashion, retail, and marketing companies.

STUDY ABROAD
Available

NOTABLE ALUMNI
Not reported

STUDENT ACTIVITIES AND ORGANIZATIONS
Young Menswear Association, Fashion & Apparel, Art & Design (FAAD), Art-to-Wear Fashion Show, Threads Fashion Show, African-American Fashion Expose, ReDress Raleigh Eco-Friendly Fashion Show, and a variety of other fashion- and retail- related activities.

FACULTY SPECIALIZATIONS AND RESEARCH
Not reported

COMMUNITY COLLEGE TRANSFERS
Transfer students from a community college must have at least 30 transferable credit hours and a 2.8 transfer gpa in order to enter our program. Transferring into the Fashion Development concentration beyond the Sophomore year is not allowed.

SCHOLARSHIPS / FINANCIAL AID
The College of Textiles has one of the largest college-based scholarship programs at NC State University. The majority of scholarship support comes from the North Carolina Textile Foundation. The North Carolina Textile Foundation (NCTF) was established in December 1942 to aid and promote all types of textile education and research at North Carolina State University in Raleigh, NC. One of the most important forms of support provided for the College of Textiles by the Foundation is the Scholarship Program. Established by the board of directors in 1980, the program has four components: the NCTF Centennial Scholars Program (created in 1999), NCTF Scholarships, NCTF Prestige Scholarships, and the NCTF Merit Graduate Fellowship Program.

Students Receiving Scholarships or Financial Aid: 60%

University of North Carolina at Greensboro

Department of Consumer, Apparel, & Retail Studies

210 Stone Building, P.O. Box 26170, Greensboro, NC 27402 | 336-334-5250 | www.uncg.edu/crs

UNIVERSITY PROFILE
Public
Urban
Commuter
Semester Schedule
Co-ed

STUDENT DEMOGRAPHICS
Undergraduate: 14,350
Graduate: 3,225

Male: 33%
Female: 67%

Full-time: 41%
Part-time: 59%

EXPENSES
Tuition: varies by resident or nonresident
Room & Board: Not reported

ADMISSIONS
P.O. Box 26170
Greensboro, NC 27402-6170
336-334-5243
ltwhite2@uncg.edu

DEGREE INFORMATION

Major / Degree / Concentration	Enrollment	Requirements for entry	Graduation rate
Consumer, Apparel, & Retail Studies Bachelor of Science Apparel Product Design	81	Successful completion of the Sewing Proficiency Examination	Not reported
Consumer, Apparel, & Retail Studies Bachelor of Science Retailing & Consumer Studies	144	Admission to the University	Not reported
Consumer, Apparel, & Retail Studies Bachelor of Science Global Apparel & Related Industries Studies	20	Admission to the University. Foreign language requirement	Not reported

TOTAL PROGRAM ENROLLMENT
Undergraduate: 255
Graduate: 30

Male: 5%
Female: 95%

Full-time: 92%
Part-time: 8%
Online: 0%

International: 8.5%
Minority: 31%

Job Placement Rate: Not reported

SCHOLARSHIPS / FINANCIAL AID
See opposite page for more info.

TOTAL FACULTY: 11
Full-time: 73%
Part-time: 27%

FASHION DESIGN ADMINISTRATION
Gwendolyn S. O'Neal, Professor and
Head, Department of Consumer,
Apparel, & Retail Studies

PROFESSIONAL / ACADEMIC AFFILIATIONS
International Textile and Apparel
Association
American Apparel and Footwear
Association
American Collegiate Retailing
Association

PROGRAM DESCRIPTION AND PHILOSOPHY

We believe that the route to excellence is to focus the course of study under the close supervision of qualified faculty. Faculty are involved in teaching, research, and service where they spend a significant amount of time advising and mentoring students. Practical learning experiences, community engagement, and global learning experiences complement academic programs. The student internship program prepares students for the real world and provides the industry with employees prepared for global careers.

FACILITIES

Computer labs, design studios, museums, historic costume collection, apparel analysis lab, extensive library resources, and databases.

ONLINE / DISTANCE LEARNING

We do not offer an online degree in the major. Some courses are offered online.

COURSES OF INSTRUCTION

- Culture, Human Behavior, and Clothing
- Textiles
- Introduction to Apparel & Consumer Retailing
- Quality Analysis of Consumer Goods
- Internship
- Fundamentals of Retail Buying & Merchandising
- Multicultural & Multichannel Retailing
- Global Sourcing of Apparel & Related Consumer Products
- Economics of the Textile & Apparel Complex
- Design Principles Applied to Textile Products
- Product Design Studio I, II, III, IV
- Portfolio Development
- Entrepreneurship in Apparel Retailing & Design

INTERNSHIPS

Required of majors at the Junior level. Interns are typically placed at companies such as VF Corporation, Tommy Hilfiger, Target, Cone Denim, Kellwood Global, Wells Hosiery, Hanes Brands, Nordstrom, Macys, Wrangler, Kayser Roth, DolceVita Life Styles, Banana Republic, *Harper's Bazaar*, Anthropologie, Kurt Salmon Associates, Burlington Worldwide, Renfro Corporation, JCPenney, and Kayser-Roth.

STUDY ABROAD

Short term study trips abroad and long tern (1 sem./1 yr.) student exchange opportunities to countries all over the world.

NOTABLE ALUMNI

All of them!

STUDENT ACTIVITIES AND ORGANIZATIONS

THREADS is the major student organization in the department. There are close to two hundred affiliated clubs and organizations, including honor societies, national societies, service organizations, professional, religious, and general groups, and Greek sororities and fraternities.

FACULTY SPECIALIZATIONS AND/ OR RESEARCH

Technical design, consumer behavior, international retailing, multi-channel multi culture retailing, entrepreneurship, social psychology of dress, history of dress, dress and identity, women and industry employment

COMMUNITY COLLEGE TRANSFERS

For consideration as a transfer, students must have at least a 2.0 or higher grade point average on a 4.0 scale on all previous work attempted from a regionally accredited college or university. Grade point averages are recalculated to determine admissibility. Transfer students must be in good standing and eligible to return to their last attended undergraduate institution.

SCHOLARSHIPS / FINANCIAL AID

UNCG administers an extensive financial aid program which provides assistance to more than half the University's enrolled undergraduates. Available aid includes scholarships, grants, loans, and work study. Eligibility for need-based programs is determined through an analysis of family financial information provided on the Free Application for Federal Student Aid [FAFSA]. For information on programs, services, and application procedures contact: UNCG Financial Aid Office at http://fia.uncg.edu

North Dakota State University

Department of Apparel, Design, & Hospitality Management

Department #2610, P.O. Box 6050, Fargo, ND 58108 | 701-231-8604 | www.ndsu.edu/adhm

UNIVERSITY PROFILE
Public
Urban
Residential
Semester Schedule
Co-ed

STUDENT DEMOGRAPHICS
Undergraduate: 11,666
Graduate: 2,189

Male: 54.7%
Female: 45.3%

Full-time: 89%
Part-time: 11%

EXPENSES
Tuition: $5,448 (ND resident)
Room & Board: $6,568

ADMISSIONS
Ceres 114
P.O. Box 6050
Fargo, ND 58108
701-231-8643
www.ndsu.edu/.prospective_
students/

DEGREE INFORMATION

Major / Degree / Concentration	Enrollment	Requirements for entry	Graduation rate
Apparel & Textiles Bachelor of Science Apparel Studies	58	2.0 gpa	73%
Apparel & Textiles Bachelor of Science Retail Merchandising:Textile Product Merchandising	75	2.5 gpa	73%
Apparel & Textiles Bachelor of Science Retail Merchandising: Interior Merchandising	14	2.5 gpa	73%
Merchandising Master of Science	6	Not reported	Not reported

TOTAL PROGRAM ENROLLMENT
Undergraduate: 148
Graduate: 4

Male: 9%
Female: 91%

Full-time: 92%
Part-time: 8%
Online: n/a

International: 6%
Minority: 4%

Job Placement Rate: 95%

SCHOLARSHIPS / FINANCIAL AID
A limited number of scholarships are designated for students majoring in the department; additional scholarships are available to all college majors. For further information on scholarships, contact the Director of Student Services and Advancement.
Students Receiving Scholarships or Financial Aid: 55%

TOTAL FACULTY: 6
Full-time: 83%
Part-time: 17%

FASHION DESIGN ADMINISTRATION
Holly E. Bastow-Shoop, Ph.D., Department Head
Virginia Clark Johnson, Ph.D., Dean

PROFESSIONAL / ACADEMIC AFFILIATIONS
International Textile and Apparel Association
American Collegiate Retailing Association

PROGRAM DESCRIPTION AND PHILOSOPHY

Our programs are professionally based and have elements of design, technology, and management interlaced into our majors. In addition, a strong general education component is provided for all majors, which aids students in learning to integrate all of their educational components. Course work in all of our majors provides students with "real life" projects. For example, students frequently work on design solutions on campus or in the community. Students in our visual merchandising class undertake display work with local retailers.

FACILITIES

The ADHM Department is housed in EML and the FLC on the NDSU campus. Facilities provide well-equipped classrooms as well as one of the finest textiles testing laboratories in the region. The Emily P. Reynolds Historic Costume Collection provides an excellent resource for students' projects and reports. Clusters of microcomputers are located in the Family Life Center for students' convenience.

ONLINE / DISTANCE LEARNING

The Master's program in Merchandising is fully online. Its faculty are from five universities in the Great Plains-Interactive Distance Educational Alliance (Great Plains IDEA) including North Dakota State University, South Dakota State University, Colorado State University, Oklahoma State University, and Kansas State University.

COURSES OF INSTRUCTION

- Fashion Dynamics
- Product Development
- Textiles
- Global Fashion Economics
- Apparel/Textiles Capstone

INTERNSHIPS

Required of majors after the summer of Junior Year. Interns are typically placed at companies such as Abercrombie & Fitch, Ann Taylor, *Vanity*, Old Navy, Macy's, Talbot's, Target Corp., Shop NBC

STUDY ABROAD

We offer study tours regionally, nationally, and internationally to such places as Kansas City ; Chicago; New York; Los Angeles; Las Vegas, London and Paris. In December 2008, a trip to India was offered. Students may also choose to attend schools in such places as New York City or London, England, or Geneva, Switzerland for a summer, a semester, or for a year. In addition, numerous other study abroad programs around the world are available to our student via the office of International Programs. Students work with an advisor to ensure that the transfer of credits occurs prior to taking advantage of one of these opportunities.

NOTABLE ALUMNI

Karen Schneider, Director of Women's Fashions, Pringle of Scotland, London, England

Britta Cabanos, Designer, Nike Swim USA, Beaverton, OR

Shauna Caufield, Director of Boys, Layettes & Infants Product Development, OshGosh B'Gosh, NYC.

STUDENT ACTIVITIES AND ORGANIZATIONS

The Fashion, Apparel, and Business Organization (FABO), allows interested students additional contacts with professionals and opportunities for leadership. Other organizations in the college and university provide further opportunities for personal and professional growth.

FACULTY SPECIALIZATIONS AND RESEARCH

Recent research of benefit to North Dakota and the region includes adolescent issues related to dress and behavior, bison wool as a textile product, and historic clothing as evidence of the social history of the Upper Great Plains. Studies in fashion awareness, country of origin as a criterion for apparel selection, and costs of shoplifting to the consumer provide information for area businesses. A database for the historic clothing is being developed at North Dakota State University for the growing Emily P. Reynolds Historic Costume Collection. A special focus of the collection includes items from the Germans from Russia ethnic group. Linkages with culturally diverse populations through exchanges of apparel and textiles information has been a recent theme of scholarship research.

Montclair State University

Fashion Studies Program, Department of Art & Design

Valley Rd., Montclair, NJ 07043 | 973-655-4000 | www.montclair.edu/arts/dept/artdesign

UNIVERSITY PROFILE
Public
Suburban
Residential
Semester
Co-ed

STUDENT DEMOGRAPHICS
Undergraduate: 18,000
Graduate: Not reported

Male: Not reported
Female: Not reported

Full-time: Not reported
Part-time: Not reported

EXPENSES
Tuition: Not reported
Room & Board: Not reported

ADMISSIONS
Montclair State University
Admissions
Valley Rd.
Montclair, NJ 07043
973-655-4000

DEGREE INFORMATION

Major / Degree / Concentration	Enrollment	Requirements for entry	Graduation rate
Fashion Studies Bachelor of Arts	300	Not reported	Not reported

TOTAL PROGRAM ENROLLMENT
Undergraduate: 300
Graduate: Not reported

Male: Not reported
Female: Not reported

Full-time: Not reported
Part-time: Not reported
Online: Not reported

International: Not reported
Minority: Not reported

Job Placement Rate: Not reported

SCHOLARSHIPS / FINANCIAL AID
Not reported

TOTAL FACULTY: 17
Full-time: 12%
Part-time: 88%

FASHION ADMINISTRATION
Scott Gordley, Department Chair

PROFESSIONAL / ACADEMIC AFFILIATIONS
International Textile and Apparel
  Association

PROGRAM DESCRIPTION AND PHILOSOPHY

The goal of the Fashion Studies program is to prepare students for a wide variety of careers in the Fashion Industry. Students find opportunities in the retail as well as the wholesale apparel industry. Because of our proximity to NY most students seek positions with designers in New York. There are approximately 300 students majoring in Fashion Studies at Montclair State.

The Fashion Studies program prepares students who are successful while conducting their careers in a socially responsible manner. The focus of the program is to prepare professionals who are able to provide wanted goods to consumers while safeguarding the interest of employees, suppliers, and the environment.

Students complete a variety of courses directly related to the various aspects of the fashion industry ... textiles, the textile and apparel industry, marketing of fashion, historic costume, apparel design, and clothing and culture. Students also complete a group of courses in Business and Art that enrich their preparation for careers in the Fashion Industry. In addition to course work, students are required to work full time in an internship position for 10 weeks. Students choose an internship that is compatible with their long-range career goals.

Students earn a BA degree in which approximately half their coursework is in GER requirements. Students have a solid liberal arts preparation in addition to preparation for a career in fashion.

FACILITIES

Computer lab, fashion design studio

ONLINE / DISTANCE LEARNING

Some courses are offered online

COURSES OF INSTRUCTION

- Clothing and Culture
- Textile Apparel Industry
- Evaluation of Apparel Quality
- Textiles
- Fashion Merchandise Math
- Historic Analysis of Costume
- Marketing of Fashion
- Consumer
- Internship

INTERNSHIPS

Required of majors

STUDY ABROAD

Available

NOTABLE ALUMNI

Not reported

STUDENT ACTIVITIES AND ORGANIZATIONS

Fashion Club

FACULTY SPECIALIZATIONS AND RESEARCH

Business, Socio-Psychological Aspects of Fashion

COMMUNITY COLLEGE TRANSFERS

Transfer students are accepted.

International Academy of Design & Technology— Las Vegas

Fashion Merchandising Department

2495 Village View Dr., Henderson, NV, 89074 | 702-990-0150 | www.iadtvegas.com

UNIVERSITY PROFILE
Private
Suburban
Commuter
Quarter Schedule
Co-ed

STUDENT DEMOGRAPHICS
Undergraduate: 550
Graduate: n/a

Male: Not reported
Female: Not reported

Full-time: Not reported
Part-time: Not reported

EXPENSES
Tuition: $405.00 per credit
Room & Board: n/a

ADMISSIONS
2495 Village View Dr.
Henderson, NV 89074
702-990-0150
www.iadtvegas.com

DEGREE INFORMATION

Major / Degree / Concentration	Enrollment	Requirements for entry	Graduation rate
Fashion Design Bachelor of Fine Arts Associate of Science	198	High school diploma or GED	Not reported
Fashion Merchandising Bachelor of Fine Arts	New in 2010	High school diploma or GED	Not reported

TOTAL PROGRAM ENROLLMENT
Undergraduate: 198
Graduate: n/a

Male: Not reported
Female: Not reported

Full-time: Not reported
Part-time: Not reported
Online: Not reported

International: 0.7%
Minority: 62.4%

Job Placement Rate: Not reported

SCHOLARSHIPS / FINANCIAL AID
Financial Aid is available to those who qualify.

TOTAL FACULTY: 13
Full-time: Not reported
Part-time: Not reported

FASHION ADMINISTRATION
Carolyn Ann Thomas, PhD, Fashion Program Chair

PROFESSIONAL / ACADEMIC AFFILIATIONS
International Textile and Apparel Association
Fashion Group International

PROGRAM DESCRIPTION AND PHILOSOPHY

The Fashion Design program engages students in the process of apparel conceptualization, illustration, construction, and marketing. The students will experiment with lines, colors, patterns, textures, functions, and style in the design and creation of original garments. A study of the evolution of fashion provides the basis for the predictive skills in consumer behavior and trend forecasting. The fashion design program provides students with an interest in the fashion design industry the opportunity to enhance creative skills and to develop the technical competencies for employment in the field.

The Fashion Merchandising program allows students to partner their interest in the world of fashion with the development of key business competencies critical to employment in today's global marketplace. While students develop skills in merchandising, management, marketing, and buying, they will also have the opportunity to explore the evolution of fashion, fashion trend forecasting, fashion media, and fashion promotion. The program requires integration of conceptual and creative abilities with business practices to prepare students for entry-level positions.

FACILITIES

The students have access to both an on-ground library as well as online library resources (CECybrary); they also have computer labs, sewing labs, patterns drafting labs.

ONLINE / DISTANCE LEARNING

The Fashion Merchandising program is offered online from IADT Online through a consortium agreement. Students could take up to 75% of their coursework in the online format if attending IADT Las Vegas.

COURSES OF INSTRUCTION

- Intro to Fashion
- Fashion Sketching
- Evolution of Fashion
- Computer Graphics for Fashion Design
- Textiles for Fashion
- Fashion Marketing and Consumer Behavior
- Entrepreneurship
- Trend Forecasting

Fashion Design
- Fashion Deisgn I-IV
- Pattern Drafting
- Draping

Fashion Merchandising
- Visual Merchandising
- Buying
- Selling
- Accounting

INTERNSHIPS

Required of majors

STUDY ABROAD

Available

NOTABLE ALUMNI

Not reported

STUDENT ACTIVITIES AND ORGANIZATIONS

Organized program activities include a Fashion Club, Design Series Lectures, bus trips to Los Angeles, CA, to visit fabric resources and industry manufactures, Fashion Shows, biannual MAGIC conferences, & other related Trade Shows.

FACULTY SPECIALIZATIONS AND RESEARCH

Fashion Design Construction, Merchandising, and Fashion Show Production

Cornell University

Fiber Science & Apparel Design, College of Human Ecology

206 Martha Van Rensselear Hall, Ithaca, NY 14853 | 607-255-3196 | www.human.cornell.edu

UNIVERSITY PROFILE
Private
Rural
Residential
Semester Schedule
Co-ed

STUDENT DEMOGRAPHICS
Undergraduate: 13,931
Graduate: 6,702

Male: 52.8%
Female: 47.2%

Full-time: 100%
Part-time: Not reported

EXPENSES
Tuition: $21,814 (resident)
$37,954 (non-resident)
Room & Board: $12,160

ADMISSIONS
172 Martha Van Rensselear
Hall
Ithaca, NY 14853
607-255-2532
humec_admissions@cornell.
edu

DEGREE INFORMATION

Major / Degree / Concentration	Enrollment	Requirements for entry	Graduation rate
Fiber Science and Apparel Design Bachelor of Science Apparel Design	48	Portfolio required See Web site for guidlines and other admission requirements.	93%
Fiber Science and Apparel Design Bachelor of Science Apparel/Textile Management	41	Same as Apparel Design. Portfolio highly recommended.	93%
Fiber Science and Apparel Design Bachelor of Science Fiber Science	2	Same as Apparel Design. No Design Index or Portfolio required.	93%

TOTAL PROGRAM ENROLLMENT
Undergraduate: 91
Graduate: 23

Male: 11%
Female: 89%

Full-time: 100%
Part-time: 0%
Online: 0%

International: 10%
Minority: 14%

Job Placement Rate: 87%

SCHOLARSHIPS / FINANCIAL AID
Types of Aid available to students are:
Federal Direct Student Loans, Federal
Family Education Loans, Federal and
State Scholarships, Federal and State
Grants, and Student employment.
Admission to Cornell is "need-blind."
Individual award offers are developed
for families with demonstrated financial
need. Cornell has initiated program to
reduce or eliminate need-based loans
for some families. Currently, 52% of our
students are receiving financial aid, and
each financial aid package meets 100%
of the student's assessed need.

TOTAL FACULTY: 12
Full-time: 100%
Part-time: Not reported

FASHION ADMINISTRATION
Alan Mathios, Dean, College of Human
Ecology
Ann Lemley, Chair, Department of Fiber
Science & Apparel Design
Charlotte Jirousek, Director of
Undergraduate Studies

PROFESSIONAL / ACADEMIC AFFILIATIONS
International Textile and Apparel
Association
Fashion Group International
International Surface Design Association
The Textile/Clothing Technology
Corporation
American Association of Textile
Chemists and Colorists
The Concept to Consumer Groups
The Costume Society of America

PROGRAM DESCRIPTION AND PHILOSOPHY

Apparel Design prepares for careers in design through a series of studio courses that encourage the development of the student's individual approach to apparel design, and the development of a personal design philosophy.

Fashion Design Management applies management/marketing principles to this specialized industry through courses in the development, manufacture, and marketing of apparel and textiles, with emphasis on consumer behavior, product development, communication, entrepreneurship, finance, globalization, and social responsibility in the industry.

Fiber Science explores the physical, chemical, and engineering properties of fibrous materials and textiles for many applications including performance and protective clothing.

FACILITIES

Design studios that include a variety of production equipment such as dress forms, industrial lockstitch machines, sergers, cover-stitch machines, and industrial irons and steamers. Computer technology is available to students 24/7 including color printers, digitizers, scanners, video cameras, and digital cameras. Industry standard software is available for fashion illustration, surface design, product development, apparel patternmaking/grading/marker making, and 3D modeling. Research labs include Fiber Science labs, textiles testing, and an ergonomics lab with 3D body scanners. The Department of FSAD has a costume and textile collection with more than 9,000 items used for teaching and research.

ONLINE / DISTANCE LEARNING

Not available

COURSES OF INSTRUCTION

- Fashion Graphics
- Fibers, Fabrics, and Finishes
- Art, Design, and Visual Thinking
- Patternmaking for Fashion Design
- Aesthetics and Meaning in World Dress
- Fashion Presentation: Portfolio Development
- Senior Collection

INTERNSHIPS

Not required, but students have held internships at companies such as: American Eagle Outfitters; Burberry, Inc.; Club Monaco; Frieda Mara Couture; Malia Mills; Marc Jacobs International, LLC; Michael Kors; Next Boutique; Nike; Perry Ellis; Polo Ralph Lauren; Proenza Schouler;

STUDY ABROAD

Most FSAD students spend a semester abroad. Undergraduates can study in any program or location that is approved by their faculty advisor and the college. The College of Human Ecology also has international exchange programs with The Hong Kong Polytechnic University and Massey University in New Zealand.

NOTABLE ALUMNI

Owners of "The Laundress" NYC; V.P. Sales-Oscar de la Renta, Via Spiga & Laura Ashley Handbags, NYC; Color, Print & Fabric Research & Development, Theory, NYC; Senior Director, Accessories Design, Polo Ralph Lauren, NYC; Director of Planning, Roberto Cavalli, NYC; V.P. of Women's Merchandising, Calvin Klein Collections, NYC; Wardrobe Mistress & Designer, Joffrey Ballet, Chicago; Design/Product Development, Michael Kors, NYC; Executive Department Editor-*Glamour* magazine, *Life & Style Weekly*, NYC; Senior Footwear Designer, The North Face, San Leandro, CA, Los Angeles, CA; Product Development Manager, Ann Taylor, NYC; Associate Curator Costume Institute, Metropolitan Museum of Art, NYC; Associate Curator, FIT Museum, NYC; Designer, Priscilla of Boston Wedding Gowns, NYC; Technical Designer, Nike,Portland, OR

STUDENT ACTIVITIES AND ORGANIZATIONS

The Cornell Design League (CDL) was formed to give students with an interest in design a chance to express their creativity outside of the classroom by producing a fashion show every Spring. Students from many fields, not just fashion, come together to create the show with over 60 students participating as designers and over 175 students participating as models.

CiFI: Careers in the Fashion Industry is a student run organization that works to bring members of the fashion industry to Cornell to discuss their career paths and industry experiences.

The Journal Club was formed by graduate students to give them an opportunity to read and discuss new research papers important to the field of fiber science and apparel design.

FACULTY SPECIALIZATIONS AND RESEARCH

Faculty conduct research in the following areas: studies of masculinities, fashion blogs, sustainable fashion design practice, and the fashion underground; conceptual design, and cognitive and computational models of design process; apparel sizing and fit, functional design, and the use of full-body three-dimensional scanning in the apparel industry; historical and cultural aspects of the design of Turkish textiles and dress, and their impact worldwide; innovative uses of digital technology for the industry; understanding fundamental phenomena at the nanoscale that are of relevance to Fiber and Polymer Science; rapidly renewable polymers as engineering materials and interfacing fiber science and nanotechnology; fiber reinforced composites that are used commonly in many applications in place of metals because of their high specific properties; biologically active bioabsorbable polymers and fibers.

Fashion Institute of Technology

Department of Accessories Design

Seventh Ave. & 27th St., New York, NY 10001 | 212-217-3760 | www.fitnyc.edu/accessoriesdesign

UNIVERSITY PROFILE
Public
Urban
Residential
Semester Schedule
Co-ed

STUDENT DEMOGRAPHICS
Undergraduate: 10,207
Graduate: 206

Male: 16%
Female: 84%

Full-time: 70%
Part-time: 30%

EXPENSES
Tuition: $3,714 (in-state)
Room & Board:
$9,650 - $17,520

ADMISSIONS
Seventh Ave. and 27th St.
New York, NY 10001
212 217.3760
fitinfo@fitnyc.edu

DEGREE INFORMATION

Major / Degree / Concentration	Enrollment	Requirements for entry	Graduation rate
Accessories Design Associate of Applied Science	Not reported	A portfolio and a high school diploma or a General Equivalency Diploma (GED). SAT scores are required for placement in English and math classes.	Not reported
Accessories Design & Fabrication Bachelor of Fine Arts	Not reported	AAS from FIT; associates or bachelor's degree from a regionally accredited college in a program that is equivalent to the FIT Accessories Design AAS program; or at least 60 credits toward a bachelor's degree in an equivalent program at a regionally accredited college.	Not reported

TOTAL PROGRAM ENROLLMENT
Undergraduate: 226
Graduate: n/a

Male: 12%
Female: 88%

Full-time: 92%
Part-time: 8%
Online: n/a

International: 12%
Minority: 23%

Job Placement Rate: 90%

SCHOLARSHIPS / FINANCIAL AID
The college directly administers its own institutional grants and scholarships, which are provided by The Educational Foundation for the Fashion Industries. College-administered federal funding includes Federal Pell Grants, Federal Perkins Loans, Federal Supplemental Educational Opportunity Grants, Federal Work-Study Program awards, and the Federal Family Educational Loan Program, which includes student and parent loans. New York State residents who meet state guidelines for eligibility may also receive Tuition Assistance Program (TAP) and/or Educational Opportunity Program (EOP) grants. Financial aid applicants must file the Free Application for Federal Student Aid (FAFSA), through which they apply for the Federal Pell Grant, and should also apply to all available outside sources of aid.

TOTAL FAULTY: 18
Full-time: Not reported
Part-time: Not reported

FASHION ADMINISTRATION
Ellen Goldstein, chair

PROFESSIONAL / ACADEMIC AFFILIATIONS
Not reported

PROGRAM DESCRIPTION AND PHILOSOPHY

Some people just notice the clothes, but accessories make the difference. Top designers know this too; that's why so many have lucrative accessory collections. The center of the accessories world is New York City—home to the major design studios and sales offices. And FIT has close ties to the industry and to the people and places that can help launch a great career. At FIT, students design and produce a full range of accessories, from high-fashion shoes and handbags to athletic footwear. They'll create boots, belts, and billfolds and carrying gear for sports. Each undergraduate program also includes a core of traditional liberal arts courses, providing students with a global perspective, critical-thinking skills, and the ability to communicate effectively, and students have the option of completing liberal arts minor.

Faculty bring their professional expertise into the classroom from all areas of the industry—from sports bags to foot anatomy to illustration, bringing technical, design, and business. In hands-on classes students learn about materials, construction, and presentation— and produce a professional-quality accessories line.

FACILITIES

FIT's campus provides its students with classrooms, laboratories, and studios that reflect the most advanced educational and industry practices. The Fred P. Pomerantz Art and Design Center houses drawing, painting, photography, printmaking, and sculpture studios; display and exhibit design rooms; a model-making workshop; and a graphics printing service bureau. The Peter G. Scotese Computer-Aided Design and Communications facility provides the latest technology in computer

graphics, photography, and the design of advertising, fashion, interiors, textiles, and toys. Other facilities include a professionally equipped fragrance-development laboratory, cutting and sewing labs, a design/research lighting laboratory, knitting lab, broadcasting studio, multimedia foreign languages laboratory, and 23 computer labs, in addition to several other labs with computers reserved for students in specific programs. Throughout the David Dubinsky Student Center are lounges, a game room, a student radio station, the Style Shop (a student-run boutique), a dining hall, student government and club offices, a comprehensive health center, two gyms, a dance studio, a weight room, and a counseling center. Four residence halls house approximately 2,300 in fully furnished single-, double-, triple-, and quad-occupancy rooms. Each residence hall has lounges and laundry facilities; the George and Mariana Kaufman Residence Hall also provides an on-site fitness center.

ONLINE / DISTANCE LEARNING

Not reported

COURSES OF INSTRUCTION

- Leather and Materials Technology
- Anatomy for Accessories
- Theatrical and Character Footwear
- Screen Printing: Scarves

INTERNSHIPS

Required of majors. Past sponsors include Coach, Kenneth Cole, Liz Claiborne, and Nine West.

STUDY ABROAD

The study abroad experience provides students with the opportunity to immerse themselves in diverse cultures and prepares them to live and work in a global community. Accessories Design students can study in countries such as England.

NOTABLE ALUMNI

Kari Sigerson and Miranda Morrison of Sigerson Morrison and Bob Webber of Nina Footwear.

STUDENT ACTIVITIES AND ORGANIZATIONS

The college is home to more than 60 clubs, societies, and athletic teams—everything from major-related organizations to hobby groups to a ski and snowboard club. Each organization is open to all students who have paid their activity fee. The Student Council, the governing body of the Student Association, grants all students the privileges and responsibilities of citizens in a self-governing college community. FIT has intercollegiate teams in basketball, cross-country, half-marathon, outdoor track, dance, table tennis, tennis, swimming and diving, and volleyball.

FACULTY SPECIALIZATIONS AND RESEARCH

FIT's faculty is drawn from top professionals in academia, art, design, communications, and business, providing a curriculum rich in real-world experience and traditional educational values. Student-instructor interaction is encouraged, with a maximum class size of 25, and courses are structured to foster participation, independent thinking, and self-expression.

COMMUNITY COLLEGE TRANSFERS

Transfer students must submit official transcripts for credit evaluation. Students may qualify for a one-year AAS option if they hold a Bachelor's degree or if they have a minimum of 30 transferable credits from a regionally accredited institution, including 24 credits equivalent to FIT's liberal arts requirements. Students seeking admission to a baccalaureate program must hold an AAS degree from FIT or an equivalent college degree, or at least 60 credits toward a Bachelor's degree in an equivalent program at a regionally accredited college.

Fashion Institute of Technology

Department of Fashion Design

Seventh Ave. & 27th St., New York, NY 10001 | 212-217-3760 | www.fitnyc.edu/fashiondesign

UNIVERSITY PROFILE

Public
Urban
Residential
Semester Schedule
Co-ed

STUDENT DEMOGRAPHICS

Undergraduate: 10,207
Graduate: 206

Male: 16%
Female: 84%

Full-time: 70%
Part-time: 30%

EXPENSES

Tuition: $3,714 (in-state)
Room & Board:
$9,650 - $17,520

ADMISSIONS

Seventh Ave. and 27th St.
New York, NY 10001
212 217.3760
fitinfo@fitnyc.edu

DEGREE INFORMATION

Major / Degree / Concentration	Enrollment	Requirements for entry	Graduation rate
Fashion Design Associate of Applied Science	Not reported	A portfolio and a high school diploma or a General Equivalency Diploma (GED). SAT scores are required for placement in English and math classes.	Not reported
Fashion Design Bachelor of Fine Arts Children's Wear Intimate Apparel Knitwear Special Occasion Sportswear	Not reported	AAS from FIT; associate's or bachelor's degree from a regionally accredited college in a program that is equivalent to the FIT Fashion Design AAS program; or at least 60 credits toward a bachelor's degree in an equivalent program at a regionally accredited college.	Not reported

TOTAL PROGRAM ENROLLMENT

Undergraduate: 1,189
Graduate: n/a

Male: 10%
Female: 90%

Full-time: 84%
Part-time: 16%
Online: n/a

International: 18%
Minority: 25%

Job Placement Rate: 90%

SCHOLARSHIPS / FINANCIAL AID

The college directly administers its own institutional grants and scholarships, which are provided by The Educational Foundation for the Fashion Industries. College-administered federal funding includes Federal Pell Grants, Federal Perkins Loans, Federal Supplemental Educational Opportunity Grants, Federal Work-Study Program awards, and the Federal Family Educational Loan Program, which includes student and parent loans. New York State residents who meet state guidelines for eligibility may also receive Tuition Assistance Program (TAP) and/or Educational Opportunity Program (EOP) grants. Financial aid applicants must file the Free Application for Federal Student Aid (FAFSA), through which they apply for the Federal Pell Grant, and should also apply to all available outside sources of aid.

TOTAL FACULTY: 107

Full-time: Not reported
Part-time: Not reported

FASHION ADMINISTRATION

Colette Wong, chair

PROFESSIONAL / ACADEMIC AFFILIATIONS

Not reported

PROGRAM DESCRIPTION AND PHILOSOPHY

For many people around the world, fashion education means just one thing: FIT. Our Fashion Design program has been preparing students for success at every level, from haute couture to ready-to-wear to mass market, for more than 65 years. The program keeps evolving along with fashion itself, but some FIT traditions are forever: First, our close ties to the industry let us immerse students in what's happening now in this fast-changing field. And our own brand of fashion education nurtures creativity while providing a rigorous grounding in the practical and technical skills needed for career success. Each undergraduate program also includes a core of traditional liberal arts courses, providing students with a global perspective, critical-thinking skills, and the ability to communicate effectively, and students have the option of completing a liberal arts minor.

Students are exposed to the real demands and practices of the fashion world. Students learn the fundamentals of professional draping, patternmaking, and sewing techniques. They'll master computer-aided design (CAD), and learn how to take a design from concept to finished garment. Fashion Design at FIT provides students with the skills and knowledge to become not only designers with their own creative vision, but professionals prepared to take their place in this challenging industry.

FACILITIES

FIT's campus provides its students with classrooms, laboratories, and studios that reflect the most advanced educational and industry practices. The Fred P. Pomerantz Art and Design Center houses drawing, painting, photography, printmaking, and sculpture studios; display and exhibit design rooms; a model-making workshop; and a graphics printing service bureau. The Peter G. Scotese Computer-Aided Design and Communications facility provides the latest technology in computer graphics, photography, and the design of advertising, fashion, interiors, textiles, and toys. Other facilities include a professionally equipped fragrance-development laboratory, cutting and sewing labs, a design/research lighting laboratory, knitting lab, broadcasting studio, multimedia foreign languages laboratory, and 23 computer labs, in addition to several other labs with computers reserved for students in specific programs.

ONLINE / DISTANCE LEARNING
Not reported

COURSES OF INSTRUCTION
- Draping
- Model Drawing for Fashion Design
- Fashion Past and Present
- Sewing Techniques

INTERNSHIPS
Required of majors. Past sponsors include Donna Karan, Calvin Klein, Tommy Hilfiger, and Ralph Lauren.

STUDY ABROAD
The study abroad experience provides students with the opportunity to immerse themselves in diverse cultures and prepares them to live and work in a global community. Fashion Design students can study in countries such as Australia, China, England, and Italy.

NOTABLE ALUMNI
Fashion designers Amsale Aberra, Reem Acra, Francisco Costa of Calvin Klein Collection, Calvin Klein, Nanette Lepore, and Ralph Rucci.

STUDENT ACTIVITIES AND ORGANIZATIONS
The college is home to more than 60 clubs, societies, and athletic teams—everything from major-related organizations to hobby groups to a ski and snowboard club. Each organization is open to all students who have paid their activity fee. The Student Council, the governing body of the Student Association, grants all students the privileges and responsibilities of citizens in a self-governing college community. FIT has intercollegiate teams in basketball, cross-country, half-marathon, outdoor track, dance, table tennis, tennis, swimming and diving, and volleyball.

FACULTY SPECIALIZATIONS AND RESEARCH
FIT's faculty is drawn from top professionals in academia, art, design, communications, and business, providing a curriculum rich in real-world experience and traditional educational values. Student-instructor interaction is encouraged, with a maximum class size of 25, and courses are structured to foster participation, independent thinking, and self-expression.

COMMUNITY COLLEGE TRANSFERS
Transfer students must submit official transcripts for credit evaluation. Students may qualify for a one-year AAS option if they hold a bachelor's degree or if they have a minimum of 30 transferable credits from a regionally accredited institution, including 24 credits equivalent to FIT's liberal arts requirements. Students seeking admission to a baccalaureate program must hold an AAS degree from FIT or an equivalent college degree, or at least 60 credits toward a bachelor's degree in an equivalent program at a regionally accredited college.

Fashion Institute of Technology

Department of Fashion Merchandising Management

Seventh Ave. & 27th St., New York, NY 10001 | 212-217-3760 | www.fitnyc.edu/fmm

DEGREE INFORMATION

Major / Degree / Concentration	Enrollment	Requirements for entry	Graduation rate
Fashion Merchandising Management Associate of Applied Science	Not reported	A high school diploma or a General Equivalency Diploma (GED). SAT scores are required for placement in English and math classes.	Not reported
Fashion Merchandising Management Bachelor of Science	Not reported	AAS from FIT; associate's or bachelor's degree from a regionally accredited college in a program that is equivalent to the FIT Fashion Merchandising Management AAS program; or at least 60 credits toward a bachelor's degree in an equivalent program at a regionally accredited college.	Not reported

TOTAL PROGRAM ENROLLMENT
Undergraduate: 2,229
Graduate: n/a

Male: 6%
Female: 94%

Full-time: 89%
Part-time: 11%
Online: 0.3%

International: 7.5%
Minority: 17%

Job Placement Rate: 90%

SCHOLARSHIPS / FINANCIAL AID
The college directly administers its own institutional grants and scholarships, which are provided by The Educational Foundation for the Fashion Industries. College-administered federal funding includes Federal Pell Grants, Federal Perkins Loans, Federal Supplemental Educational Opportunity Grants, Federal Work-Study Program awards, and the Federal Family Educational Loan Program, which includes student and parent loans. New York State residents who meet state guidelines for eligibility may also receive Tuition Assistance Program (TAP) and/or Educational Opportunity Program (EOP) grants. Financial aid applicants must file the Free Application for Federal Student Aid (FAFSA), through which they apply for the Federal Pell Grant, and should also apply to all available outside sources of aid.

TOTAL FACULTY: 102
Full-time: Not reported
Part-time: Not reported

FASHION ADMINISTRATION
Renee Cooper, Acting Chair

PROFESSIONAL / ACADEMIC AFFILIATIONS
Not reported

PROGRAM DESCRIPTION AND PHILOSOPHY

Every season, designers show their latest creations, "looks" that eventually make it from runways to store racks all over the world. It's the job of the merchandise manager to choose the best of these looks and trends, mixing and matching colors, sizes, and silhouettes to give customers what they want at a price they're willing to pay. It's a challenging and rewarding career that combines creative skills and analytical thinking. Merchandising management is where fashion meets business. New York City provides the best setting for any student who is fascinated with fashion merchandising. Instructed by experienced industry professionals, students have the opportunity to learn real-world skills beyond the classroom by visiting showrooms, specialty shops, and buying offices throughout the city. Internships and capstone classes provide additional firsthand experience and networking opportunities. Working individually and in teams, students study fashion marketing, product development, planning, and fashion management. Each undergraduate program also includes a core of traditional liberal arts courses, providing students with a global perspective, critical-thinking skills, and the ability to communicate effectively, and students have the option of completing a liberal arts minor.

FIT graduates master the skills needed in global retail operations and management, and learn how to combine their sense of style with business acumen to lead them to career success.

FACILITIES

FIT's campus provides its students with classrooms, laboratories, and studios that reflect the most advanced educational and industry practices. The Fred P. Pomerantz Art and Design Center houses drawing, painting, photography, printmaking, and sculpture studios; display and exhibit design rooms; a model-making workshop; and a graphics printing service bureau. The Peter G. Scotese Computer-Aided Design and Communications facility provides the latest technology in computer graphics, photography, and the design of advertising, fashion, interiors, textiles, and toys. Other facilities include a professionally equipped fragrance-development laboratory, cutting and sewing labs, a design/research lighting laboratory, knitting lab, broadcasting studio, multimedia foreign languages laboratory, and 23 computer labs, in addition to several other labs with computers reserved for students in specific programs.

ONLINE / DISTANCE LEARNING

FIT offers a two-year online associate degree in Fashion Merchandising Management.

COURSES OF INSTRUCTION

- Advertising and Promotion
- Fundamentals of Textiles
- Introduction to Fashion Marketing
- Business Writing
- Fashion Inventory Management

INTERNSHIPS

Required of majors. Past sponsors include Doneger, JCPenney, Macy's, Perry Ellis, and Ross Stores.

STUDY ABROAD

The study abroad experience provides students with the opportunity to immerse themselves in diverse cultures and prepares them to live and work in a global community. Fashion Merchandising Management students can study in countries such as England, France, and Italy.

NOTABLE ALUMNI

Edward Menicheschi of *Vanity Fair*, Candy Pratts Price of Style.com, and Lisa Versacio of Brocade Home.

STUDENT ACTIVITIES AND ORGANIZATIONS

The college is home to more than 60 clubs, societies, and athletic teams—everything from major-related organizations to hobby groups to a ski and snowboard club. Each organization is open to all students who have paid their activity fee. The Student Council, the governing body of the Student Association, grants all students the privileges and responsibilities of citizens in a self-governing college community. FIT has intercollegiate teams in basketball, cross-country, half-marathon, outdoor track, dance, table tennis, tennis, swimming and diving, and volleyball.

FACULTY SPECIALIZATIONS AND/OR RESEARCH

FIT's faculty is drawn from top professionals in academia, art, design, communications, and business, providing a curriculum rich in real-world experience and traditional educational values. Student-instructor interaction is encouraged, with a maximum class size of 25, and courses are structured to foster participation, independent thinking, and self-expression.

COMMUNITY COLLEGE TRANSFERS

Transfer students must submit official transcripts for credit evaluation. Students may qualify for a one-year AAS option if they hold a bachelor's degree or if they have a minimum of 30 transferable credits from a regionally accredited institution, including 24 credits equivalent to FIT's liberal arts requirements. Students seeking admission to a baccalaureate program must hold an AAS degree from FIT or an equivalent college degree, or at least 60 credits toward a bachelor's degree in an equivalent program at a regionally accredited college.

Fashion Institute of Technology

Department of Global Fashion Management

Seventh Ave. & 27th St., New York, NY 10001 | 212-217-4300 | www.fitnyc.edu/2865.asp

UNIVERSITY PROFILE
Public
Urban
Residential
Semester Schedule
Co-ed

STUDENT DEMOGRAPHICS
Undergraduate: 10,000
Graduate: 200

Male: Not reported
Female: Not reported

Full-time: Not reported
Part-time: Not reported

EXPENSES
Tuition: Varies
Room & Board: Not reported

ADMISSIONS
Seventh Ave. and 27th St.
New York, NY 10001
212-217-4300

DEGREE INFORMATION

Major / Degree / Concentration	Enrollment	Requirements for entry	Graduation rate
Global Fashion Management Master of Professional Studies (MPS)	20 per year	3.0 undergraduate gpa; minimum three years' experience in the apparel industry; essay; recommendations; personal interview	95%

TOTAL PROGRAM ENROLLMENT
Undergraduate: Not reported
Graduate: 20

Male: 20%
Female: 80%

Full-time: Not reported
Part-time: Not reported
Online: Not reported

International: 30%
Minority: Not reported

Job Placement Rate: 100%

SCHOLARSHIPS / FINANCIAL AID
As a state university, financial aid is limited to state and federal grants and loans.

TOTAL FACULTY: 10
Full-time: Not reported
Part-time: Not reported

FASHION ADMINISTRATION
Pamela Ellsworth, Department Chairperson

PROFESSIONAL / ACADEMIC AFFILIATIONS
Fashion Group International

PROGRAM DESCRIPTION AND PHILOSOPHY

FIT's Global Fashion Management is a graduate program focusing on the business of the apparel industry with the objective of moving professionals into executive positions. Almost all students entering the program work in the industry in some capacity including international students (approximately 30%) who leave their jobs to study in the three-semester GFM program in New York. Partner institutions include Institut Francais de la Mode (Paris) where students study the luxury industry, and Hong Kong Polytechnic University where supply chain and production is emphasized. A two-week seminar takes place for each of three semesters in the partner institution's respective city offering students the opportunity to develop a global network of colleagues.

FACILITIES

FIT's campus provides its students with classrooms, laboratories, and studios that reflect the most advanced educational and industry practices. The Fred P. Pomerantz Art and Design Center houses drawing, painting, photography, printmaking, and sculpture studios; display and exhibit design rooms; a model-making workshop; and a graphics printing service bureau. The Peter G. Scotese Computer-Aided Design and Communications facility provides the latest technology in computer graphics, photography, and the design of advertising, fashion, interiors, textiles, and toys. Other facilities include a professionally equipped fragrance-development laboratory, cutting and sewing labs, a design/research lighting laboratory, knitting lab, broadcasting studio, multimedia foreign languages laboratory, and 23 computer labs, in addition to several other labs with computers reserved for students in specific programs.

ONLINE / DISTANCE LEARNING

Not available

COURSES OF INSTRUCTION

- Production Management and Supply Chain
- Fashion for Global Markets
- Culture and International Business
- Politics and World Trade
- Finance
- Advanced Topics in Marketing
- Seminar in Paris
- Seminar in Hong Kong
- Seminar in New York

INTERNSHIPS

Not required

STUDY ABROAD

The program is international in scope

NOTABLE ALUMNI

Not reported

STUDENT ACTIVITIES AND ORGANIZATIONS

The college is home to more than 60 clubs, societies, and athletic teams—everything from major-related organizations to hobby groups to a ski and snowboard club. Each organization is open to all students who have paid their activity fee. The Student Council, the governing body of the Student Association, grants all students the privileges and responsibilities of citizens in a self-governing college community. FIT has intercollegiate teams in basketball, cross-country, half-marathon, outdoor track, dance, table tennis, tennis, swimming and diving, and volleyball.

FACULTY SPECIALIZATIONS AND/OR RESEARCH

Several faculty own and operate businesses in the apparel industry; faculty hold MBAs (finance and marketing) and PhDs (trade and politics) depending on their specialization

Fashion Institute of Technology

Menswear Department

Seventh Ave. & 27th St., New York, NY 10001 | 212-217-3760 | www.fitnyc.edu/menswear

UNIVERSITY PROFILE
Public
Urban
Residential
Semester Schedule
Co-ed

STUDENT DEMOGRAPHICS
Undergraduate: 10,207
Graduate: 206

Male: 16%
Female: 84%

Full-time: 70%
Part-time: 30%

EXPENSES
Tuition: $3,714
Room & Board: $9,650—
$17,520

ADMISSIONS
Seventh Ave. and 27th St.
New York, NY 10001
212-217-3760
fitinfo@fitnyc.edu

DEGREE INFORMATION

Major / Degree / Concentration	Enrollment	Requirements for entry	Graduation rate
Menswear Associate of Applied Science	Not reported	Portfolio and a high school diploma or a General Equivalency Diploma (GED). SAT scores are required for placement in English and math classes.	Not reported

TOTAL PROGRAM ENROLLMENT
Undergraduate: 81
Graduate: n/a

Male: 73%
Female: 27%

Full-time: 96%
Part-time: 4%
Online: n/a

International: 25%
Minority: 23%

Job Placement Rate: 90%

TOTAL FACULTY: 8
Full-time: Not reported
Part-time: Not reported

FASHION ADMINISTRATION
Mark-Evan Blackman, Chair

PROFESSIONAL / ACADEMIC AFFILIATIONS
Not reported

SCHOLARSHIPS / FINANCIAL AID
The college directly administers its own institutional grants and scholarships, which are provided by The Educational Foundation for the Fashion Industries. College-administered federal funding includes Federal Pell Grants, Federal Perkins Loans, Federal Supplemental Educational Opportunity Grants, Federal Work-Study Program awards, and the Federal Family Educational Loan Program, which includes student and parent loans. New York State residents who meet state guidelines for eligibility may also receive Tuition Assistance Program (TAP) and/or Educational Opportunity Program (EOP) grants. Financial aid applicants must file the Free Application for Federal Student Aid (FAFSA), through which they apply for the Federal Pell Grant, and should also apply to all available outside sources of aid.

PROGRAM DESCRIPTION AND PHILOSOPHY

To succeed in menswear—one of fashion's fastest growing fields— students need to understand every phase, from concept and design to production and delivery. The only one of its kind in the country, FIT's Menswear program immerses students in the industry in a way that's possible only in New York City. In courses taught by successful menswear professionals, they'll gain invaluable real-world insight while learning everything from basic sewing to advanced tailoring. Students master a wide range of design techniques, from pencil sketching to a variety of computer formats, and the patternmaking skills essential to producing high-quality men's apparel. Each undergraduate program also includes a core of traditional liberal arts courses, providing students with a global perspective, critical-thinking skills, and the ability to communicate effectively, and students have the option of completing a liberal arts minor.

Menswear students will discover that the real challenge is not designing a great outfit, but creating a balanced clothing line, with the right number of pieces at the right cost, that suits the market and the season. And they'll learn to create wearable clothes that sell, leading to an array of opportunities in this fast-changing, highly competitive field.

FACILITIES

FIT's campus provides its students with classrooms, laboratories, and studios that reflect the most advanced educational and industry practices. The Fred P. Pomerantz Art and Design Center houses drawing, painting, photography, printmaking, and sculpture studios; display and exhibit design rooms; a model-making workshop; and a graphics printing service bureau. The Peter G. Scotese Computer-Aided Design and Communications facility provides the latest technology in computer graphics, photography, and the design of advertising, fashion, interiors, textiles, and toys. Other facilities include a professionally equipped fragrance-development laboratory, cutting and sewing labs, a design/research lighting laboratory, knitting lab, broadcasting studio, multimedia foreign languages laboratory, and 23 computer labs, in addition to several other labs with computers reserved for students in specific programs.

ONLINE / DISTANCE LEARNING

Not reported

COURSES OF INSTRUCTION

- Menswear Design
- Tailoring the Jacket
- Fundamentals of Textiles
- Marketing of Menswear
- Digital Art for Menswear

INTERNSHIPS

Required of majors. Past sponsors include DKNY, Calvin Klein, Helmut Lang, and Marc Jacobs.

STUDY ABROAD

The study abroad experience provides students with the opportunity to immerse themselves in diverse cultures and prepares them to live and work in a global community. Menswear students can study in countries such as France and Italy.

NOTABLE ALUMNI

Fashion designer John Bartlett.

STUDENT ACTIVITIES AND ORGANIZATIONS

The college is home to more than 60 clubs, societies, and athletic teams—everything from major-related organizations to hobby groups to a ski and snowboard club. Each organization is open to all students who have paid their activity fee. The Student Council, the governing body of the Student Association, grants all students the privileges and responsibilities of citizens in a self-governing college community. FIT has intercollegiate teams in basketball, cross-country, half-marathon, outdoor track, dance, table tennis, tennis, swimming and diving, and volleyball.

FACULTY SPECIALIZATIONS AND RESEARCH

FIT's faculty is drawn from top professionals in academia, art, design, communications, and business, providing a curriculum rich in real-world experience and traditional educational values. Student-instructor interaction is encouraged, with a maximum class size of 25, and courses are structured to foster participation, independent thinking, and self-expression.

COMMUNITY COLLEGE TRANSFERS

Transfer students must submit official transcripts for credit evaluation.

Fashion Institute of Technology

Department of Technical Design

27th St. & 7th Ave., New York, NY 10001 | 212-217-4410 | www.fitnyc.edu

UNIVERSITY PROFILE
Public
Urban
Residential
Semester Schedule
Co-ed

STUDENT DEMOGRAPHICS
Undergraduate: 10,000
Graduate: 2,000

Male: 8%
Female: 92%

Full-time: 90%
Part-time: 10%

EXPENSES
Tuition: Not reported
Room & Board: Not reported

ADMISSIONS
27th St & 7th Ave.
New York, NY 10001
212-217-4410
www.fitnyc.edu

DEGREE INFORMATION

Major / Degree / Concentration	Enrollment	Requirements for entry	Graduation rate
Technical Design Associate of Applied Science	22	Not reported	99%

TOTAL PROGRAM ENROLLMENT
Undergraduate: 22
Graduate: Not reported

Male: 20%
Female: 80%

Full-time: 100%
Part-time: Not reported
Online: Not reported

International: Not reported
Minority: Not reported

Job Placement Rate: 100%

SCHOLARSHIPS / FINANCIAL AID
The college directly administers its own institutional grants and scholarships, which are provided by The Educational Foundation for the Fashion Industries. College-administered federal funding includes Federal Pell Grants, Federal Perkins Loans, Federal Supplemental Educational Opportunity Grants, Federal Work-Study Program awards, and the Federal Family Educational Loan Program, which includes student and parent loans. New York State residents who meet state guidelines for eligibility may also receive Tuition Assistance Program (TAP) and/or Educational Opportunity Program (EOP) grants. Financial aid applicants must file the Free Application for Federal Student Aid (FAFSA), through which they apply for the Federal Pell Grant, and should also apply to all available outside sources of aid.

TOTAL FACULTY: 3
Full-time: 2
Part-time: 1

FASHION ADMINISTRATION
Deborah Beard Acting Associate Chair
 Technical Design

PROFESSIONAL / ACADEMIC AFFILIATIONS
Not reported

242

PROGRAM DESCRIPTION AND PHILOSOPHY
This is new program.

FACILITIES
FIT's campus provides its students with classrooms, laboratories, and studios that reflect the most advanced educational and industry practices. The Fred P. Pomerantz Art and Design Center houses drawing, painting, photography, printmaking, and sculpture studios; display and exhibit design rooms; a model-making workshop; and a graphics printing service bureau. The Peter G. Scotese Computer-Aided Design and Communications facility provides the latest technology in computer graphics, photography, and the design of advertising, fashion, interiors, textiles, and toys. Other facilities include a professionally equipped fragrance-development laboratory, cutting and sewing labs, a design/research lighting laboratory, knitting lab, broadcasting studio, multimedia foreign languages laboratory, and 23 computer labs, in addition to several other labs with computers reserved for students in specific programs.

ONLINE / DISTANCE LEARNING
Not available

COURSES OF INSTRUCTION
- Advanced Patternmaking
- Computer Patternmaking
- Technical Design
- Advanced Textiles
- Computer corrections and fits

INTERNSHIPS
Required of majors. Interns are typically placed at all companies that need technical designers which is all companies

STUDY ABROAD
Not available

NOTABLE ALUMNI
Not reported

STUDENT ACTIVITIES AND ORGANIZATIONS
The college is home to more than 60 clubs, societies, and athletic teams—everything from major-related organizations to hobby groups to a ski and snowboard club. Each organization is open to all students who have paid their activity fee. The Student Council, the governing body of the Student Association, grants all students the privileges and responsibilities of citizens in a self-governing college community. FIT has intercollegiate teams in basketball, cross-country, half-marathon, outdoor track, dance, table tennis, tennis, swimming and diving, and volleyball.

FACULTY SPECIALIZATIONS AND RESEARCH
FIT's faculty is drawn from top professionals in academia, art, design, communications, and business, providing a curriculum rich in real-world experience and traditional educational values. Student-instructor interaction is encouraged, with a maximum class size of 25, and courses are structured to foster participation, independent thinking, and self-expression.

Genesee Community College

Business/Fashion Merchandising Management

One College Rd., Batavia, NY 14020 | 585-343-0055 ext. 6390 | **www.genesee.edu**

UNIVERSITY PROFILE
Public
Rural
Commuter
Semester Schedule
Co-ed

STUDENT DEMOGRAPHICS
Undergraduate: 7,208
Graduate: n/a

Male: 37%
Female: 63%

Full-time: 48%
Part-time: 52%

EXPENSES
Tuition: $3,400
Room & Board: $5,300

ADMISSIONS
One College Rd.
Batavia, NY 14020-9704
585-345-6800
admission@genesee.edu

DEGREE INFORMATION

Major / Degree / Concentration	Enrollment	Requirements for entry	Graduation rate
Fashion Merchandising Management Associate of Applied Science	33	Not reported	12%

TOTAL PROGRAM ENROLLMENT
Undergraduate: 7,208
Graduate: n/a

Male: 37%
Female: 63%

Full-time: 48%
Part-time: 52%
Online: 4%

International: 2%
Minority: 9%

Job Placement Rate: 75%

SCHOLARSHIPS / FINANCIAL AID
Financial Aid: $19 million awarded in
2008; 84% full-time students receive aid
Scholarships: $265,488 awarded in 2008

Students Receiving Scholarships or
Financial Aid: 84%

TOTAL FACULTY: 342
Full-time: 24%
Part-time: 76%

FASHION ADMINISTRATION
Dr. Stuart Steiner, President
Dr. Eunice Bellinger, Executive Vice
  President for Academic Affairs
Mr. Michael Stoll, Associate Vice
  President for Academic Affairs/Dean

PROFESSIONAL / ACADEMIC AFFILIATIONS
Not reported

PROGRAM DESCRIPTION AND PHILOSOPHY

The Fashion Merchandising Management program provides the skills you need to succeed in a fast-paced and ever-changing industry. Career opportunities are plentiful in areas such as fashion buying, coordinating, merchandising, advertising, display, public relations, styling, sales, marketing and e-commerce.

Every year Genesee's fashion merchandising students plan and produce an original, traditional runway fashion show–the largest in Western New York. You will produce radio and television commercials in the College's studios, develop Web pages and create a fashion portfolio using library periodicals for an up-to-date outlook on the field. Class trips to New York City and Toronto reinforce the creative approach to fashion buying and merchandising-and enhance your ability to spot fashion trends. Students benefit from Distributive Education Clubs of America (DECA) activities such as arranging visits to designer showrooms and buyers' offices and coordinating for guest speakers on campus.

All students participate in an off-campus full-time cooperative work experience. This affords them the opportunity to gain first-hand experiences in a variety of fashion-related assignments that can take place in well-known fashion centers.

FACILITIES

122 Classrooms and Laboratories
80 Smart Classrooms, including 7 Distance Learning Labs
33 Computer Labs

ONLINE / DISTANCE LEARNING

Not reported

COURSES OF INSTRUCTION

- Principles of Fashion
- Fashion Trends & Design
- Textiles
- Advertising
- Merchandise Planning & Control
- Business Topics Seminar
- Fashion Show Production

INTERNSHIPS

Required of majors at entry level. Interns are typically placed at all major retailers.

STUDY ABROAD

Not available

NOTABLE ALUMNI

Not reported

STUDENT ACTIVITIES AND ORGANIZATIONS

There are 44 Student Clubs and Organizations available to all Genesee Community College students. 10 intercollegiate men's and women's teams include Baseball, Basketball, Lacrosse, Soccer, Softball, Swimming, Volleyball, and Golf.

FACULTY SPECIALIZATIONS AND RESEARCH

Not reported

COMMUNITY COLLEGE TRANSFERS

Top Five Transfer Institutions: SUNY Brockport, SUNY Geneseo, SUNY Buffalo, SUNY Buffalo State, Rochester Institute of Technology. Fashion Merchandising Management students also transfer to FIT, LIM, Buffalo State, FIDM, and Villa Maria College. 91% of recent graduates are either employed or have transferred to a four-year college

Herkimer County Community College

Business: Fashion Buying & Merchandising

100 Reservoir Rd., Herkimer, NY 13350 | 315-866-0300 Ext. 8240 | www.herkimer.edu/academics/

UNIVERSITY PROFILE
Public
Rural
Residential & Commuter
Semester Schedule
Co-ed

STUDENT DEMOGRAPHICS
Undergraduate: 3,726
Graduate: 0

Male: 42%
Female: 58%

Full-time: 68%
Part-time: 32%

EXPENSES
Tuition: $3,240
Room & Board: $7,750

ADMISSIONS
100 Reservoir Rd.
Herkimer, NY 13350
315-866-0300 Ext. 8278
admissions@herkimer.edu

DEGREE INFORMATION

Major / Degree / Concentration	Enrollment	Requirements for entry	Graduation rate
Fashion Buying and Merchandising Associate of Applied Science	60	High School Degee	Not reported

TOTAL PROGRAM ENROLLMENT
Undergraduate: 53
Graduate: 0

Male: 19%
Female: 81%

Full-time: 96%
Part-time: 4%
Online: 4%

International: 2%
Minority: 42%

Job Placement Rate: 27%

SCHOLARSHIPS / FINANCIAL AID
77% of students receive federal and/or state financial aid. Some scholarships opportunities are available for continuing students.

Students Receiving Scholarships or Financial Aid: 77%

TOTAL FACULTY: 2
Full-time: 94%
Part-time: 6%

FASHION ADMINISTRATION
Michael Oriolo, Associate Dean of Academics
Janice Jenny, Professor of Business
Janet Ciccarelli, Professor of Business

PROFESSIONAL / ACADEMIC AFFILIATIONS
Not reported

PROGRAM DESCRIPTION AND PHILOSOPHY

Our program is under the auspices of the Business Division where the students will get a strong background in Business courses, allowing them the opportunity to transfer in the areas of Marketing, Retailing, Merchandising, Public Relations, etc. It is merchandising, as opposed to design, although we do offer an elective in Fashion Illustration.

FACILITIES

Vintage clothing collection

ONLINE / DISTANCE LEARNING

Not reported

COURSES OF INSTRUCTION

- Introduction to Fashion Merchandising
- History of Costume
- Retail Buying
- Introduction to Retailing
- Understanding Textiles

INTERNSHIPS

Not required. Most interns are ultimately hired by retailers.

STUDY ABROAD

Not available

NOTABLE ALUMNI

Sabrina King Crowley, Designer for Alfred Dunner

STUDENT ACTIVITIES AND ORGANIZATIONS

Fashion Club; Fashion Show Production Course with a fashion show in the Spring; 3-Day Trip to NYC in the Fall to visit various sites and showrooms in the Garment District

FACULTY SPECIALIZATIONS AND RESEARCH

Business Management

COMMUNITY COLLEGE TRANSFERS

Business Management

LIM College

Fashion Merchandising

12 E. 53rd St., New York, NY 10022 | 1-800-677-1323 | www.limcollege.edu

UNIVERSITY PROFILE
Private
Urban
Residential
Semester Schedule
Co-ed

STUDENT DEMOGRAPHICS
Undergraduate: 1,357
Graduate: 43

Male: 6%
Female: 94%

Full-time: 95%
Part-time: 5%

EXPENSES
Tuition: $20,900
Room & Board: $15,875
(room only)

ADMISSIONS
12 E. 53rd St.
New York, NY 10022
1-800-677-1323
admissions@limcollege.edu

DEGREE INFORMATION

Major / Degree / Concentration	Enrollment	Requirements for entry	Graduation rate
Fashion Merchandising Bachelor of Business Administration Bachelor of Professional Studies Associate of Applied Science Associate of Occupational Studies	913	Not reported	Not reported
Marketing Bachelor of Business Administration	275	Not reported	Not reported
Visual Merchandising Bachelor of Business Administration	115	Not reported	Not reported
Management Bachelor of Business Administration	54	Not reported	Not reported
Fashion Merchandising & Entrepreneurship Master of Business Administration	Not reported	Not reported	Not reported

TOTAL PROGRAM ENROLLMENT
Undergraduate: 1,357
Graduate: 43

Male: 6%
Female: 94%

Full-time: 95%
Part-time: 5%
Online: Not reported

International: 1%
Minority: 36%

Job Placement Rate: 91%

SCHOLARSHIPS / FINANCIAL AID
LIM College offers scholarships, grants, loans and work study options to over 75% of our student population.

Students Receiving Scholarships or Financial Aid: 75%

TOTAL FACULTY: 170
Full-time: 15%
Part-time: 85%

FASHION ADMINISTRATION
Michael Londrigan, Department Chair

PROFESSIONAL / ACADEMIC AFFILIATIONS

International Textile and Apparel Association

American Apparel and Footwear Association

Fashion Group International

PROGRAM DESCRIPTION AND PHILOSOPHY

When you enter LIM College, you're entering the only college in the United States dedicated to the business side of fashion. LIM College focuses exclusively on preparing you for a career in the fashion industry. We provide a solid curriculum that combines liberal arts learning with practical and relevant real-world experience. This is accomplished through immediate industry exposure on field trips, internships, and through guest lecture series. In addition to your professional fashion courses, you also complete courses in Liberal Arts and Business to provide a well-rounded general education. And what better place to live and learn about fashion than New York City! Students leave LIM College with a degree and a résumé.

FACILITIES

The college has four academic buildings with classrooms, computer and visual labs, student lounges, materials labs, college library, coffee shop, student service offices, and a Center for Career Development. The College's residence hall which houses 1/3 of our population is located on the Upper East Side of Manhattan. Our students report that New York City feels like an extended campus and being centrally located in midtown Manhattan allows them access to many fashion industry resources.

ONLINE / DISTANCE LEARNING

Not reported

COURSES OF INSTRUCTION

- Fashion Fundamentals
- Retailing
- Management
- Advertising
- Public Relations
- Product Development
- Accounting
- Business Law
- Merchandise Planning and Control
- Textiles
- Buying
- CAD for Merchandising
- Marketing
- Visual Merchandising
- Statistics
- English Composition

INTERNSHIPS

Required of majors at Freshman, Sophomore, and Senior years. Students have interned with companies such as Saks Fifth Ave., Gucci, NBC, Cotton Inc, Kenneth Cole, *InStyle* magazine, *Teen Vogue*, Juicy Couture, Bergdorf Goodman Marc Jacobs, Stella McCartney, Ralph Lauren, and MTV Networks.

STUDY ABROAD

Students have options to study in London, Paris, China and many other cities and countries around the world. There are also different options to study for an entire semester or just for 2-3 weeks.

NOTABLE ALUMNI

Not reported

STUDENT ACTIVITIES AND ORGANIZATIONS

Fashion Club, The Ultimate Choir, LIM College Dance Team, Sigma Beta Delta Honor Society, SLAB (Student Life Activities Board), Honors Program, Styling Club, Fashion Design, Visual Club, Intramural Sports Team, Student Government Association, SIFE (Students In Free Enterprise), Drama Club, Book Club

FACULTY SPECIALIZATIONS AND RESEARCH

Not reported

Marist College

The Fashion Program

Donnelly Hall #254, Poughkeepsie, NY 12601 | 845-575-3124 | www.marist.edu/commarts/fashion

UNIVERSITY PROFILE
Private
Suburban
Residential
Semester Schedule
Co-ed

STUDENT DEMOGRAPHICS
Undergraduate: Not reported
Graduate: Not reported

Male: Not reported
Female: Not reported

Full-time: Not reported
Part-time: Not reported

EXPENSES
Tuition: Not reported
Room & Board: Not reported

ADMISSIONS

DEGREE INFORMATION

Major / Degree / Concentration	Enrollment	Requirements for entry	Graduation rate
Fashion Design Bachelor of Professional Studies Fashion Merchandising or Product Development Minors Available	100	Entry portfolio–see Web site	Not reported
Fashion Merchandising Bachelor of Professional Studies Business Minor included, Product Development Minor Available	300	Entry portfolio–see Web site	Not reported

TOTAL PROGRAM ENROLLMENT
Undergraduate: 400
Graduate: Not reported

Male: Not reported
Female: Not reported

Full-time: 100%
Part-time: Not reported
Online: Not reported

International: Not reported
Minority: Not reported

Job Placement Rate: 98%

SCHOLARSHIPS / FINANCIAL AID
Scholarships are funded by fashion and educational foundations and student-generated activities.

TOTAL FACULTY: 18
Full-time: 6
Part-time: 12

FASHION ADMINISTRATION
Radley Cramer, Fashion Program Director

PROFESSIONAL / ACADEMIC AFFILIATIONS
Fashion Group International

PROGRAM DESCRIPTION AND PHILOSOPHY

A unique campus that is just 90 minutes from New York City. Classic campus life with a curriculum that blends fashion courses with liberal arts study. Very strong internship program and opportunities for international study.

FACILITIES

High-tech computer labs, working professional design studios, many cultural facilities in New York City and the Hudson River Valley.

ONLINE / DISTANCE LEARNING

Selected online courses

COURSES OF INSTRUCTION

A blending of fashion design and merchandising courses with liberal arts study

INTERNSHIPS

Not required, but students that elect to participate are typically placed at leading fashion companies, both large and small in the NYC area with internship opportunities on the West Coast as well as in England.

STUDY ABROAD

Short-term studies to Europe, Southeast Asia, and S. America. Full semesters at many locations all over the globe.

NOTABLE ALUMNI

Not reported

STUDENT ACTIVITIES AND ORGANIZATIONS

Not reported

FACULTY SPECIALIZATIONS AND RESEARCH

Not reported

Pratt Institute

Fashion Design Department

200 Willoughby Ave., Brooklyn, NY 11205 | 718-636-3600 | www.pratt.edu

UNIVERSITY PROFILE
Private
Urban
Residential
Semester Schedule
Co-ed

STUDENT DEMOGRAPHICS
Undergraduate: Not reported
Graduate: Not reported

Male: Not reported
Female: Not reported

Full-time: Not reported
Part-time: Not reported

EXPENSES
Tuition: Not reported
Room & Board: Not reported

ADMISSIONS
200 Willoughby Ave.
Brooklyn, NY 11205
800-331-0834

DEGREE INFORMATION

Major / Degree / Concentration	Enrollment	Requirements for entry	Graduation rate
Fashion Design Bachelor of Fine Arts	134	Not reported	Not reported

TOTAL PROGRAM ENROLLMENT
Undergraduate: 134
Graduate: Not reported

Male: Not reported
Female: Not reported

Full-time: 100%
Part-time: Not reported
Online: Not reported

International: Not reported
Minority: Not reported

Job Placement Rate: Not reported

SCHOLARSHIPS / FINANCIAL AID
Not reported

TOTAL FACULTY: 22
Full-time: Not reported
Part-time: Not reported

FASHION DESIGN ADMINISTRATION
Rebeccah Pailes-Friedman, Acting Chair
Robin Mollicone, Assistant Chair

PROFESSIONAL / ACADEMIC AFFILIATIONS
Not reported

PROGRAM DESCRIPTION AND PHILOSOPHY

The Fashion Design department at Pratt has been an innovator for over 95 years. The department's first fashion show was held at Wanamaker's department store in 1924. By the early 1940's, the Institute had become the first school in the United States to grant a degree in Fashion Design. Today the Fashion Design program is one of the most prestigious in the country.

Pratt's industry-centered program inspires creative expression while providing students with solid technical skills in areas such as pattern making, draping, construction and sketching as well as CAD. Interdisciplinary and collaborative opportunities are available to Fashion Design students through other departments in the School of Art and Design. Students are exposed to the European design industry through an exchange program with Nuova Accademia di Belle Arti (NABA) in Milan, Italy, as well as a Fashion in Europe class, led by Pratt faculty, in which students visit design houses, fabric manufacturers, and museums in cities such as London, Paris, Milan, Florence, and Antwerp. In addition, the Fashion Design department offers a wide variety of elective courses in menswear, millinery, leather, jewelry design, marketing, and shoe design to compliment the core curriculum.

New York City resources provide students with unique opportunities to gain important hands-on experience outside of the classroom. Field trips to design showrooms and museums, internships with top design companies such as Armani Exchange, Kate Spade New York, DKNY, Brooklyn Industries and *Harper's Bazaar*, design competitions and critiques with professional designers like Alfredo Cabrera, Renee Hunter, and others are just some of the opportunities to which students can look forward.

The faculty is professionally active and accomplished. Their designs have been featured in a wide range of publications including *The New York Times*, *Essence* Magazine, and the *New Yorker* and seen on stage at the Metropolitan Opera, Broadway, HERE! TV and Bravo TV. They have worked for companies such as Nike, Fila USA, Champion, Liz Claiborne, Nautica, and Ralph Lauren among others. Design studios are equipped with industrial grade sewing machines and specialty machines so students can learn on the same equipment used by professionals in the industry.

FACILITIES

Sewing studios, computer lab, resource library, fabric resource room, vintage clothing collections

ONLINE / DISTANCE LEARNING

Not available

COURSES OF INSTRUCTION

Classes such as Light, Color and Design, Textiles, and Fashion Sketching teach students how to think visually while Fundamentals of Patternmaking teaches basic drafting and sewing skills.

INTERNSHIPS

Required of majors at the Junior and Senior Year

STUDY ABROAD

Available

NOTABLE ALUMNI

Not reported

STUDENT ACTIVITIES AND ORGANIZATIONS

Not reported

FACULTY SPECIALIZATIONS AND RESEARCH

Costume Design, Apparel Design, Jewelry Design, Couture, Bridal, Eveningwear, Lingerie, Activewear, Shoe Design, Millinary

COMMUNITY COLLEGE TRANSFERS

Transfer students are accepted into the program.

SUNY Westchester Community College

Department of Fashion Merchandising

75 Grasslands Rd., Valhalla, NY 10595 | 914-606-6996 | www.sunywcc.edu/fashion

UNIVERSITY PROFILE
Public
Suburban
Commuter
Semester Schedule
Co-ed

STUDENT DEMOGRAPHICS
Undergraduate: 20,000
Graduate: n/a

Male: 48%
Female: 52%

Full-time: Not reported
Part-time: Not reported

EXPENSES
Tuition: $3,500
Room & Board: n/a

ADMISSIONS
75 Grasslands Rd.
Valhalla, NY10595
914-606-6880
Phyllis.Fein@sunywcc.edu

DEGREE INFORMATION

Major / Degree / Concentration	Enrollment	Requirements for entry	Graduation rate
Fashion Merchandising Associate of Applied Science	250	Open Enrollment	Not reported
Fashion Technology & Construction Associate of Applied Science	NEW- Fall 2010	Portfolio Review and Interview	Not reported

TOTAL PROGRAM ENROLLMENT
Undergraduate: 250
Graduate: n/a

Male: 15%
Female: 85%

Full-time: 64%
Part-time: 36%
Online: 15%

International: 15%
Minority: 50%

Job Placement Rate: 85%

SCHOLARSHIPS / FINANCIAL AID
Generous Foundation Scholarships

Students Receiving Scholarships or Financial Aid: 65%

TOTAL FACULTY: 5
Full-time: 3
Part-time: 2

FASHION DESIGN ADMINISTRATION
Professor Phylis Fein, Curriculum Chairperson
Professor John Christesen, Business Chairperson
Jeffrey Conte, Associate Dean

PROFESSIONAL / ACADEMIC AFFILIATIONS
Fashion Group International

PROGRAM DESCRIPTION AND PHILOSOPHY

Students who love style, have an interest in merchandising, or a desire to work in textiles and fashion marketing, will find a variety of career opportunities in the dynamic, creative, and challenging world of fashion. The Fashion Merchandising program, which combines fashion studies with business courses, will prepare students for positions in resident buying offices, fashion manufacturers, designers' showrooms, retail stores, fashion publications, and other firms associated with the fashion industry. After graduation, students may either begin their careers or may choose to transfer to bachelor's degree programs in colleges which offer Fashion Merchandising degrees, such as the upper division of the Fashion Institute of Technology (FIT), Berkeley College, or The Laboratory Institute of Merchandising (LIM) and other four-year colleges which offer fashion-related degrees.

FACILITIES

Garment Construction Lab, CAD Software Design Technology Lab, Fashion Resource Room

ONLINE / DISTANCE LEARNING

Not reported

COURSES OF INSTRUCTION

- Garment Construction
- Introduction to the Fashion Industry
- International Fashion Buying
- Visual Merchandising
- Textiles Development in the Global Marketplace

INTERNSHIPS

Required of majors.

Interns are typically placed at companies such as Eileen Fisher, Isaac Mizrahi, USACOUTURE International, Scoop, Stella McCarthy, The Wag, *Westchester* magazine

STUDY ABROAD

Italy/Paris Study Abroad-Summer Only

NOTABLE ALUMNI

Liz Carvahlo-Fashion Designer
Brenda Greving- Ralph Lauren Visual Merchandising

STUDENT ACTIVITIES AND ORGANIZATIONS

DECA Fashion Club, Fashion Group International Junior Memberships, Alpha Beta Gamma

FACULTY SPECIALIZATIONS AND RESEARCH

New Product Development, Trend Research, Fashion Animation

COMMUNITY COLLEGE TRANSFERS

FIT, LIM, Cornell, Marist, CUNY Baruch, Parsons, FIDM

Villa Maria College

Fashion Design & Merchandising Department

240 Pine Ridge Rd., Buffalo, NY 14225 | 716-896-0700 | www.villa.edu

UNIVERSITY PROFILE
Private
Urban
Commuter
Semester Schedule
Co-ed

STUDENT DEMOGRAPHICS
Undergraduate: 25
Graduate: n/a

Male: 10%
Female: 90%

Full-time: 75%
Part-time: 25%

EXPENSES
Tuition: $14,000
Room & Board: $8,000

ADMISSIONS
240 Pine Ridge Rd.
Buffalo, NY 14225
716-961-1805
admissions@villa.edu

DEGREE INFORMATION

Major / Degree / Concentration	Enrollment	Requirements for entry	Graduation rate
Fashion Design & Merchandising Bachelor of Fine Arts	Not reported	Not reported	Not reported

TOTAL PROGRAM ENROLLMENT
Undergraduate: Not reported
Graduate: Not reported

Male: Not reported
Female: Not reported

Full-time: Not reported
Part-time: Not reported
Online: Not reported

International: Not reported
Minority: Not reported

Job Placement Rate: Not reported

SCHOLARSHIPS / FINANCIAL AID
Not reported

TOTAL FACULTY: NOT REPORTED
Full-time: Not reported
Part-time: Not reported

FASHION DESIGN ADMINISTRATION
Not reported

PROFESSIONAL / ACADEMIC AFFILIATIONS
Not reported

PROGRAM DESCRIPTION AND PHILOSOPHY

The Fashion Design and Merchandising program allows students to reflect their individual and cultural values and perspectives through fashion design and imagery. The program insures students possess the creative, critical thinking, technology, portfolio presentation, and oral communication skills required in the industry. Beginning in the Sophomore year students have the option to follow a design or a merchandising track.

FACILITIES

Fashion lab/classroom

ONLINE / DISTANCE LEARNING

Not reported

COURSES OF INSTRUCTION

- Introduction to Fashion Design
- History of Fashion Design
- Elements of Fashion Design
- Sewing Techniques
- Textiles
- Introduction to Fashion Sketching
- Grading Techniques
- Advanced Sewing Techniques
- Fashion Merchandising
- Visual Merchandising
- Fashion Analysis and Trends
- CAD I
- Marker Rendering
- CAD II
- Flat Pattern Making
- Draping
- International Retailing
- Fashion Entrepreneurship
- Fashion Accessories
- Fashion Illustration
- Tailoring Techniques
- Fashion Show Production & Promotion
- Couture Techniques
- Knitwear Design
- Fashion Retail Buying
- Senior Portfolio
- Internship
- Senior Capstone Show

INTERNSHIPS

Required of majors

STUDY ABROAD

Not reported

NOTABLE ALUMNI

Not reported

STUDENT ACTIVITIES AND ORGANIZATIONS

Not reported

FACULTY SPECIALIZATIONS AND RESEARCH

Not reported

Kent State University

Shannon Rodgers & Jerry Silverman School of Fashion Design & Merchandising

P.O. Box 5190, 226 Rockwell Hall, Kent, OH 44242 | 330-672-3010 | www.fashionschool.kent.edu

UNIVERSITY PROFILE
Public
Suburban
Residential
Semester Schedule
Co-ed

STUDENT DEMOGRAPHICS
Undergraduate: 39,870
Graduate: Not reported

Male: Not reported
Female: Not reported

Full-time: Not reported
Part-time: Not reported

EXPENSES
Tuition: $8,730 (in-state)
$16,418 (out-of-state)
Room & Board: $7,940

ADMISSIONS
161 Schwartz Center
Kent State University
P.O. Box 5190
Kent, Ohio 44242-0001

DEGREE INFORMATION

Major / Degree / Concentration	Enrollment	Requirements for entry	Graduation rate
Fashion Design Bachelor of Arts Track I–Conceptual	Not reported	2.75 gpa; portfolio review after Sophomore year	Not reported
Fashion Design Bachelor of Arts Track II–Technical	Not reported	Not reported	Not reported
Fashion Merchandising Bachelor of Science	Not reported	2.75 gpa	Not reported

TOTAL PROGRAM ENROLLMENT
Undergraduate: 1,280
Graduate: 0

Male: 10%
Female: 90%

Full-time: 98%
Part-time: 2%
Online: Not reported

International: 1%
Minority: 36%

Job Placement Rate: 95%

SCHOLARSHIPS / FINANCIAL AID
There are over 45 scholarships available to students in the School of Fashion Design & Merchandising amounting to over $45,000.

TOTAL FACULTY: 33
Full-time: 60%
Part-time: 40%

FASHION ADMINISTRATION
J.R. Campbell, Director and Professor
Emily Aldredge, NYC Studio Director
Bill Hauck, Assistant to the Director

PROFESSIONAL / ACADEMIC AFFILIATIONS
International Textile and Apparel Association
Fashion Group International
American Collegiate Retailing Association

PROGRAM DESCRIPTION AND PHILOSOPHY

The Shannon Rodgers and Jerry Silverman School of Fashion Design and Merchandising, founded in 1983, is dedicated to providing excellence in fashion education. The School offers the B.A., Fashion Design, and the B.S., Fashion Merchandising. The School also participates in the Combined B.S., Fashion Merchandising/M.B.A. Program where students can earn up to 12 credits in graduate-level coursework toward a M.B.A while earning the B.S., Fashion Merchandising. At the Graduate level, the School offers courses which comprise a concentration in Fashion Design and Merchandising within the MBA Program in the College of Business.

The School's unique characteristics include selective admission, an industry-based curriculum, and a symbiotic relationship with the Kent State University Museum which serves as a learning laboratory for the students of the School as well as students from disciplines across the campus.

Selective admission to the School is limited to those students who have demonstrated at the secondary level their ability to meet the rigorous requirements of the four-year curriculum. The faculty of the School, drawn from leading fashion schools, major universities, and the fashion industry, strongly support the basic premise of a liberal arts education; that is, to develop in students intellectual flexibility, curiosity, creativity, and a life-long love of learning. A strong and viable liberal arts program forms the foundation for the professional industry-based components in design and merchandising. Of critical importance is the School's commitment to maintaining currency in fashion technology.

Throughout the programs, the merchandising and design curricula emphasize professional standards of achievement. Lectures and seminars by visiting fashion professionals supplement the course offerings, while study tours throughout the United States and abroad, and internships in

the fashion industry offer students a broad perspective and experience in international education. Underlying the philosophy of the School is a commitment to honor its founders by becoming a world-class center of fashion education.

FACILITIES

The June Mohler Fashion Library; CAD lab–30 workstations with industry specific design software; PC Lab–30 workstations with the full range of off-the-shelf software; Industry-equipped design studios; Fully-wireless environments; Kent State University Museum; and TechStyleLAB–a commercial service, research lab and learning/teaching space focused on applications of textile and clothing design technologies.

ONLINE / DISTANCE LEARNING

Not reported

COURSES OF INSTRUCTION

Fashion Design:
- Fashion Fundamentals
- Fashion Fabrics I
- Fashion Visuals
- Foundations of Fashion Drawing
- Workroom Techniques I & II
- Fashion Drawing I & II
- Flat Pattern/Draping I & II
- History of Costume
- Fashion Design I & II
- Internship
- Fashion Studio I & II
- Professional Seminar
- CAD for Fashion Applications
- Marketing
- Fashion Portfolio I-IV

Fashion Merchandising:
- Fashion Fundamentals
- Fashion Fabrics I
- Fashion Apparel Analysis
- Fashion Merch. Presentations
- Fashion Retail Industry
- Marketing
- Professional Seminar
- Product Development
- Internship
- Fashion Marketing
- Computer Applications in Retailing
- Fashion Merch. Planning and Buying
- Fashion Forecasting

- Fashion Merchandise Seminar
- Apparel in the Global Economy

INTERNSHIPS

Required of majors at the Junior/Senior level. Interns are typically placed at companies such as Abercrombie & Fitch, Anna Sui, Badgley Mischka, Betsy Johnson, Claiborne, Cynthia Rowley, Diane von Furstenberg, Dillard's, Ellen Tracy, Elie Tahari, Frost French, Funky Kids, Gap, Inc., Goodyear Hall Tailors, Husqvarna-Viking, Ishii New York, Isabel Toledo, JCPenney Co., JCrew, Kenneth Cole, Kohl's, Lane Bryant, Limited Too, Macy's, Michael Kors, Nanette Lepore, Old Navy, Oscar de la Renta, Ralph Lauren Womenswear, Saks, Inc., Sears, United Bamboo, Vera Wang, Victoria's Secret, Walt Disney World Company, Yeohlee, Zac Posen

STUDY ABROAD

We focus on semester-long study away experiences and have our own studio on 39th St. in NYC; our own studio in Florence, Italy; send students to Hong Kong Polytechnic University; and we have a direct link with Paris American Academy in which our students continue to pay KSU tuition while studying in Paris. Approximately 200 of our students study away at one of our other locations annually.

NOTABLE ALUMNI

Suede (Stephen Whitney Baum), Karen Barbiere, Bibi Okoh, Tad Boetcher

STUDENT ACTIVITIES AND ORGANIZATIONS

Fashion Student Organization, Modista (Fashion Student Group to support minority populations)

FACULTY SPECIALIZATIONS AND RESEARCH

Fashion design, construction, textile design, merchandising, costume and textile history, branding, retail management, merchandising, visual merchandising, social responsibility, sustainable practices, applications of technology

University of Central Oklahoma

Human Environmental Sciences

100 N. University Dr., Edmond, OK 73034 | 405-974-5551 | **www.uco.edu**

UNIVERSITY PROFILE
Public
Urban
Commuter
Semester Schedule
Co-ed

STUDENT DEMOGRAPHICS
Undergraduate: 13,364
Graduate: 1,740

Male: 41%
Female: 59%

Full-time: 65.3%
Part-time: 34.7%

EXPENSES
Tuition: $140 per hour
Room & Board: several packages

ADMISSIONS
100 North University Dr.
Edmond, OK 73034
405-974-5551

DEGREE INFORMATION

Major / Degree / Concentration	Enrollment	Requirements for entry	Graduation rate
Fashion Marketing Bachelor of Science	140	2.0	Not reported

TOTAL PROGRAM ENROLLMENT
Undergraduate: Not reported
Graduate: Not reported

Male: 33%
Female: 67%

Full-time: 67%
Part-time: 33%
Online: Not reported

International: 5.7%
Minority: Not reported

Job Placement Rate: Not reported

SCHOLARSHIPS / FINANCIAL AID
Tuition Fee Waivers, Foundation Scholarships, Presidential Partners, First Time Student Scholarships (dependent on SAT scores)

TOTAL FACULTY: 631
Full-time: 50%
Part-time: 50%

FASHION DESIGN ADMINISTRATION
Dr. Kaye Sears, Chair
Dr. Darlene Kness, Program Coordinator
Dr. Susan Miller, Associate Professor

PROFESSIONAL / ACADEMIC AFFILIATIONS
Fashion Group International
American Association of Family & Consumer Science

PROGRAM DESCRIPTION AND PHILOSOPHY

Graduates receive a Bachelor of Science degree with a minor in business. We are close to a large metropolitan area, which gives students access to business internships and job placement.

Helping students learn so that they may become productive, creative, ethical, engaged citizens and leaders.

The University of Central Oklahoma is a learning-centered organization committed to transformative education through active engagement in the teaching-learning interchange, scholarly and creative pursuits, leadership, global competency, and service to others.

FACILITIES

Department costume museum, several computer labs

ONLINE / DISTANCE LEARNING

Some courses are available online.

COURSES OF INSTRUCTION

- Intro to Textiles
- Fashion Marketing
- Creative Problem Solving
- Global Protocol
- Hard Goods Merchandising
- Decorative Textiles
- Advertising and Promotion
- Fashion Accessories
- Entrepreneurship
- Buying and Analysis

INTERNSHIPS

Required of majors at the Junior level. Interns are typically placed at companies such as Dillard's, Nordstrom, and many local boutiques.

STUDY ABROAD

Europe, China, Australia

NOTABLE ALUMNI

Not reported

STUDENT ACTIVITIES AND ORGANIZATIONS

Department major club, honor society, Greek system, field trips to Dallas and New York City

FACULTY SPECIALIZATIONS AND RESEARCH

Technology, apparel manufacturing

COMMUNITY COLLEGE TRANSFERS

All 2-year Oklahoma Community College transfer students who graduate have the general education courses waived.

The Art Institute of Portland

Department of Apparel Design

1122 NW Davis St., Portland, OR 97209 | 503-228-6528 | www.artinstitutes.edu/portland/

UNIVERSITY PROFILE
Private
Urban
Commuter
Quarter Schedule
Co-ed

STUDENT DEMOGRAPHICS
Undergraduate: Not reported
Graduate: 0

Male: Not reported
Female: Not reported

Full-time: Not reported
Part-time: Not reported

EXPENSES
Tuition: $28,020
Room & Board: $620-800 per month

ADMISSIONS
1122 NW Davis St.
Portland, OR 97209
1-888-228-6528

DEGREE INFORMATION

Major / Degree / Concentration	Enrollment	Requirements for entry	Graduation rate
Apparel Design Associate of Applied Arts Bachelor of Fine Arts Optional Sustainable minors	Not reported	Not reported	Not reported
Accessory Design Associate of Applied Arts Bachelor of Fine Arts Optional Sustainable minors	Not reported	Not reported	Not reported
Fashion Marketing Associate of Applied Arts Bachelor of Fine Arts Optional Sustainable minors	Not reported	Not reported	Not reported

TOTAL PROGRAM ENROLLMENT
Undergraduate: Not reported
Graduate: 0

Male: Not reported
Female: Not reported

Full-time: Not reported
Part-time: Not reported
Online: Not reported

International: Not reported
Minority: Not reported

Job Placement Rate: Not reported

SCHOLARSHIPS / FINANCIAL AID
Federal Work-Study, The Art Institutes
Awards, Grants, and Scholarships,
Federal Loans, Federal Grants

TOTAL FACULTY: NOT REPORTED
Full-time: Not reported
Part-time: Not reported

FASHION ADMINISTRATION
Sue Bonde, Department Director
Melanie Risner, Assistant Department Director

PROFESSIONAL / ACADEMIC AFFILIATIONS
Not reported

PROGRAM DESCRIPTION AND PHILOSOPHY

In the Apparel Design degree program at The Art Institute of Portland, students have an opportunity to develop skills in clothing design, sketching and illustration, patternmaking and draping, garment construction, textiles, critical analysis, and computer-aided design. The curriculum for the bachelor's degree program offers exposure to business practices, entrepreneurship, marketing, and presentation. Students will learn to develop their own collections and have opportunities to exhibit their creations in fashion shows and competitions. Graduates will be prepared to seek entry-level positions such as fashion designer, patternmaker, or apparel developer.

With a degree in Apparel Accessory Design, you can learn to create the right fashion accessory to complete the perfect outfit. The bachelor's degree program in Apparel Accessory Design at The Art Institute of Portland offers students an opportunity to develop skills in design, sketching and illustration, patternmaking and prototyping, construction, textile and material knowledge, and computer aided design. The curriculum also offers instruction in business and entrepreneurship, marketing, and presentation. Students will have the opportunity to learn to design dynamic yet functional accessories from concept to finished prototype. Graduates of the Apparel Accessory Design program can seek entry-level positions such as design assistants, freelance designers, or entrepreneurs, or to work in areas such as CAD operations or merchandising.

Our bachelor's degree program in Fashion Marketing takes a well-rounded approach to fashion, offering an expanded curriculum that allows students to develop the necessary knowledge and skills in business, marketing, fashion, and design to be competitive in today's fashion market. The fashion industry's growing need for employees educated in computer technology, advanced-level business, and sales marketing is at the core of this program. Students are offered the opportunity to enhance their skills in product development, consumer behavior, appropriate technology and software, graphic communications, and trends and concepts in fashion. As a graduate, you are prepared to seek entry-level positions such as a buyer, stylist, merchandiser, special events coordinator, visual merchandiser, as well as positions in management and sales promotion.

FACILITIES
Computer labs, fabric printing, plotter, industrial sewing labs

ONLINE / DISTANCE LEARNING
Various courses are offered online.

COURSES OF INSTRUCTION
- Fashion Illustration
- Patternmaking
- Technical Sketching
- Draping
- Couture
- Sewn Construction
- Digital Surface Design
- Fashion Forecasting
- Tailoring
- Fashion Event Production
- Concept & Development

INTERNSHIPS
Required of majors. Interns are typically placed at companies such as Adidas, Columbia, Nike, and Jantzen.

STUDY ABROAD
Available

NOTABLE ALUMNI
Not reported

STUDENT ACTIVITIES AND ORGANIZATIONS
Entwine fashion club

FACULTY SPECIALIZATIONS AND RESEARCH
Not reported

Oregon State University

Department of Design & Human Environment

224 Milam Hall, Corvallis, OR 97331 | 541-737-3796 | www.hhs.oregonstate.edu/dhe/

UNIVERSITY PROFILE
Public
Rural
Residential
Quarter Schedule
Co-ed

STUDENT DEMOGRAPHICS
Undergraduate: 18,067
Graduate: 3,902

Male: 52.3%
Female: 47.7%

Full-time: 81.3%
Part-time: 18.7%

EXPENSES
Tuition: $6,725
Room & Board: $8,352

ADMISSIONS
Oregon State University
104 Kerr Administration
Building
Corvallis, OR 97331-2106
541-737-4411
http://oregonstate.edu/
admissions/index.php

DEGREE INFORMATION

Major / Degree / Concentration	Enrollment	Requirements for entry	Graduation rate
Apparel Design Bachelor of Science Honors Bachelor of Science	168	Professional program application after 1st year. Minimum of 2.4 gpa to apply.	Not reported
Interior Design & Housing Studies Bachelor of Science Honors Bachelor of Science	260	Professional program application after 1st year. Minimum of 2.4 gpa to apply	Not reported
Merchandising Management Bachelor of Science Honors Bachelor of Science	266	Not reported	Not reported
Design & Human Environment Master of Arts Master of Science Doctor of Philosophy	29	Not reported	Not reported

TOTAL PROGRAM ENROLLMENT
Undergraduate: 694
Graduate: 29

Male: Not reported
Female: Not reported

Full-time: Not reported
Part-time: Not reported
Online: Not reported

International: Not reported
Minority: Not reported

Job Placement Rate: DHE graduates are very successful in securing jobs in their area of study upon graduation.

SCHOLARSHIPS / FINANCIAL AID
University Financial Aid: http://
oregonstate.edu/financialaid/
College and Department Financial Aid
and Scholarships: www.hhs.oregonstate.
edu/students/scholarships

TOTAL FACULTY: 13
Full-time: 85%
Part-time: 15%

FASHION DESIGN ADMINISTRATION
Leslie Davis Burns, PhD, Chair

PROFESSIONAL / ACADEMIC AFFILIATIONS
International Textile and Apparel
  Association
American Collegiate Retailing
  Association

PROGRAM DESCRIPTION AND PHILOSOPHY

Graduates of Design and Human Environment mesh creative confidence, technical skill, evidence-based knowledge, and socially responsible ethics to effectively approach the design and merchandising processes from innovation/design solution to market/user acceptance.

FACILITIES

Design studios, state-of-the-art computer labs, textile testing and quality assurance lab, historic/cultural textile and apparel collection

ONLINE / DISTANCE LEARNING

Not reported

COURSES OF INSTRUCTION

A complete listing of DHE courses can be found at: http://catalog.oregonstate.edu/CourseList.aspx?subjectcode=DHE&level=undergrad&campus=corvallis

INTERNSHIPS

Not required. Students obtain internships with a variety of regional, national, and international companies including (but not limited to) Abercrombie & Fitch, Anthropologie, Arbor Custom Homes, BCBG MaxAzria, Columbia Sportswear, Crate& Barrel, Donna Karan, *Glamour*, Guess, Herman Miller, IKEA, JCPenney, lucy activewear, Macy's, Nike, Nordstrom, The Northface, Pendleton, REI, Walmart, and many smaller companies.

STUDY ABROAD

Short-term study tours, AIU affiliation, international internships

NOTABLE ALUMNI

Alumni of the Department are in design, marketing, and management positions in regional, national, and international companies.

STUDENT ACTIVITIES AND ORGANIZATIONS

OSU Fashion Organization, Student Chapter of American Society of Interior Designers, Home Building and Design Club, Student Chapter of International Interior Design Association

FACULTY SPECIALIZATIONS AND RESEARCH

Design and Human Environment Signature Research/Creative Activity Areas Designing Human Environments

- Addressing the needs of children, seniors, people with health problems, and other special populations
- Implementing enabling technologies
- Using environmentally responsible textiles and materials
- Considering historic, cultural, social, psychological, aesthetic, economic, and marketing factors

Understanding Consumers and Users of Designed Environments

- Decision making processes
- Responses to and satisfaction with apparel, interiors, and housing
- Perceptions of environmental quality
- Influence of historic, cultural, social, psychological, aesthetic, economic, and marketing factors in designed environments

Applications of DHE Research and Creative Activity

- Product development
- Practices of individuals, organizations, and companies
- Informed policy making
- Pedagogy
- Theory development

COMMUNITY COLLEGE TRANSFERS

We work individually with transfer students to assure an effective transfer process. More information for transfer students can be found at: http://oregonstate.edu/admissions/transfer.php

Albright College

Fashion Department

Thirteenth and Bern St., Reading, PA 19612 | 610-921-7811 | www.albright.edu/fashion

UNIVERSITY PROFILE
Private
Suburban
Residential
Semester Schedule
Co-ed

STUDENT DEMOGRAPHICS
Undergraduate: 1,625
Graduate: Not reported

Male: 60%
Female: 40%

Full-time: 99%
Part-time: 1%

EXPENSES
Tuition: $31,940
Room & Board: $8,770

ADMISSIONS
Thirteenth and Bern St.
Reading, PA 19612
610-921-7700

DEGREE INFORMATION

Major / Degree / Concentration	Enrollment	Requirements for entry	Graduation rate
Fashion Bachelor of Arts Tracks in Design, Merchandising, Costume Design, Design & Merchandising	120	No Portfolio required	Fashion

TOTAL PROGRAM ENROLLMENT
Undergraduate: Not reported
Graduate: Not reported

Male: 40%
Female: 60%

Full-time: 99%
Part-time: 1%
Online: 0%

International: 8%
Minority: 17%

Job Placement Rate: Not reported

SCHOLARSHIPS / FINANCIAL AID
Not reported

TOTAL FACULTY: 118
Full-time: 100%
Part-time: 0

FASHION ADMINISTRATION
Dr. Lex McMillan, President
Dr. Andrea Chapdelaine, Chief Academic Officer
Doreen Burdalski, MBA, Chair of Fashion Department

PROFESSIONAL / ACADEMIC AFFILIATIONS
International Textile and Apparel Association
Fashion Group International
American Collegiate Retailing Association

PROGRAM DESCRIPTION AND PHILOSOPHY

Albright's Fashion department is located within a liberal arts college. Our philosophy is to develop our students into good citizens who will be successful and contribute to their profession. They will be lifelong learners with the ability to think critically and adjust to the changing times.

FACILITIES

Fashion Computer labs, Sewing/design labs, textile library,

ONLINE / DISTANCE LEARNING

Not available

COURSES OF INSTRUCTION

All Fashion Students:
- Fashion Fundamentals
- Textile Fundamentals
- History of Costume
- Visual Literacy
- Internships
- Senior Seminar

Design Students:
- Patternmaking
- Draping
- CAD
- Concept Development
- Fashion Illustration

Merchandising Students:
- Fashion Business
- Apparel Product Development
- Fashion Merchandising Communications
- Retailing
- Visual Merchandising

INTERNSHIPS

Required of majors at 4th year. Internships vary greatly by location and type of business. Albright students have interned in New York, Philadelphia, Florida, London and Italy to name a few locations. Types of businesses include apparel manufacturing and design, retail buying, retail visual merchandising, retail management, public relations, and marketing.

STUDY ABROAD

Available

NOTABLE ALUMNI

Scott French

STUDENT ACTIVITIES AND ORGANIZATIONS

Club Vogue student organization, *Seventh on 13th* fashion newsletter

FACULTY SPECIALIZATIONS AND/ OR RESEARCH

Costume design for theatre, visual merchandising, retail buying, apparel product development, computer aided design

The Art Institute of Philadelphia

Department of Fashion Design

2300 Market St., Philadelphia, PA 19103 | 215-405-6782 | www.artinstitutes.edu/philadelphia

UNIVERSITY PROFILE
Private
Urban
Commuter
Quarter Schedule
Co-ed

STUDENT DEMOGRAPHICS
Undergraduate: 3,500
Graduate: Not reported

Male: Not reported
Female: Not reported

Full-time: Not reported
Part-time: Not reported

EXPENSES
Tuition: Not reported
Room & Board: Not reported

ADMISSIONS
2300 Market St.
Philadelphia, PA 19103
215.405.6782

DEGREE INFORMATION

Major / Degree / Concentration	Enrollment	Requirements for entry	Graduation rate
Fashion Design Associate of Science Bachelor of Science	Not reported	Open Enrollment	Not reported
Fashion Marketing Associate of Science Bachelor of Science	Not reported	Open Enrollment	Not reported
Visual Merchandising Associate of Science	Not reported	Open Enrollment	Not reported

TOTAL PROGRAM ENROLLMENT
Undergraduate: Not reported
Graduate: Not reported

Male: Not reported
Female: Not reported

Full-time: Not reported
Part-time: Not reported
Online: Not reported

International: Not reported
Minority: Not reported

Job Placement Rate: Not reported

SCHOLARSHIPS / FINANCIAL AID
Not reported

TOTAL FACULTY: NOT REPORTED
Full-time: Not reported
Part-time: Not reported

FASHION ADMINISTRATION
Crystal Shamblee, Academic Director of
Fashion Design

PROFESSIONAL / ACADEMIC AFFILIATIONS
International Textile and Apparel
Association
American Apparel and Footwear
Association
Fashion Group International
American Collegiate Retailing
Association

PROGRAM DESCRIPTION AND PHILOSOPHY

The bachelor's degree program in Fashion Design at The Art Institute of Philadelphia takes a well-rounded approach to the fashion industry. It offers an expanded curriculum that allows students to develop the knowledge and skills in business, design, fashion, technology, and marketing to be competitive in today's market. Technological trends in fashion design are also reflected in the curriculum. To maintain a balance between technology and creativity, students take such courses as accessory design, knitting and weaving, and life drawing to better understand design and their craft. The Fashion Design program prepares graduates to seek career-entry positions such as assistant designer, stylist, visual display artist, and fashion illustrator. More technical career options might include manufacturing production assistant, computer marking and grading technician, patternmaker, and technical designer.

Our bachelor's degree program in Fashion Marketing takes a well-rounded approach to fashion, offering an expanded curriculum that allows students to develop the necessary knowledge and skills in business, marketing, fashion, and design to be competitive in today's fashion market. The fashion industry's growing need for employees educated in computer technology, advanced-level business, and sales marketing is at the core of this program. Students are offered the opportunity to enhance their skills in product development, consumer behavior, appropriate technology and software, graphic communications, and trends and concepts in fashion. As a graduate, you are prepared to seek entry-level positions such as a buyer, stylist, merchandiser, special events coordinator, visual merchandiser, as well as positions in management and sales promotion.

The associate's degree program in Visual Merchandising at The Art Institute of Philadelphia blends the business and psychology of fashion marketing principles with technical skills in prop building, signage, visual presentation, and design techniques. Students learn, through hands-on experience, how to design and draft a rendering of a display, how to build necessary props and accessories, and how to carry the project through to completion. Graduates are prepared for entry-level positions in department stores, specialty stores, and boutiques as visual merchandisers, marketing coordinators, and in sales and/or management.

FACILITIES
Not reported

ONLINE / DISTANCE LEARNING
Not reported

COURSES OF INSTRUCTION
Fashion Design:
- Life Drawing
- Portfolio Foundations Fashion Design
- Introduction to Apparel Design
- Clothing Construction I & II
- Fashion Design Sketch I & II
- Patternmaking I-III
- Draping
- Computer Patternmaking
- Portfolio Preparation
- Graphics for Fashion Designers I & II
- Collection Development
- Design Presentation
- Special Topics in Fashion Design
- Menswear
- Advanced Draping
- Tailoring
- Advanced Patternmaking
- Portfolio I & II
- Knitting and Weaving
- Accessory Design
- Fashion History I & II
- Survey of Fashion Industry
- Textiles & Fabrics
- Business Management
- Introduction to Manufacturing
- Consumer Behavior
- Trends and Concepts in Apparel
- Entrepreneurship
- Product Development
- International Marketing
- Current Designers
- Color Theory
- Internship I & II

Fashion Marketing:
- Portfolio Foundations Fashion Marketing
- Introduction to Retailing
- Retail Math I & II
- Apparel Evaluation and Construction
- Elements of Retail Operation
- Fashion Show Production
- Merchandise Management
- Business Ownership I & II
- Business Operations
- Special Topics in Fashion Marketing
- Merchandising Menswear
- Advertising
- Fashion Drawing
- Portfolio I & II
- Marketing Research
- Marketing in an Electronic Environment
- Fashion History I & II
- Survey of Fashion Industry
- Textiles & Fabrics
- Visual Merchandising
- Business Management
- Introduction to Manufacturing
- Sales Promotion
- Marketing
- Store Planning
- Graphic Communication in Fashion
- Consumer Behavior
- Trends and Concepts in Apparel
- Entrepreneurship
- Product Development
- International Marketing
- Current Designers
- Color Theory
- Internship I & II

INTERNSHIPS
Required of majors

STUDY ABROAD
Not reported

NOTABLE ALUMNI
Not reported

STUDENT ACTIVITIES AND ORGANIZATIONS
Not reported

FACULTY SPECIALIZATIONS AND RESEARCH
Not reported

Drexel University

Department of Fashion & Design & Merchandising

33rd & Market St., Philadelphia, PA 19104 | 215-895-2390 | www.drexel.edu/westphal

UNIVERSITY PROFILE
Private
Urban
Residential
Quarter Schedule
Co-ed

STUDENT DEMOGRAPHICS
Undergraduate: Not reported
Graduate: Not reported

Male: Not reported
Female: Not reported

Full-time: Not reported
Part-time: Not reported

EXPENSES
Tuition: Not reported
Room & Board: Not reported

ADMISSIONS
3141 Chestnut St.
Philadelphia, PA 19104
215.895.2000
www.drexel.edu/admissions

DEGREE INFORMATION

Major / Degree / Concentration	Enrollment	Requirements for entry	Graduation rate
Fashion Design Bachelor of Science	140	3.0 gpa Portfolio review	90%
Design & Merchandising Bachelor of Science	250	3.0 gpa	90%
Product Design Bachelor of Science	6	3.0 gpa	n/a

TOTAL PROGRAM ENROLLMENT
Undergraduate: 350
Graduate: 30-40

Male: 10%
Female: 90%

Full-time: 98%
Part-time: 2%
Online: n/a

International: 2%
Minority: 10%

Job Placement Rate: Not reported

SCHOLARSHIPS / FINANCIAL AID
Financial aid packages are both need based and merit based.

TOTAL FACULTY: 25-28
Full-time: 18
Part-time: 7-10

FASHION ADMINISTRATION
Roberta H. Gruber, Department Head, FD&M

PROFESSIONAL / ACADEMIC AFFILIATIONS
International Textile and Apparel Association
Fashion Group International
American Collegiate Retailing Association

PROGRAM DESCRIPTION AND PHILOSOPHY

Drexel's Fashion Design program is nationally recognized as a top-flight program. The rigorous curriculum consists of a unique six-month Co-op experience that complements coursework in conceptual design, presentation skills, CAD, and manufacturing procedures. The curriculum covers all facets of fashion design, from men's, women's, and children's wear, to swimwear and couture and prepares students for careers in fashion design, styling, advertising, and computer-aided and technical design. Small studio classes simulating the professional world are the core of a student's education with final critiques by practicing designers.

The Design & Merchandising program at the Drexel University Westphal College of Media Arts and Design prepares students for the challenges of the business and design world. Students learn to create and merchandise fashion and design products, and also obtain practical knowledge in the areas of marketing, promotion, and distribution. Our faculty and staff are committed to providing students with the skills to adapt to an ever-changing and increasingly fast-paced industry.

The Product Design program prepares students to become designers through experiential studio learning, skill development, and design thinking. Drexel's BS in product design specializes in multidisciplinary design research focused on product development and commercialization. It will also encourage collaboration in green design, sustainability and innovation in product development, facilitating and combining the fields of art, business, engineering and technology. Product designers work in a wide range of industries including consumer electronics, housewares and furniture, fashion accessories, medical devices, toys, automotive and transportation.

FACILITIES

Full design studios, computer labs/technology, fashion/fabric technology lab, Charles Evans FD&M Library, Drexel Historic Costume Collection (DHCC), Digimuse online Museum, Philadelphia Museum of Art, Leonard Pearlstein Gallery, University Library

ONLINE / DISTANCE LEARNING

Not available

COURSES OF INSTRUCTION

- Survey of the Fashion Industry
- Fashion Design Studio Courses
- Figure Drawing
- Fashion Illustration
- Portfolio Development
- Textiles
- Retail Merchandise Management
- Product Development
- Media Merchandising
- Analysis of Product

INTERNSHIPS

Required of majors at the Junior level. Interns are typically placed at companies such as Neiman Marcus, Urban Outfitters, Anthropologie, Desination Maternity, Michael Kors, Alexander McQueen, Shoshana.

STUDY ABROAD

1 term–London College of Fashion, and 1 term–London, Summer term in Prague, Montpellier, France or Australia

NOTABLE ALUMNI

Carole Hochman, Shelley Steffee, Megan Stein, Nicole Cashman,

STUDENT ACTIVITIES AND ORGANIZATIONS

DART–Design Arts Student organization, FAD–Fashion and Design student Organization

FACULTY SPECIALIZATIONS AND RESEARCH

Textile Technology, Fabric and Fashion Sustainability, Fashion Branding, Fashion Career development, Digitaliziation of Historic Costume and Fashion figures

Indiana University of Pennsylvania

Fashion Merchandising Program, Human Development, & Environmental Studies

Ackerman Hall, Room 207, 911 S. Dr., Indiana, PA 15705 | 724-357-2336 | www.iup.edu/

UNIVERSITY PROFILE
Public
Rural
Residential
Semester Schedule
Co-ed

STUDENT DEMOGRAPHICS
Undergraduate: 12,291
Graduate: 2,347

Male: 44%
Female: 56%

Full-time: Not reported
Part-time: Not reported

EXPENSES
Tuition: $7,209 (in-state)
Room & Board: $6,324

ADMISSIONS
117 Sutton Hall
Indiana, PA 15705
724-357-2230
admissions-inquiry@iup.edu

DEGREE INFORMATION

Major / Degree / Concentration	Enrollment	Requirements for entry	Graduation rate
Fashion Merchandising Bachelor of Science	275	2.0 gpa	Not reported
Business Administration Minor Marketing Concentration Small Business Management Concentration			

TOTAL PROGRAM ENROLLMENT
Undergraduate: 275
Graduate: 0

Male: Not reported
Female: Not reported

Full-time: Not reported
Part-time: Not reported
Online: Not reported

International: Not reported
Minority: Not reported

Job Placement Rate: Not reported

SCHOLARSHIPS / FINANCIAL AID
Betty Wood Scholarship, Susan B. Shubra Memorial Scholarship, Joan Schmitt Fashion Scholarship. Each given out yearly to a Sophomore-Senior.

TOTAL FACULTY: 5
Full-time: 3
Part-time: 2

FASHION ADMINISTRATION
Mary Swinker, Ph.D, Department Chair
Janet A. Blood, Ph.D, Fashion Merchandising Program Coordinator

PROFESSIONAL / ACADEMIC AFFILIATIONS
International Textile and Apparel Association

PROGRAM DESCRIPTION AND PHILOSOPHY

The Fashion Merchandising program prepares individuals for careers associated with design, production, quality control, distribution, merchandising, and promotion of apparel and related products as determined by changing global, societal, and environmental needs.

The changing and challenging world of fashion is one of the most practical and competitive fields in which to pursue a career. Successful people in fashion merchandising have a flair for both fashion and business. The Fashion Merchandising program at IUP provides courses that emphasize apparel production and distribution, textiles, apparel merchandising and promotion, ready-to-wear analysis, quality control in production, textile testing, historic costume and textiles, aesthetics, global issues in textiles and apparel, visual merchandising, color theory and application, and apparel construction and design.

FACILITIES

Mobile Computer Lab, Historic Costume Collection, Ready to Wear Collection, Sewing Lab

ONLINE / DISTANCE LEARNING

Two program courses are offered online: Global Issues in Textiles and Apparel and Seminar in Fashion Merchandising

COURSES OF INSTRUCTION

- Introduction to Fashion
- Fundamentals of Clothing Construction
- Textiles
- Historic Costume
- Ready to Wear Analysis
- Seminar in Fashion Merchandising

INTERNSHIPS

Not required; Interns are typically placed at companies such as Target, Nordstrom, Caffeine Culture, QVC, Nautica, Maurices

STUDY ABROAD

Available

NOTABLE ALUMNI

Not reported

STUDENT ACTIVITIES AND ORGANIZATIONS

IUP Fashion Association, IUP Sew Club

FACULTY SPECIALIZATIONS AND RESEARCH

Janet A. Blood, Ph.D. : Apparel Design, Historic/Cultural Aspects of Dress and Appearance, Costume Design, Adult Education, Family and Consumer Science Education

Mary E. Swinker, Ph.D.: Historic Costume and Textiles

Eun Jin Hwang, Ph.D: Fashion Merchandising, Buying, Apparel and Textile Trade, Strategic Management, Consumer Behavior

Jin Su, Ph.D: Fashion Merchandising, Global Sourcing

Philadelphia University

Department of Fashion Design

School House Lane & Henry Ave., Philadelphia, PA 19144 | 215-951-2751 | www.philau.edu/fashiondesign/

UNIVERSITY PROFILE
Private
Suburban
Residential
Semester Schedule
Co-ed

STUDENT DEMOGRAPHICS
Undergraduate: 2,892
Graduate: 605

Male: 40%
Female: 60%

Full-time: Not reported
Part-time: Not reported

EXPENSES
Tuition: $28,800
Room & Board: $9,284

ADMISSIONS
School House Lane &
Henry Ave.
Philadelphia, PA 19144
215-951-2800
Admissions@PhilaU.edu

DEGREE INFORMATION

Major / Degree / Concentration	Enrollment	Requirements for entry	Graduation rate
Fashion Design Bachelor of Science	220	Not reported	85%
Textile Design Bachelor of Science	85	Not reported	95%

TOTAL PROGRAM ENROLLMENT
Undergraduate: 224
Graduate: Not reported

Male: 3%
Female: 97%

Full-time: 97%
Part-time: 3%
Online: Not reported

International: Not reported
Minority: 20%

Job Placement Rate: Not reported

SCHOLARSHIPS / FINANCIAL AID
Students are eligilble for a range
of federal need-based financial aid,
institutional financial aid and merit
scholarships, and private scholarships.

Students Receiving Scholarships or
Financial Aid: 90%

TOTAL FACULTY: 27
Full-time: 16%
Part-time: 84%

FASHION DESIGN ADMINISTRATION
Clara Henry, Director, Fashion Design
 Program

PROFESSIONAL / ACADEMIC AFFILIATIONS
Not reported

PROGRAM DESCRIPTION AND PHILOSOPHY

Fashion Design students study all facets of fashion design and construction, with hands-on experience and state-of-the-art computerized design and production equipment. The University's unique strengths in textile materials and design helps make this one of the best programs in the country.

FACILITIES

Numerous design labs and workrooms, including sewing machines and equipment, knitting machines, computer-assisted design labs, access to The Design Center's historical textile and costume archives

ONLINE / DISTANCE LEARNING

Not available

COURSES OF INSTRUCTION

- Fashion Figure Drawing
- Garment Structures
- Flat Pattern and Construction
- Fashion Design Problem Solving
- History of Textiles and Costumes
- Draping and Construction
- Apparel CAD/CAM
- Collection Development

INTERNSHIPS

Not required

Interns are placed at major apparel firms and retailers, including Tommy Hilfiger, Macy's, Jones Apparel Group, Urban Outfitters, and the *Saturday Night Live* costume department.

STUDY ABROAD

Philadelphia University design programs in Rome and Milan, and opportunities to go almost anywhere else.

NOTABLE ALUMNI

William Calvert, couterier designer, N.Y., Jay McCarroll, winner of *Project Runway*

STUDENT ACTIVITIES AND ORGANIZATIONS

Fashion Industries Association (FIA) is a very active group on campus that includes Fashion Design, Fashion Merchandising and Fashion Industry Management majors. FIA members help produce Philadelphia University's gala Annual Fashion Show.

FACULTY SPECIALIZATIONS AND RESEARCH

Fashion design, pattern-making, textile design, accessories design, costume history

Philadelphia University

Fashion Industry Management

4201 Henry Ave., Philadelphia, PA 19144 | 1-215-951-2700 | www.philau.edu/schools/tmt/Ugrad_Majors/fim/

UNIVERSITY PROFILE
Private
Urban
Residential & Commuter
Semester Schedule
Co-ed

STUDENT DEMOGRAPHICS
Undergraduate: Not reported
Graduate: Not reported

Male: Not reported
Female: Not reported

Full-time: Not reported
Part-time: Not reported

EXPENSES
Tuition: $28,000
Room & Board: $10,000

ADMISSIONS
4201 Henry Ave.
Philadelphia, PA 19144
215-951-2800
admissions@philau.edu

DEGREE INFORMATION

Major / Degree / Concentration	Enrollment	Requirements for entry	Graduation rate
Fashion Industry Management Bachelor of Science	180	2.5 gpa	95%
Fashion Design Bachelor of Science	225	Not reported	Not reported
Fashion Merchandising Bachelor of Science	300	Not reported	Not reported

TOTAL PROGRAM ENROLLMENT
Undergraduate: 2,500
Graduate: 500

Male: Not reported
Female: Not reported

Full-time: Not reported
Part-time: Not reported
Online: Not reported

International: Not reported
Minority: Not reported

Job Placement Rate: 70%

SCHOLARSHIPS / FINANCIAL AID
Not reported

TOTAL FACULTY: NOT REPORTED
Full-time: Not reported
Part-time: Not reported

FASHION DESIGN ADMINISTRATION
Natalie W. Nixon, Program Director, Associate Professor
Nioka Wyatt, Assistant Professor
Leslie Browning-Samoni, Assistant Professor

PROFESSIONAL / ACADEMIC AFFILIATIONS
International Textile and Apparel Association
American Apparel and Footwear Association
Fashion Group International

PROGRAM DESCRIPTION AND PHILOSOPHY

The curriculum combines the fundamentals of business, including accounting, economics, marketing, finance, and management, with textile and apparel courses. Students learn the process of apparel design and manufacture from fiber to final apparel product, and become familiar with the application of computers in information retrieval, integrated apparel manufacture and design. Graduates earn the respect of employers who are familiar with the University's expertise in fashion industry management.

FACILITIES

Computer labs, CAD tech labs, costume archive at The Design Center, ETON Garment construction lab

ONLINE / DISTANCE LEARNING

Not available

COURSES OF INSTRUCTION

- Survey of the Global Apparel Industry
- Apparel & Textile Sourcing
- Economics
- Accounting
- Garment Development
- Merchandising Management
- Quality Control

INTERNSHIPS

Not required. All students are advised and encouraged to have completed at least 2 internships by graduation. Assistance & guidance is given by the faculty and career development office.

Interns are typically placed at companies such as Urban Outfitters, Anthropologie, QVC, The Limited Brands, Federated/Macy's, Calvin Klein, Tommy Hilfiger, Charming Shoppes, Phillips Van Heusen.

STUDY ABROAD

Hong Kong, London, Milan, Rome, Shanghai

NOTABLE ALUMNI

Not required

STUDENT ACTIVITIES AND ORGANIZATIONS

Fashion Industry Association and FAME which produce the fashion show. Also the textile fraternity Phi Psi.

FACULTY SPECIALIZATIONS AND/ OR RESEARCH

Quality control, sourcing, design management, print design

University of Rhode Island

Department of Textiles, Fashion Merchandising & Design

55 Lower College Rd, Kingston, RI 02881 | 401-874-4574 | www.uri.edu/hss/tmd

DEGREE INFORMATION

Major / Degree / Concentration	Enrollment	Requirements for entry	Graduation rate
Textiles, Fashion Merchandsing and Design Bachelor of Science	400	Admission to URI	Unknown
Textile Marketing Bachelor of Science	50	Admission to URI	Unknown
Textiles, Fashion Merchandsing and Design Master of Science	20	RE, TOEFL, 4 yr degree, 3.0 gpa	90

TOTAL PROGRAM ENROLLMENT
Undergraduate: 450
Graduate: 20

Male: 5%
Female: 95%

Full-time: Not reported
Part-time: Not reported
Online: Not reported

International: Not reported
Minority: Not reported

Job Placement Rate: Not reported

SCHOLARSHIPS / FINANCIAL AID
A variety of scholarships are offered.
Financial Aid is determined by the
university's financial aid office.

TOTAL FACULTY: 12
Full-time: 8
Part-time: 4

FASHION DESIGN ADMINISTRATION
Linda Welters (until 7/1/10)
Martin Bide (7/1/10-7/1/11)

PROFESSIONAL / ACADEMIC AFFILIATIONS
International Textile and Apparel
Association
American Apparel and Footwear
Association

PROGRAM DESCRIPTION AND PHILOSOPHY
We offer a broad exposure to the textile/fashion industry that combines textile knowledge with merchandising and design.

FACILITIES
Apparel lab, textile lab, gallery, historic textile and costume collection, American Association of Textile Chemists and Colorists

ONLINE / DISTANCE LEARNING
Not reported

COURSES OF INSTRUCTION
- Textile Products
- Textile Science
- Fashion Merchandising
- Textile Markets
- Seminar

INTERNSHIPS
Not required. Interns are typically placed at companies such as Coach, Brioni, TJX Corp.

STUDY ABROAD
Available

NOTABLE ALUMNI
Not reported

STUDENT ACTIVITIES AND ORGANIZATIONS
Not reported

FACULTY SPECIALIZATIONS AND RESEARCH
Cultural aspects of dress, biomedical textiles, archaeological textiles, retailing

COMMUNITY COLLEGE TRANSFERS
We have a transfer articulation agreement with Community College of RI. Many students transfer to us.

University of South Carolina

Department of Retailing

700 Assembly, Columbia, SC 29208 | 803-777-3805 | www.hrsm.sc.edu/retail/

UNIVERSITY PROFILE
Public
Urban
Residential
Semester Schedule
Co-ed

STUDENT DEMOGRAPHICS
Undergraduate: 19,000
Graduate: 6,000

Male: 46%
Female: 46%

Full-time: 93%
Part-time: 7%

EXPENSES
Tuition: SC resident = $9,156
(fall, spring)
Room & Board: Housing
ranges from $3,800 to $4,300
Meals range from $2,300 to
$2,700

ADMISSIONS
902 Sumter, Lieber College
Building
Columbia, SC 29208
803-777-7700

DEGREE INFORMATION

Major / Degree / Concentration	Enrollment	Requirements for entry	Graduation rate
Retailing Bachelor of Science Emphasis in Retail Management	100	2.0 gpa if entering as a freshmen; 2.5 gpa if transferring into the university or the department from across campus	Estimated at a 97% rate
Retailing Bachelor of Science Emphasis in Fashion Merchandisng	300	2.0 gpa if entering as a freshmen; 2.5 gpa if transferring into the university or the department from across campus	Estimated at a 99% rate

TOTAL PROGRAM ENROLLMENT
Undergraduate: 400
Graduate: 6

Male: 23%
Female: 77%

Full-time: 98%
Part-time: 2%
Online: Not reported

International: Not reported
Minority: Not reported

Job Placement Rate: 100%

SCHOLARSHIPS / FINANCIAL AID
In excess of 100 scholarships are given out annually to students in the College. In addition to university scholarships, scholarships specific to the fashion students are funds provided by the following companies a) Piggly Wiggly Scholarship b) Target Scholarship and c) Department of Retailing Scholarship

TOTAL FACULTY: 15
Full-time: 64%
Part-time: 33%

FASHION DESIGN ADMINISTRATION
Dr. Marianne C. Bickle, Chair and Professor
Dr. Richard Clodfelter, Undergraduate Coordinator and Professor

PROFESSIONAL / ACADEMIC AFFILIATIONS
International Textile and Apparel Association
Fashion Group International
American Collegiate Retailing Association

PROGRAM DESCRIPTION AND PHILOSOPHY

We are the only department that ONLY offers retailing–this is unique. We have a large base of male student body. Most departments of our kind do not have 100+ men in the program. We are able to place 100% of our students.

FACILITIES

Computer labs, museums, category management software, consumer data

ONLINE / DISTANCE LEARNING

We are in the process of placing our minor in Fashion Merchandising and the Minor in Retail Management online. We anticipate these programs to be effective in taught effective spring 2011. All of the courses required for the minor are also required for the major.

COURSES OF INSTRUCTION

Online courses will probably include: Principles of Retailing, Principles of Fashion Merchandising (Fashion Marketing course), The Art of Fashion (History of Fashion course), Retail Promotion, Sales Strategies, Small Business

INTERNSHIPS

Required of majors. Interns are typically placed at companies such as Kohl's, Target, Biltmore Estate, Paris Fashion Institute, Tiffany's, Bed, Bath & Beyond, Dillard's, Firestone, Levi's, Old Navy, Ralph Lauren, Bergdorf-Goodman, Belk, Banana Republic, Victoria Secret, etc. REMEMBER –our students are either FASHION or RETAIL MANAGEMENT–some student prefer the "glamourous" stores; other prefer companies like Lowes.

STUDY ABROAD

Each year we take students abroad to Italy, London, Paris

NOTABLE ALUMNI

Not reported

STUDENT ACTIVITIES AND ORGANIZATIONS

We work with the American InterContinental University

FACULTY SPECIALIZATIONS AND/ OR RESEARCH

Consumer buying patterns, cross channel shopping, counterfeit merchandise, international retail patronage

COMMUNITY COLLEGE TRANSFERS

Most of the students who transfer into the program have taken courses from Midlands Technical College.

East Tennessee State University

Department of Management & Marketing

P.O. Box 70625, Johnson City, TN 37614 | 423-439-4422 | http://business.etsu.edu/mgmtmkt/academics

UNIVERSITY PROFILE
Public
Suburban
Commuter
Semester Schedule
Co-ed

STUDENT DEMOGRAPHICS
Undergraduate: 11,648
Graduate: 2,222

Male: 58%
Female: 42%

Full-time: 85%
Part-time: 15%

EXPENSES
Tuition: $250 per credit hour (in-state)
$747 per credit hour (out-of-state)
Room & Board: varies

ADMISSIONS

DEGREE INFORMATION

Major / Degree / Concentration	Enrollment	Requirements for entry	Graduation rate
Management & Marketing Bachelor of Business Administration Merchandising Concentration	60	Minimum of 60 credit hours completed, with a 2.0 overall gpa, completion of three specified general education courses, and a grade of "C" or better in six specified business courses.	90%

TOTAL PROGRAM ENROLLMENT
Undergraduate: 60
Graduate: 0

Male: 10%
Female: 90%

Full-time: 100%
Part-time: Not reported
Online: Not reported

International: 5%
Minority: 5%

Job Placement Rate: 75%

SCHOLARSHIPS / FINANCIAL AID
Hope Scholarships are available to Tennessee residents through the Tennessee Lottery System. In addition, over $74,000 in endowed scholarships is awarded annually to business students, with $10,000 designated specifically for marketing majors.

Students Receiving Scholarships or Financial Aid: 95%

TOTAL FACULTY: 2
Full-time: 100%
Part-time: 0%

FASHION ADMINISTRATION
Dr. Linda Garceau, Dean
Dr. Phil Miller, Chair

PROFESSIONAL / ACADEMIC AFFILIATIONS
International Textile and Apparel Association
American Collegiate Retailing Association

PROGRAM DESCRIPTION AND PHILOSOPHY

An interest in buying, selling or promoting products defines the merchandising major. Merchandising provides students with skills necessary to plan, develop, and present product lines for exciting careers within the retail industry.

The merchandising program at East Tennessee State University provides students with product knowledge and merchandising skills necessary for diverse career opportunities within the apparel, textiles, and retailing industries. The study of merchandising emphasizes both creativity and development of merchandising expertise enabling the graduate to function successfully in the dynamic and fast-paced retail industry.

Emphasis is placed on personal and professional growth and development, written and oral communication skills, decision-making, and problem-solving. Numerous opportunities are offered to set goals and effectively work with others to develop leadership skills and flexibility.

Favorable employment opportunities in merchandising are found locally, nationally, and internationally. The successful merchandiser can find many fulfilling and lucrative career opportunities with potential for rapid advancement. Upon completion of the program, the student receives a Bachelor of Business Administration degree with a major in marketing and a concentration in merchandising.

FACILITIES

Tuition and fees paid by East Tennessee State University/College of Business and Technology majors support state of the art computer labs and classroom technology. Sherrod Library, Reece Museum, and the Archives of Appalachia provide cultural enrichment and student research opportunities.

ONLINE / DISTANCE LEARNING

Individual courses are available online.

COURSES OF INSTRUCTION

- Perspectives on Dress, Culture, & Society
- Fashion Fundamentals
- Consumer Textiles
- Fashion Merchandising
- Apparel Product Analysis
- Visual Merchandising
- Merchandising Study Tour (New York City)
- Advertising and Promotion
- Merchandising Internship
- Merchandise Planning and Buying

INTERNSHIPS

Required of majors at the Senior level. National/international internship placements include Gap, GapKids, Buckle, Belk, Victoria's Secret, and Wet Seal. Local or privately owned internship placements include Mahoney's Outfitter's, Weddings by Eda, Ciao Bella Boutique, and Massengill Specialty Shop.

STUDY ABROAD

ETSU has established Study Abroad agreements with over 18 countries, including England, France, China, and Japan. Opportunities with private study abroad companies are also available.

NOTABLE ALUMNI

Not reported

STUDENT ACTIVITIES AND ORGANIZATIONS

The Collegiate Merchandising Association promotes the merchandising program at East Tennessee State University, acquaints students with information and skills needed to facilitate professional development, and provides merchandising service/consultation to the community. Leadership opportunities contribute valuable professional experience and enhance internship and career placements.

CMA Members attend AmericasMart in Atlanta and numerous local fieldtrips to learn about the fashion industry and possible careers. Activites such as development of a "Dress for Success" pod cast and decoration of a "Mitten Tree" at Christmas (covered with donated mittens, hats, and scarves for the Salvation Army) provide service to the community.

In April, 2010, the Collegiate Merchandising Association received East Tennessee State University Summit Awards for Outstanding Service Program and Program of the Year.

FACULTY SPECIALIZATIONS AND/OR RESEARCH

Dr. Kelly Atkins specializes in teaching consumer behavior, merchandise planning and buying, and supervising internship classes. Her primary area of research is consumer behavior. Specifically, Dr. Atkins has published on topics related to consumer efficiency, consumer decision making, and consumer perceptions of virtual communities and mixed-use developments.

Dr. Anna Roberts specializes in textiles, apparel product analysis, advertising and promotion, and visual merchandising. Research interests include creation of original apparel design for juried exhibition and documentation of outsider textile art.

International Academy of Design & Technology—Nashville

Fashion Design & Merchandising

One Bridgestone Park, Nashville, TN 37210 | 615-232-7384 | www.iadtnashville.com

UNIVERSITY PROFILE
Private
Suburban
Commuter
Quarter Schedule
Co-ed

STUDENT DEMOGRAPHICS
Undergraduate: 713
Graduate: 0

Male: Not reported
Female: Not reported

Full-time: Not reported
Part-time: Not reported

EXPENSES
Tuition: $350 per credit hour
Room & Board: n/a

ADMISSIONS
One Bridgestone Park
Nashville, TN 37210
615-232-7384
www.iadtnashville.com

DEGREE INFORMATION

Major / Degree / Concentration	Enrollment	Requirements for entry	Graduation rate
Fashion Design & Merchandising Associate of Applied Science	74	High School Diploma	79%
Fashion Design & Merchandising Bachelor of Applied Science	65	High School Diploma	78%

TOTAL PROGRAM ENROLLMENT
Undergraduate: 713
Graduate: 0

Male: 51%
Female: 49%

Full-time: 54%
Part-time: 46%
Online: 12.5%

International: Not reported
Minority: 50%

Job Placement Rate: Not reported

SCHOLARSHIPS / FINANCIAL AID
See opposite page for more info.

TOTAL FACULTY: 11
Full-time: 36%
Part-time: 64%

FASHION ADMINISTRATION
Dr. Dianne Tatara, Program Chair of Fashion Design and Merchandising
Mr. Richard Wechner, President

PROFESSIONAL / ACADEMIC AFFILIATIONS
International Textile and Apparel Association
American Apparel and Footwear Association
Fashion Group International
American Collegiate Retailing Association

PROGRAM DESCRIPTION AND PHILOSOPHY

IADT-Nashville's Fashion Design and Merchandising Program prepares students to create fashion designs, develop patterns and select fabrics for the fashions, make the sample garments, and have the products manufactured and distributed.

FACILITIES

Facilities available to our students include two garment construction labs with 16 industrial single needle machines, 3 sergers, and 1 coverstitch machine in each lab; two pattern drafting labs with 60" wide drafting/cutting tables; 25 dress forms in a variety of shapes and sizes; two computer labs with 20+ computers, a scanner, and color printer available for each lab; a computer with computer projector in each classroom and Internet access for teaching in each classroom; fabric library for learning fabrics and for cutting swatches; and a library with over 1,200 fashion related titles including magazines such as *Threads* and newspapers such as *WWD* and *DNR*.

ONLINE / DISTANCE LEARNING

All general education courses are offered online.

COURSES OF INSTRUCTION

- Clothing Construction I & II
- Pattern Drafting I & II
- Draping I & II
- Sketching I & II
- Fashion Design
- History of Clothing
- Visual Merchandising
- Retail Management
- Salesmanship

INTERNSHIPS

Required of majors for AAs & BAs. Interns are typically placed at custom clothiers and independent boutiques in the Nashville area

STUDY ABROAD

Available

NOTABLE ALUMNI

Not reported

STUDENT ACTIVITIES AND ORGANIZATIONS

Our students are active participants in the monthly fashion shows produced in Nashville. The students manage and create a large fashion show each year for the school. In 2010, over 200 outfits were presented on the runway. A portion of proceeds benefitted Ronald McDonald House Charities.

FACULTY SPECIALIZATIONS AND RESEARCH

Our faculty members have a wide array of experience from working in costume production and management at Opryland for 20 years to creating clothing for rock and roll musicians that are now on exhibit at the Rock and Roll Hall of Fame in Cleveland, OH. One of our faculty members co-founded a software company which creates and sells software for making sewing patterns. One member worked at Anna Sui in NYC before joining us. One has experience in global sourcing with *Vanity Fair*. Each of our instructors has experience to back the subject they are teaching.

SCHOLARSHIPS / FINANCIAL AID

IADT participates in the following Title IV programs Federal Pell Grant, Federal Supplemental Educational Opportunity Grant (SEOG) Federal Family Educational Loan Program (FFELP) and Direct Loan program which provide Stafford Loans, Federal and Direct PLUS loan, Academic Competitiveness Grant and Federal Work study. All of the above require that the student have completed a Free Application for Federal Student Aid (FAFSA). IADT is also approved for Veteran's Educational Benefits including the yellow ribbon program which was established in 2009. Other Grants/Scholarships offered through IADT to students meeting the eligibility requirements are the Tennessee Student Assistance Award (TSAA), Senior Day Scholarship, and the Career Education Scholarship Funds. Students who meet the required credit requirements can also apply for private alternative loans. These loans are awarded up to the cost of attendance minus other aid awarded to the student.

Students Receiving Scholarships or Financial Aid: 73%

Middle Tennessee State University

Department of Human Sciences

1301 E. Main St., Box 86, Murfreesboro, TN 37132 | 615-898-2884 | www.mtsu.edu/humansciences/

UNIVERSITY PROFILE
Public
Suburban
Residential
Semester
Co-ed

STUDENT DEMOGRAPHICS
Undergraduate: 25,188
Graduate: 1,811

Male: 46.63%
Female: 53.37%

Full-time: 80%
Part-time: 20%

EXPENSES
Tuition: $6,000
Room & Board: $6,000—$10,000

ADMISSIONS
1301 E. Main St.
208 Cope Administration Bldg.
Middle Tennessee State University
Murfreesboro, TN 37132
615-898-2111
admissions@mtsu.edu

DEGREE INFORMATION

Major / Degree / Concentration	Enrollment	Requirements for entry	Graduation rate
Textiles, Merchandising, & Design Bachelor of Science Apparel Design	80	2.0 gpa; application to program after 30 credit hours of specified courses.	90%
Textiles, Merchandising, & Design Bachelor of Science Fashion Merchandising	120	2.0 gpa; application to program after 30 credit hours of specified courses.	Not reported

TOTAL PROGRAM ENROLLMENT
Undergraduate: 200
Graduate: 0

Male: 10%
Female: 90%

Full-time: 90%
Part-time: 10%
Online: Not reported

International: 3%
Minority: 25%

Job Placement Rate: Not reported

SCHOLARSHIPS / FINANCIAL AID
The Human Sciences Department offers private scholarships that total $45,000 annually

Students Receiving Scholarships or Financial Aid: 75%

TOTAL FACULTY: 5
Full-time: 5
Part-time: 0

FASHION DESIGN ADMINISTRATION
Dr. Teresa B. Robinson, Coordinator, Textiles, Merchandising & Design

PROFESSIONAL / ACADEMIC AFFILIATIONS
International Textile and Apparel Association
American Apparel and Footwear Association
American Collegiate Retailing Association

286

PROGRAM DESCRIPTION AND PHILOSOPHY

The Textiles, Merchandising, & Design program prepares students for career opportunities in fashion-related industries; the academic program combines traditional classroom instruction with experiential learning offering students industry specific learning opportunities. Graduates enter the workforce with a sense of reality and preparation; graduate placements include buyers, patternmakers, designers, stylists, etc.

FACILITIES

TXMD computer lab, Design studios, Historic clothing collection, Textile Testing laboratory

ONLINE / DISTANCE LEARNING

Online courses are offered within the program; no online degree is offered.

COURSES OF INSTRUCTION

- Introduction to the Fashion Industry
- Fashion Forecasting
- History of Fashion
- Fashion Branding
- Fashion Buying
- Social Aspects of Clothing
- Fashion Illustration
- Apparel Manufacturing & Sourcing
- Patternmaking
- Computer Aided Design

INTERNSHIPS

Not required but available to students at the Junior/Senior level. Interns are typically placed at companies such as VF Corporation, Zac Posen, Buckle, Hot Flops,

STUDY ABROAD

International Study Tour offered annually during Summer terms.

NOTABLE ALUMNI

Not reported

STUDENT ACTIVITIES AND ORGANIZATIONS

F.A.D.S. (Fashion & Design Students), Kappa Omicron Nu, AAFCS

FACULTY SPECIALIZATIONS AND RESEARCH

TXMD faculty have diverse professional and academic backgrounds from design, manufacturing, textiles, wholesaling, retailing, and related industry experiences.

Tennessee State University

Department of Family & Consumer Sciences

Box 9598, 3500 John A. Merritt Blvd., Nashville, TN 37209 | 615-963-5601 | http://agfacs.tnstate.edu/

UNIVERSITY PROFILE
Public
Urban
Residential
Semester
Co-ed

STUDENT DEMOGRAPHICS
Undergraduate: 7,000
Graduate: 2,000

Male: Not reported
Female: Not reported

Full-time: Not reported
Part-time: Not reported

EXPENSES
Tuition: $2,852 (in-state)
$9,116 (out-of-state)
Room & Board: Not reported

ADMISSIONS
3500 John A. Merritt Blvd.
Nashville, TN 37209
616-963-5101
gejohnson@tnstate.edu

DEGREE INFORMATION

Major / Degree / Concentration	Enrollment	Requirements for entry	Graduation rate
Family and Consumer Sciences Bachelor of Science Fashion Merchandising	25	Same as University requirements	Not reported
Family and Consumer Sciences Bachelor of Science Design	20	Same as University requirements	Not reported

TOTAL PROGRAM ENROLLMENT
Undergraduate: 200
Graduate: Not reported

Male: 20%
Female: 80%

Full-time: 80%
Part-time: 20%
Online: 20%

International: Not reported
Minority: Not reported

Job Placement Rate: Not reported

SCHOLARSHIPS / FINANCIAL AID
Various scholarships are available for students enrolled in the department. Scholarships vary in requirements and monetary amounts.

TOTAL FACULTY:
Full-time: 90%
Part-time: 10%

FASHION ADMINISTRATION
Gearldean Johnson, Chair
Sue Ballard de Ruiz, Director of Design Program
Jung Im Seo, Fashion Merchandising

PROFESSIONAL / ACADEMIC AFFILIATIONS
International Textile and Apparel Association
American Apparel and Footwear Association
Fashion Group International
American Collegiate Retailing Association

PROGRAM DESCRIPTION AND PHILOSOPHY

The Design and Merchandising programs provide small class sizes and individual guidance that allows students to focus on areas of interest within the field of Design and Fashion. Support courses in business, merchandising, and art broaden students' exposure to various areas in the field.

FACILITIES

Computer labs, resource library (fabrics and finishes), construction/ sewing laboratory, drafting and design labs

ONLINE / DISTANCE LEARNING

Not reported

COURSES OF INSTRUCTION

- Fashion Illustration
- Costume and Fashion Design
- Textiles
- Experimental Textile and Apparel Design
- Cultural Interpretation of Dress
- CAD, History of Costume
- Apparel Construction

INTERNSHIPS

Required of majors at Junior/Senior level

STUDY ABROAD

Faculty work with other schools to place interested students in appropriate programs.

NOTABLE ALUMNI

Reco Chapple–Bravo's *Fashion Show* finalist

STUDENT ACTIVITIES AND ORGANIZATIONS

The Fashion Guild is a campus student organization that organizes and supports fashion shows and related events

FACULTY SPECIALIZATIONS AND RESEARCH

Professor Jung Im Seo specializes in e-marketing and business, as well as clothing construction. Professor Ballard de Ruiz has a professional background in Interior Design and Illustrating, as well as Sustainable Design practices.

Tennessee Technological University

School of Human Ecology
P.O. Box 5037, Cookeville, TN 38505 | 931-372-3157 | www.tntech.edu/hec

UNIVERSITY PROFILE
Public
Rural
Residential
Semester Schedule
Co-ed

STUDENT DEMOGRAPHICS
Undergraduate: 8,500
Graduate: 2,500

Male: 49%
Female: 51%

Full-time: 80%
Part-time: 20%

EXPENSES
Tuition: Not reported
Room & Board: Not reported

ADMISSIONS
PO Box 5006
Cookeville, TN 38505
800-255-8881
admissions@tntech.edu

DEGREE INFORMATION

Major / Degree / Concentration	Enrollment	Requirements for entry	Graduation rate
Human Ecology Bachelor of Science Merchandising & Design	40	See Admissions Office for current requirements	75%
Human Ecology Bachelor of Science Housing & Design	50	See Admissions Office for current requirements	75%

TOTAL PROGRAM ENROLLMENT
Undergraduate: 200
Graduate: Not reported

Male: 5%
Female: 95%

Full-time: 90%
Part-time: 10%
Online: Not reported

International: 1%
Minority: 3%

Job Placement Rate: 70%

SCHOLARSHIPS / FINANCIAL AID
Most students receive the TN Hope Scholarship funded via the TN Lottery System valued at 3000-4000. The unit has approximately 20 scholarships ranging from $500-$2,500. Most of these are from endowments. There are a few work scholarships. The due date for applying is December 15th each year.

Students Receiving Scholarships or Financial Aid: 80%

TOTAL FACULTY: 10
Full-time: 7
Part-time: 3

FASHION DESIGN ADMINISTRATION
Dr. Sue Bailey, CFCS

PROFESSIONAL / ACADEMIC AFFILIATIONS
International Textile and Apparel Association

PROGRAM DESCRIPTION AND PHILOSOPHY

A general undergraduate program in merchandising which provides an overall introduction to the profession and preparation of the graduate for entrance into the world of retailing or graduate school.

FACILITIES

Computer labs, clothing design labs, textiles and costume collection, study tours, Market trips

ONLINE / DISTANCE LEARNING

Some courses, but not all are online.

COURSES OF INSTRUCTION

- Apparel Design
- Aspects of Dress
- Fashion Promotion
- Merchandising
- Textiles
- Fashion Display
- Marketing

INTERNSHIPS

Not required.

A practicum is required at the Sophomore level. Seniors may enroll in internship during the Senior year.

STUDY ABROAD

Not reported

NOTABLE ALUMNI

Wil Crider, Oshkosh b'Gosh, Inc. Global Fabric Sourcing Specialist Melissa Phelps, Designer, Doll Fashions, www.etsy.com/shop/love2sew

STUDENT ACTIVITIES AND ORGANIZATIONS

Student organizations: the TN Tech Association of Family and Consumer Sciences and the Merchandising Association

FACULTY SPECIALIZATIONS AND RESEARCH

Strengths include leadership including networking, textiles research, and creative apparel design.

COMMUNITY COLLEGE TRANSFERS

American Association of Family and Consumer Sciences; Association of Career and Technical Education; and AATCC

The Art Institute of Dallas

Fashion Design Department

8080 Park Lane, Dallas, TX 75231 | 800-275-4243 | www.artinstitutes.edu/dallas

UNIVERSITY PROFILE
Private
Urban
Commuter
Quarter
Co-ed

STUDENT DEMOGRAPHICS
Undergraduate: 2,000
Graduate: 0

Male: Not reported
Female: Not reported

Full-time: Not reported
Part-time: Not reported

EXPENSES
Tuition: $28,440
Room & Board: n/a

ADMISSIONS
8080 Park Lane
Dallas, TX 75231
1-800-275-4243

DEGREE INFORMATION

Major / Degree / Concentration	Enrollment	Requirements for entry	Graduation rate
Fashion Design Associate of Applied Arts	51	Not reported	Not reported
Fashion Design Bachelor of Fine Arts	127	Not reported	Not reported

TOTAL PROGRAM ENROLLMENT
Undergraduate: 181
Graduate: 0

Male: 10%
Female: 90%

Full-time: 50%
Part-time: 50%
Online: 0%

International: Not reported
Minority: Not reported

Job Placement Rate: 92%

SCHOLARSHIPS / FINANCIAL AID
Quarterly Merit Scholarship: Each quarter scholarships are awarded to continuing students (one per program). Departmental Scholarship : Each quarter departments award a $500 scholarship to honor an outstanding student in each program of study. The Mildred M. Kelley Scholarship: Awarded each quarter to one outstanding upper quarter student at The Art Institute of Dallas or The Art Institute of Ft. Worth. The Art Institutes Passion for Fashion Scholarship Competition: High school seniors interested in Fashion Design or Fashion Marketing & Merchandising at The Art Institutes are eligible to participate in this competition.
Evelyn Keedy Memorial Scholarship: High school seniors may apply.

TOTAL FACULTY: 10
Full-time: 60%
Part-time: 40%

FASHION ADMINISTRATION
Donna Sapp, Director, School of Fashion Design

PROFESSIONAL / ACADEMIC AFFILIATIONS
International Textile and Apparel Association

PROGRAM DESCRIPTION AND PHILOSOPHY

Students are introduced to sewing, flat pattern drafting, and draping to provide a solid foundation in the fundamentals of apparel production. Design courses emphasize the principles and aspects of good design and the drawing and illustration techniques essential for design communication. Advanced course work in design allows students to take ideas from concept to completion. Students gain personal satisfaction from building their creative expressions into realities through the development of products, lines, and collections. Computer Aided Design plays an important role in the preparation of Fashion Design students. Students learn computer pattern drafting, grading, and marker making through training on program specific software and hardware. A thorough understanding of all facets of apparel manufacturing allows students to critique their creations from many viewpoints: as art, as fashion statements, and as saleable products.

CAD systems are also integrated into course work for printed, woven, and knitted textile design, as well as collateral materials. Business practices, industry procedures, and client relations are studied to support the creative side of design and provide students with a realistic view of the world of work. The College also produces a quarterly fashion show that highlights the fashion design work of students.

FACILITIES

The Art Institute of Dallas is located in the Dallas/Fort Worth area, which has one of the lowest cost-of-living indexes of any major metropolitan area. This metropolis offers diverse cultural and recreational activities, including the Dallas Symphony, Mesquite Rodeo, Six Flags, Lone Star Park, concerts in the West End, and national sports teams. Many major employers have relocated to the Dallas/Fort Worth area due to its positive economic environment. Facilities in the school include labs offering PC and Macintosh computers for student use. The library supports the student community's information and imaging needs and has a collection of more than 20,000 books, 4,000 periodical titles in both print and full-text electronic versions, 1,450 videotapes, 12,500 photographic slides, and 11,000 Visual Reference Cards. In addition, it provides reference services and instruction in the use of library services and facilities, electronic database searching, and research techniques. The Academic Improvement Center provides tutoring services in the areas of general study skills, mathematics, writing, reading, and basic computer application skills. The center is open Monday through Friday and provides academic testing (ASSET, Learning Styles Assessment) on a weekly basis.

ONLINE / DISTANCE LEARNING

Not available

COURSES OF INSTRUCTION

- Construction I-III
- Drawing I-IV
- The Fashion Industry
- Patternmaking I-III
- Fashion Design Basics
- Textiles I & II
- Tailoring
- Draping
- Fashion Presentation Techniques
- Color In Fashion
- Computer Pattern I & II
- Computer Design I-III
- Manufacturing Processes
- Fashion History I & II
- Apparel Grading
- Apparel Marker
- Surface Design
- Fashion Show Production
- Concept and Line Development
- Apparel Structure & Fit
- Fashion Styling
- Trends and Concepts in Apparel
- Collection
- Costing & Specifications
- Portfolio I & II
- Apparel Marketing
- Internship
- Fundamentals of Business
- College Orientation
- Computer Applications
- Career Development
- Behavioral Science Elective
- Sportswear Design Studio
- Bridal Design Studio
- Theatrical Design Studio
- Menswear Design Studio
- Childrenswear Design Studio
- Knitwear Design Studio
- Humanities Elective

INTERNSHIPS

Required of BFA majors. Students are typically placed at companies such as, Haggar, St. Pucchi, Cooper by Courtney, Abi Ferrin, Sharrari Couture, Billy Reid, Manuel Designs, Tandy Brands Accessories, St. Maartin, RSC Productions, Jan Strimple, Meridian Sourcing, Bolt Productions. Career-entry positions such as assistant designer, stylist, visual display artist and fashion illustrator. More technical career options might include manufacturing production assistant, computer marking and grading technician, patternmaker, and technical designer. Opportunities are also available working in both wholesale and retail markets.

STUDY ABROAD

Available via the Art Institutes Study Abroad Consortium. For more information, contact the Art Institute of Dallas Study Abroad Coordinator: Evilu Pridgeon, epridgeon@aii.edu 214-692-8080.

NOTABLE ALUMNI

William Reid, Rhonda Sargent Chambers

STUDENT ACTIVITIES AND ORGANIZATIONS

The Student Council promotes the quality of the educational experience and represents the student body. This organization hosts a number of social events every quarter.

The Design Dallas organization allows fashion students to socialize and network with fellow students as well as with employers in their field of study.

Students are also encouraged and given the opportunity to join local, regional, national organizations representing fields in the school's different disciplines.

FACULTY SPECIALIZATIONS AND RESEARCH

Not reported

Baylor University

Family & Consumer Sciences: Fashion Division

1224 S. 8th St., Waco, TX 76798 | 254-710-3626 | www.baylor.edu/fcs

UNIVERSITY PROFILE
Private
Urban
Residential
Semester Schedule
Co-ed

STUDENT DEMOGRAPHICS
Undergraduate: 12,149
Graduate: 2,465

Male: 44%
Female: 56%

Full-time: 96%
Part-time: 4%

EXPENSES
Tuition: $26,966
Room & Board: $8,331

ADMISSIONS
One Bear Pl. #97056
Waco, TX 76798
254-710-3435
800-229-5678
admissions@baylor.edu.htm

DEGREE INFORMATION

Major / Degree / Concentration	Enrollment	Requirements for entry	Graduation rate
Fashion Design Bachelor of Arts	3	Courses in major available starting the Freshman year. Nine hours in apparel production required before design classes may be taken	98%
Fashion Design Bachelor of Science Family & Consumer Science	51	Same as above	99%
Fashion Merchandising Bachelor of Arts	9	Not reported	Not reported
Fashion Merchandising Bachelor of Science Family & Consumer Science	117	Not reported	Not reported

TOTAL PROGRAM ENROLLMENT
Undergraduate: 180
Graduate: 0

Male: 2%
Female: 98%

Full-time: 98%
Part-time: 2%
Online: 0%

International: 4%
Minority: 8%

Job Placement Rate: 88%

SCHOLARSHIPS / FINANCIAL AID
Financial aid is available through
financial services and is based on need.
Academic achievement scholarships are
granted to merit scholars.

TOTAL FACULTY: 9
Full-time: 90%
Part-time: 10%

FASHION ADMINISTRATION
Suzy Weem, PhD Department Chair
Judith Lusk, PhD Fashion Program
 Coordinator

PROFESSIONAL / ACADEMIC AFFILIATIONS
International Textile and Apparel
 Association
Fashion Group International

PROGRAM DESCRIPTION AND PHILOSOPHY

The Design program at Baylor University is committed to:

- Creative apparel design education and application
- Apparel design for specific target markets
- Network opportunities with professionals in the apparel industry
- Diversity of classroom experiences
- Critical problem solving and application in the apparel design process
- Strong liberal arts background
- Study abroad programs
- Design competitions and fashion shows
- Discipline specific apparel construction and computer labs
- Student membership in Fashion Group International
- Fashion design internships

Fashion Merchandising
The Fashion Merchandising program at Baylor University focuses on developing professional skills, such as communication, analytical thinking, teamwork, and ethical behavior. These skills help sustain graduates as they apply management and marketing theory and business principles to the global fashion industry. The Fashion Merchandising program at Baylor University not only teaches students the professional skills they will need to succeed in a variety of jobs in the fashion industry, but also life skills that will help them succeed both on and off the job.

FACILITIES

Computer Labs, Gerber CAD, Digital Printer

ONLINE / DISTANCE LEARNING

Not available

COURSES OF INSTRUCTION

- Principles of Art and Design
- Apparel Production and Evaluation
- Creative Techniques in Apparel Production
- Apparel in Today's Society
- Introduction to the Fashion Industry
- Textile Science
- Fashion Illustration

INTERNSHIPS

Required of majors after course work is completed or between the Junior and Senior year; Interns are typically placed at companies such as Nordstroms; Dillards; Shoshanna; Jodi Arnold; Betsey Johnson; Condé Nast; MTV; Academy Sport; Quik Silver; Haggar; Sharon Young; Dallas Cowboys; Campus Couture and Greek

STUDY ABROAD

Study abroad trips occur every other year and students may take 3–6 hours of study or they may choose to study their foreign language abroad.

NOTABLE ALUMNI

Jodi Arnold, NYC; Cheryl McMullin: Double D Ranch,

STUDENT ACTIVITIES AND ORGANIZATIONS

Student chapter of Fashion Group

FACULTY SPECIALIZATIONS AND/ OR RESEARCH

Consumer Behavior and Personal Appearance; Cotton and other sustainable fiber research.

El Paso Community College

Department of Fashion Technology

P.O. Box 20500, El Paso, TX 79998 | 915-831-5057 | www.epcc.edu

UNIVERSITY PROFILE
Public
Urban
Commuter
Semester Schedule
Co-ed

STUDENT DEMOGRAPHICS
Undergraduate: 27,600
Graduate: n/a

Male: 30%
Female: 70%

Full-time: Not reported
Part-time: Not reported

EXPENSES
Tuition: $1,700
Room & Board: n/a

ADMISSIONS
PO Box 20500
El Paso, TX 79998
915-831-2580
dhendry@epcc.edu

DEGREE INFORMATION

Major / Degree / Concentration	Enrollment	Requirements for entry	Graduation rate
Fashion Technology Associate of Applied Science Fashion Merchandising	15	Open entry	90%
Fashion Technology Associate of Applied Science Fashion Design	60	Open entry	90%
Fashion Technology Associate of Applied Science Fashion Illustration	1	Open entry	90%
Fashion Technology Certificate of Completion Industrial Patternmaking Certificate	4	Open entry	90%

TOTAL PROGRAM ENROLLMENT
Undergraduate: 80
Graduate: 0

Male: 40%
Female: 60%

Full-time: 42%
Part-time: 58%
Online: Not reported

International: 3%
Minority: 89%

Job Placement Rate: 92%

SCHOLARSHIPS / FINANCIAL AID
See opposite page for more info.

TOTAL FACULTY: 1,446
Full-time: 30%
Part-time: 70%

FASHION ADMINISTRATION
Trish Winstead, Fashion Technology
 Coordinator

PROFESSIONAL / ACADEMIC AFFILIATIONS
Not reported

PROGRAM DESCRIPTION AND PHILOSOPHY

Fashion Technology at EPCC is dedicated to developing skills in pattern-perfect and industry-ready patternmaking techniques, including computer aided apparel design, marking, and grading. The EPCC Fashion student is charged with the challenge of thinking creatively in a cost- effective and industry-efficient manner. Students are encouraged to understand all aspects of costing, sourcing, and business expensing.

FACILITIES

Fashion Technology laboratory equipped with CAD patternmaking software (Microdynamics and Assyst); CAD design software (Fashion Studio Plus); Adobe, etc.; dress forms; sewing machines, etc. There is also a dedicated fashion technology computer lab. Local museums include the El Paso Museum of Art and the El Paso Museum of History.

ONLINE / DISTANCE LEARNING

Not available at this time.

COURSES OF INSTRUCTION

- Fashion Collection Design
- Fashion Collection Production
- Apparel Product Development
- Computer Aided Apparel Design
- Draping
- Flat Patternmaking
- Fashion Retailing
- Fashion Buying
- Fashion Sketching
- Fashion Illustration Media
- Garment Construction
- Fashion Promotion
- Fashion History
- Textiles

INTERNSHIPS

Not required. Students have interned at companies such as AmeriTech and Levi's.

STUDY ABROAD

Not available

NOTABLE ALUMNI

Jose D. Saenz, winner of the Paris Fashion Institute Scholarship; Edith Clary, winner of the Paris American Academy Scholarship

STUDENT ACTIVITIES AND ORGANIZATIONS

Not reported

FACULTY SPECIALIZATIONS AND RESEARCH

We are a small program with two faculty members, both have owned their own apparel companies and continue to stay active in the industry. Trish Winstead is a member of Surface Design International.

COMMUNITY COLLEGE TRANSFERS

Fashion Technology courses transfer to most other community colleges in the state of Texas. Our courses also transfer to four year institutions such as Texas Tech University and New Mexico State University.

SCHOLARSHIPS / FINANCIAL AID

The Fashion Technology scholarship is funded by The Woman's Department of the Greater El Paso Chamber of Commerce and administered through the Fashion Technology program. Financial aid is available from a number of sources including the state of Texas and Veterans Affairs.

Students Receiving Scholarships or Financial Aid: 78%

Houston Community College, Central College

Lifestyle Arts & Design Careers Division

1300 Holman St., SJAC 325A, Houston, TX 77004 | 713-718-6152 | http://central.hccs.edu/lifestylearts

UNIVERSITY PROFILE
Public
Urban
Commuter
Semester Schedule
Co-ed

STUDENT DEMOGRAPHICS
Undergraduate: 21,000
Graduate: n/a
Male: 41%
Female: 59%

Full-time: 25%
Part-time: 75%

EXPENSES
Tuition: $2,061 (in-district)
Room & Board: n/a

ADMISSIONS
1300 Holman St., LHSB
Houston, TX 77004
713-718-6111
annette.lott@hccs.edu

DEGREE INFORMATION

Major / Degree / Concentration	Enrollment	Requirements for entry	Graduation rate
Fashion Design Associate of Applied Science Theatrical Costume Design Specialization	658	High School Diploma or GED	91%
Fashion Merchandising Associate of Applied Science	234	High School Diploma or GED	93%

TOTAL PROGRAM ENROLLMENT
Undergraduate: 1,837
Graduate: n/a

Male: 18%
Female: 82%

Full-time: 26%
Part-time: 72%
Online: 2%

International: 7%
Minority: 76%

Job Placement Rate: 100% except international students who are not permitted to work in the US.

SCHOLARSHIPS / FINANCIAL AID
All college student Federal and State Financial Aid programs are available to HCC students. The HCC Foundation provides annual scholarships to both incoming and enrolled students. Through the annual Passion for Fashion fundraiser and the Design Society community support group, the Fashion Design and Fashion Merchandising Programs award scholarships to selected students currently enrolled in the programs.

Students Receiving Scholarships or Financial Aid: 53%

TOTAL FACULTY: 23
Full-time: 17%
Part-time: 83%

FASHION ADMINISTRATION
Kay King, Division Chair, Lifestyle Arts & Design Careers
Suzette Brimmer, Associate Chair, Fashion Programs

PROFESSIONAL / ACADEMIC AFFILIATIONS
Fashion Group International

PROGRAM DESCRIPTION AND PHILOSOPHY

HCC fashion students consistently compete and win fashion competitions on a national level. The HCC fashion degrees and certificates are designed to completely prepare students for employment in the fashion industry, but HCC's nationally accredited courses are also transferable to universities.

FACILITIES

The Historical Fashion Collection storage facility houses over 2,000 objects dating from the 18th century to the 21st century, focusing on designer fashion and international costume. It is accessible to faculty and students and it can be searched online at http://library.hccs.edu/ Fashion. Items from the collection are exhibited annually in the HCC Fine Arts Gallery. The Apparel Computer Lab features a plotter, drafting board, and computers with the Gerber Garment Technology Accumark Software System for Pattern Design, Pattern Grading, and Marker Making. There are separate computers with Creative Suite 4 software to teach design. All labs and lecture spaces have wireless projection systems. Apparel Construction Labs have state-of-the-art cutting tables, commercial sewing and pressing equipment, and dress forms for 20 students. The Art Lab includes equipment for textile dying, visual merchandising, and fashion illustration. A complete millinery studio with a large selection of wooden hat blocks was acquired to provide the equipment necessary to teach this course.

ONLINE / DISTANCE LEARNING

Individual courses in both the Fashion Design and Fashion Merchandising programs are offered online. These include Fashion History, Fashion Trends, Fashion Selling, Fashion Buying, Fashion Retail and Fashion Advertising.

COURSES OF INSTRUCTION

Core Fashion Courses:
- Introduction to Fashion
- Textiles
- Fashion History
- Art for Fashion
- Apparel Computer Systems
- Ready-to-Wear Construction
- Internship.

Fashion Design:
- Fashion Sketching
- Design Construction Techniques
- Apparel Alterations
- Flat Pattern Design
- Custom Patterns
- Pattern Grading
- Draping
- Couture Dressmaking
- Men's Tailoring
- Millinery
- Bustier Construction
- Knit Construction
- Fabric Manipulation
- Fabric Design
- Fashion Collection Design & Production

Fashion Merchandising:
- Fashion Buying
- Fashion Selling
- Fashion Retailing
- Fashion Advertising
- Fashion Trends
- Fashion Promotion
- Visual Merchandising
- Fashion Image

INTERNSHIPS

Required of majors as capstone course in final semester. Interns are typically placed at companies such as Neiman-Marcus, Macy's, Forever 21, Cesar Galindo, Betsey Johnson, Carlton-Hall, Gayla Bentley, Walt Disney World Costume Shop, Paper City, Parker School Uniforms, Houston Grand Opera Costume Shop, Houston Ballet Costume Shop, Thimblefingers, Mikel Marketing, MLD Designs, Stage Stores.

STUDY ABROAD

Fashion Study Abroad Tours are organized by the faculty every other year, alternating with a New York Fashion Study Tour during the alternate years. Global study tour destinations include Paris, Milan, Madrid, Hong Kong, Bangkok, Tokyo, Beijing and London.

NOTABLE ALUMNI

Chloe Dao, *Project Runway* Winner, Season 2

STUDENT ACTIVITIES AND ORGANIZATIONS

Fashion students are student members of Fashion Group International of Houston and are also members of Delta Epsilon Chi (DEX). They participate in annual fashion competitions by Fashion Group International in Houston and Dallas, and at the Arts of Fashion Foundation and the DEX international competitions. They recently won Best of Show in Houston (Paris American Academy full scholarship), two 1st place awards in Dallas and several DEX awards. HCC annually sponsors the Flash & Trash Fashion Show and the Fashion Show of Student Designs that are televised locally on HCC TV.

FACULTY SPECIALIZATIONS AND RESEARCH

Kay King is National Past President of the Costume Society of America. Suzette Brimmer is Texas President of Delta Epsilon Chi. All full-time and part-time faculty have many years of fashion industry experience. Part-time faculty are currently working in the field, making the instruction by HCC fashion faculty completely relevant to the "real world of fashion."

COMMUNITY COLLEGE TRANSFERS

About 25% of our graduates transfer to Senior institutions. The other 75% go directly to work in the fashion industry. Of the students who transfer, most of the fashion design students transfer to Fashion Institute of Technology in New York, most of the fashion merchandising students transfer to University of Houston. In both cases most HCC courses transferred, leaving only two more years to complete the bachelor's degree. Other popular transfer choices by our students include U. of North Texas and Fashion Institute of Design and Merchandising in Los Angeles.

International Academy of Design & Technology— San Antonio

Fashion Design & Merchandising

4511 Horizon Hill Blvd. #100, San Antonio, TX 78229 | 210-530-9449 | www.iadtsanantonio.com

UNIVERSITY PROFILE
Private
Suburban
Commuter
Quarter Schedule
Co-ed

STUDENT DEMOGRAPHICS
Undergraduate: 569
Graduate: n/a

Male: Not reported
Female: Not reported

Full-time: Not reported
Part-time: Not reported

EXPENSES
Tuition: $15,000
Room & Board: n/a

ADMISSIONS
4511 Horizon Hill Blvd. #100
San Antonio, TX 78229
210-530-9449
ngarcia@iadtsanantonio.com

DEGREE INFORMATION

Major / Degree / Concentration	Enrollment	Requirements for entry	Graduation rate
Fashion Design and Merchandising Associate of Applied Science	70	Application for Admission H.S. Diploma or Equivalent Enrollment Agreement Payment of Application Fee Disclosure Form	Not reported
Fashion Design and Merchandising Bachelor of Fine Arts	190	Application for Admission H.S. Diploma or Equivalent Enrollment Agreement Payment of Application Fee Disclosure Form	Not reported

TOTAL PROGRAM ENROLLMENT
Undergraduate: 260
Graduate: n/a

Male: 35%
Female: 65%

Full-time: 95%
Part-time: 5%
Online: n/a

International: n/a
Minority: 70%

Job Placement Rate: Not reported

SCHOLARSHIPS / FINANCIAL AID
See opposite page for more info.

TOTAL FACULTY: 27
Full-time: 25%
Part-time: 75%

FASHION ADMINISTRATION
Gilbert De Leon, Director of Education
Cynthia Rangel, Program Chair for Fashion Design
Jacqueline Benavides, Lead Instructor for Fashion Design

PROFESSIONAL / ACADEMIC AFFILIATIONS
Fashion Group International
American Collegiate Retailing Association

PROGRAM DESCRIPTION AND PHILOSOPHY

The Fashion Design and Merchandising Program prepares students for entry-level positions in fashion, retail, and merchandising. The interdisciplinary program allows students the opportunity to develop skills in market and trend research, apparel design, pattern drafting, and draping, and clothing construction. Students will have the opportunity to further develop basic skills in business and retail management, merchandise displays, and publicity and promotion.

FACILITIES

Computer Labs, Pattern Drafting Lab, Construction Lab, Display Windows, and Gerber Lab.

ONLINE / DISTANCE LEARNING

Not available

COURSES OF INSTRUCTION

- Fashion Sketching I & II
- Clothing Construction I & II
- Fashion Publicity & Promotion
- Textile Design
- Computer Graphics for Fashion Design
- Draping I & II

INTERNSHIPS

Required of majors

STUDY ABROAD

Available to schools in the UK, Italy, and France

NOTABLE ALUMNI

Not reported

STUDENT ACTIVITIES AND ORGANIZATIONS

Di Moda Fashion Club, Stitch Fashion Club, and Gepetto Fashion Show Production Club

FACULTY SPECIALIZATIONS AND RESEARCH

Fashion Design Construction, Merchandising, and Fashion Show Production

SCHOLARSHIPS / FINANCIAL AID

Financial Aid is available for those who qualify. The International Academy of Design and Technology participates in a variety of financial aid programs including Federal Pell and Supplemental Grants, Student Loans, Work Study, and VA Educational Benefit programs. The International Academy of Design and Technology administrates its financial aid programs in accordance with federal and state laws and its own institutional policies. In order to remain eligible for financial aid, a student must maintain satisfactory academic progress as defined in this catalog. Students who want additional information and guidance should contact the Financial Aid Office.

Students Receiving Scholarships or Financial Aid: 90%

Sam Houston State University

Department of Family & Consumer Sciences

Box 2177 SHSU, Huntsville, TX 77341 | 936-294-1242 | www.shsu.edu/~hec_www

UNIVERSITY PROFILE
Public
Rural
Residential
Semester Schedule
Co-ed

STUDENT DEMOGRAPHICS
Undergraduate: 13,312
Graduate: 2,241

Male: 42.6%
Female: 57.4%

Full-time: 74.4%
Part-time: 25.6%

EXPENSES
Tuition: $7,000
Room & Board: $1,500 – $1,700

ADMISSIONS
Box 2418
Sam Houston State University
Huntsville, TX 77341
936-294-1828
admissions@shsu.edu

DEGREE INFORMATION

Major / Degree / Concentration	Enrollment	Requirements for entry	Graduation rate
Fashion Merchandising Bachelor of Arts	30	2.0 gpa or undergraduate admission	90%
Fashion Merchandising Bachelor of Science	60	2.0 gpa or undergraduate admission	90%

TOTAL PROGRAM ENROLLMENT
Undergraduate: 90
Graduate: 0

Male: 5%
Female: 95%

Full-time: 80%
Part-time: 20%
Online: 0%

International: 5%
Minority: 40%

Job Placement Rate: 85%

SCHOLARSHIPS / FINANCIAL AID
See opposite page for more info.

TOTAL FACULTY: 4
Full-time: 75%
Part-time: 25%

FASHION DESIGN ADMINISTRATION
Dr. Janis H. White, Chair, Department of Family and Consumer Sciences
Dr. Jerry Bruce, Associate Dean of Undergraduates, College of Humanities & Social Sciences
Dr. John de Castro, Dean, College of Humanities & Social Sciences

PROFESSIONAL / ACADEMIC AFFILIATIONS
Fashion Group International

PROGRAM DESCRIPTION AND PHILOSOPHY

The Fashion Merchandising Program at Sam Houston State University has strong bases in content and knowledge of apparel and in business operations management. Students leave the program with an understanding of apparel items in the "product" sense and a background in business operations. One program strength is the course in Patternmaking and Apparel Production that includes a laboratory where students develop a trend board, a collection board, and then go through the patternmaking and product development process with a specific apparel item from the collection. This course helps to prepare students to be part of a product development team. Another strength is the business core (four courses) required of all Fashion Merchandising majors.

FACILITIES

Computer labs (many of them 24-hour - there is also one in the department), Clothing Construction laboratory, 20th Century Costume Collection

ONLINE / DISTANCE LEARNING

Some courses are offered online, but not entire programs.

COURSES OF INSTRUCTION

- Fashion and Society
- Fashion Merchandising
- Merchandising Control
- Introductory Soft-Textiles Construction
- Patternmaking and Apparel Production
- Introduction to Textiles
- Textile Science
- Basic Design
- Fashion Promotion
- Seminar in Fashion, Textiles, & Merchandising
- Marketing
- Management
- Accounting
- Economics

INTERNSHIPS

Required of majors at the Senior year level.

Interns are typically placed at companies such as Charming Charlie, Dillard's, Nordstrom, Forever 21, and Impressions Bridal all recruit and encourage SHSU students to apply for their internship programs. The responsibility for finding a suitable internship position rests with the student, and is considered to be part of the internship process.

STUDY ABROAD

Available

NOTABLE ALUMNI

Alicia Macha, Fashion Jewelry Buyer for Charming Charlie; Kim Polak, Regional Manager for Visuals at Forever 21; Tracey Fasholz, Buyer for JCPenney

STUDENT ACTIVITIES AND ORGANIZATIONS

Fashion Merchandising Club, Kappa Omicron Nu

FACULTY SPECIALIZATIONS AND RESEARCH

Not reported

COMMUNITY COLLEGE TRANSFERS

Articulation agreements are available with many of the community colleges in the State of Texas, especially Lone Star College that serves the Houston Metropolitan Area, Blinn College, and some of the community colleges that serve the Dallas-Fort Worth Metroplex.

SCHOLARSHIPS / FINANCIAL AID

There are multiple scholarships for students majoring in any program area in the Department of Family and Consumer Sciences, and there is one specifically for Fashion Merchandising majors (J. E. "Bo" Crews Award in Fashion Merchandising). Most scholarship recipients have at least a 3.0 gpa and are juniors or seniors at the time the monies are awarded. Financial aid is through the completion of a FAFSA and is widely available for those who qualify.

Students Receiving Scholarships or Financial Aid: 40%

Stephen F. Austin State University

School of Human Sciences

P.O. Box 13014, SFA Station, Nacogdoches, TX 75962 | 936-468-4502 | www.sfasu.edu/go/human-sciences

UNIVERSITY PROFILE
Public
Rural
Residential
Semester Schedule
Co-ed

STUDENT DEMOGRAPHICS
Undergraduate: 10,404
Graduate: 1,586

Male: 38%
Female: 62%

Full-time: 81%
Part-time: 19%

EXPENSES
Tuition: $6,732 (resident)
$15,042 (non-resident)
Room & Board: $7,377

ADMISSIONS
P.O. Box 13051, SFA Station
Nacogdoches, TX 75962
936-468-2504
admissions@sfasu.edu

DEGREE INFORMATION

Major / Degree / Concentration	Enrollment	Requirements for entry			Graduation rate
Fashion Merchandising Bachelor of Science	100	HS Rank	SAT	ACT	Data not available
		1st Qtr	(no minimum score)		
		2nd Qtr	850	18	
		3rd Qtr	1050	23	
		4th Qtr	1250	28	

TOTAL PROGRAM ENROLLMENT
Undergraduate: 100
Graduate: 0

Male: 6%
Female: 94%

Full-time: 91%
Part-time: 9%
Online: 0%

International: 2%
Minority: 41%

Job Placement Rate: no data available

SCHOLARSHIPS / FINANCIAL AID
Not reported

TOTAL FACULTY: 3
Full-time: 100%
Part-time: Not reported

FASHION DESIGN ADMINISTRATION
Lynda Martin, Ph.D., Director, School of Human Sciences
Rebecca Greer, Ph.D., Asst. Director, School of Human Sciences & Fashion Merchandising Program Coordinator

PROFESSIONAL / ACADEMIC AFFILIATIONS
International Textile and Apparel Association
Fashion Group International
American Collegiate Retailing Association

PROGRAM DESCRIPTION AND PHILOSOPHY

The SFASU School of Human Sciences emphasizes enhanced student achievement, a strong commitment to total lifelong learning and development, and interactive/innovative instruction, research, and service. The fashion merchandising program teaches all the activities needed to provide customers with fashion apparel and accessories. It is the only Fashion program offered which allows the focus to be more specialized. Students are prepared with strong product knowledge for careers in the buying and selling of apparel and accessories for men, women, and children in retailing, wholesaling, or manufacturing. Program has a low instructor/student ratio. Hands-on class projects are based on industry standards and some may lead to entries in industry-sponsored student competitions.

FACILITIES

500+ piece twentieth-century costume collection, visual merchandising cases and forms, computer labs, classrooms have Internet-projection capabilities.

ONLINE / DISTANCE LEARNING

Some of the courses for the General Education Core classes and the minor may be taken online.

COURSES OF INSTRUCTION

- Intro. to Fashion Merchandising
- Apparel I & II
- Aesthetics
- Cultural Aspects of Clothing
- Twentieth Century Costume
- Apparel Design
- Merchandising Applications
- Textiles Science
- Advanced Textiles
- Specialty Merchandising
- Visual Merchandising
- Merchandising Procedures
- Internship
- Fashion Entrepreneurship Management
- Fashion Promotion

INTERNSHIPS

Required of majors at the Senior level. Interns are typically placed at department stores (Neiman-Marcus, Dillards, Nordstrom, Macy's, Palais Royal/Beall's, Belk, JCPenney, Saks Fifth Ave.), specialty stores (Forever 21, Cache, Gap, Old Navy, Victoria's Secret, American Eagle Outfitters, Anthropologie, Buckle, Benetton, Maurice's, Limited, White House Black Market), designer boutiques (Chanel, Hermes, Kate Spade, Cole Hahn, Betsey Johnson), discount stores (Target, Walmart) and fashion market showrooms (Poleci, Select Showroom).

STUDY ABROAD

The School of Human Sciences offers study abroad opportunities annually; recent trips have included Italy, London, & Thailand.

NOTABLE ALUMNI

Amy Harper, Senior Marketing Manager–Retail Development, Dallas Market Center and Regional Director, Fashion Group International, Inc.; Emily Kampner, Niche Media, New York; Craig Navarro, Hermès, Dallas (honored in 2010 as one of top 10 Hermès sales personnel internationally).

STUDENT ACTIVITIES AND ORGANIZATIONS

Fashion Merchandising Club and Phi Upsilon Omicron Honor Society

FACULTY SPECIALIZATIONS AND RESEARCH

Consumer behavior, textiles, apparel production, and merchandising

Texas Christian University

Department of Design, Merchandising & Textiles

2722 W. Berry St., Fort Worth, TX 76109 | 817-257-7499 | www.demt.tcu.edu

UNIVERSITY PROFILE
Private
Urban
Residential
Semester Schedule
Co-ed

STUDENT DEMOGRAPHICS
Undergraduate: 7,640
Graduate: 1,213

Male: 41%
Female: 59%

Full-time: 88%
Part-time: 12%

EXPENSES
Tuition: $30,000
Room & Board: $6,200

ADMISSIONS
2800 S. University Dr. # 112
Fort Worth, TX 76129
817-257-7490
frogmail@tcu.edu

DEGREE INFORMATION

Major / Degree / Concentration	Enrollment	Requirements for entry	Graduation rate
Fashion Merchandising Bachelor of Science	232	2.5 gpa	98%

TOTAL PROGRAM ENROLLMENT
Undergraduate: 232
Graduate: 0

Male: 2.6%
Female: 97.4%

Full-time: 100%
Part-time: 0%
Online: 0%

International: 2.5%
Minority: 14.2%

Job Placement Rate: 92.3%

SCHOLARSHIPS / FINANCIAL AID
Scholarships are available through Phi Upsilon Omicron Beta Zeta chapter for undergraduate for members and alumni. TCU also offers many general scholarship opportunities and financial aid.

TOTAL FACULTY: 5.5
Full-time: 100%
Part-time: 0%

FASHION DESIGN ADMINISTRATION
Dr. Janace Bubonia. Department Chair

PROFESSIONAL / ACADEMIC AFFILIATIONS
International Textile and Apparel
  Association
American Apparel and Footwear
  Association
Fashion Group International
American Collegiate Retailing
  Association

PROGRAM DESCRIPTION AND PHILOSOPHY

Fashion Merchandising program offers students a hands-on education covering all aspects of the supply chain. Students are engaged in activities related to the development, buying, and selling of merchandise. This major will develop skills associated with buying, product development, apparel production, selection and coordination, fibers and fabrics, computer aided design, product compatibility, quality assessment and control.

The Center for Merchandising Education and Research was launched in 2009. The Center's purpose is to forge meaningful industry partnerships that enhance the education and development of TCU merchandising students and faculty. Programs sponsored by the center include the JCPenney's Executive in Residence Day, Merchandising Matters Career Symposium, and speakers' forum with corporate CEOs.

FACILITIES

25 station CAD lab, software Lectra's Kaledo Style, Print, Knit, & Weave, Catalogue Builder; Adobe Creative Suite; Microsoft Office, Textile testing lab, Costume collection over 2,000 items catalogued for teaching and display purposes.

ONLINE / DISTANCE LEARNING

Fashion Internship. Most courses contain a Web component.

COURSES OF INSTRUCTION

- Merchandising Principles
- Clothing Construction
- Fashion Illustration
- Textile Fundamentals
- Promotion Principles
- Product Development
- Merchandise Buying
- CAD for Apparel
- Entrepreneurship
- Career Development
- History of Costume
- History of Contemporary Dress
- Textile Testing & Analysis
- International Trade
- Clothing in Society
- Fashion Internship

INTERNSHIPS

Required of majors at the Junior level.

Interns are typically placed at companies such as Pier 1 Imports Corporate Offices, Zale Corporate Headquarters, JCPenney Headquarters, Neiman Marcus Corporate Buying Office; Nordstrom; Donna Karan, Louis Vuitton, Chanel, Ralph Lauren, Tommy Hilfiger, Kenneth Cole, Henri Bendel, Escada, Tobe Report, Williamson-Dickies Mfg. Co, Bergdorf Goodman, Trina Turk, Sonia Rykiel, Jimmy Choo, Carolina Herrera, Nicole Miller, Lafayette 148, Elie Tahari, Dallas Market Center, Elle Magazine, Fossil, Inc, Texas Rangers Merchandise DEpt., Kate Spade, Rebecca Taylor, Anthropologie, LaRok, Chan Luu, RUCA, Calypso-St. Barts.

STUDY ABROAD

Semester study abroad programs for merchandising students are available in Florence, Italy; Paris, France; and London, England.

NOTABLE ALUMNI

Kent Cummins, Celebrity stylist LA & NYC; Stacy Caldwell, Global Wholesale Director Thakoon; Ajiri Aki, US Operations Director Orange Films, Inc.

STUDENT ACTIVITIES AND ORGANIZATIONS

Beta Zeta Chapter of Phi Upsilon Omicron National Honor Society

FACULTY SPECIALIZATIONS AND RESEARCH

Clothing Construction, Philanthropy, Branding & Product Development; Portfolio Development, Textile Testing, Refurbishment, Performance of Consumer Goods; Global Trade in Textiles and Apparel, Entrepreneurial Ventures, Socio-psychology of Clothing and Appearances, Social Responsibility, and Retail Channel Strategy.

Texas State University

Department of Family & Consumer Sciences

601 University Dr., San Marcos, TX 78666 | 512-245-2155 | www.txstate.edu/fcs

UNIVERSITY PROFILE
Public
Suburban
Residential
Semester Schedule
Co-ed

STUDENT DEMOGRAPHICS
Undergraduate: 30,000
Graduate: 3,000

Male: Not reported
Female: Not reported

Full-time: Not reported
Part-time: Not reported

EXPENSES
Tuition: Not reported
Room & Board: Not reported

ADMISSIONS
601 University Dr.
San Marcos, TX 78666
512-245-2364
www.vpfss.txstate.edu/acct/
studentinfo.html

DEGREE INFORMATION

Major / Degree / Concentration	Enrollment	Requirements for entry	Graduation rate
Fashion Merchandising Bachelor of Science Minor in Business	375	Completion of 9 hours of prescribed courses with an average of 2.25. Maintain a 2.5 to advance	Not reported

TOTAL PROGRAM ENROLLMENT
Undergraduate: 375
Graduate: Not reported

Male: Not reported
Female: 90%

Full-time: 60%
Part-time: 40%
Online: Not reported

International: Not reported
Minority: Not reported

Job Placement Rate: 80%

SCHOLARSHIPS / FINANCIAL AID
Many types of scholarships and financial aid are available.

TOTAL FACULTY: 7
Full-time: 100%
Part-time: Not reported

FASHION DESIGN ADMINISTRATION
Dr. Maria Canabal, Department Chairman
Dr. Ann DuPont, Program Coordinator

PROFESSIONAL / ACADEMIC AFFILIATIONS
International Textile and Apparel Association
American Collegiate Retailing Association

PROGRAM DESCRIPTION / PHILOSOPHY

The Fashion Merchandising program at Texas State University prepares students for careers in the merchandising, production, and promotion of fashion goods and services.

FACILITIES

Computer labs, resource labs, textile conservation lab, historic textiles and apprarel study collection and gallery.

ONLINE / DISTANCE LEARNING

Various courses are offered online from time to time

COURSES OF INSTRUCTION

- Introduction to Fashion
- Textiles
- Buying I & II
- Consumer Behavior
- Fashion History
- Aesthetics and Design
- Fashion Economics
- Enterprise Development
- Product Development
- Visual Merchandising

INTERNSHIPS

Leading national retailers, wholesalers, and fashion communications firms

STUDY ABROAD

Available

NOTABLE ALUMNI

Many former students are now buyers, general merchandise mangers, and store managers with top-ranked retailers.

STUDENT ACTIVITIES AND ORGANIZATIONS

Fashion merchandising related student organizations include Fashion Merchandising Association, FashioNation, and student AATCC chapter as well as Phi Upsilon honorary.

FACULTY SPECIALIZATIONS AND RESEARCH

Faculty research areas include consumer behavior, sustainability in product design and social marketing, international trade, history of fashion, entrepreneurship, and aesthetics.

Texas Tech University

College of Human Science, Department of Design

Apparel Design & Manufacturing Program, Box 41220, Lubbock, TX 79409 | 806-742-3050

www.depts.ttu.edu/hs/dod/adm/index.php

UNIVERSITY PROFILE

UNIVERSITY PROFILE
Public
Suburban
Residential
Semester Schedule
Co-ed

STUDENT DEMOGRAPHICS

Undergraduate: 24,236
Graduate: 10,000

Male: Not reported
Female: Not reported

Full-time: Not reported
Part-time: Not reported

EXPENSES

Tuition: Not reported
Room & Board: Not reported
See admission website:
www.admissions.ttu.edu/
fastfacts.pdf

ADMISSIONS

Office of Undergraduate
Admissions
Texas Tech University, Box
45005
Lubbock, TX 79409-5005
806-742-1480
admissions@ttu.edu

DEGREE INFORMATION

Major / Degree / Concentration	Enrollment	Requirements for entry	Graduation rate
Apparel Design & Manufacturing Bachelor of Science	120	None	90%

TOTAL PROGRAM ENROLLMENT

Undergraduate: 120
Graduate: n/a

Male: 10%
Female: 90%

Full-time: Not reported
Part-time: Not reported
Online: 0%

International: Not reported
Minority: Not reported

Job Placement Rate: 90%

SCHOLARSHIPS / FINANCIAL AID

The Department of Design, in conjunction with the College of Human Sciences, offers a variety of undergraduate and graduate scholarships of different amounts. In order for a student to receive a scholarship from the Department of Design, it is the College of Human Sciences requirement that the student completes an undergraduate or graduate scholarship application via the university's scholarship Web sites.

TOTAL FACULTY: 5

Full-time: 60%
Part-time: 40%

FASHION DESIGN ADMINISTRATION

Dr. Su Shin, Director of Apparel Design & Manufacturing (ADM) Program
Dr. Zane Curry, Director of Interior Design (ID) Program
Dr. Cherif Amor, Interim Chair, Department of Design

PROFESSIONAL / ACADEMIC AFFILIATIONS

International Textile and Apparel Association
American Apparel and Footwear Association
Fashion Group International

PROGRAM DESCRIPTION AND PHILOSOPHY

The Apparel Design and Manufacturing program at Texas Tech University provides the key to entering the glamorous world of fashion. Students learn to create and produce their own designs, research, and apply the latest trends, manage product development, apparel design, or design and construct costumes or stage. A variety opportunities and jobs are possible with a degree in Apparel Design and Manufacturing.

FACILITIES

Students have access to well-equipped design and production laboratories, a computer laboratory that features state-of-the-art apparel design, and pattern making. Available technologies and software: [TC]2 3D-body scan technology, Gerber AccuMark System for CAD, and Adobe Creative Design.

ONLINE / DISTANCE LEARNING

Not reported

COURSES OF INSTRUCTION

- Introduction to Apparel Design
- Intermediate Clothing Construction
- Flat Pattern Design
- Textiles
- Advanced Flat Pattern Design
- Individual Study
- Surface Design
- Apparel Portfolio Development
- Internship in Apparel Design and Manufacturing
- Clothing Construction
- Fashion Illustration
- Design through Draping
- Computer Applications in Apparel Design
- History of Philosophy of Dress
- Apparel Manufacturing
- Apparel Product Development
- Professional Practices for Apparel Design & Manufacturing

INTERNSHIPS

Required of majors at the Senior level.

Interns are placed in major apparel companies such as Academy Sports, Inc., JCPenney, Linda Segal for CFA, Inc., Nordstrom, Jessica McClintock, Old Navy, Spiegel, BCBG, Max Azria, Donna Ricco, and more.

STUDY ABROAD

Available

NOTABLE ALUMNI

Not reported

STUDENT ACTIVITIES AND ORGANIZATIONS

Hi-Tech Fashion Group is a student organization in Apparel Design & Manufacturing (ADM) Program to promote knowledge of professional fields in the fashion industry.

FACULTY SPECIALIZATIONS AND/ OR RESEARCH

- Dr. Su Shin, Professor, Program Director: Specialties in Apparel Technologies, 3D body scan, Computer Applications for Apparel Design (CAD), Apparel Design, and Apparel Manufacturing. Research is being conducted to develop standard sizing systems for mass customization/production, fit and body shape analysis using 3D body scan technology.
- Ms. Rachel Anderson, Instructor: Specialties in Draping, Patternmaking, and Creative Design.
- Ms. Laura Haynie, Instructor: Specialties in Knit Design and Apparel Industry.
- Dr. Samina Khan, Professor: Specialties in Textiles, History and Philosophy of Clothing.

University of Houston

Department of Human Development and Consumer Sciences

4800 Calhoun, Houston, TX 77004　|　713-743-4110　|　www.tech.uh.edu/Programs/Consumer_Merchandising

UNIVERSITY PROFILE
Public
Urban
Residential
Commuter
Semester Schedule
Co-ed

STUDENT DEMOGRAPHICS
Undergraduate: 27,600
Graduate: 5,500

Male: 49%
Female: 51%

Full-time: 74%
Part-time: 26%

EXPENSES
Tuition: $8,530
Room & Board: $7,890

ADMISSIONS
4888 Calhoun
Houston, TX 77004
713 743 1010
www.uh.edu/admissions

DEGREE INFORMATION

Major / Degree / Concentration	Enrollment	Requirements for entry	Graduation rate
Consumer Science & Merchandising Bachelor of Science	260	Admission to the University of Houston (see www.uh.edu/admissions/undergraduate/index.php)	Not reported
Consumer Science & Merchandising Certificate	10	Admission to the University of Houston (see www.uh.edu/admissions/undergraduate/index.php)	Not reported

TOTAL PROGRAM ENROLLMENT
Undergraduate: 260
Graduate: n/a

Male: 40%
Female: 60%

Full-time: 68%
Part-time: %32
Online: 50%

International: 5%
Minority: 55%

Job Placement Rate: 90%

SCHOLARSHIPS / FINANCIAL AID
U.S. Federal, Texas State, University of Houston, and College of Technology scholarship and financial aid funds are available (see www.uh.edu/financial/).

Students eceiving Scholarships or Financial Aid: 95%

TOTAL FACULTY: 11
Full-time: 36%
Part-time: 54%

FASHION DESIGN ADMINISTRATION
Dr. Carole Goodson, Professor & Chair Human Development & Consumer Sciences
Dr. Marcella Norwood, Associate Professor & Coordinator Consumer Science & Merchandising

PROFESSIONAL / ACADEMIC AFFILIATIONS
International Textile and Apparel Association
Fashion Group International
American Collegiate Retailing Association

PROGRAM DESCRIPTION AND PHILOSOPHY

Consumer Science and Merchandising at the University of Houston is a unique on-campus/online undergraduate program for those seeking to understand consumers and merchandising. It focuses on consumer-oriented business practices in the fields of merchandising, technology entrepreneurship, retailing, e-tailing, sales, customer services, and public relations.

The Consumer Science and Merchandising curriculum is designed to develop professionals who can integrate knowledge of consumers and merchandising processes and apply that knowledge to technology-based consumer practices. in the fields of merchandising, technology entrepreneurship, retailing/e-tailing, sales/consumer service, and training and development.

The program offers specializations in Consumer Science and Merchandising, Technology Entrepreneurship, e-Tailing, Training and Development, and Professional Studies. The professional studies option is designed for students who have completed an associate's degree or an extensive content block and wish to build upon this content to complete their bachelor's degree. The program builds on prior academic experience, providing additional knowledge in merchandising, consumer science, sales and training, and development.

FACILITIES

Internships in the major retail centers of metropolitan Houston; student instructional labs including student tutoring and support; and multiple student computer laboratories and technical support services.

ONLINE / DISTANCE LEARNING

All Consumer Science and Merchandising content courses are offered online. All courses in the major field are offered online. Required general education courses may be online or transferred from approved, accredited institutions.

COURSES OF INSTRUCTION

- Merchandising & Consumer Science
- Consumer Science
- Visual Merchandising
- Entrepreneurship
- Merchandising Systems
- Merchandising
- Communications Strategies
- Strategies in E-tailing
- Industrial/Consumer Sales

INTERNSHIPS

Required of majors at Senior year.

Interns are typically placed at companies such as Macy's, Target, Stage Stores, Inc., Neiman Marcus, Jos A Bank Clothiers, Al's Formal Wear, *Houston* magazine, BB1 Classic, New Living, Porsche, Aeros, HEB, Bath Junkie, Elie Tahari, Honeywell, Lot 8, Mixx Sixty, Dillard's, CVS Pharmacy, Memorial Herman Healthcare System.

STUDY ABROAD

Independent options exist

NOTABLE ALUMNI

Victor Costa, designer; retail buyers and merchandise managers; Macy's; store managers; sales managers; corporate executives; retail owners; wholesale managers

STUDENT ACTIVITIES AND ORGANIZATIONS

Collegiate DECA: leadership development, collegiate competitive events, student judging of high school competitions, career days, travel study New York and Dallas. Star Awards: recognition events highlighting leaders in retailing. Retail Forum: career speakers, panels, resume and interviewing skills workshops, and job interviews.

FACULTY SPECIALIZATIONS AND RESEARCH

Retail management, visual merchandising and display, consumer marketing, entrepreneurship, technology entrepreneurship, distance education, online teaching and learning, international consumer behavior, adult education, career planning

COMMUNITY COLLEGE TRANSFERS

The University of Houston has articulation agreements with numerous community colleges and encourages student transfer from community colleges.

University of North Texas

School of Merchandising & Hospitality Management

1155 Union Circle # 311100, Denton, TX 76203 | 940-565-2436 | www.smhm.unt.edu

UNIVERSITY PROFILE
Public
Suburban
Residential
Semester Schedule
Co-ed

STUDENT DEMOGRAPHICS
Undergraduate: 28,474
Graduate: 7,649

Male: 44.47%
Female: 55.53%

Full-time: 66.84%
Part-time: 33.16%

EXPENSES
Tuition: $7,606 (in-state)
Room & Board: $6,600
(estimated)

ADMISSIONS
1147 Union Circle
Denton, TX 76203
940-565-2681
admissins@unt.edu

DEGREE INFORMATION

Major / Degree / Concentration	Enrollment	Requirements for entry	Graduation rate
Merchandising Bachelor of Science	608	2.25 gpa	Not reported
Home Furnishings Merchandising Bachelor of Science	71	2.25 gpa	Not reported
E-Merchandising Bachelor of Science	35	2.25 gpa	Not reported
Merchandising Master of Science	63	2.8 gpa on all undergraduate work or 3.0 for last 60 hours; GRE or GMAT score; 3 Letters of recommendation; essay	Not reported
Merchandising Graduate Certificate	6	2.8 gpa on all undergraduate work or 3.0 for last 60 hours; OR a 3.4 gpa on previous master's degree.	Not reported
Merchandising/ Business Master of Business Administration	9	2.8 gpa on all undergraduate work or 3.0 for last 60 hours; GMAT score; 3 letters of recommendation; essay	Not reported

TOTAL PROGRAM ENROLLMENT
Undergraduate: 714
Graduate: 63

Male: 5%
Female: 95%

Full-time: 81%
Part-time: 19%
Online: 0%

International: 2%
Minority: 40%

Job Placement Rate: 86%

SCHOLARSHIPS / FINANCIAL AID
School of Merchandising & Hospitality Management Scholarships are awarded each year. The deadline for application is February 1. See www.smhm.unt.edu for details.

TOTAL FACULTY: 20
Full-time: 60%
Part-time: 40%

FASHION DESIGN ADMINISTRATION
Tammy Kinley, Chair
Christy Crutsinger, Associate Dean
Judith Forney, Dean

PROFESSIONAL / ACADEMIC AFFILIATIONS

International Textile and Apparel Association

American Apparel and Footwear Association

Fashion Group International

American Collegiate Retailing Association

PROGRAM DESCRIPTION / PHILOSOPHY

The University of North Texas merchandising program is a dynamic program offering classroom and experiential opportunities incorporating all areas of the merchandising industry. Strategically located in the Dallas/Fort Worth Metroplex, University of North Texas offers exciting internship opportunities and job placements with large internationally recognized companies. Students engage in dynamic relationships with faculty, staff, classmates, and industry professionals that create lifelong friendships and networking opportunities. We are proud to be the largest merchandising program in the country as well as the only institution to offer a Digital Merchandising degree.

The mission of the Merchandising Division is to integrate education, leadership, and research experiences that contribute to the critical analyses of merchandising strategies as they relate to the development, distribution, evaluation, and use of fashion-oriented products in the consumer-driven global market. Core competencies are archived through innovative curricula, laboratory experiences, applied technology, research activities, and industry involvement. Five concepts frame the merchandising program: (1) merchandising foundations; (2) product evaluation; (3) consumer segmentation; (4) industry analysis; and (5) merchandising applications.

FACILITIES

In addition to traditional university facilities, we have a dedicated computer lab and a sample room for the Home Furnishings Merchandising program.

ONLINE / DISTANCE LEARNING

The Merchandising M.S. and the Graduate Certificate in Merchandising are both offered with a 100% online option.

COURSES OF INSTRUCTION

Undergraduate:
- Fashion Theory & Trend Analysis
- Consumer Studies
- Historic & Contemporary Styles of Apparel
- Apparel Quality Analysis
- Textiles
- Profit-Centered Merchandising
- Advanced Merchandising Applications

Graduate:
- Merchandising Strategies
- Consumer Theory
- Managing Customer Experiences
- Promotions
- Global Retailing
- E-Merchandising

INTERNSHIPS

Required of majors at the Senior level. Interns are typically placed at companies such as Nordstrom, JCPenney, Fossil, Dillard's, and Target.

STUDY ABROAD

We offer a 3-week study abroad to Hong Kong/China each Summer.

NOTABLE ALUMNI

Not reported

STUDENT ACTIVITIES AND ORGANIZATIONS

The undergraduate students are encouraged to join Merchandising, Inc., our professional development student organization. They are also encouraged to become student members of Fashion Group International.

FACULTY SPECIALIZATIONS AND RESEARCH

Consumer Behavior, M-Commerce, Brand Equity, Retail Employees, Merchandising Strategies, Body Image and Clothing, Rural Retailing, Internationalization, Multichannel Retailing.

COMMUNITY COLLEGE TRANSFERS

We gladly accept coursework from other institutions. Students will work with advisors pretransfer to ensure all courses completed elsewhere will articulate to our degree plans.

The Art Institute of Virginia Beach

Department of Fashion & Retail Management

4500 Main St., Virginia Beach, VA 23462-3358 | 757-493-6700 | www.artinstitutes.edu/virginia-beach/

UNIVERSITY PROFILE
Private
Urban
Commuter
Quarter Schedule
Co-ed

STUDENT DEMOGRAPHICS
Undergraduate: 105
Graduate: n/a

Male: 38%
Female: 62%

Full-time: 72%
Part-time: 29%

EXPENSES
Tuition: $30,208
Room & Board: n/a

ADMISSIONS
4500 Main St. Ste. 100
Virginia Beach, VA 23462-3358
757-493-6700
aiva adm@aii.edu

DEGREE INFORMATION

Major / Degree / Concentration	Enrollment	Requirements for entry	Graduation rate
Fashion Retail Management Bachelor of Arts	120	2.5 gpa Portfolio assessment following quarter 4, 7, and 11	95%

TOTAL PROGRAM ENROLLMENT
Undergraduate: 101
Graduate: n/a

Male: 38%
Female: 62%

Full-time: Not reported
Part-time: Not reported
Online: n/a

International: 0%
Minority: Not reported

Job Placement Rate: n/a

SCHOLARSHIPS / FINANCIAL AID
Federal student loans, periodic organization-sponsored contests.

Students Receiving Scholarships or Financial Aid: 95%

TOTAL FACULTY: 16
Full-time: 6%
Part-time: 94%

FASHION ADMINISTRATION
Marilyn H. Burstein, President
Sharon L. Youngue, Dean of Academic Affairs
Jonelle Tate, Sr. Director of Admissions

PROFESSIONAL / ACADEMIC AFFILIATIONS
Not reported

PROGRAM DESCRIPTION AND PHILOSOPHY

The Fashion Marketing and Retail Management program provides graduates with relevant industry and professional development skills needed for entry-level careers within the retail industry. Course work will provide graduates with a strong academic and professional foundation through both applied coursework and technological applications. The market-driven curriculum teaches students to utilize problem solving and critical thinking skills, which meet the expressed needs of the retail industry. Focusing on marketing, management, and interpersonal skills, graduates are prepared to work in the retail industry.

FACILITIES

MAC and PC Labs, display closet, classrooms, technology, research resources, local museums/archives

ONLINE / DISTANCE LEARNING

We do not offer online courses at this location.

COURSES OF INSTRUCTION

- Introduction to Retailing
- Fashion History I & II
- Fashion Drawing
- Retail Math
- Design Elements
- Introduction to Marketing
- Fundamentals of Business
- Textiles
- Consumer Behavior
- Accounting
- Apparel Evaluation and Construction
- Brand Strategy & Marketing
- Visual Merchandising
- English
- Algebra
- Professional Communication
- Public Speaking
- Critical Thinking

INTERNSHIPS

Not required. Students may take an internship in their 12th Quarter.

The Art Institute of Virginia Beach began their first quarter Fashion Retail Management curriculum in January, 2010. Companies offering internships have not yet been determined.

STUDY ABROAD

Not available.

We anticipate joining the Ai Study Abroad Consortium within the next year.

NOTABLE ALUMNI

Not reported

STUDENT ACTIVITIES AND ORGANIZATIONS

Not reported

FACULTY SPECIALIZATIONS AND/ OR RESEARCH

Not reported

Marymount University

Fashion Design & Merchandising

2807 N. Glebe Rd., Arlington, VA 22207 | 703-522-5600 | www.marymount.edu/academics

UNIVERSITY PROFILE

Private
Suburban
Residential
Semester Schedule
Co-ed

STUDENT DEMOGRAPHICS

Undergraduate: 2,224
Graduate: 1,256

Male: 26%
Female: 74%

Full-time: 85%
Part-time: 15%

EXPENSES

Tuition: $22,370
Room & Board: $9,745

ADMISSIONS

2807 N. Glebe Rd.
Arlington, VA 22207
800-548-7638
703-284-1500
admissions@marymount.edu

DEGREE INFORMATION

Major / Degree / Concentration	Enrollment	Requirements for entry	Graduation rate
Fashion Design Bachelor of Arts	94	2.5 gpa	Not reported
Fashion Merchandising Bachelor of Arts	121	2.5 gpa	Not reported

TOTAL PROGRAM ENROLLMENT

Undergraduate: 215
Graduate: Not reported

Male: Not reported
Female: Not reported

Full-time: Not reported
Part-time: Not reported

International: 13%
Minority: Not reported

Job Placement Rate: Not reported

SCHOLARSHIPS / FINANCIAL AID

Ninety per cent of first-time, full-time freshmen at Marymount University receive financial aid. Merit scholarships and awards are earned at the upper class level from external organizations and specifically designated endowment.

TOTAL FACULTY: 10

Full-time: 50%
Part-time: 50%

FASHION DESIGN ADMINISTRATION

Janice Ellinwood, Department Chair, Fashion Design and Merchandising

PROFESSIONAL / ACADEMIC AFFILIATIONS

International Textile and Apparel Association
Fashion Group International

PROGRAM DESCRIPTION AND PHILOSOPHY

The Fashion Design program educates students for entry into the fashion industry as assistant designers in manufacturing and product development firms. The Fashion Merchandising program prepares students to enter fields like management, buying, visual merchandising, public relations and fashion events, writing and media, product development, and international trade. The programs provide a personal environment, and courses are taught only by the professors themselves. Fashion Club, the fashion show, and study abroad opportunities create a sense of community.

FACILITIES

- Swing/pattern-making studios
- Computer labs stocked with Illustrator, Photoshop, Wild Ginger, Lectra
- Marymount Historic Costume Collection
- Membership in Washington, DC, Consortium of Colleges and Universities
- Accessibility to Washington, DC, museums such as the Smithsonian and the National Gallery of Art

ONLINE / DISTANCE LEARNING

Not reported

COURSES OF INSTRUCTION

Fashion Design:
- Apparel Design I, II, and III
- Fashion Illustration I, II
- Product Development
- Digital Presentation for Fashion
- Senior Fashion Design Portfolio

Fashion Merchandising:
- Retailing
- Buying Fashion Apparel
- Fashion Show Production
- Fashion Research and Communication
- Product Development
- Fashion in the Global Marketplace
- Senior Seminar

INTERNSHIPS

Required of majors at the senior level.

Interns are typically placed at companies such as Michael Kors, Betsey Johnson, Anna Sui, Washington Opera, Theory, Saks Fifth Ave., Burberry Ltd., Athropologie, Nordstrom, Bloomingdale's

STUDY ABROAD

Marymount University has programs of study in Paris, London, Florence, and internships throughout the world.

NOTABLE ALUMNI

Not reported

STUDENT ACTIVITIES AND ORGANIZATIONS

Marymount's prestigious fashion show, Portfolio in Motion, entertains 2000 people annually and is filmed for cable television. MU's Designer of the Year Award is given annually to noted designers, such as Michael Kors, Carolina Herrera, and Oscar de la Renta, who review the seniors' fashion design portfolios. Fashion Club is Marymount University's student organization that works behind the scenes at Washington DC area fashion shows and galas, brings members of industry to speak on campus, and travels into the NYC apparel market.

During recent charity fundraisers and promotional events, students worked with Nanette Lepore, Lela Rose, Christian Laboutin, Tim Gunn, and Oscar de la Renta.

FACULTY SPECIALIZATIONS AND RESEARCH

Faculty Awards: Fulbright Scholar 2001; ITAA 2008 Lectra Outstanding Faculty Award in Fashion Design; ITAA 2008 Sandra Hutton Award for Excellence in Fiber Art. Research: The Artistic Decision-Making of Fashion Designers; Media Campaigns in the Fashion Industry; Integration of Trend Research into the Design of High Runway Showpieces; Research and Analysis for Color Marketing; Color Theory and Textile Design; Marketing and E-tailing for Fair Trade Organizations; Prototype Development for Mature Female Tenniswear.

COMMUNITY COLLEGE TRANSFERS

Tranfers enjoy the transition into Marymount's fashion programs. The same top internships, activities with Fashion Club, the outstanding fashion show, and stimulating courses are available to transfers as they are to first-year freshmen.

Virginia Commonwealth University

Department of Fashion Design & Merchandising

325 N. Harrison St., Richmond, VA 23284-3087 | 804-828-1699 | www.vcu.edu/arts/fashion/dept/

UNIVERSITY PROFILE
Public
Urban
Residential
Semester Schedule
Co-ed

STUDENT DEMOGRAPHICS
Tuition: $7,117 (in-state)
Room & Board: $8,325 (in-state)

EXPENSES
Tuition: $7,500
Room & Board: Varies, avg. $7,000

ADMISSIONS
821 W. Franklin St.
Richmond, VA 23284-2526
804-828-1222
ugrad@vcu.edu

DEGREE INFORMATION

Major / Degree / Concentration	Enrollment	Requirements for entry	Graduation rate
Fashion Design Bachelor of Fine Arts	104	Portfolio and completion into Art Foundation program	85%
Fashion Merchandising Bachelor of Arts	260	1,000 SAT and 3.0 gpa minimum	88%

TOTAL PROGRAM ENROLLMENT
Undergraduate: 365
Graduate: 0

Male: 5%
Female: 95%

Full-time: 98%
Part-time: 2%
Online: 0%

International: 1%
Minority: 38%

Job Placement Rate: 85%

SCHOLARSHIPS / FINANCIAL AID
Numerous types of scholarships available including traditional sources but also Presidential, Provost, and Dean's scholarships. Once enrolled, there are several scholarship for fashion majors based on gpa and talent
www.vcu.edu/arts/prospective_students/scholarships/

TOTAL FACULTY: 20
Full-time: 10%
Part-time: 10%

FASHION DESIGN ADMINISTRATION
Karen M. Videtic, Chairperson
Donna W. Reamy, Associate Chairperson
Mike Etto, Administrative Tech Specialist

PROFESSIONAL / ACADEMIC AFFILIATIONS
Fashion Group International

PROGRAM DESCRIPTION AND PHILOSOPHY

Prepare students to seamlessly enter the fashion industry with a global perspective and the ability to analyze and solve merchandising issues and problems. Courses are project and simulation drive with critics or clients driving the contemporary issues.

FACILITIES

Costume collection, Lectra computer lab, design labs

ONLINE / DISTANCE LEARNING

Not reported

COURSES OF INSTRUCTION

- Fashion Forecasting
- Contemporary Fashion
- Retail Buying
- Fashion Economics
- Line Development
- Advanced Store Development (Entrepreneurship)
- Principles of Marketing
- International Marketing
- Textiles
- Import/Exporting

INTERNSHIPS

Not required, but available at the Junior level. Interns are typically placed at companies such as Stylesight, Armani Exhange, Nordstroms, Ana Sui, Betsy Johnson, Ralph Lauren, and numerous others in NYC, London, Paris.

STUDY ABROAD

London, Florence, Paris, Qatar, and summer programs in Paris and Florence Guatemala. Students can study in any accredited university worldwide.

NOTABLE ALUMNI

Don Wan Harrell: creator/owner of AKADEMICS and PRPS

STUDENT ACTIVITIES AND ORGANIZATIONS

Extensive field trips in Europe and Asia as well as NYC and MAGIC/POOL/Project in Las Vegas.

FACULTY SPECIALIZATIONS AND RESEARCH

Buying, Fashion Economics, Branding, Product Development, Historic Costume, Import Exporting (faculty authored textbooks in all of these areas)

Virginia Polytechnic Institute & State University

Department of Apparel, Housing, & Resource Management

240 Wallace Hall, Blacksburg, VA 24061 | 540-231-6164 | www.ahrm.vt.edu

UNIVERSITY PROFILE
Public
Rural
Residential
Semester Schedule
Co-ed

STUDENT DEMOGRAPHICS
Undergraduate: 24,000
Graduate: 5,000

Male: 60%
Female: 40%

Full-time: 80%
Part-time: 20%

EXPENSES
Tuition: $9,500 (in-state)
Room & Board: $6,400-$9,800

ADMISSIONS
201 Burruss Hall
Blacksburg, VA 24061
540-231-6267

DEGREE INFORMATION

Major / Degree / Concentration	Enrollment	Requirements for entry	Graduation rate
Apparel, Housing, & Resource Management Bachelor of Science Apparel Product Development & Merchandising Management	180	2.0 gpa	98%

TOTAL PROGRAM ENROLLMENT
Undergraduate: 180
Graduate: n/a

Male: 10%
Female: 90%

Full-time: 98%
Part-time: 2%
Online: Not reported

International: 6%
Minority: 23%

Job Placement Rate: A high percent

SCHOLARSHIPS / FINANCIAL AID
Financial Aid information would be available from the Financial Aid office at Virginia Tech. Apparel scholarships available to students include the Oris Glisson Scholarship, the Sutherland Purdy Scholarship, the Belk Scholarship, the American Association of Textile Chemists and Colorists Scholarship.

Students Receiving Scholarships or Financial Aid: 70%

TOTAL FACULTY: 7
Full-time: 100%
Part-time: Not reported

FASHION DESIGN ADMINISTRATION
Julia Beamish, Professor & Department Chairperson

PROFESSIONAL / ACADEMIC AFFILIATIONS
International Textile and Apparel Association
American Collegiate Retailing Association

PROGRAM DESCRIPTION AND PHILOSOPHY

The program of apparel product development and merchandising management addresses the domestic and international concerns of apparel and textile manufactures and retailers and their consumers. Basic to these concerns are the social, cultural, political, economic, and technological factors that affect consumer satisfaction with apparel/textile and fashion products and the contributions the apparel and textile industries make to the national and global economics.

The program prepares students for careers in business, industry, and governmental services, such as buyers, fashion coordinators, fashion forecasters, product development managers, merchandise managers, store managers, and visual merchandisers. The program core courses are intended to provide students with a broad liberal education and with knowledge and skills fundamental to the development, production, merchandising, distribution, and use of apparel/textile and fashion products. Through coursework, internships, study tours, student organizations, and interaction with industry experts, students prepare for careers in the field.

FACILITIES

We have a number of special facilities for apparel student, including a dedicated computer lab, a high-tech CAD lab, textile and conditioning laboratories, display galleries, the Oris Glisson Historic Costume and Textile Collection, and several dedicated product development laboratories.

ONLINE / DISTANCE LEARNING

We have select courses offered online, this varies from year to year.

COURSES OF INSTRUCTION

- Clothing and People
- Structure and Fit
- Introduction to Textiles
- Apparel Textiles Lab
- Introduction to the Fashion Industry
- Fashion Presentation Techniques
- History of Costume
- Apparel Production
- Fashion Retailing Concepts
- Introduction to Textile Evaluation
- Clothing Behavior Patterns
- Economics of the Textile and Apparel Industry
- Fashion Analysis and Communication
- Apparel Quality Evaluation
- Merchandising Strategies
- Multichannel Retailing
- Advanced Apparel Assembly
- Small Apparel Business Management
- Entrepreneurship
- New York Fashion Study Tour
- European Fashion Study Tour

INTERNSHIPS

Not required but suggested at the Junior level. Students have interned in a wide variety of companies including retailers, designers, manufacturers, product developers,

STUDY ABROAD

European Fashion Study Abroad

NOTABLE ALUMNI

All of our alums are notable to us and have been employed by companies such as The Limited, Nike, Ralph Lauren, Liz Claiborne, Norma Kamali, Di Lorenzo Designs, Calvin Klein, Etienne Aigner, Woolrich, Macy's, Nordstrom's, and Oscar de la Renta.

STUDENT ACTIVITIES AND ORGANIZATIONS

We have a very active student organization titled the Fashion Merchandising and Design Society; and the American Association of Textile Chemists and Colorists Student Association.

FACULTY SPECIALIZATIONS AND RESEARCH

Our faculty specialize in the following areas: apparel; consumer behavior; marketing and textiles; retail entrepreneurship; business management; international economic development; merchandising and product development; non-store retailing; quick response strategies; textile and apparel economics.

Central Washington University

Family & Consumer Sciences

400 E. University Way, Ellensburg, WA 98926-7565 | 509-963-2067 | www.cwu.edu/~fandcs/fcsa/

DEGREE INFORMATION

Major / Degree / Concentration	Enrollment	Requirements for entry	Graduation rate
Major in Fashion Merchandising Bachelor of Science	65	2.3 gpa, 45 credits	100%
Minor in Fashion Merchandising	10	2.3 gpa, 45 credits	100%
Minor in Apparel Design	5	2.3 gpa, 45 credits	100%

TOTAL PROGRAM ENROLLMENT
Undergraduate: 72
Graduate: n/a

Male: 7%
Female: 93%

Full-time: 100%
Part-time: n/a
Online: n/a

International: 2%
Minority: 24%

Job Placement Rate: 100%

SCHOLARSHIPS / FINANCIAL AID
See opposite page for more info.

TOTAL FACULTY: 2
Full-time: 85%
Part-time: 15%

FASHION ADMINISTRATION
Andrea Eklund, Program Coordinator & Assistant Professor

PROFESSIONAL / ACADEMIC AFFILIATIONS
International Textile and Apparel Association

PROGRAM DESCRIPTION AND PHILOSOPHY

Central Washington University's Fashion Merchandising program is designed to help students gain the knowledge you need to recognize industry trends, analyze market and consumer behavior, and evaluate retail needs. Guest speakers, industry field trips, and attending trade shows allow students to have contact with fashion industry professionals. Students also gain additional hands-on professional experience during summer internships.

FACILITIES

Computer labs, apparel design lab, program reference library, advisory board for networking

ONLINE / DISTANCE LEARNING

No complete degrees offered online, some courses offered online

COURSES OF INSTRUCTION

- Basic Accounting
- Business Math Applications
- Program Management & Planning
- Applied Research
- Fashion Show Production
- Basic Sewing Techniques
- Intro to the Fashion Industry
- Sociocultural Aspects of Apparel
- Sewn Product Analysis
- Consumer Textiles
- Fashion Trend Analysis
- History of Fashion
- Retail Buying
- Principles of Selling
- Internship

INTERNSHIPS

Required of majors at Junior and Senior level; Interns are typically placed at companies such as Disney College Program, Nordstrom, Valcom, Gap, Pacific Northwest Costumes, Zumies, Buckle, regional boutiques and many other locations.

STUDY ABROAD

Study abroad to Italy, Australia, and Ireland

NOTABLE ALUMNI

Not reported

STUDENT ACTIVITIES AND ORGANIZATIONS

Student Fashion Society

FACULTY SPECIALIZATIONS AND RESEARCH

Apparel Design, Socio-Cultural Aspects of Apparel

SCHOLARSHIPS / FINANCIAL AID

Carolyn Schactler Scholarship: full-time student, majoring in Fashion Merchandising, Theatre Costume Design or minoring in Apparel Design, Minimum 3.3 cumulative gpa, upper division standing (preferably Junior) and have at least 2 quarters remaining at CWU after spring quarter 2010, one letter of recommendation from a professor.

Eugene Kosy Scholarship: full-time student, majoring in Information Technology & Administrative Management, Business or Marketing Education, or Fashion Merchandising, 3.0 gpa, and attained junior or senior standing at the time of receiving the scholarship.

Multiple other scholarships available that are non-program specific.

Washington State University

Department of Apparel, Merchandising, Design, & Textiles

P.O. Box 642020, Pullman, WA 99164-2020 | 509-335-1233 | http://amdt.wsu.edu/

DEGREE INFORMATION

Major / Degree / Concentration	Enrollment	Requirements for entry	Graduation rate
Apparel, Merchandising & Textiles **Bachelor of Arts** Apparel Design	87	2.7 gpa Portfolio review during Sophomore year	100%
Apparel, Merchandising & Textiles **Bachelor of Arts** Merchandising	167	2.7 gpa 24 credits	100%

TOTAL PROGRAM ENROLLMENT
Undergraduate: 254
Graduate: 11

Male: 6%
Female: 94%

Full-time: 100%
Part-time: 0%
Online: 0%

International: 21%
Minority: 21%

Job Placement Rate: 90%

SCHOLARSHIPS / FINANCIAL AID
See opposite page for more info.

TOTAL FACULTY: 9
Full-time: 100%
Part-time: 0%

FASHION DESIGN ADMINISTRATION
Karen K. Leonas, Professor & Chair

PROFESSIONAL / ACADEMIC AFFILIATIONS
International Textile and Apparel Association
Fashion Group International
American Collegiate Retailing Association

PROGRAM DESCRIPTION AND PHILOSOPHY

The Department of Apparel, Merchandising, Design, and Textiles at Washington State University provides students with opportunities to learn about the apparel/fashion/retail industry in a comprehensive manner with an understanding of the industry from concept to consumer. The field is interdisciplinary and requires the integration of designing and merchandising apparel and textile products with an understanding of the people who use those products. Students study a variety of areas including design, supply-chain management, international trade regulations, marketing, consumer behavior, analytical retail practices, interrelationships between culture, gender and dress, textile chemistry, textile physics and product development. The program involves many experiential based learning opportunities and employs research based problem solving strategies addressing current issues related to design, production, distribution and consumption of products, services, and experiences in a global context. The department is the only 4-year program at a state school in Washington with merchandising and design options. Washington State and the Puget Sound area are home to numerous fashion/apparel/retails companies which support our students in their learning experiences.

FACILITIES

Computer laboratory with apparel design and business software; apparel design software by Lectra; Plotter, Historic Textile and Costume Collection containing over 5000 pieces; Textile Research Laboratory fully renovated in 2009; two apparel design studios; two design work rooms; visual merchandising laboratory; 3D body-scanner; photography studio.

ONLINE / DISTANCE LEARNING

Not available

COURSES OF INSTRUCTION

- Introduction to Apparel, Merchandising, Design, & Textiles
- Visual Merchandising & Promotion
- Textile Specifications
- Apparel Quality & Product Analysis
- Consumer Behavior in Fashion
- Fashion Forecasting
- Merchandise Buying & Planning
- International Trade in Textiles & Apparel
- Multicultural Perspectives Body/Dress
- History of Fashion Design

INTERNSHIPS

Required of majors, preferred Junior year. Interns are typically placed at companies such as Nordstrom, The Buckle, Hollister, Cold Water Creek, Macy's, Gap, Eddie Bauer, Ann Taylor

STUDY ABROAD

Washington State University provides more than 1,200 education abroad choices for students that are appropriate with his/her academic and personal goals for the abroad experience.

NOTABLE ALUMNI

Not reported

STUDENT ACTIVITIES AND ORGANIZATIONS

International Textiles and Apparel Association student chapter; American Association of Textiles and Colorists student chapter, Mom's Weekend Fashion Show

FACULTY SPECIALIZATIONS AND RESEARCH

Apparel/Textile product development: High-performance textiles, Specialized end-use apparel, Fit and function. Creative scholarship & design. Merchandising; International trade, Sustainability, Economic development, Retail studies. Consumer studies; Sociopsychological, Cultural and ethnic, Historical, Consumer behavior, Textile sciences

SCHOLARSHIPS / FINANCIAL AID

The Office of Financial Aid and Scholarships is committed to making the financial aid process as transparent and understandable as possible. The information listed below will assist students and parents in making sense of the process. Scholarships are awarded based on combinations of a wide range of criteria. These may include academic merit, financial need, areas of study, group affiliations and many others.

Madison College

Fashion Marketing

3550 Anderson St., Madison, WI 53704 | 608-246-6486 | http://matcmadison.edu/program-info/fashion-marketing

UNIVERSITY PROFILE
Public
Suburban
Commuter
Semester Schedule
Co-ed

STUDENT DEMOGRAPHICS
Undergraduate: 40,000
Graduate: n/a

Male: Not reported
Female: Not reported

Full-time: Not reported
Part-time: Not reported

EXPENSES
Tuition: $2,000
Room & Board: n/a

ADMISSIONS
3550 Anderson St.
Madison, WI 53704
608-246-6000

DEGREE INFORMATION

Major / Degree / Concentration	Enrollment	Requirements for entry	Graduation rate
Fashion Marketing Associate of Applied Science	100	High School Diploma or Equivalent Compass, ACT, or SAT scores	50%

TOTAL PROGRAM ENROLLMENT
Undergraduate: 100
Graduate: n/a

Male: 5%
Female: 95%

Full-time: 20%
Part-time: 80%
Online: n/a

International: 2%
Minority: 8%

Job Placement Rate: 100%

SCHOLARSHIPS / FINANCIAL AID
Madison College Foundation has an account for the Fashion Marketing Program that students can apply for. Regular national and state scholarships and aid are also available.

Students Receiving Scholarships or Financial Aid: 2%

TOTAL FACULTY: 4
Full-time: 1
Part-time: 3

FASHION ADMINISTRATION
Betty Hurd, Director Fashion Marketing

PROFESSIONAL / ACADEMIC AFFILIATIONS
Fashion Group International

PROGRAM DESCRIPTION AND PHILOSOPHY

Fashion Marketing is a two-year associate degree program designed for people with a creative flair and an interest in business and fashion. The program presents exciting career opportunities for people who have the ability and interest to create, develop and promote new fashion products and services. Opportunities in retail, wholesale, manufacturing and related marketing fields are available to graduates of the program. Professional courses stress an understanding of marketing activities and knowledge of fashion products and practices. Study tours to markets and fashion centers such as Italy, New York, Chicago, and Minneapolis as well as guest lecturers enrich class studies and enable students to explore career opportunities. Second-year students enroll in the Internship course during the summer semester and receive supervised work experience.

Students take a variety of courses in Fashion Marketing, General Marketing, and Arts and Sciences. Sixty-seven credits are required for graduation. The program offers articulation agreements with many local high schools and transferability with some four-year colleges.

The Fashion Marketing program is directed by an advisory committee of people from area businesses, including Lands' End, Famous Footwear, Talbot's, Kohl's, Younkers, JCPenney, Target, Limited Express, Old Navy, The Boston Store, Marshall Field's, and The Gap. These companies employ many program graduates and often offer internships to Madison College Fashion Marketing students.

FACILITIES
Computers, Cad

ONLINE / DISTANCE LEARNING
Many courses are offered as hybrid

COURSES OF INSTRUCTION
Apparel Marketing, Fashion Analysis, CAD Textiles, Visual Merchandising, Merchandise Planning and Control, Store Operations, Store Management, Portfolio Presentations

INTERNSHIPS
Required of majors. Interns are typically placed at retailers, local, designers, and marketing companies.

STUDY ABROAD
International Business in Fashion – Italy

NOTABLE ALUMNI
Not reported

STUDENT ACTIVITIES AND ORGANIZATIONS
Marketing Club

FACULTY SPECIALIZATIONS AND RESEARCH
JDA software

COMMUNITY COLLEGE TRANSFERS
All general education courses are available at the college transfer level. All Fashion classes transfer to some, but not all 4-year colleges.

Milwaukee Area Technical College

Department of Marketing

6665 S. Howell Ave., Oak Creek, WI 53154 | 414-571-4507 | http://oncampus.matc.edu/luchta/fashionretail/

UNIVERSITY PROFILE
Public
Suburban
Commuter
Semester Schedule
Co-ed

STUDENT DEMOGRAPHICS
Undergraduate: 57,000
Graduate: n/a

Male: 47.5%
Female: 52.5%

Full-time: 10%
Part-time: 90%

EXPENSES
Tuition: $3,450 (in-state)
Room & Board: No Campus Housing

ADMISSIONS
6665 S. Howell Ave.
Oak Creek, WI 53154
414-571-4566

DEGREE INFORMATION

Major / Degree / Concentration	Enrollment	Requirements for entry	Graduation rate
Fashion Marketing Associate of Applied Science Fashion Track	70	2.0 gpa and 18 cummulative score on ACT or passing on Accuplacer	Not reported
Fashion Marketing Associate of Applied Science Retail Management Track	25	2.0 gpa and 18 cummulative score on ACT or passing on Accuplacer	Not reported

TOTAL PROGRAM ENROLLMENT
Undergraduate: 90-100
Graduate: n/a

Male: 10%
Female: 90%

Full-time: 12%
Part-time: 80%
Online: 8%

International: 0%
Minority: 20%

Job Placement Rate: 98%

SCHOLARSHIPS / FINANCIAL AID
See opposite page for more info.

TOTAL FACULTY: 11
Full-time: 7%
Part-time: 4%

FASHION DESIGN ADMINISTRATION
Ann Lucht, Program Advisor/Instructor
Deb Jansky, Program Advisor/Instructor

PROFESSIONAL / ACADEMIC AFFILIATIONS
Not reported

PROGRAM DESCRIPTION AND PHILOSOPHY

Fashion/Retail Marketing is a two-year associate degree program that prepares students for a career in stores, specialty shops, and boutiques. Fashion marketing courses emphasize the creative aspects of selling apparel, and the retail management courses emphasize the managerial and financial aspects of more general retailing. Trained fashion/retail applicants are continually recruited for supervisory, management, and merchandising positions at stores ranging from huge discounters to fashion boutiques. Job responsibilities vary with career emphasis; however, typical positions include visual merchandiser, sales representative, buyer, district/divisional manager, and store manager.

FACILITIES

Computer labs, visual merchandising lab, community based projects

ONLINE / DISTANCE LEARNING

Not reported

COURSES OF INSTRUCTION

- Marketing Principles
- Advertising Principles
- Textiles
- Special Event Management
- Apparel Marketing
- Retail Management
- Visual Merchandising
- Fashion Analysis
- Selling Principles

INTERNSHIPS

Required of majors after 2 semesters, after 1st year. Interns are typically placed at most major retailers in the Milwaukee area, Goodwill Ind.

STUDY ABROAD

Not available

NOTABLE ALUMNI

Not reported

STUDENT ACTIVITIES AND ORGANIZATIONS

Marketing Management Club

FACULTY SPECIALIZATIONS AND RESEARCH

All faculty have Master's Degrees in Marketing or Business.

COMMUNITY COLLEGE TRANSFERS

Transfer agreements with UW-Stout, Franklin College and Mt. Mary College.

SCHOLARSHIPS / FINANCIAL AID

Financial aid is available from federal, state, and private resources. There are four primary types of financial aid programs: grants, scholarships, loans and federal work-study.

- Grants and scholarships are free money you will not have to pay back.
- Loans are money you will have to pay back.
- Federal work-study is money you will not have to pay back. You earn federal work-study money by working a job approved through the MATC JOBshop. You can use this earned money to help pay for your education-related expenses.

Students Receiving Scholarships or Financial Aid: 98%

Mount Mary College

Fashion Department

2900 N. Menomonee River Pkwy, Milwaukee, WI 53222 | 414-258-4810 | www.mtmary.edu/dept_fashion.htm

STUDENT DEMOGRAPHICS
Undergraduate: 1,925 total undergrads and grads

Male: 0%
Female: 100%

Full-time: Not reported
Part-time: Not reported

EXPENSES
Tuition: $21,668
Room & Board: Not reported

ADMISSIONS
2900 N. Menonomee River Pkwy.
Milwaukee, WI 53222
800-321-6265
admiss@mtmary.edu

DEGREE INFORMATION

Major / Degree / Concentration	Enrollment	Requirements for entry	Graduation rate
Apparel Product Development Bachelor of Arts Creative Design Concentration	Not reported	Not reported	Not reported
Apparel Product Development Bachelor of Arts Technical Design Concentration	Not reported	Not reported	Not reported
Merchandise Management Bachelor of Arts	Not reported	Not reported	Not reported

TOTAL PROGRAM ENROLLMENT
Undergraduate: 50
Graduate: 0

Male: 0%
Female: 100%

Full-time: 80%
Part-time: 20%

International: 0%
Minority: 18%

Job Placement Rate: Not reported

SCHOLARSHIPS / FINANCIAL AID
Students in the fashion program may apply for the following scholarships: Harold Winston Memorial Scholarship; Florence Eiseman Memorial Scholarship; Sophie Yoerg Schroeder Memorial Scholarship; Hilda J. and Leonard L. Bartell Scholarship; Aileen Ryan Fashion Scholarship; Charles Kleibacker Scholarship; Fashion Department Scholarships; Stella and Rosemary Kleffman Endowed Scholarship Fund for Fashion; Antionette Totero Italian Fashion Scholarship

TOTAL FACULTY: 18
Full-time: 4
Part-time: 14
Online: 0

FASHION ADMINISTRATION
Sandra Keiser, Professor & Chair

PROFESSIONAL / ACADEMIC AFFILIATIONS
International Textile and Apparel Association

PROGRAM DESCRIPTION AND PHILOSOPHY

Students interested in working toward a fashion-related career will find that the Fashion department at Mount Mary College offers a variety of options for study within the industry.

Rated as one of the top programs in the country, Mount Mary's fashion program melds the excitement of change, the challenges of new technology, and a sensitivity to design, manufacturing, and merchandising which enhances student ability to create innovative and functional solutions.

Through the program, fashion students are introduced to real-world experiences and use state-of-the-art computers to gain a working knowledge of industry technology. The Fashion Department offers two unique majors–Apparel Product Development and Merchandise Management. Post-Baccalaureate certificate programs are also available.

FACILITIES

- Historic Costume Collection contains more than 9,000 objects for children and adults dating from 1750 to the present.
- Fashion Computer Lab features 16 stations equipped with Lectra U4ia, Adobe Photoshop, and Adobe Illustrator.
- Patternmaking Laboratory utilizes Gerber Accumark software for use in patternmaking, pattern grading, and marker making.

ONLINE / DISTANCE LEARNING

No online major

COURSES OF INSTRUCTION

- Introduction to Fashion Careers
- Textiles
- History of Western Costume
- Product Analysis
- Fashion Show Coordination
- Apparel Industry Seminar

Apparel Product Development:
- Fashion Experience
- Pattern Construction I-III
- Computer Graphics I
- Computer Graphics-Kaledo
- Fashion Drawing
- Design Development & Rendering
- Fashion Design I & II
- Fashion Collections I & II
- Introduction to Machine Knitting
- Tailoring
- Designing with Leather
- Computer-Aided Patternmaking
- Historic Pattern Reproduction
- Machine Knitting Techniques
- Pattern Grading & Marker Making
- Special Problems in Patternmaking
- Merchandise Management:
- Trend Analysis
- Retail Management
- Training Supervision, Customer Service
- Buying & Assortment Planning
- Visual Presentation
- Inventory Management
- Retail Strategies
- Financial Accounting
- Microeconomics
- Human Resource Management
- Principles of Marketing
- Consumer Behavior
- Advertising & Promotion
- Principles of Management

INTERNSHIPS

Required of majors

STUDY ABROAD

Mount Mary faculty partner with faculty from the Paris American Academy to offer students a study tour to Paris every other January during Winter Break. Mount Mary's Fashion Department also sponsors a study tour to New York City, every other year in the Fall.

Additionally, through Mount Mary's International Studies Office fashion students can study in China, Ireland, Italy, England, Nicaragua, and Peru. The College has an affiliation agreement with American Intercontinental University in London where students have the option to take classes or complete an internship for a semester or over a summer. The Peru study abroad program offers fashion majors the opportunity to complete an internship in Peru's cotton or alpaca industry.

NOTABLE ALUMNI

Alumni are employed at the following companies: ABS by Allen Schwartz; Kohl's Department Stores; Donna Ricco; Land's End; Florence Eiseman, Inc.; Macy's; The Gap; Patagonia; Harley-Davidson, Inc.; Ralph Lauren; Jockey International; Target Corporation

STUDENT ACTIVITIES AND ORGANIZATIONS

Annual fashion show is student-produced and features apparel designs by fashion majors.

FACULTY SPECIALIZATIONS AND RESEARCH

Not reported

University of Wisconsin-Stout

Department of Apparel Design & Development

Heritage Hall, Menomonie, WI 54751 | 715-232-1106 | www.uwstout.edu/programs/bsadd/index.cfm

UNIVERSITY PROFILE
Public
Rural
Residential
Semester Schedule
Co-ed

STUDENT DEMOGRAPHICS
Undergraduate: 7,971
Graduate: 1,044

Male: 49%
Female: 51%

Full-time: Not reported
Part-time: Not reported

EXPENSES
Tuition: Not reported
Room & Board: Not reported

ADMISSIONS
Not reported

DEGREE INFORMATION

Major / Degree / Concentration	Enrollment	Requirements for entry	Graduation rate
Apparel Design & Development Bachelor of Science	250	Not reported	100%

TOTAL PROGRAM ENROLLMENT
Undergraduate: 250
Graduate: Not reported

Male: 2%
Female: 98%

Full-time: Not reported
Part-time: Not reported
Online: Not reported

International: Not reported
Minority: Not reported

Job Placement Rate: 100%

SCHOLARSHIPS / FINANCIAL AID
Students Receiving Scholarships or
Financial Aid: 5%

TOTAL FACULTY: 6
Full-time: 100%
Part-time: Not reported

FASHION DESIGN ADMINISTRATION
Dr. Gindy Neidermyer, Program Director

PROFESSIONAL / ACADEMIC AFFILIATIONS
International Textile and Apparel
  Association
American Apparel and Footwear
  Association

PROGRAM DESCRIPTION AND PHILOSOPHY

The Apparel Design and Development program will help prepare you for the fast-paced exciting apparel industry. Students may choose from three concentrations: Apparel Design, Apparel Development, and Apparel Product Management. Knowledgeable faculty and up-to-date laboratories make UW-Stout a great place to develop your talents. *Bobbin* magazine described UW-Stout's apparel major as "one of the best kept secrets in apparel education."

FACILITIES

Computer labs, historic gallery, pattern lab, textile testing

ONLINE / DISTANCE LEARNING

Not reported

COURSES OF INSTRUCTION

- Quality Analysis
- Pattern Development
- Apparel Construction
- Functional Clothing Design
- Knit Design & Technology

INTERNSHIPS

Required of majors at the Junior/Senior level. Interns are typically placed at companies such as Target, Kohls, Dallin Chase, Anna Sui, Burton, Gander Mountain, WSI Sports, Under Armour

STUDY ABROAD

Available

NOTABLE ALUMNI

Not reported

STUDENT ACTIVITIES AND ORGANIZATIONS

Not reported

FACULTY SPECIALIZATIONS AND/ OR RESEARCH

Not reported

Pierpont Community & Technical College

School of Human Services

1201 Locust Ave., 137 ED, Fairmont, WV 26554　|　304-367-4919　|　**www.pierpont.edu/schoolofhumanservices/**

UNIVERSITY PROFILE
Public
Rural
Residential & Commuter
Semester Schedule
Co-ed

STUDENT DEMOGRAPHICS
Undergraduate: 3,000
Graduate: Not reported

Male: 40%
Female: 60%

Full-time: 65%
Part-time: 35%

EXPENSES
Tuition: $1,766 (in-state);
$4,216 (out-of-state)
Room & Board: $3,510

ADMISSIONS
1201 Locust Ave.
Fairmont, WV 26554
304-367-4892
Memori.Dobbs@pierpont.edu

DEGREE INFORMATION

Major / Degree / Concentration	Enrollment	Requirements for entry	Graduation rate
Fashion Design Associate of Applied Science	60	ACT score or Compass test and HS diploma or GED	38%

TOTAL PROGRAM ENROLLMENT
Undergraduate: 60
Graduate: 0

Male: 20%
Female: 80%

Full-time: 75%
Part-time: 25%
Online: 0%

International: 2%
Minority: 20%

Job Placement Rate: 70%

SCHOLARSHIPS / FINANCIAL AID
First, understand PCTC and FSU are
an excellent value. We keep our tuition
reasonable, plus we offer an outstanding
education that combines diverse
programs, high-quality instruction, and
real-world experiences. More than 80
percent of our students receive some
sort of scholarship or financial aid.

TOTAL FACULTY: 8
Full-time: 2
Part-time: 6

FASHION DESIGN ADMINISTRATION
Beth A. Newcome, PhD, Dean, School of
 Human Services

PROFESSIONAL / ACADEMIC AFFILIATIONS
Not reported

PROGRAM DESCRIPTION AND PHILOSOPHY

The Fashion students, who complete the 2-year degree, enter the workforce into various design businesses, retailing, fashion/bridal consulting, and specialized work in their field such as visual merchandising, design, marketing and sales, while some graduates open their own businesses. One recent graduate now owns and operates two bridal salons in the Charleston, WV area, while another graduate just opened a fashion boutique in downtown Fairmont, WV. The placement of our students is excellent with starting salaries ranging from $28-34,000 depending on experience. We encourage all of our fashion students to work part-time (even as little as 10 hours per week) to build experience into their resumes, along with their educational credentials.

Our Fashion program has included many student activities this year, such as a "project runway," "extreme makeover" fashion event, and a "look for less" fashion show, where our students put together designer looks for a fraction of the cost from area retailers. Every student participates in a practicum at local retail stores to get on-the-job experience in fashion marketing and sales. We believe that students need the opportunity to "practice" classroom theory and knowledge.

FACILITIES

Pierpont Community & Technical College shares a 120-acre main campus in Fairmont, West Virginia, with Fairmont State University. Partnership allows us to better serve our combined 7,450 students. Partnership provides students with the opportunity to find their future from more than 145 skill sets, certificates, associate degrees, bachelor's degrees, and graduate programs. Pierpont offers a variety of courses at more than 15 sites in North Central West Virginia. We value scholarship, opportunity, achievement and responsibility. The campus includes multiple dorms, on campus food service, bookstore, computer labs, recreational center, and library with Internet café. The campus is located within walking distance of the city of Fairmont with retail and community services.

ONLINE / DISTANCE LEARNING

Not available

COURSES OF INSTRUCTION

- Introduction to Fashion Business
- Apparel Design I & II
- Textiles
- Design Concepts
- Visual Merchandising
- History of Fashion
- Computer Design for Fashion
- Clothing & Culture
- Practicum Experience
- Small Business Fundamentals
- Graphics electives

INTERNSHIPS

Required of majors at the Senior year level.

Interns are typically placed at companies such as American Eagle, Gap, New York and Co., JCPenny, many locate fashion businesses.

STUDY ABROAD

Study Abroad programs are available in conjunction with the partner institution, Fairmont State University.

NOTABLE ALUMNI

Not reported

STUDENT ACTIVITIES AND ORGANIZATIONS

PCTC and FSU have more than 80 student organizations ranging from Student Government, professional and honorary organizations to fraternities, sororities, music groups, religious clubs and arts organizations, including a ballroom dance team. About 50 percent of our students participate in Intramurals—we offer 24 sports such as flag football, softball, horseshoes and backgammon.

FACULTY SPECIALIZATIONS AND RESEARCH

Dr. Beth Newcome is a professor of Textiles and Clothing, and Applied Design at the Pierpont Community and Technical College at Fairmont State University. She serves as Dean for the School of Human Services and is the advisor and coordinator of the Fashion and Interior Design associate degree program. She received her BS and MS in Home Economics Education from West Virginia University, with an emphasis in textiles and clothing and received her Ph.D. from The Ohio State University in Human Ecology. While at Ohio State, she completed a major in Higher Education Administration for Family and Consumer Sciences with minors in educational technology and historic textiles. She is the curator for both the Masquer's Historical Costume Collection (1850-1975) and the Commodity Cotton Bag and Feed Sacks Collection (1920-1970). Much of her research on feed sacks was done in conjunction with her study in historical textiles while at Ohio State University.

COMMUNITY COLLEGE TRANSFERS

Over the years PCTC has graduated many students with the associate degree in Fashion. Some students opt to complete a bachelor degree through our partner institution, Fairmont State University with a BS degree in Family and Consumer Sciences Fashion Merchandising through a 2+2 articulation with no loss of credit.

West Virginia University

Division of Design & Merchandising

702 Allen Hall, Morgantown, WV 26508 | 304-293-3402 | www.design.wvu.edu

UNIVERSITY PROFILE
Public
Rural
Residential
Semester Schedule
Co-ed

STUDENT DEMOGRAPHICS
Undergraduate: 22,000
Graduate: 7,000

Male: Not reported
Female: Not reported

Full-time: Not reported
Part-time: Not reported

EXPENSES
Tuition: $5,500
Room & Board: $7,500

ADMISSIONS
P.O. Box 6009
Morgantown, WV 26506
304-293-2121
go2wvu@mail.wvu.edu

DEGREE INFORMATION

Major / Degree / Concentration	Enrollment	Requirements for entry	Graduation rate
Fashion Design & Merchandising Bachelor of Science Fashion Design Track	Not reported	2.25 gpa	Not reported
Fashion Design & Merchandising Bachelor of Science Merchandising Track	Not reported	2.25 gpa	Not reported

TOTAL PROGRAM ENROLLMENT
Undergraduate: Not reported
Graduate: Not reported

Male: Not reported
Female: Not reported

Full-time: Not reported
Part-time: Not reported

International: Not reported
Minority: Not reported

Job Placement Rate: Not reported

SCHOLARSHIPS / FINANCIAL AID
Numerous scholarships are available through the university, college, and private concerns. The Fashion Design & Merchandising program currently offers one scholarship, the Ruth E. Weibel Memorial Scholarship.

TOTAL FACULTY: 5
Full-time: Not reported
Part-time: Not reported
Online: Not reported

FASHION ADMINISTRATION
Dr. Barbara McFall, Division Director

PROFESSIONAL / ACADEMIC AFFILIATIONS
International Textile and Apparel Association

PROGRAM DESCRIPTION AND PHILOSOPHY

The Fashion Design & Merchandising (FDM) program offers two tracks, Fashion Design and Fashion Merchandising. Students obtain a broad-based background in fashion design and merchandising. Our students have been successful in gaining admission for advanced work in areas such as historic costume and textiles, social-psychology of dress, apparel design, textile design, and business. With additional study at the graduate level, students may secure positions with fiber and fabric producers, museums which exhibit and preserve textiles and apparel, and with colleges and universities.

FACILITIES

Computer labs equipped with scanners, printers, and color plotters; studio spaces. Please note: there is a laptop requirement for all Fashion Design & Merchandising students after the Sophomore level.

ONLINE / DISTANCE LEARNING

Not reported

COURSES OF INSTRUCTION

- Introduction to Design
- Introduction to the Fashion Business
- Design Concepts of Dress
- Figure & Fabric Drawing
- Introduction to Textiles
- Fashion & Dress through History
- Fashion, the Body, and Culture
- Apparel Production & Fit
- Product Development
- Flat Pattern Design
- Applied History of Fashion & Dress
- Visual Merchandising
- Knitting for Design
- Basic Garment Construction
- Merchandising Practicum
- Fashion Study Tour
- Draping
- Fashion Merchandising
- Merchandise Planning & Control
- Fashion Design Portfolio
- Global Issues & Fashion
- Merchandising Internship
- Couture Techniques
- Fashion Presentation
- Trend Forecasting & Brand Management
- Media Communication & Fashion

INTERNSHIPS

Required of merchandising majors at Junior/Senior level.

STUDY ABROAD

Available to European fashion capitals of Milan, Italy, or London, England. An elective New York study tour enables students to observe textile, apparel, and retail industry sites, view historic costume collections and network with graduates of the FDM program.

NOTABLE ALUMNI

Not reported

STUDENT ACTIVITIES AND ORGANIZATIONS

Fashion Business Association student chapter, Annual Fashion Show

FACULTY SPECIALIZATIONS AND RESEARCH

Social psychology of dress; professional development in the apparel industry, gender and sub-cultural studies; branding; consumer behavior; history of costume; functional apparel design; teaching for creativity; interdisciplinary, cross-cultural, study abroad education; cross-cultural and transnational apparel design; 3D body-scanning technology; sustainable fashion; pedagogy of dress, specifically focusing on undergraduate research as a tool for developing professional skills in students

Algonquin College of Applied Arts and Technology

School of Part-time Studies

Room #C137, 1385 Woodroffe Ave., Ottawa, Ontario K2G 1V8, Canada | 613-727-4723 | www.algonquincollege.com

UNIVERSITY PROFILE
Public
Urban
Commuter
Semester Schedule
Co-ed

STUDENT DEMOGRAPHICS
Undergraduate: Not reported
Graduate: Not reported

Male: Not reported
Female: Not reported

Full-time: Not reported
Part-time: Not reported

EXPENSES
Tuition: Not reported
Room & Board: Not reported

ADMISSIONS
1385 Woodroffe Ave.
Ottawa, Ontario K2G 1V8
Canada
613-727-0002
AskAlgonquin@
algonquincollege.com

DEGREE INFORMATION

Major / Degree / Concentration	Enrollment	Requirements for entry	Graduation rate
Fashion Design Certificate	Not reported	Not reported	Not reported

TOTAL PROGRAM ENROLLMENT
Undergraduate: Not reported
Graduate: Not reported

Male: Not reported
Female: Not reported

Full-time: Not reported
Part-time: Not reported
Online: Not reported

International: Not reported
Minority: Not reported

Job Placement Rate: Not reported

SCHOLARSHIPS / FINANCIAL AID
Our Fashion courses are offered part-time (evenings and weekends). Students pay for each course that they take at that time. Some students take two or three of the courses offered under the program. Some only take one. There is financial aid support offered by our Financial Aid office.

TOTAL FACULTY: NOT REPORTED
Full-time: Not reported
Part-Time: Not reported

FASHION ADMINISTRATION
Laura Daub, Program Coordinator, Fashion Design)
Erin Sample, Program Support Officer – Administrative, Fashion Design
Larry White, Academic Manager, Media and Design

PROFESSIONAL / ACADEMIC AFFILIATIONS
Not reported

PROGRAM DESCRIPTION AND PHILOSOPHY

Interested in working in the exciting fashion design industry? This certificate program provides students with the theory, techniques, and hands-on skills to conceptualize and produce clothing in a variety of styles that are suitable for commercial use. The curriculum is designed to provide students with the additional specialty skills needed to excel in fashion design and offers courses on tailoring techniques, pattern construction, millinery, and the history of costume.

To qualify for this certificate, you must complete eleven compulsory courses and one elective within six years.

FACILITIES

We have a special classroom which is stocked with sewing machines, mannequins, etc. Everything the students will need to be successful in the program. Each semester we try to purchase some new machines, supplies for the program.

ONLINE / DISTANCE LEARNING

Not reported

COURSES OF INSTRUCTION

- Flat Pattern and Design I and II
- Clothing Construction I and II
- Tailoring I and II
- Fashion Illustration
- Millinery
- Basic Textiles
- Fashion Merchandising
- Design Concepts
- Portfolio Presentation
- History of Costume
- Fashion Draping

INTERNSHIPS

Not required

STUDY ABROAD

Not available

NOTABLE ALUMNI

Not reported

STUDENT ACTIVITIES AND ORGANIZATIONS

Not reported

FACULTY SPECIALIZATIONS AND RESEARCH

Not reported

Blanche Macdonald Centre for Applied Design

Department Fashion Merchandising/Fashion Design

460 Robson St., Vancouver, British Columbia V6B 2B5, Canada | 604-685-0337 | www.blanchemacdonald.com

UNIVERSITY PROFILE
Private
Urban
Commuter
Semester Schedule
Co-ed

STUDENT DEMOGRAPHICS
Undergraduate: 200
Graduate: n/a

Male: 6%
Female: 94%

Full-time: 100%
Part-time: n/a

EXPENSES
Tuition: $13,000-$16,000
Room & Board: n/a

ADMISSIONS
460 Robson St.
Vancouver, British Columbia
V6B 2B5
Canada
604-685-0337
info@blanchemacdonald.com

DEGREE INFORMATION

Major / Degree / Concentration	Enrollment	Requirements for entry	Graduation rate
Fashion Merchandising Diploma	140	Must be 19 years of age or have graduated from high school. Must possess good written and verbal English skills. Must have an interest in the fashion and apparel industries.	80%
Fashion Design Diploma	60	Must be 19 years of age or have graduated from high school. Must possess good written and verbal English skills. Must have an interest in the fashion and apparel industries. Must have basic or better sewing skills.	90%

TOTAL PROGRAM ENROLLMENT
Undergraduate: 200
Graduate: n/a

Male: 6%
Female: 94%

Full-time: 100%
Part-time: n/a
Online: n/a

International: 15%
Minority: n/a

Job Placement Rate: 80-90%

SCHOLARSHIPS / FINANCIAL AID
Nor reported

TOTAL FACULTY: 30
Full-time: 13%
Part-Time: 87%

FASHION ADMINISTRATION
Peggy Morrison, Executive Program Director
Donna Baldock, Program Director
Amanda Craig, Program Associate

PROFESSIONAL / ACADEMIC AFFILIATIONS
Not reported

PROGRAM DESCRIPTION AND PHILOSOPHY

Statement of Purpose: Our purpose is to provide quality education that is industry relevant within a positive and creative learning environment.

Student Success Policy: Your success is our success. At the Blanche Macdonald Centre we commit to providing our students with an education that incorporates passionate instruction with an industry relevant curriculum delivered in and environment of personal empowerment and respect. We offer ongoing career support and opportunities to connect with the Centre and the industry long after graduation.

FACILITIES

Computer lab, sewing lab, museums, libraries, marts

ONLINE / DISTANCE LEARNING

Not available

COURSES OF INSTRUCTION

Fashion Merchandising program:
- Textiles
- Fashion Awareness
- Marketing
- Business
- Visual Merchandising
- Fashion Illustration
- Fashion Show Production
- Retail Buying
- Fashion Elements
- Fashion Styling
- Manufacturing & Wholesaling

Fashion Design program:
- Pattern Making
- Garment Construction
- Textiles
- Fashion Awareness
- Fashion History
- Fashion Elements
- Fashion Illustration
- Design Collections
- Manufacturing

INTERNSHIPS

Not required, but students have held internships at companies such as small manufacturing sites, wholesale agencies, and special event companies.

STUDY ABROAD

Not available

NOTABLE ALUMNI

Please refer to Blanche Macdonald Centre Web site

STUDENT ACTIVITIES AND ORGANIZATIONS

Not reported

FACULTY SPECIALIZATIONS AND RESEARCH

Not reported

COMMUNITY COLLEGE TRANSFERS

Transfer of credits is discussed and reviewed on an individual basis. Marketing, Business, and Textile courses with a 75% passing grade or higher may be transferrable. Review of the institution's course outline, curriculum, reference material, & textbook listing as well as mark breakdown is required. Methods of learner evaluation must be varied and include formal exams.

George Brown College

School of Fashion Studies

C 442, 160 Kendal Ave., Casa Loma Campus, Toronto, Ontario M5T 2T9 Canada | 416-415-5000 x 4840

www.georgebrown.ca/fashionstudies/

UNIVERSITY PROFILE

Public
Urban
Commuter
Semester Schedule
Co-ed

STUDENT DEMOGRAPHICS

Undergraduate: 19,000
Graduate: n/a

Male: Not reported
Female: Not reported

Full-time: 95%
Part-time: 5%

EXPENSES

Tuition: $4,000 CAD
Domestic Fees; $11,000 CAD
international fees
Room & Board: n/a

ADMISSIONS

Registrar
P.O. Box 1015, Stn. B
Toronto Ontario M5T 2T9
Canada
1-877-515-5559
fashionstudies@georgebrown.ca

DEGREE INFORMATION

Major / Degree / Concentration	Enrollment	Requirements for entry	Graduation rate
Fashion Management Diploma	300	Ontario Secondary School Diploma with minimum level of math and English (see Web site for details)	90%
Fashion Business Industry Diploma	250	Ontario Secondary School Diploma with minimum level of math and English (see Web site for details)	90%
Fashion Techniques & Design Diploma	259	Ontario Secondary School diploma with min level of math and English, plus sewing test (see Web site for details)	90%
International Fashion Development & Management Advanced Diploma	25	Fashion or Business degree or diploma or combination of education and experience (see Web site for details)	90%

TOTAL PROGRAM ENROLLMENT

Undergraduate: 1,000
Graduate: NA

Male: 10%
Female: 90%

Full-time: 95%
Part-time: 5%
Online: n/a

International: 14%
Minority: 50%

Job Placement Rate: 80%

SCHOLARSHIPS / FINANCIAL AID

Information is available at: www.georgebrown.ca/financialaid/

TOTAL FACULTY: 25

Full-time: 40%
Part-time: 60%

FASHION ADMINISTRATION

Marilyn McNeil-Morin, Chair , School of Fashion Studies and Performing Arts
Rosa Fracassa, Program Coordinator, Fashion Studies programs

PROFESSIONAL / ACADEMIC AFFILIATIONS

International American Apparel and Footwear Association
Fashion Group International

PROGRAM DESCRIPTION AND PHILOSOPHY

Fashion Techniques and Design program simulates the standards, practices, and facilities used in the apparel industry and focuses on sewing and drafting skills. Study of textiles, technical specifications, fashion illustration, pattern grading, use of computer technology, history of costume, and design fundamentals provide depth to student understanding of clothing design, manufacture, and apparel development.

Students have the opportunity to volunteer for Fashion Week, interact with industry leaders in class or on field trips, participate in fashion industry events, and enter design competitions. An annual fashion show showcases garments designed and constructed in the program. Students are involved with research projects.

Fashion Management and Fashion Business Industry diplomas are also offered to provide students with business management skills and knowledge of the entire supply chain of apparel production from concept to development, production and sale to the consumer. The postgraduate certificate, International Fashion Development and Management prepares students for careers in the global fashion business.

FACILITIES

Computer labs, sewing labs, drafting labs, drafting technology lab, library, gymnasium, etc.

ONLINE / DISTANCE LEARNING

Not available

COURSES OF INSTRUCTION

- Textiles Science
- World of Fashion
- Visual Merchandising
- Principles of Accounting
- Apparel Marketing
- Economics
- History of Costume
- Apparel Sourcing
- Logistics for the Apparel Industry
- Computer Applications
- Adobe Illustrator
- Fashion Merchandising and Buying
- Drafting
- Apparel Construction
- Product Development and Costing
- Fashion Show Production

INTERNSHIPS

Required of majors. Interns are typically placed at companies that deal with retail, manufacturing, apparel production, import-export, wholesale, etc.

STUDY ABROAD

Available

NOTABLE ALUMNI

Kimberly Newport-Mimran–Pink Tartan
Doug Burkman–Burkman Bros.

STUDENT ACTIVITIES AND ORGANIZATIONS

Student Affairs and student-run clubs

FACULTY SPECIALIZATIONS AND RESEARCH

Not reported

Humber College

Fashion Institute

205 Humber College Blvd., Toronto, Ontario M9W 5L7, Canada | 416-675-6622 | www.humber.ca

UNIVERSITY PROFILE
Public
Suburban
Residential
Semester Schedule
Co-ed

STUDENT DEMOGRAPHICS
Undergraduate: 18,000
Graduate: Not reported

Male: Not reported
Female: Not reported

Full-time: Not reported
Part-time: Not reported

EXPENSES
Tuition: Not reported
Room & Board: Not reported

ADMISSIONS
205 Humber College Blvd.
Toronto, Ontario M9W 5L7
Canada
416-675-6622

DEGREE INFORMATION

Major / Degree / Concentration	Enrollment	Requirements for entry	Graduation rate
Fashion Arts Diploma	450	Grade 12 English	90%
Cosmetic Management Diploma	40	Grade 12 English	90%
Esthetician Spa Management Diploma	100	Grade 12 English	90%

TOTAL PROGRAM ENROLLMENT
Undergraduate: 590
Graduate: 0

Male: 5%
Female: 95%

Full-time: 98%
Part-time: 2%
Online: 0%

International: 2%
Minority: 95%

Job Placement Rate: 80%

SCHOLARSHIPS / FINANCIAL AID
Students receiving Scholarships or
Financial Aid: 1%

TOTAL FACULTY: 30
Full-time: 10%
Part-time: 90%

FASHION ADMINISTRATION
Pauline Ashworth
Antonietta Perretta

PROFESSIONAL / ACADEMIC AFFILIATIONS
Fashion Group International

PROGRAM DESCRIPTION AND PHILOSOPHY

To develop employable skills for successful business careers for fashion and beauty.

FACILITIES

Computer labs, spa, retail

ONLINE / DISTANCE LEARNING

Not reported

COURSES OF INSTRUCTION

- Supervision
- Ethics in the Cosmetic Industry
- Cosmetic Product Launches and Event Planning
- Counter Sales Management
- Spa Finance
- Introduction to the Cosmetic Industry
- Colour Theory
- Computer Applications for Fashion
- Retail Buying
- Retail Operations
- International Trade
- Photo Styling
- New Venture Development

INTERNSHIPS

Required of majors at second level. Interns are typically placed at major retailers, manufacturers, magazines, event planning companies, and spas.

STUDY ABROAD

Not available

NOTABLE ALUMNI

Not reported

STUDENT ACTIVITIES AND ORGANIZATIONS

Not reported

FACULTY SPECIALIZATIONS AND RESEARCH

Not reported

COMMUNITY COLLEGE TRANSFERS

Degree program at alternate campus

Kwantlen Polytechnic University

Fashion Design & Technology

8771 Lansdowne Rd., Richmond, British Columbia V6X 3V8 Canada | 604-599-2543 | **www.kwantlen.ca/fashion**

DEGREE INFORMATION

Major / Degree / Concentration	Enrollment	Requirements for entry	Graduation rate
Fashion & Technology Bachelor of Design	160	www.kwantlen.ca/calendar/programs/fash-bc.html	Not reported
Fashion Marketing Diploma	40	www.kwantlen.ca/calendar/programs/FASHION_MARKETING_DIPLOMA.html	Not reported

TOTAL PROGRAM ENROLLMENT
Undergraduate: 150
Graduate: 40

Male: 2%
Female: 98%

Full-time: 100%
Part-time: Not reported
Online: Not reported

International: 2%
Minority: Not reported

Job Placement Rate: 90%

SCHOLARSHIPS / FINANCIAL AID
See opposite page for more info.

TOTAL FACULTY: 14
Full-time: 50%
Part-time: 50%

FASHION ADMINISTRATION
Barbara Duggan, Dean of Faculty of Design
Evelyn May, Fashion Program Coordinator
Vanessa Fors, Program Assistant

PROFESSIONAL / ACADEMIC AFFILIATIONS
Not reported

PROGRAM DESCRIPTION AND PHILOSOPHY

As the only program of its kind in western Canada, Kwantlen's Bachelor of Design in Fashion & Technology program prepares students for careers in the global apparel economy in fashion design, production, marketing, and computer technology. This dynamic program features integrated comprehensive industry-based education and training using leading-edge technology; class projects facilitated by prominent apparel companies such as lululemon athletica; and an extensive internship that results in employment.

FACILITIES

Computer labs, Fashion library, and Sewing Labs

ONLINE / DISTANCE LEARNING

Not available

COURSES OF INSTRUCTION

- Fundamentals in Fashion Design
- Drafting and Sewing
- Textile Science
- History of Costume
- Technical Fashion Drawing
- Computer Aided Pattern Making
- Fashion Design and Drawing

INTERNSHIPS

Required of majors by the 3rd year. Interns are typically placed at companies such as lululemon, Arcteryx, Mountain Equipment co-op, Christine Designs.

STUDY ABROAD

Finland, UK, Taiwan

NOTABLE ALUMNI

Carlie Wong–contestant on Project Runway, Phaedra Godchild –Aritzia, Raymond Boutet–Evan& Dean

STUDENT ACTIVITIES AND ORGANIZATIONS

Student Union, student class representatives, opportunity to represent students at faculty meetings

FACULTY SPECIALIZATIONS AND RESEARCH

Faculty attend conventions and seminars across North America regularly and bring their research back to share with students.

SCHOLARSHIPS / FINANCIAL AID

Kwantlen students may apply for a number of general scholarships and awards. For more information go to www.kwantlen.ca/awards.

Fashion specific scholarships go to deserving fashion students on an annual basis. Award recipients are selected by the fashion faculty and are recognized for their academic standing, volunteer work in the community and apparel industry, and contribution to the Kwantlen program area & community.

Students receiving Scholarships or Financial Aid: 10%

Olds College Calgary Campus

Department of Apparel Technology

4500 - 50th St., Olds, Alberta T4H 1K7 Canada | 1-800-661-6537 | www.oldscollege.ca

UNIVERSITY PROFILE
Public
Rural
Commuter & Residential
Semester Schedule
Co-ed

STUDENT DEMOGRAPHICS
Undergraduate: Not reported
Graduate: Not reported

Male: 40%
Female: 60%

Full-time: Not reported
Part-time: Not reported

EXPENSES
Tuition: Not reported
Room & Board: Not reported

ADMISSIONS
4500 - 50 St.
Olds, Alberta, T4H 1K7
Canada
1-800-661-6537
info@oldscollege.ca

DEGREE INFORMATION

Major / Degree / Concentration	Enrollment	Requirements for entry	Graduation rate
Apparel Technology Diploma	Not reported	High School diploma; 50% or better in English Language Arts 30-1 or 30-2; 50% or better in Pure Math or Applied Math 20	Not reported

TOTAL PROGRAM ENROLLMENT
Undergraduate: 60
Graduate: Not reported

Male: 3%
Female: 97%

Full-time: 80%
Part-time: 20%
Online: Not reported

International: Not reported
Minority: Not reported

Job Placement Rate: Not reported

SCHOLARSHIPS / FINANCIAL AID
Olds College students have over $400,000 of Internal Olds College awards that can be applied for after Registration Day.

TOTAL FACULTY: 6
Full-time: 70%
Part-time: 30%

FASHION DESIGN ADMINISTRATION
Lisa Sorestad, Coordinator

PROFESSIONAL / ACADEMIC AFFILIATIONS
Not reported

PROGRAM DESCRIPTION AND PHILOSOPHY

The two-year, Apparel Technology Diploma program prepares its graduates to produce custom apparel for the fashion or the performing Arts and entertainment industries. Made-to-measure pattern making and apparel construction projects are completed using both industrial and domestic sewing equipment. Class sizes for labs are maximum 24, to enable instructors to assist students on an individual basis. Focus is on "hands-on" training, with students completing both samples and projects to demonstrate their abilities.

FACILITIES

Four fully-equipped sewing labs, computer/technology labs, Fine Arts Centre, Gym/running track, Swimming pool

ONLINE / DISTANCE LEARNING

Not available

COURSES OF INSTRUCTION

- Apparel Construction
- Pattern Design
- Textiles
- History of Clothing
- Tailoring
- Designing with Knits

INTERNSHIPS

Not required

STUDY ABROAD

Not available

NOTABLE ALUMNI

Not reported

STUDENT ACTIVITIES AND ORGANIZATIONS

Annual Open House Fashion Show in April to showcase student work. Fashion Club run by students to fundraise and provide activities.

FACULTY SPECIALIZATIONS AND RESEARCH

Not reported

COMMUNITY COLLEGE TRANSFERS

Transfers are assessed on a

Olds College Calgary Campus

School of Business

4500 - 50th St., Olds, Alberta T4H 1R6, Canada | 1-800-661-6537 | www.oldscollege.ca

UNIVERSITY PROFILE
Public
Urban
Commuter
Semester Schedule
Co-ed

STUDENT DEMOGRAPHICS
Undergraduate: 30-50
Graduate: Not reported

Male: 5%
Female: 95%

Full-time: 95%
Part-time: 5%

EXPENSES
Tuition: $6,050
Room & Board: n/a

ADMISSIONS
4500 - 50 Street
Olds Alberta T4H 1R6
Canada
1-800-661-6537
info@oldscollege.ca

CALGARY CAMPUS
640 14th Ave. S.E.,
Calgary, AB T2G 1E8

DEGREE INFORMATION

Major / Degree / Concentration	Enrollment	Requirements for entry	Graduation rate
Fashion Marketing Certificate	50	High School Diploma or its equivalent; 50% or better in English Language Arts 30-1 or 30-2; 50% or better in Pure or Applied Math 20; Alternate Admission status call 1-800-661-6537	90%

TOTAL PROGRAM ENROLLMENT
Undergraduate: 50
Graduate: Not reported

Male: Not reported
Female: 95%

Full-time: Not reported
Part-time: Not reported
Online: Not reported

International: Not reported
Minority: Not reported

Job Placement Rate: 90%

SCHOLARSHIPS / FINANCIAL AID
See opposite page for more info.

TOTAL FACULTY: 5
Full-time: 80%
Part-time: 20%

FASHION DESIGN ADMINISTRATION
Terry Males, Chair of School of Business
Anne Blackburn, Coordinator of Fashion Marketing Program

PROFESSIONAL / ACADEMIC AFFILIATIONS
Not reported

PROGRAM DESCRIPTION AND PHILOSOPHY

Students in the Fashion Retail program aspire to work in the creative and managerial positions in the fashion industry. Students learn by exploring business theory and practices, experimenting through hands-on experience and interacting with industry members. The nine-month intensive program prepares students for entry-level management positions in areas like store management, sales, buying, promotions and marketing, or visual design. Graduates are often successful in finding employment in chain stores and with independents. It is an excellent program for anyone wishing to become self-employed in the retail industry. The demand for well-trained retail and fashion people is greater than ever. The Fashion Marketing program strives to equip students with analytical and managerial competencies, and to create an awareness of the importance of highly effective interpersonal skills. Our graduates have an approximately 100% success rate in securing employment in their field. Many move into management within six months to one year after graduating.

FACILITIES

City Central Library, Computer Labs, Transit systems

ONLINE / DISTANCE LEARNING

The Olds College Fashion Marketing Online program is currently under development with courses already available. Call 1-800-661-6537 for details.

COURSES OF INSTRUCTION

- Visual Design and Merchandising
- Garment Analysis
- Fashion Promotions
- Introduction to Image Consulting
- Principles of Marketing
- Retail Management

INTERNSHIPS

Not required. Interns are typically placed at companies such as Holt Renfrew and The Bay.

STUDY ABROAD

Not available

NOTABLE ALUMNI

Cheri Milaney

STUDENT ACTIVITIES AND ORGANIZATIONS

Olds College Calgary Campus Fashionista Club

FACULTY SPECIALIZATIONS AND RESEARCH

Visual Design, Retail Management, Leadership, Textiles

COMMUNITY COLLEGE TRANSFER

University of Alberta

SCHOLARSHIPS / FINANCIAL AID

Thanks to our generous program, one in three Olds College students will receive a scholarship, bursary, or award. The Olds College Awards program is designed to recognize the achievements of our students and help alleviate student financial need. The Awards guide is available on the Olds College Web site www.oldscollege.ca. Once you are registered as a full-time student (minimum 18 credits per semester) simply access the online application form through any computer on campus. Complete all the required information. Specific eligibility details are outlined in the Awards Guide.

Ryerson University

School of Fashion

40 Gould St., Toronto Ontario M5B 2K3 Canada | 416-979-5333 | www.ryerson.ca/fashion

UNIVERSITY PROFILE
Public
Urban
Commuter
Semester Schedule
Co-ed

STUDENT DEMOGRAPHICS
Undergraduate: 25,000
Graduate: 1,950

Male: Not reported
Female: Not reported

Full-time: Not reported
Part-time: Not reported

EXPENSES
Tuition: $5,821.93
Room & Board: $3,961-
$11,132

ADMISSIONS
350 Victoria St.
Toronto, Ontario M5B 2K3
Canada
416-979-5036
askme@ryerson.ca

DEGREE INFORMATION

Major / Degree / Concentration	Enrollment	Requirements for entry	Graduation rate
Fashion Design Bachelor of Design	300	Academic Non-academic portfolio	88%
Fashion Communication Bachelor of Design	300	Academic Non-academic portfolio	88%

TOTAL PROGRAM ENROLLMENT
Undergraduate: 600
Graduate: 20

Male: 1%
Female: 99%

Full-time: 100%
Part-time: 0%
Online: 0%

International: 5%
Minority: Not reported

Job Placement Rate: Not reported

SCHOLARSHIPS / FINANCIAL AID
Please visit our website: www.
ryerson.ca/currentstudents/awards/
programspecific/fashion/html

TOTAL FACULTY: 42
Full-time: 19
Part-time: 23

FASHION DESIGN ADMINISTRATION
Prof. Robert Ott, Chair
Prof. Lucia Dell'Agnese, Associate Chair
Prof. Paulette Kelly, Program Director,
Fashion Design
Prof. Shelagh Stewart, Program
Director, Fashion Communication

PROFESSIONAL / ACADEMIC AFFILIATIONS
International Textile and Apparel
Association
Fashion Group International

PROGRAM DESCRIPTION AND PHILOSOPHY

The School of Fashion's aim is to provide career-oriented education at a degree level which will ultimately lead to professional careers for men and women in all industries related to fashion.

Students of Ryerson's School of Fashion are prepared for a variety of careers in Fashion Communication and Fashion Design. The first year of the four-year program is common to all Fashion students. This foundation year is designed to give a general overview of the knowledge and skills applicable to all branches of the fashion industry. Introductory studies range from art history, textiles, clothing construction and pattern-making, design and colour, and fashion drawing. In addition, courses in liberal studies provide the broad foundation necessary for later specialization. In second year students begin their specialization in either: Fashion Communication or Fashion Design.

Students accepted into the Design program begin specialization in the second year. Within the third and fourth year there are core courses in intermediate and advanced apparel design, computer aided design, tailoring, production management, fashion and society, international marketing, grading, and materials management. In addition students may further focus on such subjects as contour and knitwear design, theatre/historical costume, surface (textile) design, and curation and exhibition through the selection of elective courses in second, third, and fourth year. Senior students work with some of Canada's most noted designers to develop their own apparel collections, which are critiqued by industry buyers and manufacturers and shown in the annual year-end fashion events. The collections may be produced individually or as part of a design team.

Specialization in Fashion Communication also begins in second year. Business-related courses in areas such as marketing, business, communication, fashion in international markets, and fashion and society are combined with professional studies in communication design, illustration, typography, curation and exhibition, photography, video production, and fashion journalism to produce a graduate who can work in all areas of fashion communication. Through the selection of elective courses in second, third and fourth year, students may elect to pursue a minor or to otherwise customize their elective package to focus on their individual career objectives. Students also work in teams to produce a series of fashion events culminating in the year-end fashion presentation, attended by over 3,500 people, including industry and media representatives.

FACILITIES

Student services, labs, Ryerson Athletic Center (RAC), visit www.ryerson.ca/student services, www.ryerson.ca/acs, firefly.ryerson.ca/sportsandrec

ONLINE / DISTANCE LEARNING

Not available

COURSES OF INSTRUCTION

- Intro to Fashion I – The Industry
- Intro to Fashion II – Concepts and Theory
- Communication Design
- Integrated Visual Communication
- Fashion Promotion
- Typography and Graphic Workflow
- Strategic Production Management
- Fundamentals of Design and Colour
- Illustration
- History of Design
- Topics in Fashion Photography
- Art Direction for Photography
- Packaging Design
- Intermediate Illustration for Communication
- Digital Illustration and Product Development
- Advertising Design
- Production Technology
- Textiles
- Textile Design
- Intermediate Fashion Design
- Computer Aided Design
- Materials Management
- Grading
- Contour Design
- Fur Design
- Knitwear Design
- Ladieswear Block Development
- Surface Design and Manipulation
- Accessories Design II
- Functional Apparel Design
- Menswear Development
- Introduction to Fashion Journalism
- Fashion in International Markets
- Internship
- Advance Colour Theory
- Design, Text, and Ideas
- Product Data Management
- Topics in Fashion History and Theory
- Visual Merchandising and Display
- Merchandise Analysis
- Fashion Event Planning
- Fashion: Creativity in Design
- Curation and Exhibition

INTERNSHIPS

Required of majors. Interns are typically placed at companies such as Abercrombie & Fitch, Danier Leather, *Elle* Magazine, *Flare* Magazine, HBC, Holt Renfrew, le Chateau, lululemon.

STUDY ABROAD

Exchange opportunities in third year of study for one semester

NOTABLE ALUMNI

Lida Baday, David Dixon, Joeffer Caoc, Paul Hardy, Tu Ly, Todd Lynn, Lucian Matis, Erdem Moralioglu, Arthur Mendonca

STUDENT ACTIVITIES AND ORGANIZATIONS

Ryerson Student Union, visit www.rsuonline.ca

FACULTY SPECIALIZATIONS AND RESEARCH

For Faculty Bios, visit www.ryerson.ca/fashion (under About Us/Faculty and Staff)

University of Alberta

Department of Human Ecology

Human Ecology Building, Edmonton, AB T6G 2N1 | 780-492-5230 | www.ualberta.ca

UNIVERSITY PROFILE
Public
Urban
Residential
Semester Schedule
Co-ed

STUDENT DEMOGRAPHICS
Undergraduate: 37,000
Graduate: 7,000

Male: 44.8%
Female: 55.2%

Full-time: 90.5%
Part-time: 8.5%

EXPENSES
Tuition: $6,000
Room & Board: Not reported

ADMISSIONS
Graduate Admissions
Coordinator
Department of Human
Ecology
302A Human Ecology Building
University of Alberta
Edmonton, AB T6G 2N1
780-492-5230
linda.mirans@ualberta.ca

DEGREE INFORMATION

Major / Degree / Concentration	Enrollment	Requirements for entry	Graduation rate
Clothing, Textiles, & Material Culture Bachelor of Science	125	Not reported	Not reported
Fashion Merchandising minor	70	Not reported	Not reported
Textile Science minor	5	Not reported	Not reported
Interiors minor	10	Not reported	Not reported
Material Culture & Design Studies minor	40	Not reported	Not reported

TOTAL PROGRAM ENROLLMENT
Undergraduate: 220
Graduate: 35

Male: 2%
Female: 98%

Full-time: 95%
Part-time: 5%
Online: 0%

International: 3%
Minority: Not reported

Job Placement Rate: 80%

SCHOLARSHIPS / FINANCIAL AID
The University of Alberta offers financial
assistance at both the Faculty and
department level, however graduate
funding is dependent on scholarship
and supervisor's availability of research
funds at the department level.

Students Receiving Scholarships or
Financial Aid: 50%

TOTAL FACULTY: 12
Full-time: 100%
Part-time: n/a

FASHION ADMINISTRATION
Deanna Williamson, Department Chair

PROFESSIONAL / ACADEMIC AFFILIATIONS

International Textile and Apparel
Association

PROGRAM DESCRIPTION AND PHILOSOPHY

The department's major in Clothing, Textiles, and Material Culture explores the material world of everday life, from textiles to home interiors. This multidisciplinary, client-centred, holistic major examines the theoretical, technical, creative, and applied aspects of the near environment, with a particular focus on clothing and textiles. After their first year, students declare a minor specialization in one of the following four areas: Textile Science; Fashion Merchandising; Material Culture and Design Studies; or Interiors.

FACILITIES

The Department of Human Ecology's Clothing and Textile Collection at the University of Alberta is the only teaching collection of its kind in Canada, and is home to over 18,500 artifacts. It features a large collection of historic Western dress and an extensive quilt collection. In addition, students have access to apparel design labs, computer labs, conservation lab, and Textile Analysis Services lab.

ONLINE / DISTANCE LEARNING

Not available

COURSES OF INSTRUCTION

- Survey of Historic Dress
- The World of Design
- Applications of Textile Science
- Apparel Design and Product Development
- Quality Assurance in Textiles and Apparel

INTERNSHIPS

Required of majors at 4th year

STUDY ABROAD

Not available

NOTABLE ALUMNI

Linda McPhee

STUDENT ACTIVITIES AND ORGANIZATIONS

Not reported

FACULTY SPECIALIZATIONS AND RESEARCH

Specializations in material culture of dress, dress and fashion history, design processes, and textile science with a focus on protective clothing and sports clothing.

Aspects of museology are also incorporated into our program via the work of the Curator for the Clothing and Textiles Collection.

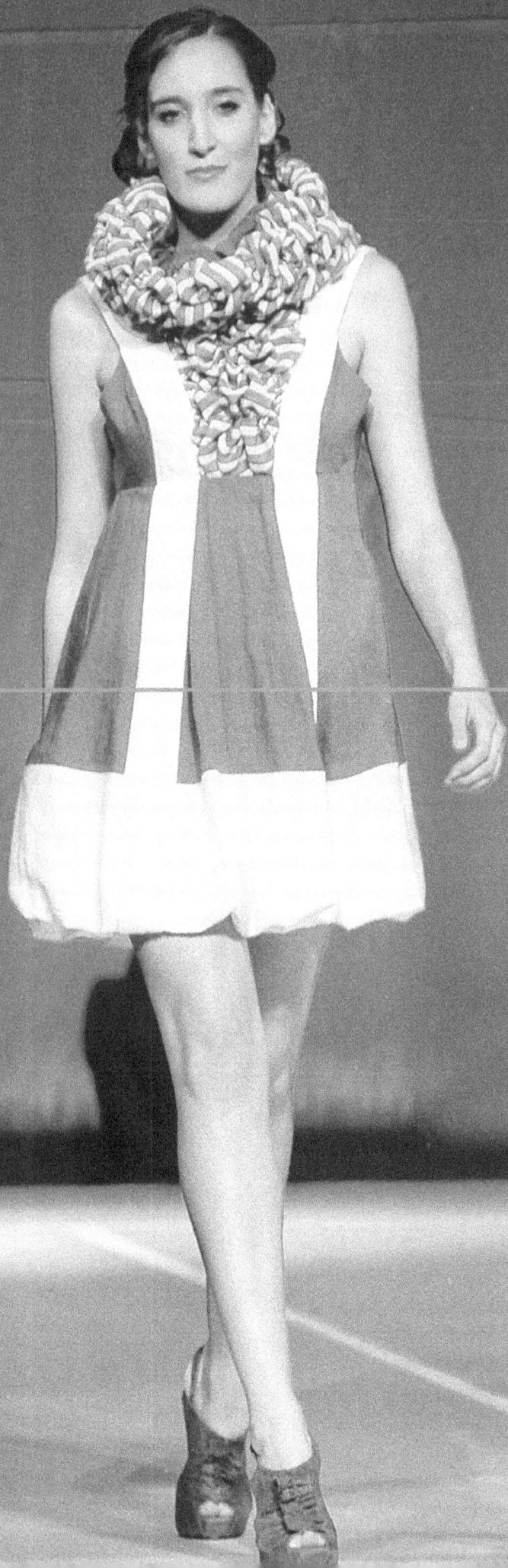

Indexes

Fashion Schools by Degrees Offered

Fashion Schools by Degrees Offered

Bachelor of Professional Studies (B.P.S.)

Bachelor of Science (B.S.)

Fashion Schools by Degrees Offered

Certificate Programs

Fashion Schools by Degrees Offered

PhD Programs

Fashion Schools by Majors, Concentrations, and/or Areas of Emphasis